SAILING SHIPS OF WAR
1400 - 1860

Frontispiece
A contemporary engraving of an English 3rd Rate of about 1730.

SAILING SHIPS OF WAR
1400 - 1860

Dr FRANK HOWARD

MAYFLOWER BOOKS
NEW YORK

Library of Congress Catalog No 79-89072
ISBN 0 8317 7656 0

MANUFACTURED IN GREAT BRITAIN
FIRST AMERICAN EDITION

CONTENTS

ILLUSTRATIONS - SOURCES & ACKNOWLEDGEMENTS

Reproduced by gracious permission of Her Majesty the Queen – 52, 247

Ashmolean Museum, Oxford – 1, 132

The Science Museum, London – 1, 55–60, 65, 66, 68, 80, 112, 113, 115, 117, 119, 126, 142, 145, 147, 152–156, 170–172, 222, 237, 273, 275–277, 304, 308, 309, 316, 319, 339, 347, 351, 360, 364, 366, 367, 284–386

The Public Records Office, London – 2, 121, 333

Deutsches Schiffahrtsmuseum – 3–5

The Mariners Mirror – (1955, *41*, p291) 6, 1923, *IX*, 83ff) 7, (1934, *XX*) 8–10, (1968, *54*, 126) 11, (1925, *XI*, 153) 12, (1925, *XI*, 152) 13, (1924, *X*, 305) 16, (1928, *XIV*, 163) 17, (1935, *41*, 191) 18, (1931, *XVII*, 335) 19, (1955, *41*, 190, 284, 293, 188) 20, 21, 31, 42, (1945, *31*, 96, 86) 23, 151, (1920, *VI*, 85–6) 43, (1961, *47*, 85) 53, (1964, *50*, 119) 54, (1921, *VII*, 110) 61, (1948, *34*, 124) 73, (1914, *IV*, 142–3) 74, (1920, *VI*, 13) 108, (1920, *VI*, 11) 109, (1919, *V*, 48) 123, (1961, *47*, 171, 175) 128, 138, (1972, *58*, p41ff) 296–298

The Pierpont Morgan Library – 14, 50

The British Library – 15, 28–30, 51, 114, 116, 118, 122, 245, 246

Drawings based on artifacts in the Sjöhistoriska Museum, Stockholm – 24, 40(e–f), 160, 161, 182

Based on originals in *Columbus' Ships* by Jose-Maria Martinez-Hidalgo – 27(a), 40(a–c), 44

Victoria and Albert Museum – 32

Drawings based on artifacts in the Tøjhus Museum, Copenhagen – 46, 220

Based on a drawing by J C Thorn in *The Cattewater Wreck*, National Maritime Museum Monograph No 13, 1974–47

Based on an illustration in *Historie des Guerres Judaiques* by Flavius Josephus, *c*1490, MS 2538, f109, in the Österreichische Nationalbibliothek, Vienna – 49

Bibliothèque Royale, Brussels – 62

National Maritime Museum – 63, 69–71, 134, 164–168, 179, 181, 224, 231, 232, 234, 235, 254, 255, 268, 278, 280, 293, 306, 334, 337, 338, 342–344, 348, 349, 368–371, 373, 376, 377, 382, 383

Based on an original in *Svenskt Skeppsbyggeri*, edited by G Halldin, Malmö, 1963–64

Pepysian Library, Magdalene College, Cambridge – 67, 150, 190, 242–244, 248–251, front endpaper

Sjöhistoriska Museum, Stockholm – 72, 133, 174, 175, 213, 336

The Bodleian Library, Oxford – 75

Cosmographie Universelle selon les Navigateurs, tant ancienc que modernes by Guillaume Le Testu, Library of the Ministère de la Guerre, Paris – 78

Based on an original by Edward D Tucker in *Underwater Archaeology: A Nascent Discipline*, published by UNESCO in 1967–107

By courtesy of Colin Martin – 110

Southsea Castle Museum – 111

Scheepvaart Museum, Amsterdam – 124, 148, 149, 173, 228, 229, 240, 305, 310, 335, 340, 346, 378, rear endpaper

From *Souvenirs de Marine* by Amiral Paris – 125, 127, 187

Rigsarkivet, Copenhagen – 129, 176–178, 188, 215, 216, 225, 226, 230, 233, 238, 260, 285, 292, 294, 295, 311, 312, 317, 321, 322, 327, 330–332, 340, 350, 374, 375, 380, 381, 387

Based on originals in the Riksarkivet, Stockholm – 130, 131

Based on originals in *Souvenirs de Marine* by Amiral Paris – 135, 352–357

Based on originals in *Regelskeppet* by G Schoermer – 136

From a drawing in *Svenskt Skeppsbyggeri*, edited by G Halldin, based on an original in the Krigsarkivet, Stockholm – 137

Frans Halsmuseum – 139–141

Based on drawings in *Old Ships' Figureheads and Sterns* by Carr Laughton – 143, 144, 146, 157, 163, 169, 223, 279, 281, 284, 288–291, 229–303, 307

From Raalamb's *Skeps Byggerij*, Stockholm, 1691 – 183, 212

Based on drawings in *Seventeenth Century Rigging* by R C Anderson – 184, 186, 189, 191, 195–197, 201–211

Based on an original in *Ship Models* by R Morton Nance – 185

The International Journal of Nautical Archaeology (1976, 5, 189–199) – 214 'L'Artillerie de Mer 1674–1856', *Triton* 84, 85, 86, 217–219, 223, 324, 328, 329

Conway Picture Library – 227, 264, 372, 388

Rijkmuseum, Amsterdam – 236, 239

Danish Shipping Museum, Kronberg Castle, Elsinore – 253

By courtesy of Basil Bathe (Science Museum models, except 259 Musée de la Marine, Paris) – 256, 259, 262

Photographs by Len Tucker (models in the National Maritime Museum) – 257, 258, 261, 263, 265, 266, 269

By courtesy of Roderick Stewart, Technical Officer, *Unicorn* project – 267, 272, 359

Photographs by the author – 271, 272

Popperfoto – 320

American Neptune (1943, *III*, 150) – 325

Based on originals in *Shipbuilding* by A Creuze – 358, 361–363, 365, 379

In the chapters following the marginal figures refer to relevant illustrations

1. A big merchantman, perhaps Flemish, of the second half of the fifteenth century. There are two decks to the forestage and two, or even three, in the aftercastle. The huge opening near the stern is a cargo port that would be closed by a strong lid. Note the numerous shrouds, set up with deadeyes; the lower deadeyes fastened by chains; and the parrels with ribs and trucks. There are no ratlines, access to the maintop being by a Jacob's Ladder up the mast, though there is none to the fore- and mizzenmasts. The hull is carvel-planked and has four wales. The ship is heavily armed, for she has 8 guns in the after-castle and a swivel in the mizzen top. This familiar illustration is by an artist known only by his initials WA. The model in the Science Museum, London is based on the WA 'kraeck'. The reconstruction of the parts not visible on WA's drawing has been based on other drawings and on what is known about later ships' internal arrangements.

INTRODUCTION

The astonishing expansion of European sea-borne trade, the formation of colonies in the Americas and Australasia and the establishment of huge Empires by the major maritime States of Europe during the four and a half centuries from AD1400 to 1860 owed its success, in the first place, to the transformation of the primitive sailing ship from a one-masted and single-sailed vessel into a three- and sometimes four-masted ship carrying a formidable armament of heavy guns and able to remain at sea for weeks and even months at a time. Without such ships to back them up the early colonists and *Conquistadores* would never have been able to hold their own against the indigenous inhabitants of the East and of America, nor would the settlement of Australia and the Pacific islands have been within the realms of possibility.

Although innumerable books have been written about the history of European expansion the story of the development of the ocean-going ship that made it possible, and which took place for the most part in little more than a century, is still known only partially and in outline before the beginning of the seventeenth century, by which time practically every feature of the classic sailing warship was present in at least rudimentary form. The detail of much of what happened before that date remains blank and is likely to remain so until the archives of the maritime States have been worked over.

When the fifteenth century opened the ships of the western and northern coasts of Europe were less developed, to judge from the available evidence, than those of the Mediterranean countries, and they belonged to a different tradition or rather, as recent archaeological discoveries have shown, to several different traditions, that had a long history behind them. Broadly speaking, the Northern ships were built with overlapping planks (clinker or lap-strake) whereas Mediterranean ships had edge-to-edge planking (carvel building). So far as we know, Northern ships had only one mast until the fifteenth century but in the Mediterranean ships with two masts had been known since classical times. Another difference between ships of the two regions was that Northern ships had square sails but, in general, Mediterranean ships had lateens. What the ships of Spain, Portugal and south-western France were like is still uncertain.

AD1400 is a convenient point at which to begin the story of the development of the Northern sailing warship. It was in the fifteenth century that the foundations of the national navies were laid; in England the credit has been given to Henry V, the Yorkist Kings and to Henry VII. It was in the same century that the transformation of the Northern ship got under way; and it was in that century that evidence for the construction, rig and armament of warships becomes available in sufficient quantity and detail to make convincing reconstructions possible. The terminal date, 1860, is fixed by the launching of HMS *Warrior*, the first iron-hulled, armoured and steam-driven warship, a vessel so heavily armed that she could successfully have tackled whole fleets of wooden sailing warships.

The amount of information that has survived from those four and a half centuries is enormous: pictures, documents, books, plans, contemporary models and, from the very end of the era, photographs. There are also examples of the ships themselves. The preservation of the *Victory* in Britain, the *Constitution* and *Constellation* in America and the *Jylland* in Denmark is well known but in the last twenty years many others have been recovered, in varying states of preservation, by underwater archaeologists. The *Wasa* in Sweden is the most famous and spectacular example, but the mediaeval cog found in the River Weser near Bremen promises to be a good runner-up. The Baltic Sea, and the Great Lakes of America, are proving to be treasure-houses of well-preserved wrecks, and the reclamation of the Zuider Zee has already yielded over 350 vessels although none, so far, has turned out to be a warship.

Of all the sources listed, pictures (which may be taken to include carvings as well) are probably the least reliable for the first two and a half centuries of our period. Their quality ranges from mediaeval illustrations that suggest that the artist had heard of ships but had never seen one to the almost photographic accuracy of Dutch marine painters. Yet even seemingly crude drawings may record some important feature however much it may have been garbled.

We know now that the cog's keel was tilted up at each end as some contemporary seals show it, and that carracks' masts were enormously thick. Nautical historians were puzzled for a long time by representations of mediaeval ships that looked as though they were built of long bricks but when the *Grace Dieu*'s remains were examined it was found that her planks were short, only 6-7ft. Paradoxically, the most detailed pictures may be as unreliable as crudely drawn ones, though for quite a different reason. When seascapes became fashionable in the late sixteenth and early seventeenth centuries the products of Dutch painters were widely sold and vendors were not above ascribing the buyer's nationality to the vessel(s) depicted. The well-known engravings of Armada ships by the Dutch artist Visscher are believed by some authorities to show Dutch ships, or at any rate to show Dutch features, and even the famous picture of the *Prince Royal* of 1612 and her consorts sailing into Flushing harbour has had the accuracy of some of its details questioned. Indeed, it is not until the establishment of an English school of marine painting after the middle of the seventeenth century that representations of English ships can be trusted to show English practice although, of course, there are exceptions to this general statement and some examples will be found in later sections of this book.

Better than pictures as evidence for the appearance of ships are the contemporary models known in Britain as 'Dockyard' or 'Navy Board' models. Splendid collections are preserved in the museums of all the European maritime countries, and in America. Britain has an unequalled range of such models dating from the early seventeenth century to the end of the sailing warship era. The principal collections are now in the Science Museum, London, and the National Maritime Museum at Greenwich but there are smaller, though valuable, collections in other museums; Merseyside museums in Liverpool and the Royal Scottish Museum in Edinburgh have important examples and there are others in private hands. One very important collection went to America in the 1920s and is now part of the Henry Huddleston Rogers Collection at the United States Naval Academy. In Europe the collection in the Sjöhistoriska Museum at Stockholm is of especial interest to students of the seventeenth century warship because of the number of models from the early part of that century preserved there. Some of the models are of English ships and represent the work of the English shipwrights there, of whom Francis Sheldon is probably the most important.

Authoritative though 'Dockyard' models appear to be, and in the majority of instances undoubtedly are, their value as evidence is not without reservations. Is the rigging original? If it is not, or if it has been restored, it may contain anachronisms. Some models, though few of those in Britain fortunately, have had damaged hulls drastically 'restored'. A feature of 'Dockyard' models that has fallen under suspicion is the manner of framing them. As most people know, it was customary to leave the lower part of the hull unplanked and the frames visible. It has been argued that the disposition of the frames in the model does not correspond with actual dockyard practice. The question has not yet been finally decided and all that need be said here is that the familiar arrangement should not be taken for granted as representing the real one. Before leaving the subject of models mention must be made of the superb modern models in museums. Based on thorough and up-to-date research, these models equal, and sometimes surpass, the quality of 'Dockyard' models. To name only two, the model of the bomb-vessel *Granado* in the National Maritime Museum and that of the *Wasa* being made at the Science Museum in London are of the very highest standard of accuracy.

Of all the sources of information about the sailing warship by far the largest is the documentary, including contemporary books and plans. The quantity is enormous and deals with every conceivable aspect of ship construction, armament, rigging, stores and so on. In Britain the principal collections are in the Public Records Office and the British Library in London and in the National Maritime Museum, but a great deal of material is in private collections. Important collections are preserved in the Danish and Swedish archives, in France and in the USA. Being official documents the information is of course authoritative. The same cannot be said unfortunately about contemporary books. Their authors were often more concerned with continuing the practices of the 'good old days' or with advocating new principles, neither of which represented contemporary official practice. So far as scientific studies of naval architecture are concerned, French authors produced some excellent work but in Britain the information put into the books was all too often out of date and copied from one book to another. Sections of Falconer's *A Universal Dictionary of the Marine*, first published in 1769, can be traced through Steel's *Elements of Mast-making, Sail-making and Rigging* of 1794 to Abraham Rees' *Naval Architecture* of 1819. Illustrations were used in the same way. 'Mr Dummer's Draught of a First Rate' that came out in 1680 was still going strong in the early nineteenth century. Nevertheless, after the middle of the eighteenth century an improvement in the quality of naval architecture books gradually came about and is exemplified by the monumental *Architectura Navalis Mercatoria* by the famous Swedish naval architect Frederic Henry af Chapman.

The most valuable documentary sources are, of course, contemporary plans for they show the ship as she was to be built, or actually built, whereas a model may be a proposed design or a presentation model that does not correspond with any actual ship. Britain is especially fortunate in having an enormous collection of plans of every kind of warship from the beginning of the eighteenth century. This, the Admiralty Collection, is now in the National Maritime Museum. Another important collection is that of the Danish Navy and among the thousands of plans are many of other nationalities' warships, some from the beginning of the 1600s. The Swedish archives likewise have much of interest to the student of the wooden warship, as do those of France, Holland and the United States.

The remaining source of information – the ships themselves – is naturally the least plentiful. Britain has the *Victory*, now in permanent drydock, and two nineteenth century frigates still afloat, the *Foudroyant* at Portsmouth and the *Unicorn* at Dundee. The *Wasa* has already been mentioned and so have the American ships *Constitution* and *Constellation*. Besides those two ships, which are to a considerable extent reconstructions, the Americans have raised several warships from the bottom of the Great Lakes and preserved them; these are ships that date from the Wars of Independence and 1812. From British waters much valuable evidence has come to light: the remains of Henry V's *Grace Dieu* lie in the Hamble River near Southampton, whilst the *Mary Rose* off Portsmouth and recently the remains of the *Dartmouth* wrecked off Mull in 1690 have been excavated with results of the greatest interest. Nor should the discovery of the remains of Armada ships be neglected, for they throw light on the structure of ships derived from a different tradition of naval architecture. Unfortunately, however, the very circumstances under which ships are wrecked means that the remains are nearly always scanty and usually confined to the bottom timbers and the more durable fittings.

If the foregoing account of the amount of historical material available has led the reader to imagine that the development of the sailing warship is adequately described, he is going to be disappointed. Shelves full of books have been written about the doings of seamen in peace and war but a definitive history of the development of the ships that enabled those things to be done has not yet appeared, although some valuable limited surveys such as, for example, of seventeenth century rigging have been produced. In Britain the best general account of the sailing warship is still the Historical Notes to the Science Museum's catalogue *Sailing Ships: their history and development* published in 1932 but now out of print. The Naval Accounts of Henry VII were published in 1896 but those of Henry VIII have not been, yet they contain over 400 pages dealing with the *Henry Grace à Dieu* alone. The marvellous collections of draughts made by the Elizabethan master-shipwright Mathew Baker, and his notes on the design of ships, have never been published in full, nor has Anthony Deane's *A Doctrine of Naval Architecture* that he wrote in 1670 for Samuel Pepys. The list could extended. Much the same comments apply to the excavations of wrecks. Until very recently few had been adequately described, if they had been recorded at all. In fact, it is probably true to say that until twenty years ago only two wrecks had been at all well reported. One was a well-preserved mediaeval coaster found in a former channel of the River Rother in Sussex in 1822 and described in Vol XX of the journal *Archaeologia* (1824), and the other was the *Grace Dieu* whose remains were surveyed under great difficulty in 1933.

It will be apparent that anyone intending to study an individual ship or a class of vessel, or to make a representative model of either, needs to know where to find the information, how extensive it is and whether it is reliable. Those needs have been taken into account in writing this book, which has a three-fold purpose: to relate how the sailing warship developed; to present essential data about construction, rigging and armament at each stage of the development; and to guide the inquirer to original sources from which the development may be studied in fuller detail than a single book will permit. Important material scattered among books and periodicals, or not yet published, has been brought together and its value assessed from the standpoint of the ships themselves. In reproducing it here, bearing in mind the limitations of space, preference has been given to the less well-known and less readily accessible material, for the general reader cannot be expected to make searches in the national archives. Consequently, more space has been given to ships of the fifteenth and the first half of the sixteenth century than to those of Armada times; to those of the first half of the eighteenth in preference to the ships of the second half; and to the nineteenth century sailing warship, about which little has appeared in popular form. The book is in essence five monographs, each one dealing with a major stage in the warship's development. As it happened, each of the five stages took place in a different century, so a chronological division can conveniently be used. Developments are described under hull and fittings, decoration, rigging and armament as they relate to the biggest class of ship, support craft and boats being treated separately. It has been assumed that the reader is familiar with the common names of the parts of a ship but unusual ones will be defined as they crop up.

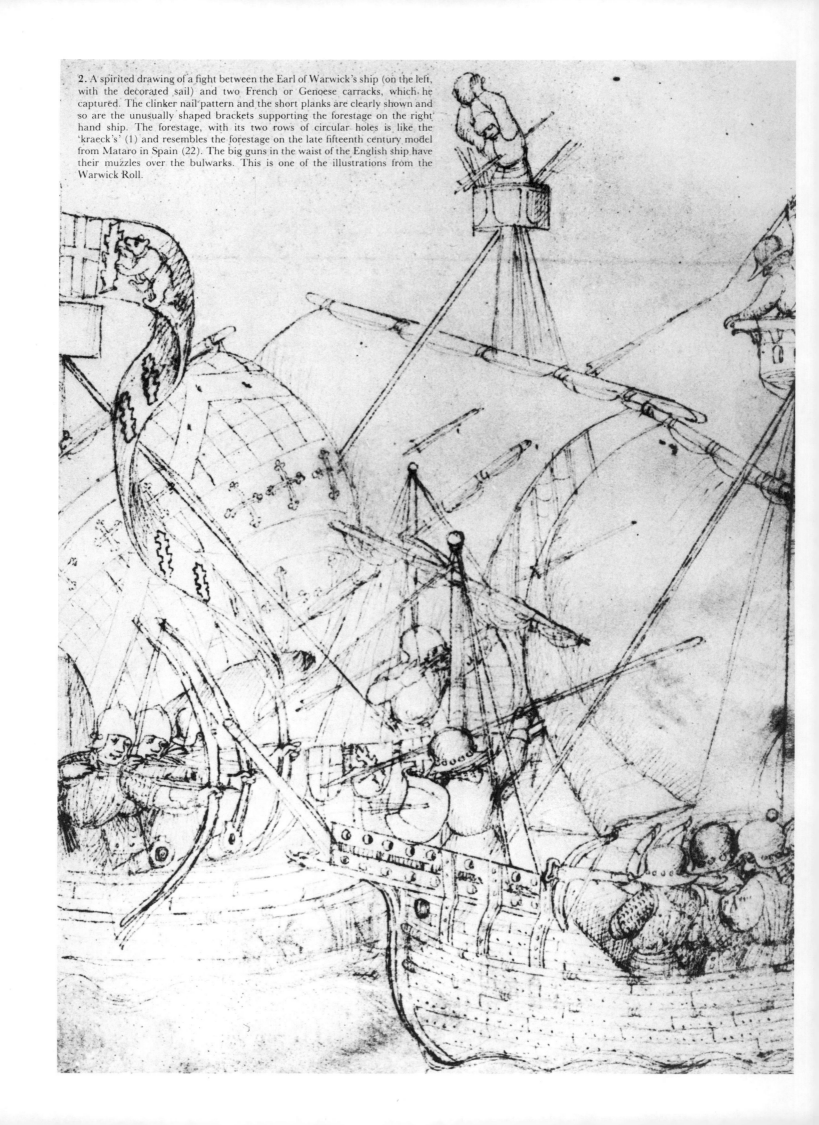

2. A spirited drawing of a fight between the Earl of Warwick's ship (on the left, with the decorated sail) and two French or Genoese carracks, which he captured. The clinker nail pattern and the short planks are clearly shown and so are the unusually shaped brackets supporting the forestage on the right hand ship. The forestage, with its two rows of circular holes is like the 'kraeck's' (1) and resembles the forestage on the late fifteenth century model from Mataro in Spain (22). The big guns in the waist of the English ship have their muzzles over the bulwarks. This is one of the illustrations from the Warwick Roll.

THE FULL RIGGED SHIP

The question whether the first steps towards the transformation of the North European one-masted ship into the ocean-going man-of-war of the sixteenth century were taken before or just after AD1400 is still in dispute but it is irrelevant to the subject of this chapter because the evidence makes it clear that only a few years either side of that date are concerned. Some significant changes in the shape of North European ships had taken place long before the fifteenth century opened. For hundreds of years those ships had been double-ended and with curved stem- and sternposts, but when the sternpost rudder was adopted in the thirteenth century the sternpost was straightened, although it still sloped backwards, and in time differences in shape between bow and stern developed, the latter becoming fuller above the waterline. One feature of the early mediaeval ship remained unchanged, at any rate in England: the hulls were built of overlapping planks in the traditional North European manner that we call clinker-building (or lapstrake). In the past the prevalence of clinker-building has been ascribed to Viking influence but the evidence of recently found wrecks suggests that it was in common use along the Channel and North Sea coasts as well as in Scandinavia. That is not to say that the Southern style of building in which the planks were set edge-to-edge (carvel-built) was unknown along the Channel coasts and beyond, for the trade between Flanders and Southampton and the Mediterranean ports would have made the Southern, carvel-built ships a familiar sight to the local seamen and shipwrights. Nevertheless, the remains of mediaeval vessels that have been found up to now are all at least partially clinker-built.

Before describing the changes that took place during the fifteenth century something must be said about the basic features of Northern warships as they were about 1400. Between the eleventh and the end of the fourteenth century oar-driven ships, descendants of Viking-style vessels, had gradually been replaced by sturdy sailing ships. A few big galleys (different in build from the Mediterranean galley) were launched in the thirteenth and fourteenth centuries and had served, usually, as special Royal ships. In England none seems to have been constructed after Edward III died in 1377. Small oared warships, about which even less is known than about the sailing ships, were in use up to the end of the fourteenth century and indeed for long afterwards, but by 1400 all the big ships of which we have records relied on sails for propulsion. The English ones had a single mast and probably only one sail, and they differed little in either hull form or rig from the bigger contemporary merchant ships. The roles of warship and merchantmen were in fact interchangeable, for the King hired or commandeered merchant ships to augment his fleet in wartime and when he was at peace he sometimes leased his ships to merchants. The main difference between the King's ships and merchantmen was size: the Royal ships were bigger. As we shall see later, some Royal ships were as big as any ships built in the sixteenth and even the early seventeenth centuries. In fact, the principal Royal ships in the fifteenth century were as big as the technology of the time and the nature of the harbours – many of which dried out at low tide and had shallow approaches – would allow.

The shape of warships, and because of the ever-present threat of piracy the shape of merchantmen too, was governed by their means of attack and defence. The ram was not adopted by the Northern seamen, so until the development of effective firearms a warship's armament was limited to bows and arrows, javelins and such objects as could be flung from the fighting tops on to the enemy's decks. A sea fight was simply a land fight on floating platforms and had features in common with an attack on, and the defence of, a castle. Warships had high sides – the equivalent of castle walls – and the high stages at bow and stern provided command and enfilading fire as a castle's towers did. The basic manoeuvre was to place the attacker's stem against the side of the enemy ship, as a siege tower was brought up to a castle wall, and to use arrows and javelins to clear the decks as a preliminary to boarding. To make the tactic more effective the bows were given an enormous forward rake (overhang) and a high forestage that sometimes had two and even three storeys projecting further forward. At the other end of the ship was the aftercastle. This was not so high as the forecastle but was much longer and was used to accommodate the important people on board. As the fifteenth century progressed the height of the forecastle was reduced until by about 1480 it was only a little higher than the aftercastle although the latter, it seems, was somewhat higher than it had been at the beginning of the century. Precisely when the reduction in height of the forecastle came about, and why, has yet to be discovered. It may be that the extraordinarily high forecastles of ships like the *Grace Dieu* of 1418 and her contemporary, the great ship being built at Bayonne for Henry V, were found to have disadvantages that outweighed their benefits and that later, when guns became an important factor in sea fights, a change in tactics made towering forecastles unnecessary (though they reappeared in the early sixteenth century, but in a different form). Unfortunately the English evidence is mostly from either the first quarter of the century or the last one, so that we are at a loss to know when several important innovations appeared. The earlier evidence deals with Henry V's ships, the *Grace Dieu* of 1400 tons, the *Jesus,* of 1000, and the *Holigost* of 760 tons, as well as some smaller craft. It covers the time when a second mast came into use but leaves the question of a third one open. When documentary evidence becomes plentiful again after about 1480 the first stage in the transformation is completed, a fact that is quite clear from the drawings of ships in that marvellous collection of sketches known as the Warwick Roll (or Rous Roll), the proper title being 'The Pageant of the Birth, Life and Death of Richard Beauchamp, Earl of Warwick, KG'[1]. Twelve of the drawings have ships in them, and three or perhaps four different kinds are shown. One sort dates from the middle of the century or earlier and another seems to be about 1470 but the ships in the pictures illustrating the latest incidents in the Earl's life are recognisably forerunners of the 'great ships' of the next century. They have four masts, carry a battery of big guns in the waist and have the characteristic early sixteenth century arched openings for guns in their upperworks. The date of the Roll is uncertain. It is not contemporary with the Earl, who died in 1439, and is said to have been made for his daughter, the Countess of Warwick, who died in 1493. Another possibility, however, is that it was made for *her* daughter, Anne, who married Richard III (1483–5). Thus its date might be before, and as much as a decade before, 1493 or it might be after that date. A close dating for the pictures is most desirable because the later ships are carefully drawn and give an impression of being 'from life'. If it could be proved that the Roll was made in King Richard's time the ships depicted are likely to be those of one or other of his predecessors and if that is the case English shipbuilding (and by implication that of other European States, for several of the ships in Richard's fleet were foreign-built) was more advanced than is usually supposed. On the other hand, if the pictures were drawn after the accession of Henry VII in 1485 they might show the *Sovereign,* which was afloat in 1488, or perhaps even the *Regent* (1497). The complement to the Warwick Roll is the information in Henry VII's naval accounts and inventories for 1485–8 and 1495–7. They contain innumerable details about the building, care and maintenance of the King's ships and although, like the accounts from the beginning of the century, they say little about the shape of the hulls, what can be inferred agrees with the Warwick Roll pictures[2].

THE HULL

Mediaeval English seamen spoke of four kinds of ships: nefs, cogs, hulks and carracks. The name nef was, at first, a general one for ships but towards the end of the Middle Ages it became an archaic word applied only to the biggest ships – the capital ships, as we would call them. The cog was a vessel of Northern origin that had been the merchant ship *par excellence* for over two centuries during which it had traded, and raided, from Scandinavia to the Mediterranean where shipbuilders had adopted some of the cog's characteristics. It had served as a warship in some of the sea fights of the Hundred Years War, notably at Sluys in 1340. Cogs are shown on the seals of several ancient seaports. They are high sided ships, have a straight stempost with a great forward rake, a small forecastle but a big aftercastle. The cogs are clinker-built and have only one mast and one sail. What appear to be the end of beams protrude through the sides of the hull and on some seals the keel is bent upwards towards each end.

Despite the cog's importance that was practically all that was known about it until 1962. In that year, whilst some improvements were being made to the channel of the River Weser, in Germany, part of an old ship was uncovered. Its importance was appreciated at once and its complete excavation taken in hand. The find proved to be the almost intact hull of a cog! From the evidence of the objects found in the hull it seems that the ship had been almost finished when a flood swept it away and carried it down the river to sink near what was then the river bank. The find confirmed what the seals showed: high sides, straight and raking stempost, clinker build, and protruding beam ends. Only the mast and yard are missing. The ship is 22.5m long, 7.5m in beam and is 5.3m high. The keel is 15.6m long, and the stem 8.4m. The planks are 0.75m wide. Part of the bottom, which is flat, is carvel-planked and the rest of the hull is clinker. But the most interesting feature is the shape of the keel: the fore and after thirds are tilted up, as some seals show. This unusual shape was adopted, it is thought, to strengthen the hull against hogging[3]. The pattern of the annual growth rings in the big timbers show that the trees from which they had been sawn were felled about AD1380. This extraordinarily fortunate find, the most complete of any ship between the Gokstad and Oseberg ships and the *Wasa*, means that we now have the information necessary to make a model of one kind of early fifteenth century warship if we add the war service forestage, which at that time was a temporary structure. It must be remembered, however, that the ship is a German one and that other nation's cogs may have differed in details. Northern ships in later centuries were basically the same but were nevertheless distinguishable at a glance to a seaman.

Towards the end of the fourteenth century cogs were being displaced by hulks for cargo carrying and probably as warships too, for Henry IV had a hulk, the *Christopher of the Tower* ('of the Tower' means that a ship belonged to the King) in 1410[4]. Hulks are some-

3. The Bremen cog being re-assembled after preservative treatment at the Deutsches Schiffahrtsmuseum, Bremerhaven. The straight stempost, raking well forwards, is about to have the false stem fitted. To the left of the photograph's centre the end of one of the tie-beams protrudes through the planking. The strakes are very wide, the uppermost in the photograph being more than 24in.

4. The after part of the cog's side. The holes for the roves that fastened the overlapping strakes together can be seen in the lower edges of the two upper strakes.

5. A preliminary model to show what the cog will look like when it has been re-assembled. Since the model was made, however, it has been discovered that the keel is not straight as on the model, but turns up towards each end. The curved keel is thought to have provided a greater resistance to hogging than a straight keel would have done. Until the reconstruction is finished no complete plans will be available.

3

4

5

6. Development of the Carrack 1400–1500. (a) 'Castles' only; (b) somercastle brought forward, tilt-frame aft; (bb) variant tilt-frame of lean-to form; (c) poop, raised on stanchions, with thwartships tilt-frame over it, forecastle tilt-frame; (cc) variant tilt-frame of longships form; (d) stage added to forecastle also, tilt-frame over it; (e) poop joined to hull, arched openings, guns on gunwale; (f) forecastle consolidated, poop built raking, guns in round open ports; (g) two counters aft, heavy forecastle.

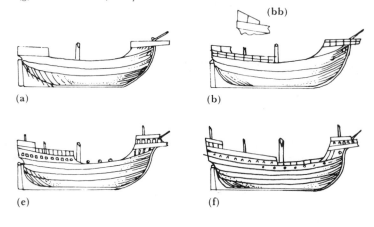
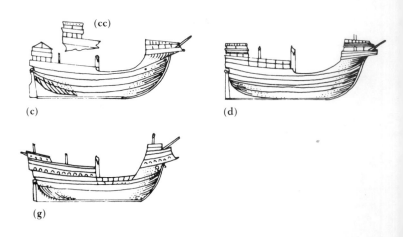

(a) (b) (c) (d)

(e) (f) (g)

thing of a mystery and little is known about their build or rig. They were often big ships, but small ones are occasionally mentioned. The slight evidence from the fourteenth and fifteenth centuries suggests that the hulk of that time was clinker-built, had a flat bottom and was probably double-ended[5]. The *Christopher of the Tower* had the same rig as a cog, for her gear included one mast, one sailyard, and one course (sail) with a bonnet (an extension to lace on to the bottom of the sail). She also had a forecastle and a somercastle (the aftercastle), both of which may have been temporary structures, and 34 pavesses (large wooden shields to protect the men on deck). The meaning of the name hulk changed during the fifteenth century, since by the sixteenth it often stood for a Northern European, as distinct from an English, merchantman and later still came to mean a worn out hull, usually a large one.

The fourth kind of ship was the carrack. She probably originated in the Mediterranean though some scholars believe that the honour may belong to Bayonne. The carrack was the biggest ship of her time and it was her size that impressed men. The general lines of the carrack's development have been established by R M Nance and Guilleux la Roërie[6], who have shown that there were differences in build and rig between Mediterranean carracks and those of Northern Europe, at least in the early stages of the carrack's history. Southern carracks, for example, were always carvel-built and had transom sterns whereas the early Flemish and English carracks, and probably all the other Northern ones, were clinker-built at the beginning of the fifteenth century and

were double-ended until the century was well under way. The principal features of a carrack were a roomy hull with a keel:beam ratio of 2:1 or 2.5:1, bluff bows with a great rake to the convexly curved stem and high sides that narrowed in above the main deck. At bow and stern were lofty 'castles' that evolved into the forecastle and quarterdeck of later centuries. The forecastle was, at first, a single-decked open platform that projected over the bows but before long it was closed in and another stage added above it. On the biggest ships there might be yet another stage. The aftercastle started out as a lightly built structure at the stern, its length being about 1/3 the length of the ship's keel. It was called (in English) the somercastle and was primarily the accommodation for the officers and important passengers. By 1480 it had become a permanent part of the hull, had been extended forward nearly to the mainmast and had, in effect, become the half-deck of later times. Right at the stern was a short poop that usually had a tilt frame over it to support an awning. On Mediterranean carracks the axis of the tilt frame was set athwartships whereas on the Northern vessels it ran fore and aft. For most of the fifteenth century the forecastle was higher, often much higher, than the aftercastle but by the last quarter of the century lower forecastles had come into fashion and the height of the aftercastles was increased.

Quantitative information about carracks is rare but two documents and part of a hull, all from the first half of the century, provide data for a partial reconstruction and give indications of how at least one hull was put together. The earliest of the two documents

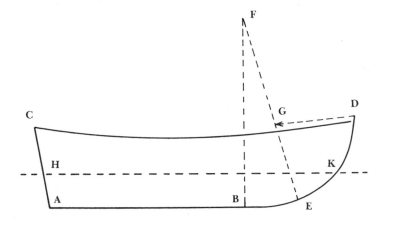

7. A reconstruction of the lower hull of the Bayonne ship of 1419. CD is the approximate line of the main deck.
AB, keel=112ft=FB, radius of inner arc
AC, post=48ft. GE, radius of outer arc=46ft=beam.
BD, stem=96ft.
Vertical height of C=47ft.
Vertical height of D=54ft.
Rake aft=10ft.
Rake forward=64ft.
HK, waterline.

8. The lines of the remains of the *Grace Dieu*, at Bursledon.

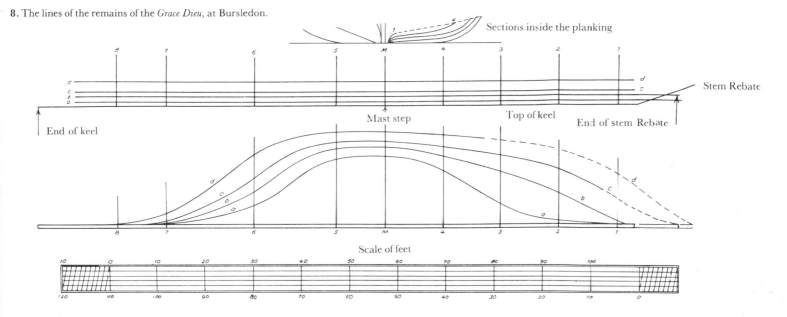

is a letter written to Henry V by John Alcetre in 1419 about a ship that was being built for the King at Bayonne. The letter was destroyed in the fire that burnt part of the famous Cottonian collection of historical documents, but a copy had been made and published in 1827[7]. The relevant part of Alcetre's letter runs: 'At the makyng of this letter yt was in this estate, that ys to wetyng, xxxvj strakes yn hyth y bordyd, on the wheche strakys byth y layde xj bemes; the mast beme ys yn leynthe xlvj comyn fete, and the beme of the hameron afore ys yn leynthe xxxix fete, and the beme of the hameron by hynde ys yn leynthe xxxij fete, fro the onemost ende of the stemme in to the Poste by hynde ys yn leynthe an hundred iiij[xx] and vj fete [186ft] and the stemme ys in hithe iiij[xx] and xvj fete [96ft]; and the Poste xlviij fete and the kele ys in leynthe an hundred and xij fete, but he is rotyt and must be chaungyd . . . '

The dimensions given by Alcetre pose more questions than they answer, and attempts to reconstruct the Bayonne ship have had only limited success, but a convincing profile of the lower hull was worked out by L G Carr Laughton[8]. He assumed that the backward rake of the sternpost (the 'Poste' of Alcetre's letter) was 10ft, and as the overall length of the hull was 186ft of which the keel accounted for 112ft, the rake of the stem was 64ft, which is slightly more than half the keel's length. Such an enormous overhang is not impossible, for English ships in the late sixteenth and early seventeenth centuries had fore rakes equal to 2/5 of their keels' lengths. The height of the stem, 96ft, must have been the length round the curve and not the vertical height above

the keel. The outline is only part of the story. Above the bows there would be the forestage which, with its bulwarks and probably another stage above, would bring the total height to about 64ft. The top of the sternpost is 47ft above the keel, and if to that are added the heights of the somercastle (half-deck) and the poop the top cannot have been far short of 57ft, which is about the same height as the *Victory*'s poop.

Attempts to reconstruct the midship section and the deck plan have failed because too many assumptions have to be made. How wide were the strakes? Were they carvel, as would be likely at Bayonne, or clinker? If we assume that the 36 strakes were carvel, that the planks were 12in wide and that the mast beam of 46ft was laid on top of the uppermost strake, a normal midship section can be drawn in which the topmost strake is about 18ft above the keel. If the strakes were laid clinker fashion and with a 4in overlap, the top one comes out about 8ft above the keel. That is a reasonable height for the beams of a lower orlop, but would a mast beam be set as low as that? It is unlikely. Moreover, the 11 beams are said to have been laid *on* the strakes which means, if taken literally, that their ends protruded through the sides. As we now know from the Bremen cog, beam ends did protrude in that way but the two alternative reconstructions for the Bayonne ship would mean that in one case the beam ends were at the waterline and in the other well below it. The beams of the 'hameron' are another puzzle. The word does not occur in dictionaries of mediaeval English or French. It has been suggested that the two hameron beams mark the ends of the waist

9. The construction of the remains of the *Grace Dieu*, at Bursledon.

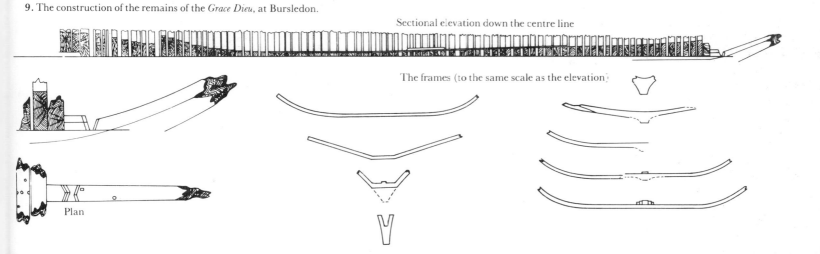

Sectional elevation down the centre line

The frames (to the same scale as the elevation)

Plan

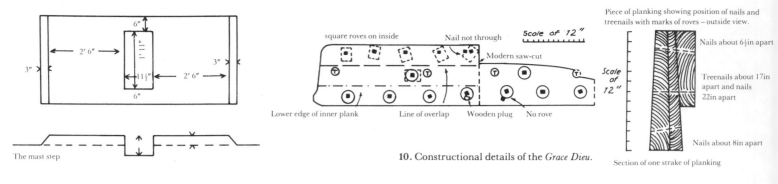

10. Constructional details of the *Grace Dieu*.

but if that is right the 'beam of the hameron behind' must have been well back for it was 13ft shorter than the mast beam. Another suggestion is that the 'hameron afore' was where the tack came aboard, and would therefore be towards the bows, but in that case what was the beam of the hameron behind?

The dimensions in Alcetre's letter seemed so incredibly large for a fifteenth century ship that it was often suspected that the original letter had been mis-copied in parts, but in 1933 the remains of an even bigger English ship, one that was afloat when the Bayonne ship was being built, were identified in the River Hamble near Southampton[9]. The conditions under which the examination was made were very difficult for the wreck is almost completely buried in mud, it lies at the edge of the river channel and is exposed for only a short time even at the lowest tides. A complete survey was impossible but enough evidence was obtained to prove that the ship was Henry V's *Grace Dieu* of 1400 tons, built in 1418 and burnt in 1439 after being struck by lightning. The keel is at least 125ft long and is probably 129ft. The maximum breadth of the remains is 37½ft but since only the bottom of the ship is left, the full breadth would probably have been about 50ft. The sternpost was inaccessible and most of the stem has gone, but what remains shows that it had had a great forward rake. Incomplete though the survey had to be, it was enough to show that the *Grace Dieu* was bigger than any other ship built in England until the seventeenth century.

The astonishing feature of the ship is the planking. It is three-layer clinker, each strake being built up from two planks 12in wide and one of 8in, their com-bined thicknesses being 4½in. The two wide planks over-lap the strake below so that at the overlap there are *five* thicknesses. The planks making up each strake are fastened together by iron nails driven through from the inside and clenched over circular roves (washers) on the outside. The fastenings have a knobbly appearance, a feature that appears in contemporary pictures. The planks were surprisingly short, only 6-7ft. Documentary evidence came to light subsequently from which it was possible to calculate that some ship planks were sawn in two lengths, about 6½ft and 10ft, and that they were about 12in wide and 1½in thick, as indeed the *Grace Dieu*'s planks are[10].

A modern reconstruction of the *Grace Dieu*'s profile has been produced and the dimensions correspond to a draught of 22ft, a freeboard to the top of the waist bulwarks of 26ft and a height from the water to the top of the poop rails of 60ft. The second deck of the forecastle is about 80ft above the keel, or 58ft above the water. If the reconstruction looks top-heavy it must be remembered that the upperworks were light structures and that few if any guns were carried in them. Unbeliev-ably large though the ship's dimensions may seem they have been confirmed from a contemporary source. In 1430 Luca di Maso degli Albizzi, the Captain of the

Florentine galleys trading to Flanders, visited the Royal ships in the Hamble River and recorded the measure-ments of the biggest one in his diary[11]. Luca di Maso said that the ship was of 1500 or even 1650 tons, about 184ft along the deck and about 50ft broad. Her forestage was 52ft above the water and another one was added to it for war service. Di Maso measured the mainmast and found it to be 22ft in circumference (or nearly 7ft in diameter) and he was told that it was 200ft high. He said that the ship was the largest and most beautiful construction that he had ever seen. A Florentine Captain of Galleys was not a man to be easily impressed and di Maso was an accomplished seaman who would have known whether the measurements that he was given were of the right order or not.

After the accounts dealing with the *Grace Dieu* and her consorts[12] come to an end there is a gap in the English records of 40 to 50 years and when evidence becomes plentiful again the extent to which develop-ment has taken place in plain to be seen. Some idea of what was going on in the Mediterranean in the first half of the fifteenth century is contained in an Italian manu-script about the building of galleys and ships that was written about 1445. The manuscript was translated by Dr R C Anderson and published in the *Mariner's Mirror*[13]. Among the data is the accompanying table of dimensions for carracks.

There are some interesting relationships between the principal dimensions in this table. The keel:beam ratios lie between 3.25:1 and 2.5:1. The sternpost:beam proportions are 1:1, or very nearly, for 1, 4, 6 and 7 and 0.7-0.75 for 2, 3 and 5, suggesting a rule that the sternpost should be the same length as the beam (as it was on the Bayonne ship) or else about 3/4 of it. The stem:beam proportion is also a simple one, roughly 4:3 except for 5, in which it is 10:9.

Nothing comparable to the Italian manu-script's information is available for Northern ships and reliable evidence is scanty until about 1470. By then carvel building was being adopted for big ships, three masts were common and cannon a normal part of a warship's armament. A mid-fifteenth century ship from the Hastings Manuscript still has the high forestage but has a pair of big gunports in the aftercastle. The well-known engraving showing the WA 'kraeck' is probably the most important evidence for the appearance and rig of carracks of the third quarter of the fifteenth century. The drawing is believed to have been based on a votive ship in a church, for the waterline is set too low as it often is on votive models. The rigging, convincing though it seems at first glance, has in fact defeated the artist. But he is in a numerous company, for few artists then or later managed to make an accurate job of rigging. The date of the ship is, unfortunately, uncertain. The picture is said to have been made about 1470 but if it was based on a church-ship the model may have been a good deal older.

For the appearance of English warships in the second half of the century the most important evidence is, without any doubt, the Warwick Roll in which three or perhaps four different ships appear. The oldest have single-decked and open forestages and the hulls are clinker-built for the characteristic nail pattern is shown; the planks are short. The forestages are supported by riders on the outside of the hulls, and from the shape of the riders it is clear that the forestage is considerably narrower than the maindeck below it. The shape of the riders is a peculiar one. If they are made of wood they seem scarcely thick enough for their job; but perhaps the

riders were made of iron, for the accounts for Henry VII's *Sovereign* record buying iron for 'bolts and clamps of iron for the forecastle, somercastle and poop of the said ship'.

There is a difference between the forestages of the two ships on one of the Warwick Roll illustrations: the English ship, to the left, has its forestage rails hung with pavesses but the other ship, which is intended to represent a French or a Genoese carrack, has its forestage bulwarks made of two bands of planking with a wide gap between them. Each band has a row of circular holes in it. Similar holes occur on the late fifteenth

DIMENSIONS FOR CARRACKS – Early Fifteenth Century

Carrack	Burden (botte*)	Keel (ft)	Stem (ft)	Sternpost (ft)	Beam (ft)	Floor (ft)	Width 3ft above keel	Width 6ft above keel	Depth (ft)	Transom (ft)
1	1000	85	45½	35	34	11	27	33**	12	–
2	700	72½	36	21	28	10	19¾	23¾	11	–
3	700	70	36	21	28	10	–	25	–	20
4	500	72½	34	25	25	9	18½	–	11	–
5	300	62½	25	15½	22½	7	15	–	7½	13
6	250	60	27	19	20½	8½	16¼	18½	8½	–
7	200	60	25	18½	18	–	–	–	–	–

*A botta was about half a ton.
**Dr Anderson believed that this figure was a mistake and should have been either 29 or 31ft.

11. The profile of the *Grace Dieu* compared with those of some other big ships, as reconstructed by Major-General M W Prynne.

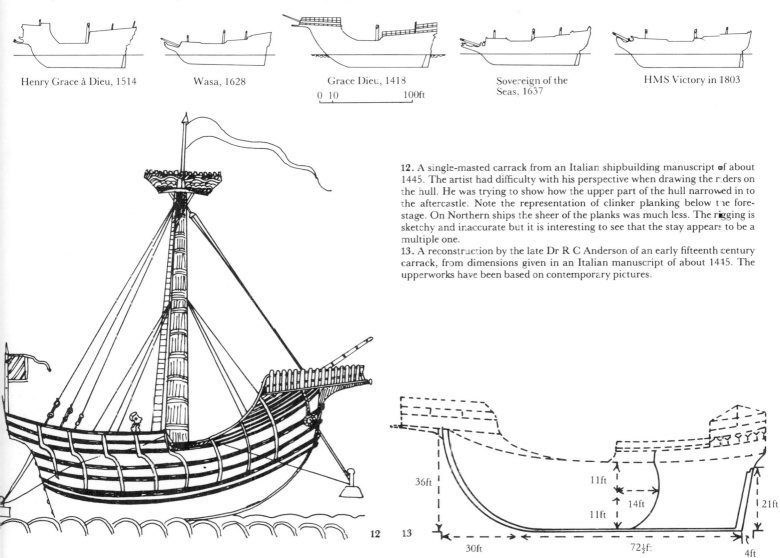

Henry Grace à Dieu, 1514   Wasa, 1628   Grace Dieu, 1418   Sovereign of the Seas, 1637   HMS Victory in 1803

0 10   100ft

12. A single-masted carrack from an Italian shipbuilding manuscript of about 1445. The artist had difficulty with his perspective when drawing the riders on the hull. He was trying to show how the upper part of the hull narrowed in to the aftercastle. Note the representation of clinker planking below the forestage. On Northern ships the sheer of the planks was much less. The rigging is sketchy and inaccurate but it is interesting to see that the stay appears to be a multiple one.

13. A reconstruction by the late Dr R C Anderson of an early fifteenth century carrack, from dimensions given in an Italian manuscript of about 1445. The upperworks have been based on contemporary pictures.

12   13

36ft   11ft   14ft   11ft   21ft   30ft   72½ft   4ft

tıf þe come ın to ııı̃. fadını deep and yf ıt be ſtrenp
fronnde ıt ıs betwene ſhıeſhaıt and cıſſe ın tħe entre
of tħe chanel of ffaandres and ſoo goo youre coıırs
tıl ye ſlaue ſtott fadnıı̃ deep. tħan goo eſt nortħe eſt
a longe tħe ſee . ♱ c̃.

14

century model from Mataro, in Catalonia, so they may have been a feature of Southern ships. The big carrack on the Warwick Roll shows an impressive degree of detail and the structural features are of great interest. The forecastle has two decks (this part of the drawing is not the artist's best – he had difficulty with the perspective), the hull has distinctly rounded sides and the sides of the somercastle narrow in sharply. There seem to be two decks above the maindeck in the aftercastle of the ship. The after part of the hull shows how the planks run in to the sternpost and how the deadwood is shaped. Rudder, tiller and rudder irons are clearly drawn. The bows cannot be seen but another picture in the Roll supplies the missing parts. The carrack's hull has some puzzling features about it. There are no wales, no nail patterns and no plank joints. If the rest of the hull had not been so clearly drawn it might be supposed that those details had been left off but it is possible that the artist was trying to record carvel planking. Other interesting features of the hull will be discussed under fittings, armament and decoration.

Ships that were at the time the last word in advanced warship design are also depicted on the Roll. Although these are still carracks they are developing into the 'great ship' of the next century. The arches in the forecastle and the aftercastle (which can now be called a half-deck) testify to the presence of guns in greater numbers than ever before. The stems have lost most of their forward rake and run nearly straight from the water to the stem knee. The aftercastle is fully integrated with the lower hull, which no longer has the excessive tumble-home that the earlier ships have. The hulls are shown as clinker-built and have a pair of wales. The combination of clinker planking and wales is unusual and might be dismissed as a mistake, but the accounts for building the *Mary Fortune,* which was clinker-built, include 'long timber for wales'[2].

14. An English warship of about the middle of the fifteenth century, from the Hastings Manuscript. She has three masts and perhaps a main topmast. The hull has the old-fashioned high forestage but the gunports in the after part are omens of the changes that would come about with the adoption of the gun as a major part of a ship's armament. The hull may have a square stern but as the picture was probably copied in the early sixteenth century from an earlier manuscript the artist may have made a mistake in drawing the stern.
15. A small carrack, probably about the middle of the fifteenth century, from the Warwick Roll. There is only one deck in the forestage; the hull is clinker-built of short planks but has two strong wales. Note the great arched entrance into the forecastle, and the way the bulwarks of the waist are constructed. The main shrouds seem to be set up with deadeyes.

The Warwick Roll ships dovetail neatly with the naval accounts for Henry VII's ships. Being concerned with what was on the ships or in the storehouses when the inventories were taken, or with purchases of materials for building or repairing the King's ships, the accounts have little to say about the shape of the ships. Some useful inferences can be drawn nevertheless. The gun list for the *Sovereign* reveals that she had at least two decks in her forecastle and two in the aftercastle. The large quantities of rove-and-clench nails bought for the new ships *Sweepstake* and *Mary Fortune* prove that substantial portions of those ships were clinker-planked. On the other hand the accounts for the *Sovereign* and the *Regent* have no references to rove-and-clench nails, and *Regent's* actually list 'carvel nails'. The implication is clear: by 1497 the biggest and most up-to-date English warships were carvel-planked, although it is possible that the *Sovereign* was clinker when she was first built (see Chapter 2). The examples just given are only a small fraction of what may be deduced from a study of the accounts, which have not yet been systematically analysed.

Before closing the section on hull development something must be said about the arrangement of decks in carracks and other fifteenth century ships. Contemporary documents rarely mention decks and when they do it is usually those in the fore- and aftercastles. The disposition of decks has to be worked out from pictures and the occasional references to the siting of key fittings. The main deck from the mainmast forward presents no difficulty. It runs flush, or else with a gentle sheer, from the aftercastle bulkhead to the bows. The Warwick pictures suggest that it also ran at the same level under the somercastle (half-deck) because one of the ships has a door in the bulkhead at maindeck level, and another has a row of stern windows at the level of the maindeck. The 'kraeck' has a similar arrangement. Two of the Warwick ships and the 'kraeck', but not the other

ships, have the tiller coming inboard a deck below the maindeck. On the big ships there would be at least two decks below the maindeck and perhaps more, for the *Grace Dieu* and the Bayonne ship were over 30ft high from the top of their keel to their maindeck. Ships of later times often had a deck at or near their waterline, so there was probably one there in the Middle Ages. On the 'kraeck' there would be a deck just below her cargo port.

So far the picture seems clear: a maindeck running uninterrupted from bow to stern with one or more decks below it, each having 5 or 6ft of headroom. In the aftercastle there would be the somercastle deck (which was *the* deck in English ships in the fifteenth and early sixteenth centuries) and above that, the poop deck. The forecastle would have one or two decks. But now a complication appears. As R M Nance pointed out[12], the hawseholes of carracks are always set so high up that a cable taken from them to a capstan in the waist would come in at such an angle that the turns would ride up the barrel. Nance therefore postulated that the capstan stood in the somercastle and that the maindeck inside the somercastle was at a higher level than in the waist. In the Warwick drawings, however, the hawseholes seem to be a whole deck higher than the waist and the 'kraeck' has a similar arrangement. The question thus remains an open one although one cannot but wonder whether a lead that would have the cable in the air 5 or 6ft above the waist was a practicable one.

HULL FITTINGS
These are grouped as outboard and inboard and described in that order from bow to stern. A few indeterminate members such as anchors and cables are dealt with as seems most convenient.

Hawseholes. Every picture of the bows of a fifteenth century ship shows the hawseholes as high up and large. The high position is understandable but why were they so large? Some must have been more than 2ft across. Round the hawsehole is a thick flange of wood.

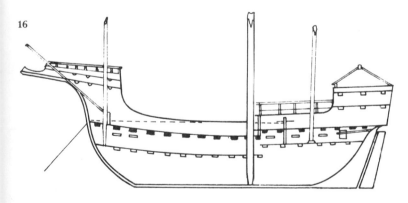

16

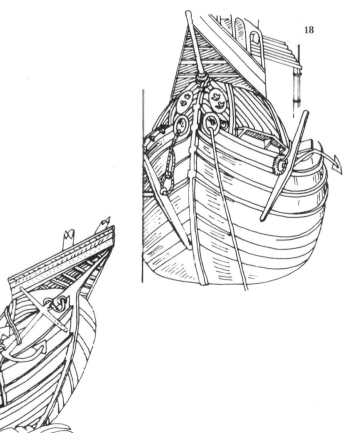

18

17

16. Suggested layout of decks in a carrack. However, this drawing is based on Mediterranean carracks – English ones, according to the Warwick Roll, had their hawseholes higher up.

17. The bows of a fifteenth century Mediterranean carrack. The small hawsehole is unusual at this date but the details of the drawing are so carefully rendered that it is probably correct. The anchor is slung from a timber-head or cleat inside the bulwark and has another lashing round its fluke. The square, mat-like object is a ropework shoe for the anchor's fluke, to stop it from damaging the ship's side. The drawing is based on a Florentine engraving, 'Three Ships at Sea', in the Albertina Museum, Vienna.

18. The bows of a Mediterranean carrack of the second half of the fifteenth century. The ship is carvel-built, has several wales, and has the space below the forestage covered with diagonal clinker planking. The huge hawseholes are set well above the maindeck and have a pair of oval covers hanging by chains from the stem. Note the davit behind the anchor stock and the little platform just in front of it. This was, presumably, for sailors to stand on when fishing the anchor. The drawing has been made after one of the scenes in Carpaccio's 'Legend of St Ursula'.

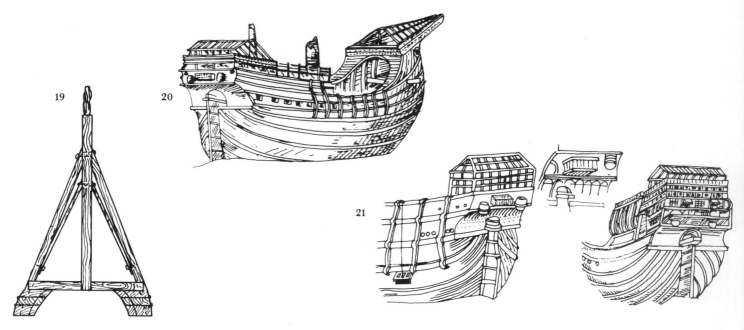

Forestage. At the beginning of the century the forestage was still, in Northern ships, an addition to the hull rather than a permanent part of it. A platform was built on the basic framework and rails set up, and sometimes the sides were boarded up. Shields were hung on the rails and sometimes on the planking. Quite early in the fifteenth century the forestage was amalgamated with the hull by planking the space between the underside of the platform and the gunwale. On Southern ships the planking was diagonally laid clinker but on the 'kraeck' and the Warwick Roll ships it follows the line of the sheer. When there was an upper storey to the forestage it was constructed in the same way but was smaller. On ships from the last quarter of the century the upper storey was supported on curved wooden stanchions.

Wales and fenders. The apparent occurrence of wales on clinker-built hulls has been mentioned. Carvel-planked ships had several wales, Mediterranean vessels usually having more than Northern ships, on which there were four. Vertical fenders in the waist appear towards the end of the century. They protected the sides of the ships from damage against a quay or when hoisting in heavy objects. The 'kraeck's' clutch of wales is shown abreast her mainmast, where they would not be much use (unless they were not fenders but riders to counter the pull of the shrouds). Perhaps the artist got his perspective wrong and they should really be at the waist.

Channels. The early history of these fittings has yet to be worked out. The 'kraeck' has main channels and a Warwick Roll carrack has them, although none of the other Warwick ships shows them. The 'kraeck's' are fixed on top of her bulwarks – an unlikely place. At main-deck level is more probable.

Scuppers. These would be on the first deck above the waterline that would keep their outer ends above water when the ship heeled. On the fifteenth century model from Mataro, and on an early wreck from the Zuider Zee, the scupper pipes are square blocks of wood, bored axially and fixed between the frames. Wooden scuppers were sometimes lined with lead, and their outer ends were covered with leather flaps. Scuppers on the upper decks might simply be holes through the bulwarks or pipes like those on the lower deck.

Cargo ports. Warships would not need cargo ports yet one of Henry IV's warships, the *Carake*, had two iron

bolts for closing the port listed in her inventory, suggesting that perhaps she was an ex-merchantman. A door the size of the 'kraeck's' would need to be securely fastened.

Rudders. While ships had only one mast the rudder had to be a big one and to have a wide sweep, and as the tiller was fixed over the rudder-head there was necessarily a wide opening in the stern to allow it to swing. Even when ships had three masts and could be more easily balanced against the wind the rudder remained large. The Italian shipbuilding manuscript already mentioned states that the rudder's width at the bottom should be 1/4 of its length and at the top 3/16. Northern ships had similar proportions. How the tiller fitted over the rudder-head can be seen on the WA 'kraek'. It would probably be strengthened by an iron strap going round it from one side to the other. We cannot say how the rudder was controlled. The whipstaff (see Chapter 2) was not in use in the fifteenth century as far as we know. Presumably big ships had a team of helmsmen, or perhaps tackles to the tiller's end. The helmsman's vision is an interesting problem, for after the middle of the century, if not earlier, he was tucked away under the half-deck and later on, if the evidence of the Warwick Roll may be trusted, he was a deck lower down.

The stern. Ships are often shown with a pair of tubs at the stern, sometimes on the taffrail and sometimes on the quarters. The tubs are said to have been for soaking the salt meat before cooking. That may be so, but on the Warwick Roll big carrack they would have been very awkward to get at. Perhaps that was the idea! The 'kraeck' has a latrine at each end of her stern gallery but it is not clear why a piece of the rigging should be led through the roof of each one.

Bulwarks and rails. The waist's bulwarks might be stanchions and rails, or planked up. Forestage bulwarks might be open rails, planked up, or half-and-half. Sometimes the planked part has rows of circular holes. The purpose of these is unknown: they are too early for hand-guns and too many for cannon. Aftercastle bulwarks were similar. Open rails were hung with large shields called pavesses, which gave some protection to the crew.

Anchors and cables. These are not strictly speaking fittings but it is convenient to deal with them as such. Medieval ships were well supplied with anchors[15]: the English *Christopher* had five in 1410-12; the *Sovereign*, in

19. The framework of a carrack's forestage. Uprights would be set into the outer members and the floor space planked over. The uprights would support an upper floor and might have the spaces between them boarded, openings being left for archers or guns.

20. A big Mediterranean carrack. It is probably a merchant ship because in the aftercastle is a row of windows. The riders on the hull served to strengthen the lighter upperworks against the pull of the shrouds and to protect the side from damage against a quay or another ship. Like all Southern carracks this one has awnings on forestage and poop, those on the latter set athwartships whereas Northern carracks had their poop awnings fore-and-aft. The framing of the interior of the forecastle, the side gangways curving up to the forestage deck, and the strong bitt-beam protruding through the sides, can be seen. The outboard part would be used as a cathead. The hawseholes are set high up, as they were on Northern ships.

21. Sterns of some Mediterranean carracks based on contemporary illustrations. The tub-like objects may be oil jars. Between them are what appear to be hen coops. The ship on the left has several small openings in her side, probably to give air and light to the cabins. Note the big cargo port near the waterline, and the large opening for the tiller in the counter.

22. A drawing based on the fifteenth century votive model from a church in Mataro, Catalonia; it was made, it is believed, at some time in the second half of the fifteenth century. The ship is carvel-built and has one mast but may have had two originally. Although the model represents a Mediterranean ship it has several points of similarity to the small ships drawn by WA. The model is now in the Prins Hendrik Museum at Rotterdam.

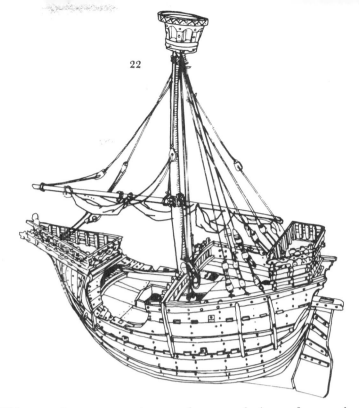

22

1495, had eight, comprising one sheet anchor, one Bristol anchor (ie a Bristol-made anchor), two bowers, two destrelles (small bowers) and two kedges. The *Sovereign's* anchors were divided equally between port and starboard and this was, no doubt, a general rule. References to the sizes of mediaeval anchors are rarely to be found, but Henry V's *Holigost*, of 760 tons, had a great anchor that was 15ft 11in long and 11ft wide. If the width was measured across the arms from tip to tip the proportion is about the same as that of a seventeenth century anchor. Pictures, with due allowance for the failings of artists when dealing with ships, suggest that fifteenth century anchors had much the same shape as the later Admiralty pattern anchor. The arms were usually arcs of a circle although straight ones were known. They met the shank at between 45° and 60°, smaller angles being more common in the earlier pictures. The arms might be half as long as the shank, sometimes a little more. Flukes were half as long as the arm. They were usually triangular but some are shown, improbably, as being barbed like an arrowhead. Anchors sometimes had a large ring at the crown whose diameter, according to pictures, was rather less than the length of a fluke. The ring was used for lashing the anchor to the ship's side and for fastening the buoy-rope. Anchor stocks were made of wood and were much the same shape as they were in later centuries.

Besides their anchors warships had at least one grapnel. It hung from the end of the bowsprit, on an iron chain that ran over a sheave or a pulley and could be dropped in a moment on to an opponent's deck. The 'kraeck's' grapnel has six arms but four is the usual number. No data are available about the size and weight of war grapnels but they would be heavy so that they could bite into the deck and so that they could not readily be picked up and thrown overboard.

Rather more is known about the cables of English ships. There was a rule in the late sixteenth century that the circumferences of a ship's biggest cable should be 1/24 of the beam, or a little less if the cable was made of Mediterranean hemp. If that rule held in the Middle Ages the *Grace Dieu*, with a beam of 50ft would have had a cable 25in in circumference. The 1000 botte ship (about 500 tons) of the Italian manuscript would have had her best cable a little less than 17in. Henry

VII's naval accounts give us the actual sizes of several cables. The *Sovereign* had two of 13½in and two of 13in, three of 10in and one slightly smaller. She may have had a 15in cable, too. The bigger *Regent* had a 15in cable and others of 13, 12 and 11in, and probably of 8in and 7½in.

The usual way of stowing anchors on big ships seems to have been to lash one arm of the anchor to the bulwarks in the waist and to leave the other end of the shank hanging from the cable. Alternatively, the anchor might be slung by the shank painter from some convenient strongpoint in the waist.

When we come to the inboard arrangements and fittings of mediaeval ships we find little contemporary evidence other than that in pictures and what follows is to a considerable degree guesswork, but it must serve until more research has been done on documents preserved in national archives.

Bulkheads. The forecastles of carracks (using the name in its modern sense, for mediaeval seamen spoke of 'under the forecastle' for that space) were partly closed off from the waist by a sloping bulkhead that the English called the cubbridge head. It had a large, arched opening in the middle, and sometimes the sides of the bulkhead seem to have had slats across them as though they were footholds for the crew to go up to the forestage deck. That might have been so on a merchant ship but on a warship like those shown on the Warwick Roll it seems more likely that the slats represent clinker planking because the high bulwarks round the forestage would make entry that way difficult. However, the *Wasa* has a similar arrangement on her beakhead bulkhead. No picture shows any door or other barricade across the bulkhead's opening although it would be essential to keep boarders out of the forecastle. Perhaps a 'war service' barricade was set up when required. The 'kraeck' has no bulkhead but a broad gangway along each side of the waist, at gunwale level, that rises up to the forestage deck is shown. None of the Warwick Roll ships has side gangways. Drawings of the after bulkhead are rare, but one of the later Warwick Roll illustrations shows it running vertically up to the poop deck and having a small, arched doorway in the centre. The aftercastles on some engravings of small merchant ships by the Flemish artist WA are open to the main deck. We have no information about internal bulkheads.

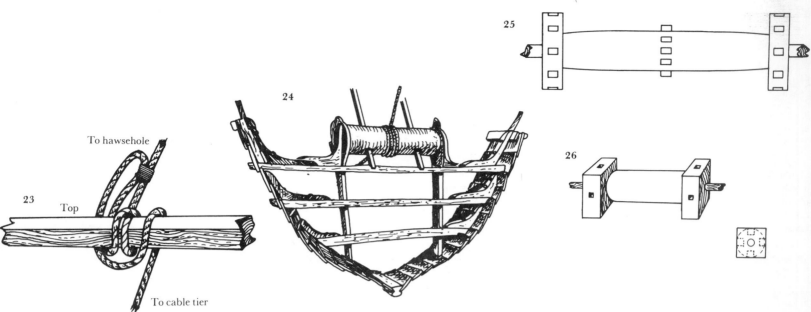

To hawsehole

Top

23

To cable tier

23. Suggested method of bitting a cable on the *catena*.

24. The windlass from a small thirteenth century ship found in Kalmar Harbour, Sweden. The bars were thrust into the slots in the barrel. There was no pawl. (Now in the Sjöhistoriska Museum, Stockholm).

25. The sort of windlass that might have been used on the bigger fifteenth century ships. The barrel's axle would be fixed between a pair of strong posts and the pawl, of wood or occasionally iron, would be attached to another post opposite the teeth set in the barrel.

26. A small windlass barrel from a wreck found in the Zuider Zee. This sort was used on boats and small craft. (Now in Ketelhavn Museum, Holland.)

Deck openings (hatchways and companionways). Hatchways in the maindeck and the deck(s) below it can be taken for granted and as a warship's provisions and water would be in tuns and barrels that were much the same size in the Middle Ages as they were until the end of the sailing ship era so, we may safely assume, were the hatchways. 8 to 10ft long and 6 to 8ft wide would be a reasonable size for the main hatch and perhaps 6ft by 5ft for the fore, if there was one. The hatches were, no doubt, covered with gratings to allow air to circulate to the lower decks, and to allow defenders below the maindeck to get at boarders with pikes. A fighting ship would obviously need some means by which armed men could pass quickly from one deck to another and to and from the after stages. Unfortunately we have no evidence of how that access was provided, and so it has to be assumed that it was by means of companionways.

Tilts for awnings. Northern and Southern ships had awnings: the former's were usually over the poop whereas Southern ships had an awning on the forestage as well as the poop. According to pictures the poop awning on a Mediterranean ship ran athwartships but on a Northern ship the axis was fore and aft. In such cases the awning might be all abaft the mizzenmast or the ridge-pole might pass to one side of the mast (to starboard on one of the Warwick Roll ships). On the 'kraeck' the forestage awning's ridge-pole is to port of the foremast.

Bitts and bitt-beams (or catenas). Some pictures of carracks show a strong, curved beam running from side to side of the forecastle and a little way forward of the bulkhead. The beam's ends are often shown protruding through the ship's side as they do on the Mataro model.
23 The beam was for bitting the cable. Although bitt-beams are not shown on the Warwick Roll ships nor are they mentioned in HenryVII's naval inventories, there are a few records of their use on English ships in the early sixteenth century and so they are likely to have been used

in the previous one. By the end of the fifteenth century, however, some English warships had bitts which were, presumably, the standard sort made of two strong uprights and a cross-beam. The *Regent* had fore-bitts in 1497 so she must have had others not recorded in her accounts.

Knights. These are rarely listed in inventories and when they are there is nothing to suggest that they were other than normal fittings. One of Henry V's ships had '2 knights with 4 sheaves' (ie each knight had two sheaves) in 1419-22. Both the *Sovereign* and the *Regent* at the end of the century had a knight with two brass (actually bronze) sheaves 'in the forecastle', which means that it stood on the forestage deck. As no other knights are listed it is possible that the foreknight was recorded because of its costly bronze sheave. As the name knight implies, the upper ends of the posts were carved to represent a helmeted head, at least on the important ships.

Davits. The arrangements for getting fifteenth century anchors on board are obscure. In 1410-12 the English warship *Christopher* had '1 hook for holding anchors at the bows' and '1 forecastle davit'⁴ and a few years later the *Holigost* had '1 davit and 2 trokelis [ie sheaves] of brass'¹². Davits are rarely shown in pictures, presumably because they were stowed away when not in use. By the end of the century big English warships had several davits. The *Sovereign* had a long davit with two brass sheaves, two short ones each with an iron sheave, and two more of unstated length, each with an iron sheave, that stood just abaft the forecastle bulkhead. Most davits were, probably, movable but these two seem to have been fixtures. The bigger *Regent* had one long davit with two brass sheaves that stood 'in the forecastle', that is, on the forestage deck. She also had two short davits with iron sheaves and one of unspecified length. The fact that long davits had two sheaves suggests that they went right across the ships and projected over each side as some eighteenth century davits did. The short ones would have their inboard ends lashed down, probably to a ringbolt or eyebolt.

Capstans and windlasses. These were in use long before 1400. A small vessel found in the harbour of Kalmar in Sweden and believed to be from the thirteenth century has a windlass and the Bremen cog has both a windlass and a capstan. Neither capstans nor windlasses make many appearances in documents of the fifteenth century. Henry IV's *Christopher* had four capstan bars among her effects and his *Carake* had two but no capstans are listed.

24

Henry V's *Cog John* had a capstan 'delightfully wrought in the manner of three fleur-de-lys'[16]. After Henry's death in 1422 there is a gap in the English records until 1485. In that year the *Mary of the Tower* had three that were no doubt the same kind as those on the *Sovereign*, namely one on the forecastle deck, a main capstan and a lift capstan. The *Regent* also had three capstans and we are told that one stood 'in the deck above the main capstan'. As the main capstan seems always to have stood abaft the mainmast the *Regent*'s main capstan must have been in the somercastle and the other one on the half-deck. The entry is unlikely to mean that the two capstans had a common spindle – double capstans were a much later invention.

The location of the main capstan under the half-deck raises the question of how the cable was brought in. So far as English ships are concerned there is no reliable evidence that the main capstan was on a higher level than the waist, so there must have been some way of overcoming the difference in height between the hawseholes and the main deck. A possible solution to the problem is suggested by the listing of three snatch pulleys among the anchor gear of the *Sovereign* and the *Regent*. If one or two were lead pulleys the cable could be brought down to maindeck level. There remains then the problem of getting in what was undoubtedly a thick cable which could not be taken round the capstan without a backing capstan to hold it taut. The third snatch pulley may have been used with a messenger cable.

Fifteenth century capstans were not the mushroom-headed sort familiar from the end of the seventeenth century, since the bars went right through the barrel. Capstans of that sort could not take many bars because they had to be at a level at which the men could exert their full strength; in other words between $3\frac{1}{2}$ and $4\frac{1}{2}$ft from the deck. At the base of the capstan would be a pawl that worked horizontally on a pivot in the deck, but whether the pawl was pivotted in the middle or at one end is not known. The former would make it easier to change the pawl's position but it could be dislodged by an accidental kick.

The history of the early windlass is even more uncertain than that of the early capstan. Henry V's *Holigost* and *Jesus* had windlasses for raising the mainsail but whether that means the sail only or the sail and its yard is not known, nor do we know where the windlass stood. The windlass on the Swedish boat mentioned above stood a little abaft the single mast. The only data about fifteenth century windlasses come from the Italian manuscript on shipbuilding of 1445. The text is difficult to understand but it appears to say that the length of a ship's windlass was equal to 1/10 the height of the mainmast above the deck and that the circumference of the barrel was $1\frac{1}{4}$ times the barrel's length. In the case of the *Grace Dieu* of 1418 the mainmast stood about 160ft above the maindeck, so her windlass (if she had one) would have been about 16ft long (a reasonable figure) but the barrel's circumference would have been 20ft, equivalent to a diameter of 6ft! Even on a much smaller ship with a mainmast of only 70ft or so, the windlass diameter, if the manuscript is to be believed, works out at nearly 3ft, which seems excessive, though not impossible. We can only guess at the shape of mediaeval windlasses on big ships, but the accompanying figure is based on fourteenth century catapult windlasses. The cogs on the barrel would have been made of hard wood, and the fact that the *Holigost*'s windlass pawl is stated to have been made of iron implies that there were wooden ones.

The windlass problem is complicated by the existence at the end of the fifteenth century and the beginning of the sixteenth of a device called 'a whele for wynding the sail up'. Only mainsails had 'wheles' and it is clear from the other gear listed that the 'whele' was not part of the yard-hoisting tackle but was used for hauling up the sail. An old meaning of wheel was a winch like those formerly used over wells, so the 'whele to wynd the sail up' may have been something of that sort. This suggests that perhaps the *Holigost*'s windlass was similar. It would be a quicker way to haul up the *sail* than a windlass or capstan although it would be impracticable as a means of hoisting the yard and sail.

Pumps. Despite the vital importance of pumps very little is known about them, but they were probably like the kind of pump used on small vessels until the end of the nineteenth century. Some early pumps did not have a handle, the plunger being pulled up and down. There are occasional references to pumps on English warships: the *Grace Dieu* had two when she was built in 1418 and 80 years later the *Regent* had a pump by her mainmast and another by the mizzenmast. The small ships *Sweepstake* and *Mary Fortune* had only one each. On big ships the pumps were below the maindeck but on smaller craft they stood in the open. Whether the pumps discharged into a trough that took the water to the scuppers or whether it was allowed to flow over the deck is not known. The *Regent*'s pumps had hoses but they could only have been short ones for half an ox hide provided sufficient material[2].

27. Small ships probably had the simple kind of pump (a), bigger vessels the more complex variety (b). The pump's pipe was a tree-trunk, or several pieces of tree-trunk, bored out and fitted with a stop valve at the bottom. Pumps like (b) were in use as late as the end of the nineteenth century on some river and estuarine barges.

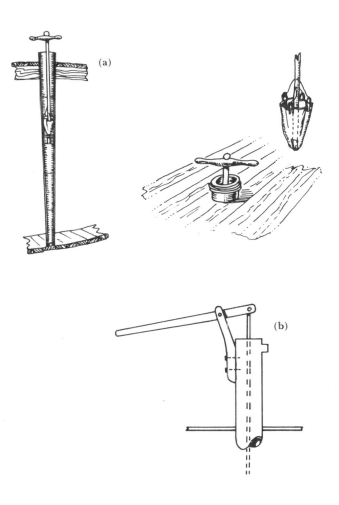

Lanterns. Whether fifteenth century ships showed lights at night is not revealed in the surviving inventories although the latter sometimes list lanterns. The English *Holigost,* for example, had two lanterns and six 'great lanterns' among her gear in 1422 and the *Sovereign* had three great lanterns and four small ones. At the same date the *Regent* had a great lantern over her fore-bitts. As these probably stood under the forecastle deck there must have been plenty of head room to keep the lantern out of harm's way. One of the Warwick Roll ships has a spherical object at each corner of the poop and possibly another on the after end of the awning's ridge-pole. These may be lanterns although none of the other Warwick ships has them.

Bells. The *Regent* had two 'watch bells' whose position is not given, but in the sixteenth century the ship's bell stood either under the half-deck or just in front of it. Except on important ships, the bells are likely to have been the simple kind made by hammering over a sheet of iron or bronze, as cow-bells are still made in some places.

The foregoing list of fittings is not, of course, anything like the full complement. Cleats, kevels, timber-heads, ringbolts and so on were just as necessary in mediaeval times as later but we know nothing about them. For the present all the can be done is to follow seventeenth century practice.

28. A big carrack from the Warwick Roll. The drawing shows the run of the stern timbers and the deadwood, the opening for the tiller, the shape of the rudder irons and the decoration of the aftercastle. Together with the other Warwick Roll illustrations it would provide enough information for an accurate model of the hull. Note the guns, at least 5 on each side, firing *through* the waist rails, and the curved riders supporting the sides of the aftercastle.

29. A big carrack, probably from the 1480s. The arches in the forestage and the aftercastle are for guns. These would be smaller than the cannon shown firing over the waist rails. If the masts have been drawn correctly true top-masts were later than the after mizzenmast (the bonaventure mizzenmast) but as both were in use in 1485 the artist may have put only token rigging in his picture. It is nevertheless an interesting possibility.

30. Two other views of the ship shown in 29 (also from the Warwick Roll). The gathering-in of the stern planking is shown in the upper drawing, and the clinker nail pattern in the lower one. The chequer-pattern round the upper forestage and the poop is intended for cloth painted with the Earl's colours, which were yellow and blue. The windows in the stern of the upper ship indicate the levels of the decks there. Note the hawsehole high up under the forestage deck. This ship appears to have a main topmast.

DECORATION

In the Middle Ages and for long afterwards paints made by suspending a pigment in a drying oil or a varnish were too expensive to be used either for weather-proofing or for decorating large surfaces. Ships timbers, if they were given any protective treatment, were coated with fish oil or some other fatty material, or else with wood tar. What little painting was done had a two-fold purpose: to display the Arms (that is, to make known the identity of the important person(s) on board) and to imitate, as far as practicable, the sumptuous furnishings of castle or manor. However, on special occasions such as a Royal voyage painting overall was the order of the day. At the beginning of the century one of Henry IV's ships, the *Trinity*, was coloured red, probably with haematite, which is a dull red, or red ochre. At the same date one of the Royal barges, the *Nicholas*, was black and 'powdered' with ostrich feathers in white with gilded stems. The *Goodgrace*, of about 1400, was painted 'red, and the cabin and stern in other colours . . . and the bulwarks in various colours'[16], although we are left guessing what the colours were. About 20 years later Henry V's *Holigost* had paintings of a swan and an antelope (two of the King's badges) and 'divers arms also, with the Royal motto called *Une sanz pluis* in divers parts of the ship'. The decorations were probably on the cabins' panelling and on the shields hung along the bulwarks. Another ship, the *Trinity*, had four shields of the King's Arms within a collar of gold, and two more with the Arms of St George within the Garter. In her cabin were two large eagles on a diapered ground.

     No details of the decoration of English ships are available from the the middle 50 years of the fifteenth century but the Warwick Roll drawings show something of the fashions, though not the colours, of the last 25 years. The older ships still have painted shields on fore- and aftercastles and along the waist rails but the big four-masters have shields only on the fore end of the poop. The after end of the poop bulwarks, the taffrail and the bulwarks to the upper deck of the forecastle are painted chequer-wise, presumably in the Earl's colours which were yellow and blue. Henry VII's naval accounts contain little information about painting. The bill for painting the *Regent* in 1497 came to £14 but as that covered board, lodging and wages for the master painter and four men, as well as the materials used, the decoration need not have been either extensive or elaborate.

     It is important to remember – especially when making a model – that the paints and other colouring matters used in mediaeval times and for long afterward, did not, except for artists' colours, have either the bright hues or the high gloss of today's paints. The pigments used then were nearly all naturally occurring ones and contained a percentage of impurities that deadened their colours. Those used to paint an English galley in 1295 were azure, red lead, vermilion, orpiment (yellow), black, blue, white, red, green, 'foreign blue', ochre and brown[17] and all these were still in use until quite recent times. The shades of the pigments would be dulled

30

further by whatever oils or varnishes were used to bind them. It is unlikely, however, that the ordinary 'paint' was a pigment-in-oil mixture. The colouring matter was more likely to have been bound with egg-white or glue size, or perhaps the casein glue that was made by grinding cheese with slaked lime; alternatively the 'paint' might simply have been a lime wash on which the designs were applied while the wash was still damp.[18] Whatever method was used, the final surface would be a matt one like the old-fashioned wall distemper or a modern undercoat – it would certainly not be bright and glossy.

     Adornment was not limited to painting; carved work was an important feature. Henry V's *Trinity* had four effigies, of St Margaret, St Katherine, St George and St Anthony, in the stern but whether they were inside or out is not stated. It is interesting to find that the 'kraeck' drawing shows three black shapes on the taffrail that resemble the outlines of three standing human figures. The shapes have been interpreted as doors with round windows above them, but three large doors in a fairly narrow taffrail seem unnecessary. Perhaps the artist was showing three paintings or statues of saints

  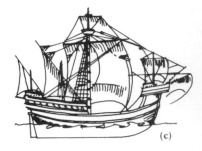

(a) (b) (c)

31. The development of the carrack's sail plan.
(a) Between the early 1400s and about 1430.
(b) About 1450.
(c) By 1500.

and if so, might not the *Trinity* have had something similar? Carvings are recorded on other English warships. The *Holigost,* about 1420, was given carvings of a swan and an antelope but their location is not stated. Carvings were also perched on the spars. The *Goodpace of the Tower,* about 1400, had 'standing on the bowsprit a great golden eagle with a crown in its beak' and a little later Henry V's *Cog John* had a crown and sceptre in her top and a wooden leopard with a gilded crown in its mouth on top of the mast. In the second part of the century, if not earlier, ships had a figurehead at the end of the stem knee. One of the Warwick ships has what looks like a duck's head with ears, and the 'kraeck' has a curious head at the end of her stem knee. Henry VII's ships seem to have had little carving. The *Sovereign* had three gilt fleurs-de-lys, apparently on her bowsprit, and the *Regent* had a crown of gilded copper.

The most spectacular adornments of mediaeval ships were the decorated streamers, banners, flags and sails. They were probably used only when there were important people on board or to impress an enemy. A fairly complete list of the *Holigost*'s flags and sails has survived[12]. This ship had a small counter-sign of the Holy Ghost embroidered on worsted for covering her sail and coverings of worsted for her bonnets, one of which was embroidered with ostrich feathers and the other with the Holy Ghost. Among her flags were three standards, the great standard with the image of St George, another with the Swan and the third with the Antelope. Both those creatures were among Henry V's badges. At various times the *Holigost* had five gitons (long narrow pendants) that had the Holy Ghost, the Swan, the Antelope, the King's Arms and St Edward embroidered on them. Decorated sails are recorded from the beginning of the century. The ship in which Henry V set out for France had the Royal Arms on its sail and another ship had the ostrich feather and stars. The *Nicholas'* sail had a swan, and the *Katherine of the Tower* had an antelope climbing up a beacon (another of the King's badges).

Henry VII's inventories have many examples of the flags and streamers supplied to his ships. In 1485 the *Mary of the Tower* had two streamers, seven standards, and nineteen pendants for the craneline to the top, as well two top armings – cloths to drape round the outside of the top, and usually having heraldic devices on them. Twelve years later the *Regent* had five top armings, three streamers, eleven banners and two gitons as well as 22 pendants decorated with red crosses and roses. The flags were made of say, which was a kind of serge.

Decorations on a model should always be in the style of the time to which the ship belonged. Books on heraldry will give typical devices for shields and sails, and for religious motifs contemporary paintings are a good source.

MASTS AND YARDS

In plotting the development of rigging during the fifteenth century three factors have to be taken into account: the uneven distribution of the evidence; the fact that inventories list what was present but rarely say what was missing; and the time lag between the first appearance of a new item and its earliest record. As an example of the last factor, the first reference to an English ship having a foresail, mainsail and mizzen dates from 1466, about 30 years after the three-mast rig had become general. Anticipating the evidence, we can provisionally summarise the development of the multi-masted ship as follows: up to about 1400, one mast; between 1400 and some time not long after 1420, two masts; from then until an unknown date before 1480, three masts, and after that four. The dates are not absolute and fresh evidence may push them all further back.

Lower masts. Until nearly the end of the fourteenth century the single mast rig had been adequate for Northern ships, which were in general smaller than those from the Mediterranean and Iberian peninsula seaports, but when Northern ships of 200 tons or more came into use the shortcomings of the simple rig were plain to be seen, and in the case of warships they were aggravated by the high fore- and aftercastles. Consequently, in about 1400, Northern shipmen added a second mast. The first English reference is from the period 1409-10, when Henry IV's *Carake* (a Southern ship) had '1 great mast, 1 small mast'. A little later (1413-20) there is a reference to a 'mesan mast' and thereafter references to the mizzen (in various spellings) are common but no English evidence for either a foremast or a foresail is earlier than 1432. It has been argued that the original meaning of mesan/mizzen signified a foresail, as it does in French[19]. Whether this is true or not a second mast, abaft the mainmast, was in use in the first quarter of the century. It seems likely in fact that a ship would be given a foremast or a mizzenmast according to whether she tended to head up into the wind or to fall off it. On warships with a high forestage the second mast was probably a mizzen (in the modern meaning of the name). The two-mast rig did not last long and in 1432 an English balinger (a swift pursuit vessel) had a foresail and mizzen bought for her. The absence of any reference to a mainsail has prompted the suggestion that the ship was a two-master, but the simplest explanation is that since she already had a mainsail it was not recorded. Altogether, the balance of evidence is that Northern ships had three masts by 1430. When exactly the fourth one was added has not yet been discovered. Four-masted ships are shown in the Warwick Roll, and 'aftermizzens' (as the fourth masts called) were recorded without comment in Henry VII's naval accounts for 1485. On the other hand the 'kraeck' has only three masts but the date of the drawing's subject is anything but definite. For English ships a fourth mast may have been in use by 1480 and perhaps a few years earlier.

The mainmast on single-masted ships and the early two-masters was stepped slightly abaft the mid-point of the maindeck and was therefore in front of the mid-point of the keel. The mainmast of the *Grace Dieu* of 1418 was 55ft from the fore end of her 125-130ft keel, slightly more than 2/5 of the length. The Italian ship-building manuscript of 1445 states that the mainmast should be 2/5 of the keel's length from the fore end and 3/7 of the ship's length between stem and sternpost[13]. The early mizzenmast was a little over half way from the mainmast to the after end of the poop but later in the century, at all events on English ships, it was somewhat further aft.

The first foremasts were small and the sail could only have served as a balancing force for its propulsive power was insignificant. No dimensions are available, unfortunately, but pictures have the height of foremasts above deck as about 1/3 (at most) of the corresponding height of the mainmast. They soon became bigger. It is impossible to be definite about the placing of the foremast in the first half of the century but the ship in the Hastings Manuscript and those in the Warwick Roll have their foremasts stepped above the point at which the waterline meets the stem, and therefore forward of the end of the keel.

The size of mediaeval mainmasts fascinated artists and they often drew masts so tall and thick that the ship would have capsized. There was some excuse for the exaggeration for mainmasts *were* enormous. The Mediterranean proportions were as follows: length equal to four times the ship's breadth, or 1.6 times the length of the keel; circumference at the deck equal to 1/14 of the length. For the *Grace Dieu*, with a keel of 125-130ft, the mainmast works out at about 180ft (we know that it was, in fact, 200ft long) and its girth at 14ft (and therefore its diameter at 4⅓ft). Luca di Maso, however, recorded the girth as 22ft (7ft diameter). The difference reflects, no doubt, the more boisterous weather to be found in the Channel. The *Grace Dieu*'s mainmast is the only fifteenth century English one of which we have a record but if the Woolwich wreck (see Chapter 2) is really the remains of Henry VII's *Sovereign* her mainmast, at least in its early sixteenth century form, was 52in in diameter *below* deck, and therefore thicker at the partners.

Mizzenmasts were much less spectacular. The Italian manuscript of 1445 states that the aftermast should be half as long as the mainmast. For mast lengths in the second half of the century pictures are the only source. The Warwick Roll ships have the length of the mainmast above the deck as about the same as the main deck's length. The above-deck height of the foremast is about half that of the mainmast and the mizzenmast's is 3/4, whilst the aftermizzen's length is a little less than half the height of the mainmast above the deck.

The construction of mainmasts can only be inferred. The numerous rope bindings (wooldings) shown in pictures, and confirmed by a reference to buying rope to make wooldings for the *Regent*'s mainmast, point to composite ('made', or built-up) masts. The Woolwich ship mentioned above had a made mast. Nothing is known about how the other masts were constructed although they were small enough to have been made from a single tree.

Bowsprit. The bowsprit has a longer history than any other spar except the mainmast on Northern ships, for it was in use in the thirteenth century. The bowsprit's original purpose seems to have been to give a better lead to the bowlines. Later, it served as a suspension point for the grapnel and had a sheave in its outer end or sometimes a block, over which the grapnel's chain ran. In the fifteenth century, if the pictorial evidence is reliable, the bowsprit had large triangular 'teeth' on its underside that served, it is supposed, to hold the bowlines forward, one passing from port to starboard and the other contrariwise. How the bowsprit was stepped remains to be discovered. Pictures show it rising from the forestage deck at a steep angle (45° in some cases) and with its heel apparently against the foremast when there was one. In reality, the bowsprit probably passed to one side of the foremast as it did in the next century, and on the starboard side in English ships. The 'kraeck' picture shows a stem lashing (the gammoning) holding the bowsprit to the stemhead but nothing of the kind is shown on the Warwick Roll ships, nor is there any mention of a gammon lashing in Henry VII's inventories. English bowsprits seem to have been nearly as long above the forestage deck as the foremasts were, and about as thick. The bowsprits of Henry VII's *Sovereign* and *Regent* were armed with a pair of sheerhooks – sickle-shaped knives intended to cut enemy rigging as the two ships came together.

A new spar came into use in the course of the century. This was the 'outligger', a stout timber projecting over the stern of the ship and used to haul out the mizzen sheet. Outliggers were in use before 1485 and possibly before about 1450 if the Hastings Manuscript is as early as that although it is curious that neither the 'kraeck' nor the Warwick Roll ships have outliggers. Their absence is not necessarily due to ignorance and carelessness. It is possible that fifteenth century mizzens

32. This carving of a carrack on a bench end from King's Lynn, Norfolk is said to date from about 1415. As the ship is a big one it is possible that the *Grace Dieu* was taken as the model. The hull is clinker-built and has projecting beam ends. The hawseholes are set high up under the forecastle, which has two stages. The aftercastle may also have two stages or perhaps one and an awning. Note the huge mainmast with its fighting top, in which the heavy iron darts (gadds) are stacked ready for use. The rigging is carefully delineated and, although simplified, is accurate. The carving is now in the Victoria and Albert Museum, London.

33. Examples of mediaeval tops.

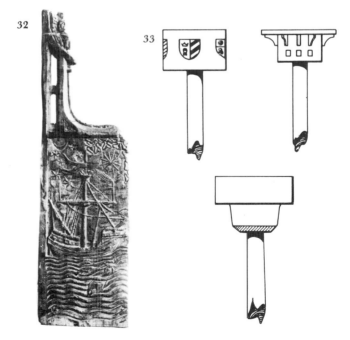

34

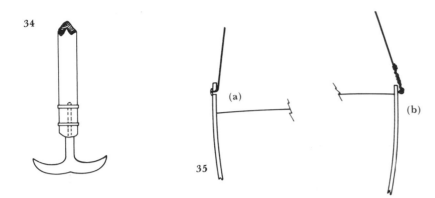

35

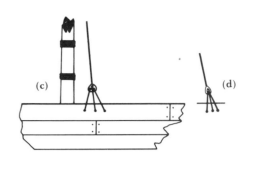

34. Sheerhooks were crescentic iron knives fixed in the ends of the mainyard, and sometimes the bowsprit. They were sharpened on the inner and outer edges so that they would cut an opponent's rigging when the ships came to close quarters.

35. Four ways in which mediaeval shrouds may have been set up.
(a) The shroud passes through the bulwark and is fastened to a toggle outboard.
(b) The shroud is taken to a ring- or eye-bolt in the side and the end wound round its standing part and made fast.
(c) The shroud's end has a deadeye turned in, and either three separate ropes go to holes in the ship's side or perhaps a lanyard is reeved between the deadeye and the holes.
(d) An arrangement similar to (c) but with a heart.

(and aftermizzens) were sometimes sheeted directly to the poop, inefficient though the arrangement may seem to us.

Tops. All late mediaeval ships had a huge top on the mainmast, and by the end of the fifteenth century smaller ones had appeared on the fore- and mizzenmasts. Tops were originally fighting platforms, as their older name, topcastle, implies. The scanty pictorial evidence points to mediaeval tops being made in much the same way as they were in the seventeenth century, that is, by building a platform on the trestletrees and crosstrees and then setting up the sides on uprights fixed to the top's floor (see Chapter 3). The 'kraeck's' top, however, seems to be set up on four brackets fixed to the masthead but if that is right it is difficult to understand how the shrouds were fitted. It was customary to drape cloths round the fighting tops, to screen the men, and the cloths bore heraldic devices. Fighting tops had a hoist for bringing up stones, 'gadds' (heavy iron javelins) and other missiles. The hoisting gear consisted of a short davit projecting over the edge of the top, and from the davit's end a rope, called the craneline, ran over a sheave and down to the deck. The 'kraeck's' cranelines are endless ropes to which loads were attached and taken off at the top but whether this was the usual arrangement is not known. As the 'kraeck' shows, guns might be mounted in the tops. None is present, however, on the Warwick Roll drawings.

So far as we know, the advent of topmasts did not bring about any change in the shape or construction of tops, and when a top was made at the head of the topmast – the topgallant – it was like the lower top.

Topmasts and topgallant masts. Although a topsail is recorded in an English poem of 1390 there is no mention of a topmast until, at the earliest, 1420 and it is not clear whether in fact it is a topmast or the lower mast that is referred to.[19] The first English picture showing a topmast is in the Hastings Manuscript. The absence of a topsail yard may mean that it had been sent down. By 1485, however, main topmasts were regular fittings on English warships (and probably on all Northern warships) and by 1495 fore topmasts had appeared but there

was no mizzen topmast. How topmasts originated is not known. Probably the idea of setting a sail from the flagstaff in the top was tried and when the advantage of the extra sail was seen the flagstaff was replaced by a small mast. It has been suggested, however, that the first topmasts were simply the upper parts of the lower mast. Whether or not that was so, the *Sovereign's* main topmast in 1495-7 was a separate spar that was fastened to the lower masthead by an iron band called a garland.

Topgallant masts were smaller versions of the topmasts. The *Regent* had a main topgallant mast in 1497 but the *Sovereign* did not, so it is likely that topgallant masts were introduced at about that date. Both topmasts and topgallant masts were fixed permanently aloft and must have been a fearful worry in a gale. No dimensions of topmasts have come to light, but the supposed topmast in the Hastings Manuscript is about half as long as the mainmast above the deck, although the drawing is not to scale. The topmasts on some of the Warwick Roll ships are probably too short.

Yards. The early fifteenth century mainyard, like its mast, was a huge spar. Pictures usually show it as being about the same length as the above-deck part of its mast, and very thick. The Italian shipbuilding manuscript of 1445 states that a mainyard should be 4/5 of the mast's length and the maximum diameter should be 1/28 of the yard's length. The mizzenyard, which carried a lateen sail, was to be half as long as the mainyard. Whether those proportions applied to Northern ships is uncertain. In view of the trade connections between Flanders, England and Italy at that time, they probably did, but by the end of the century, and no doubt well before that time, mizzenyards are a good deal longer than half the mainyard. Foreyards were much smaller than the mainyard, probably only about 1/3 of its length at first but increasing to about 1/2 by the 1470s and possibly reaching 3/5 by 1500.

The only references to the construction of the yards of Northern ships come from the first and last decades of the century. Henry IV's *Carake* in 1410 had a sailyard, presumably the mainyard but possibly the mizzen, made in two pieces. She was a Southern ship and we know that Mediterranean vessels did have their yards made of two overlapping pieces of timber. Henry VII's inventories are more definite. For the *Sovereign*, 'ij mastes to make a new mayne yard for the seyd ship' were bought in 1496. They cost £9, quite a sum of money then. The entry might be taken to mean that the masts' timber was to be used in place of new wood but an entry for the *Regent* refers to buying two masts of 'spruce tre' (Prussian trees, not necessarily spruce) to make her mainyard, and it is expressly stated that each tree was used to make one half of the yard. That must mean that the mainyards of the two ships were in two pieces that overlapped in the middle. Yards made that way were still used in 1546. Only the biggest ships had two-piece yards and the explanation is, almost certainly, that trees long enough to make a 'single stick' yard were not obtainable. Mizzenyards on Northern ships were always, so far as we know, made in one piece, and so were the topsail and topgallant yards. There were no mizzen topsail yards in the fifteenth century. Practically nothing is known about the fittings on fifteenth century yards except that mainyards had a pair of sheerhooks at each end. There were no footropes or jackstays.

One other yard appeared during the century – the spritsail yard that was slung below the bowsprit. It was in use on English warships by 1485 and may have been known in 1466[15] unless a spritsail in the modern meaning of the name is referred to, but it is curious that none of the Warwick Roll ships has a spritsail yard. When so much is uncertain, the date of the introduction of the spritsail yard can only be guessed at, but on present evidence it might be as early as 1460.

STANDING RIGGING

The rapid evolution of the multi-masted ship during the fifteenth century was accompanied by a matching development of rigging from something not much different from that of the Gokstad ship to one visibly akin to the rig of warships in the last days of sailing warships. Yet despite the wealth of references to rigging and particularly to that in use in the last twenty years of the century little is known about how it was set up.

Bowsprit. The bowsprit does not seem to have had any standing rigging other than the possible gammoning already mentioned nor do we know if the lashing was like early seventeenthcentury gammonings. Whether the lower end of the bowsprit was lashed to the foremast is also unknown.

Lower masts. Familiar names like tackles, shrouds, stays, backstays and swifters occur in English rigging inventories from even the beginning of the century but it is not always certain that the names mean the same as they did a century later. Backstays are an example, since in the fifteenth century they were lower mast rigging but by the end of the next one they had shifted up to the topmasts. Another instance is the forestay. Until ships had a foremast the forestay belonged to the mainmast and was what its name implies – the opposite to the backstay.

As would be expected from the size of mediaeval masts, their supporting rigging was abundant. The English warship *Christopher* in 1410-12 had 20 headropes (shrouds), 6 backstays and a forestay. At the same time, the *Carake* had 19 (sic) shrouds with 38 pulleys, so her shrouds were set up with tackles as they were on Mediterranean galleys. Masts also had tackles called 'pollankers' (the name is spelt in several different ways), and swifters, which may or may not have been the same as the later stay of that name. The English records are almost a blank, unfortunately, from the 1420s until 1485, when the first of Henry VII's naval inventories provide detailed lists of fittings. Some of the earliest lists, however, are set down in an irregular order and it is not always clear whether the full complement of gear was present nor whether, in some cases, it is standing or running rigging. The 1495-7 lists have much more information and inspire confidence in the completeness of the picture they give of a major warship's rigging. The *Sovereign*'s mainmast, for example, had 16 swifting tackles, 6 pollankers and 32 shrouds as well as a mainstay. She had also 4 garnets and 4 'Breton tackles', which

were probably the same thing as the later burton tackles. It is curious that none of Henry VII's ships has backstays; perhaps the swifting tackles took their place. The multiplicity of shrouds and supporting tackles is a feature of fifteenth and early sixteenth century English ships. It may have been due to the rope being weaker than that of later times, or to the need to spread the pull of the shrouds over a long stretch of topsides.

Listing the rigging items is one thing but deciding in what order it was put on is a very different one. Henry VII's inventories list the mainmast rigging in several arrangements: shrouds, swifting tackles, stay; or shrouds, swifting tackles, pollankers, stay; or shrouds, stay, pollankers, breton tackles, swifting tackles. It is doubtful, therefore, whether the order in the lists represents the rigging order, and until definite evidence comes to light it would be best to follow seventeenth century practice if a model is to be rigged. The order would then become: pollankers, shrouds, swifting tackles or backstays, and stay.

The number of pollankers for some documented fifteenth century ships is as given in the table.

POLLANKERS – Fifteenth Century		
Ship	Date	Number of pollankers
Christopher	1410–12	2
Holigost	1414–16	2*
Mary of the Tower	1485	6
Martin Garsia	1485	4
Governor	1485	4
Sovereign	1495–7	6
Regent	1495–7	8**
Mary Fortune	1497	***
Sweepstake	1497	2

*Each with 2 pulleys.
**Plus 2 on the foremast.
***None listed.

The absence of pollankers from the *Mary Fortune*'s inventory is interesting because she was a new ship, built at the same time as the *Sweepstake* and about the same size (80-100 tons). The pollankers can hardly have been missing, though they may have been overlooked, but it is quite possible that they were given up about the time the *Mary Fortune* was built, for they do not occur in the rigging lists of the principal ships of the next reign. It is not known where the pollankers' falls were made fast – perhaps to a large cleat on the bulwarks or perhaps to convenient timber-heads.

In the early English records shrouds are called headropes, a name that was later transferred to part of a sail. How the early shrouds were set up has been the subject of a good deal of inconclusive discussion[20]. The only evidence before about 1470 is pictures of doubtful reliability and which are often crudely drawn but in them it is possible to make out three ways of fastening shrouds. The first two arrangements are unlikely on big ships whether or not they were used on boats but the third *may* have been used for the shrouds supporting the smaller masts of ships. There are deadeyes on the 'kraeck' and possibly on one of the Warwick Roll ships, but at all events deadeyes were normal fittings on English ships by 1485, and taking all the evidence into account it is likely that they were in use a good while before that and possibly even before 1450. How shrouds were set up before that date remains to be discovered.

SHROUDS – Fifteenth Century

Ship	Date	Foremast		Mainmast		Mizzenmast		After or bonaventure mizzenmast	
		Shrouds*	Lower deadeyes with chains	Shrouds*	Lower deadeyes with chains	Shrouds*	Lower deadeyes with chains	Shrouds*	Lower deadeyes with chains
Christopher	1410–12	–	–	20	–	–	–	–	–
Holigost	1416	–	–	30	–	–	–	–	–
Mary of the Tower	1485	12	–	32	32	26	–	–	–
Martin Garsia	1485	8	–	26	26	12	–	–	–
Governor	1485	12	–	28	32	16	–	–	–
Sovereign	1495	16	32	32	32	12	12	8	8
Regent	1495	16	32	36	36	12	12	10	10
Mary Fortune	1497	6	–	14	14	–	–	4	–
Sweepstake	1497	8	–	18	18	–	–	4	–

*The number of shrouds is the total for both sides.

In the English records from the end of the fifteenth century lower mast deadeyes are attached to the ship's side by chains, as they are on the 'kraeck'. Whether the chains had short links, as they seem to have had on Continental ships, or whether the links were long like those on seventeenth century English ships is not known. On the 'kraeck' the fore and mizzen deadeyes also have chains. The English evidence about shrouds and how they were set up is summarised in the accompanying table.

There are some puzzling differences between the entries in the table. Deadeyes are only recorded when they have chains, no reference being made to the upper ones. Some ships, in consequence, have their shrouds recorded but without any deadeyes. Furthermore, only the two biggest ships have chains to the deadeyes of their fore- and mizzenmasts (including the after-mizzen). The specific mention of chains probably means that chains were expensive items that would attract thieves, so a note of their number was desirable. But does the absence of a reference to deadeyes of any sort mean that they were a normal piece of gear but were set up with rope to the ship's side, or does it mean that the shrouds were secured in some other way, perhaps with a tackle, galley fashion, as they sometimes were in the next century (see Chapter 2), or even secured to a convenient timber-head in the bulwarks? It is significant that, with the exception of the ships at the beginning of the century, of which we have only fragmentary records, it is the small masts that lack deadeyes.

The deadeyes on the 'kraeck's' main shrouds are fastened to the hull immediately below the channel but that must be a mistake since the chains placed thus would not counter the pull of the shrouds. Probably they should have been on the next wale down, as they appear to be on one of the Warwick Roll ships and in the picture of German carracks. Fifteenth century deadeyes were heart-shaped and were set up with their broad ends opposite one another. Nothing is known about their size. According to a seventeenth century English rule the width of a deadeye was equal to about half its mast's diameter but that is unlikely to have been the case in the fifteenth century, when masts were so much thicker. If the rule had applied then, the *Grace Dieu* of 1418 would have had deadeyes 3½ft across! The spacing of deadeyes is also unknown. On the 'kraeck' drawing they are shown close together, and in view of the numerous shrouds on fifteenth century ships' masts, or at all events their mainmasts, that is very likely correct.

For most of the century the mizzenmast was a bigger spar than the foremast, as the relative numbers of shrouds in the table confirms. But in the last few years of the century the foremast grew in size and had more shrouds than the mizzen. The table also reveals the existence of a problem concerned with mizzenmasts. The ships in the 1485 accounts of Henry VII have mizzenmasts; his two big ships *Sovereign* and *Regent* have mizzenmasts and bonaventure mizzenmasts; but the two new, small ships *Sweepstake* and *Mary Fortune* have bonaventure masts *but no mizzenmasts*. Now, the bonaventure mizzenmast is always shown, on four-masted ships, as perched right at the stern, almost over the sternpost, which is a reasonable position, but what introduces the problem is that some early sixteenth century pictures show three-masted ships with the 'mizzen' mast so placed. The drawings showing the mast so far aft are too carefully executed for its position to be put down to carelessness. The possibility exists, therefore, that towards the end of the fifteenth century, and at least on English ships, the mizzenmast on a three-masted vessel might be in the usual position, about half way between the mainmast and the taffrail, or it might be right at the after end of the poop.

BACKSTAYS AND SWIFTING TACKLES – Fifteenth Century

Ship	Date	Backstays	Swifting tackles
Christopher	1410–12	6	0
Carake	1410–12	4	0
Holigost	1416	2	0
Grace Dieu*	1485	0	0
Mary of the Tower	1485	0	8
Martin Garsia	1485	0	6
Governor	1485	0	12
Sovereign	1495	0	16**
Regent	1497	0	16***
Mary Fortune	1497	0	0
Sweepstake	1497	0	0

*The inventory is in some disorder.
**With 45 (?48) pulleys.
***With 48 pulleys.

It is surprising that the last two ships had neither backstays nor swifting tackles, for they were newly-built. Perhaps small ships did not have them. Only the *Sovereign* and *Regent* had tackles to their foremasts; the former had eight swifting tackles and the latter two and two pollankers. No foremast backstays are listed for any of Henry VII's ships.

Backstays and swifting tackles present another puzzle, for English ships that had backstays did not have swifting tackles, and vice versa, as the table shows. It is surprising that the last two ships had neither backstays nor swifting tackles, for they were newly built. Perhaps small ships did not have them. Only the *Sovereign* and *Regent* had tackles to their foremasts. The former ship had eight swifting tackles and the *Regent* had two and two pollankers. No foremast backstays are listed for any of Henry VII's ships.

If the early backstays were like seventeenth century running backstays they were simple pendants and whips. Swifting tackles were more complex. Those with three pulleys were probably as shown in the drawing. Both pieces of gear were presumably made fast to the bulwarks near the mast.

The *Sovereign* had four of the new Breton tackles, each with two pulleys, but the entries for the *Regent* are confusing, for in one list she is credited with three tackles with ten pulleys, and four pendants and four halliards for the tackles, but in another list she has only two pendants and two halliards. It is tempting to assume that her complement was incomplete and that she should have had four tackles each with three pulleys.

Stays also provide problems. Some of the early inventories list two, three or even four forestays (ie mainstays of single-mast ships) but whether this means that the ships had multiple stays, or whether the total included spares is not known. There is some evidence from the next century that stays did sometimes have more than one part. We do not know how the stays were rigged. If one may argue from the fact that topmast and topgallant mast rigging in later centuries seems to continue earlier practice on lower masts, then the stays had a large eye at their upper ends that went over the masthead. The lower end, so far as can be made out, was fastened to, or near, the stemhead but when foremasts came in the mainstay seems to have been secured near the foot of the foremast. The *Holigost* had a complex tackle at the lower end of her mainstay – '1 stay with 3 ropes and 4 tackles, each of which has 3 pulleys'. On the 'kraeck' the mainstay is set up with a pair of deadeyes. The stay passes to starboard of the foremast and appears

to be fastened to the stem knee. The records state that the *Grace Dieu* in 1485 had five deadeyes to her mainstay! Perhaps the clerk made a mistake and wrote 'v' instead of 'ij' – the figures look alike in some Tudor writing. The *Sovereign*'s mainstay had '2 tyes' (sic) and '4 double chains of iron serving for the mainstay and to the deadeyes'[2] and on the *Mary Fortune* in 1497 there was 'a collar of iron with a bolt that is annexed to the stay of the said ship'.

Forestays were set up to the bowsprit. In the Warwick Roll pictures the forestay goes nearly to the outer end of the bowsprit but on the 'kraeck' and the Hastings Manuscript ship it is much further in. Nothing is known about how it was fastened.

The history of mizzenstays is even more obscure than that of forestays. They are not mentioned in the early inventories nor is there any reference to mizzenstays in Henry VII's naval accounts, although bonaventure mizzenstays are listed for the *Sovereign* and *Regent* but not for the *Sweepstake* and *Mary Fortune*. Yet the pictorial evidence shows mizzenstays on the Warwick Roll ships, and bonaventure mizzenstays also, and the Hastings Manuscript ship has a mizzenstay. Nevertheless, there is none on the 'kraeck'. For the present, then, it must remain an open question as to whether fifteenth century ships had mizzenstays.

The last pieces of lower mast rigging (if that is what they are) are the garnets. The *Sovereign* and the *Regent* had four each but the small ships *Sweepstake* and *Mary Fortune* had only one. The doubt about the purpose of the garnets arises from the way they are recorded. On the two big ships the garnets are among the mainmast's gear but on the others they appear among the mainyard's gear, whilst on the *Mary Fortune* the single garnet is recorded as a 'garnet to the main tackle', whatever that was. No uncertainty attaches to the great garnet. It was the hoisting tackle found on seventeenth century ships and was rigged, we may assume, as shown in the drawing. Nothing in the records tells us where the garnets were made fast, and for the present seventeenth century practice will have to be followed.

Topmasts and topgallant masts. The small size of the early topmasts and topgallant masts is reflected in the

36. Backstays and tackles.
(a) Early backstay.
(b) Late fifteenth century swifting tackle.
(c) Simple Breton tackle.
(d) The *Regent's* Breton tackle?

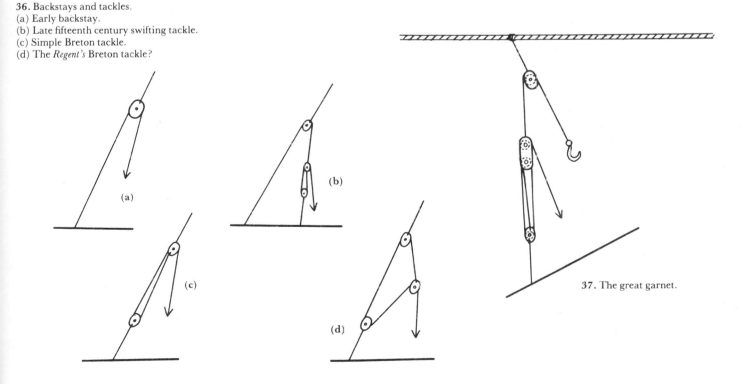

37. The great garnet.

RIGGING OF TOPMASTS AND TOPGALLANT MASTS – late Fifteenth Century								
Ship	Date	Fore topmast		Main topmast		Main topgallant mast	
		Shrouds*	Stay	Shrouds*	Stay	Shrouds*	Stay
Grace Dieu	1485	**	**	**	**	–	–
Mary of the Tower	1485	***	***	6	No	***	***
Martin Garsia	1485	***	***	6	No	***	***
Governor	1485	***	***	6	No	***	***
Sovereign	1495–7	8	Yes	12	Yes	***	***
Regent	1495–7	8	Yes	10	Yes	8	Yes
Mary Fortune	1497	***	***	4	Yes	***	***
Sweepstake	1497	***	***	8	Yes	***	***

*The number of shrouds is the total for both sides.
**It is not known whether topmasts were fitted.
***No topmast or topgallant.

simplicity of their rigging. Shrouds are few compared with the lower masts, there are no swifting tackles or backstays, and stays only appear in the records in 1495. The table summarises the available evidence. Deadeyes are recorded only for the *Regent's* main topmast, and they have chains like the lower deadeyes. That leaves open the question whether shrouds on the other masts had deadeyes secured with rope, or whether the ends of the shrouds were set up to eyebolts, for example in the rims or the floors of the tops. The main topmast shrouds on the Hastings ship are taken down the outside of the top and appear to be fastened either to the top's floor or passed under it to the masthead. On Northern ships all shrouds, upper as well as lower, had ratlines and had them, so far as we know, from the beginning of the century and probably earlier. Southern ships, because their shrouds were set up with tackles, had a Jacob's Ladder from the masthead, as the 'kraeck' has.

The main topmast stay presumably had a large eye worked in its upper end that went over the topmast head. The lower end would go to the foretop or to the masthead just below, as it did in the next century. Fore topmast stays would be set up to the outer end of the bowsprit. The *Regent's* main topgallant stay was probably taken to the foretop.

RUNNING RIGGING
This part of the rigging has been set out in two sections according to the functions of the gear. One is concerned with hoisting and controlling the yard and the other with fastening, setting, controlling and furling the sail. Each section is subdivided according to whether the gear belongs to square sails or lateens. The square sails and yards are treated first.

Fore- and mainyards. From the very beginning of the century two ways of hoisting a yard are recorded and both might be used together. These were firstly by tyes and halliards, and secondly by jeers. A tye was a strong rope fastened round the yard and passed over a block slung from the masthead, or else over a sheave in the hounds or in the mast itself. There was a block on the lower end of the tye, and a halliard ran between it and another block on the deck, probably near the mast. On the *Holigost* in 1416 the tye had two pulleys (blocks) which are likely to have had only a single sheave each, for multi-sheave pulleys are usually recorded as such. In time, the lower block was replaced by sheaves in a knight. The knights seem to have had only two sheaves to begin with but three and even four are found in later times. Scanty evidence suggests that each tye had its own

knight. The quota of tyes on late fifteenth century English ships is given in the table. Whether half-tyes were pieces of rigging in their own right or merely old tyes that had been cut in two we cannot say. It is possible, though evidence is lacking, that they were connected with the replacement of the upper block of the halliard tackle by the ramhead. In its later version the ramhead was a huge block of wood, with a hole at the top for attaching the tye, and three sheaves in the lower half for the halliard. Perhaps the early ramhead had two upper holes, one for each half-tye.

Jeers were used only on the biggest yards and are recorded in Henry VII's naval inventories for the mainyards of the *Sovereign* and *Regent* but no other ships. The *Regent's* jeer had three pulleys. The mainyard of the big ships was so heavy that it could not have been hoisted by hand even with the large crews on warships. The halliards and the jeer fall would have had to go to a capstan or a windlass. We know that at the end of the century ships had up to three capstans, so it may be assumed that two of them were used for hoisting the fore- and mainyards. At the beginning of the century, however, things may have been different. The *Holigost* had a windlass for raising her sail 'in modo carrac' (carrack fashion). Taken literally that means the *sail* – and the early Tudor ships between 1485 and about 1530 did have a device for that purpose. On the other hand 'in modo carrac' may mean that on some sorts of ship the yard was raised by a windlass and on others by a capstan.

Parrels and trusses. The history of these pieces of gear in the fifteenth century, and for the next two centuries, is intermingled and obscure. The early parrel seems to have been simply a ring of strong rope passed round mast and yard, probably with a downhaul of some sort to help the parrel over the woolings on the mast. By the begin-

TYES – late Fifteenth Century		
Ship	Foreyard	Mainyard
Grace Dieu	*	*
Mary of the Tower	2	2
Martin Garsia	1	2
Governor	1	2
Sovereign	2	2
Regent	2	2
Mary Fortune	1	2
Sweepstake	1	2

*No tyes recorded for either yard, but 2 half-tyes listed.

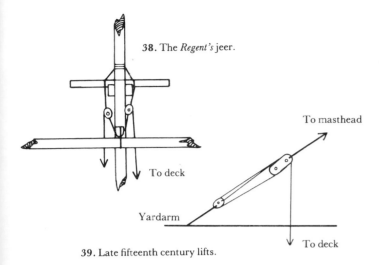

38. The *Regent's* jeer.

39. Late fifteenth century lifts.

To masthead

To deck

Yardarm

To deck

BRACES – Fifteenth Century					
Ship	Date	Foremast		Mainmast	
		Braces	Yard ropes	Braces	Yard ropes
Holigost	1416	*	*	–	2**
Grace Dieu	1485	***	***	2	–
Mary of the Tower	1485	–	2	2	–
Martin Garsia	1485	***	***	2	–
Governor	1485	***	***	2	–
Sovereign	1495–7	2	–	2	–
Regent	1497	2	–	2	–
Mary Fortune	1497	–	2	–	2
Sweepstake	1497	–	2	–	2

*No foremast.
**With 2 pulleys.
***Not listed.

ning of the fifteenth century the simple parrel (which was called a 'rack' or 'rakke') sometimes had a pair of 'susters', in other words 'sisters'. What these were is disputed[19], but the likeliest suggestion is that susters were wooden ribs with a pair or more of holes like those in the ribs of later parrels, so perhaps the parrel now consisted of two turns of rope threaded through the holes in the susters and passing round mast and yard. The susters would act as spacers for the rope and help it to ride over the wooldings. Another kind of parrel had large wooden bobbins, called trucks, threaded on the parrel rope where it passed round the mast. At some time during the century susters and trucks were combined into a more complex parrel that remained in use down to the end of the sailing warship era. It can be seen on the 'kraeck'.

Parrels soon became associated with trusses and there was also a later hybrid called a truss-parrel. What the early truss was like it is impossible to say. Basically it was a rope to haul the yard back to the mast and it was also used to haul the yard down. How these two opposing functions were combined is not clear, for even seventeenth and eighteenth century descriptions leave a lot to be desired. The problem is discussed further in Chapter 3. Whatever parrels, trusses and truss-parrels were the *Regent* had all three, for her mainyard was fitted with a main parrel, a truss-parrel and two trusses. There was also a breast-rope, which in later centuries was a rope binding the yard to the mast and acting as a preventer parrel if the main one gave way.

Besides parrels and their associates, mainyards had two other items of gear. These were 'stetyngs' and 'dryngs'. They are often recorded together but, as a general statement, stetyngs are listed more often than dryngs at the beginning of the century whereas at its end dryngs are more common. By that time, however, stetyngs may have acquired a different function (see Chapter 2). The early stetyngs may have been extra, or preventer, braces and something of the sort can be seen on the Portuguese carrack depicted in Chapter 2, although it does not follow of course that something used on a foreign ship of about 1520 was in use on English ones a century earlier. On the *Holigost* the stetyngs had a pair of pulleys each, but nothing is said about how many pulleys the *Regent's* stetyngs had.

Dryngs are recorded from 1426 when the *Holigost* had a dryng with ten pulleys, so it must have been a complex tackle. In the Tudor inventories from the last two decades of the century dryngs are almost always equal in number to trusses and until 1495, when the

Regent but not the *Sovereign* had dryngs to the foreyard, are found only among the mainyard's gear. It has been suggested[19] that dryngs were some kind of sling for the yard but that seems unlikely at the end of the century when big ships had a jeer as well as tyes to their mainyards. The juxtaposition in the inventories of dryngs with parrels and trusses points to their being a device for holding the yard back. Perhaps they were a tackle attached to the truss-rope and taken well aft. Some such arrangement can just be made out on certain pictures and it would have been a great help in holding the huge yard against the strain of a fresh wind. That dryngs were tackles is confirmed by the inventory of 1512-14 for the *Henry Grace à Dieu*. Her dryngs each had a double and a single pulley.

Lifts. These were in use from very early times and are shown, for example, in pictures of ships of about 1400. The early English records, however, do not mention lifts unless the *Holigost's* '2 old lifting ropes'[12] are lifts. By 1485 lifts with a double and a single pulley were in use.

Braces. These are so obviously necessary that it is surprising to find them missing from some inventories. In such cases their place is taken by yard ropes, as in the table. To the examples in the table can be added the spritsail yards, which had yard ropes but no braces. The distribution suggests that braces were used only on big yards and that yard ropes were fitted instead to the mainyards of small vessels. We know that braces ran through a block on a pendant from the yardarm, so perhaps yard ropes went straight to the deck from the yardarms. That would not have been the case on the *Holigost*, however.

Spritsail yard. On Henry VII's ships these yards were hoisted with a tye, apparently without a halliard. If that is correct the tye would have run over a sheave in the bowsprit, or a block fastened to it, and have come inboard to the forecastle. Neither parrels nor trusses are listed among the spritsail yard's gear. They were probably impracticable because it was customary to bring the yard into the forestage when the sail was not in use. As mentioned above, there were no spritsail yard braces.

Mizzenyards. The early history of the mizzen's rigging has yet to be worked out, but at the end of the fifteenth century the yard was rigged in much the same way as it was in the sixteenth and seventeenth centuries. Comment on it has therefore been left until the next chapter.

Topsail and topgallant yards. A topsail is mentioned in an English poem of 1390, in another of 1399 and in a third of 1420[15b] but rigging details do not appear until

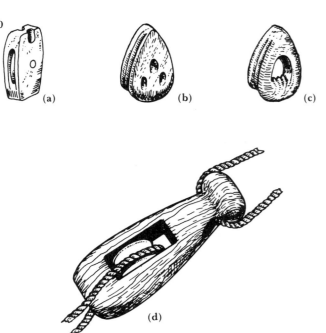

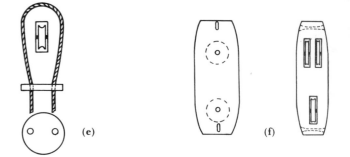

40. Mediaeval blocks and deadeyes.
(a), (b) and (c) are based on the fifteenth century model from Mataro, Spain.
(d) is a mediaeval block from Denmark. The block is made of oak and is 49cm long.
(e) is a similar block but stropped in a different way. It is in the Sjöhistoriska Museum, Stockholm and came from a late fifteenth or early sixteenth century wreck in the Baltic Sea.
(f) is based on a 3-sheave block from the *Wasa*.
41. Ramhead with two half-tyes.
42. The running rigging of a carrack's mainsail. At the side are the bowlines and the tackle, later called a martnet, that hauled the sail up for reefing (at this period, and for about two centuries more, sails were lowered to reef them). The tackles in the middle of the sail may be the stryks. They are shown in the drawing on the right, which has been taken from a contemporary Danish picture.

1485 and then are fragmentary. The *Mary of the Tower* and the *Governor* had main topsail lifts but no gear is recorded for the *Grace Dieu* and the *Martin Garsia*. None of those ships had fore topsail yards. Ten years later the inventories record:

Sovereign: Fore topsail yard – tye, halliard, parrel, lifts. No braces or yard ropes. Main topsail yard – tye, halliards, parrel, lifts, braces.
Regent: Fore topsail yard – tye, halliard, parrel, lifts. No braces or yard ropes. Main topsail yard – parrel and lifts only.
Sweepstake: Main topsail yard – tye, halliard, yard ropes.
Mary Fortune: Main topsail yard – tye, halliard, yard ropes.

The omissions are curious. Those from the 1485 lists may represent gear lost or worn out during the war just finished, and that missing from the *Regent*'s main topsail yard may have been worn out, but the rest of the absences seem to reflect the way the yards were controlled. The lack of braces or yard ropes to the *Sovereign*'s and the *Regent*'s fore topsail yards suggests that those yards were controlled by taking the topsail sheets to the lower yard, and the absence of parrels for the main topsail yards of the *Sweepstake* and the *Mary Fortune* must mean that the yards were set 'flying'. No gear is listed for the *Regent*'s main topgallant yard. In fact, no yard is listed although a topgallant sail is.

There were no footropes on any mediaeval yards. They did not appear until the late seventeenth century.

Blocks and rope. The dimensions of blocks and the sizes of rope required to fit out each kind of ship were part of the rigger's everyday knowledge and for that reason were hardly ever recorded. Even as late as the eighteenth century the sizes of blocks are not usually listed in inventories. In the fifteenth and early sixteenth centuries blocks (always called pulleys) were listed, as a rule, only when their sheaves were made of expensive bronze, and in no case is the size of the blocks recorded. Early blocks have been recovered from wrecks in the Baltic but not, so far, from British waters. The Scandinavian blocks are in many cases quite different from those familiar to us from 'Navy Board' models and contemporary paintings. Some are like the single blocks shown on the 'kraeck' drawing and on the fifteenth century model from Mataro. They

are roughly oblongs with rounded corners and have a hole at one end for fastening the block. When such blocks are part of a tackle they have a hole at each end. Other single blocks seem to be descendants of those used on the Gokstad ship. Stropped blocks have been found, and occasional references are made in the English records to multi-sheave blocks but the pictorial evidence for the latter is even vaguer than it is for single blocks. It does suggest, however, that the sheaves were set one behind another instead of side by side as in later times. Blocks of this sort were in use on the *Wasa* when she sank in 1628. In addition to blocks there would be what were later called 'bullseyes'. On the 'kraeck' they are heart-shaped or pear-shaped.

The sizes of blocks can only be guessed at but it is safe to say that they were at least as big as seventeenth century blocks (see Chapter 3). The size of a block was governed by the size of the sheave, and that was determined by the rope's thickness. Late seventeenth century English blocks had sheaves with diameters equal to about six times the rope's diameter. They would not be smaller two centuries earlier and may well have been quite a lot bigger. Blocks taking heavy loads often had bronze sheaves, and it has been calculated that some early sixteenth century sheaves on English ships were up to 20in in diameter[21]. A wooden sheave to stand the same strain would be 30in or more across.

A little more is known about the sizes of rope used on English ships than about the blocks, and a great deal more would be known if a correlation could be established between the weight of a cable, or a hawser, and its girth because there are more references to the weights of ropes in Henry VII's naval accounts. Unfortunately, the length of a fifteenth century cable is not known. For rigging a model of a fifteenth century ship the best guide for the present is the inventory of the Queen's ships taken in 1588 after the Armada campaign had finished (see Chapter 2). In order to adapt the information to ships of a century earlier several assumptions must be made. The first is that ships of the same tonnage were the same size. Early English tonnage is still very ill-defined and one ship may have several different tonnages ascribed to her. The *Sovereign* is credited with 600 tons in one source and 800 in another, and the *Regent*'s tonnage varies between 800 and 1000. The two

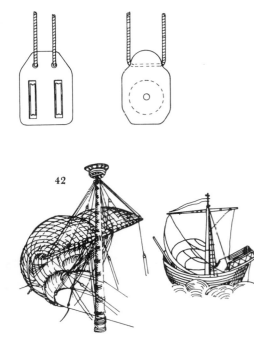

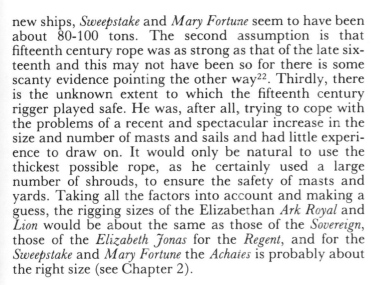

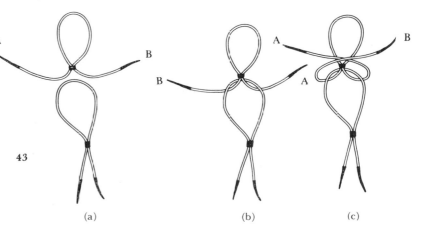

43. Mediaeval reefing.
(a) A pair of reef points, one above the other.
(b) The lower loop is hauled up and the 'legs' of the upper one passed through it from front to back. One 'leg' A is taken to the right and the other one B to the left.
(c) The 'legs' are brought round to the front and tied, presumably in a reef knot.

new ships, *Sweepstake* and *Mary Fortune* seem to have been about 80-100 tons. The second assumption is that fifteenth century rope was as strong as that of the late sixteenth and this may not have been so for there is some scanty evidence pointing the other way[22]. Thirdly, there is the unknown extent to which the fifteenth century rigger played safe. He was, after all, trying to cope with the problems of a recent and spectacular increase in the size and number of masts and sails and had little experience to draw on. It would only be natural to use the thickest possible rope, as he certainly used a large number of shrouds, to ensure the safety of masts and yards. Taking all the factors into account and making a guess, the rigging sizes of the Elizabethan *Ark Royal* and *Lion* would be about the same as those of the *Sovereign*, those of the *Elizabeth Jonas* for the *Regent*, and for the *Sweepstake* and *Mary Fortune* the *Achates* is probably about the right size (see Chapter 2).

SAILS AND THEIR GEAR

The Italian manuscript on shipbuilding states that a 'cocca's' mainsail should be half as deep as it is wide, and this is the proportion given more than two centuries later in a Spanish book on navigation and shipbuilding[27]. Whether Northern ships' sails were of the same proportions is not known, but it seems likely. Sails were made of strips of hemp canvas sewn vertically, and so far as we know the strips were 28in wide. The stitching was arranged to give sails a lot of 'bag', and to give them extra strength it was customary, at any rate on Mediterranean ships, to sew bands of canvas across the sail horizontally and vertically. The bands were sometimes coloured, giving the sail a chequered appearance. English ships had such bands in the fourteenth century but whether they had them a century later is not known.

Nearly all the gear associated with sails in later centuries was in use in at least a primitive form in the fifteenth century but there were also some items that fell out of use by the middle of the next century.

Robands. These were the lashings by which a sail was fastened to its yard and they are recorded as early as the late thirteenth century. Mediaeval pictures show the robands so widely spaced as to seem insufficient. In the seventeenth century there were two lashings to a cloth, at the first and third quarters along the width, but perhaps mediaeval sails had only one. The figures in Chapter 3 show how robands were tied in the seventeenth century but there may have been a different arrangement in the fifteenth, for an English document of about 1420 mentions '2 thin ropes called robands'. These may have been wound spirally round the yard and through eyelets in the sail[19].

Boltropes and leechropes. These were recorded before the fifteenth century. The boltrope at the top of the sail seems to have been called a headrope or sometimes a headline.

Sheets and tacks. Sheets are recorded as such from the beginning of the century but no tacks are known before about 1415. There are references to 'lollers', however, which may have been tacks under another name.

Bowlines. The *Holigost* had two bowlines to her mainsail, each with a pulley, in 1416. It is not known whether the bowlines were rigged like a brace, with a pendant and whip, or whether the pulley was merely a lead-block. Bowlines were taken to a convenient point on the bowsprit, fore bowlines, when they came into use, being placed further along than main bowlines.

Reef points. These were in use throughout the late Middle Ages and three arrangements are known from pictures. One has the reef points near the foot of the sail and another has them near the top, but in the third they are distributed all over the sail. Two sorts of reef point are shown. One is the ordinary kind, a short length of rope passed through the sail and hanging down on each side, but the other is like an inverted 'V' and may be on either side of the sail. It has been suggested that what the artists were trying to show were loops of rope that enabled a kind of bag reef to be taken in the sail.

The existence of reef points implies some means of hoisting up the slack of the sail but only two pieces of gear occur in the English inventories. One is the 'brail' (always in the singular), which was part of the square sail rigging but not, as in later times, of the lateen mizzen. The mediaeval brail seems, in fact, to have been a primitive buntline and was used to haul up the foot of the sail and it is recorded only on foresails and mainsails.

Some of Henry VII's ships had a 'wheel for to wind up the mainsail' and associated with it in the lists is a strong 'wheelrope'. Occasionally two wheelropes are

44
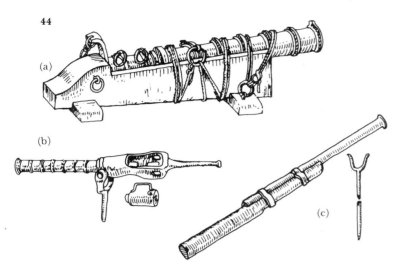

44. Fifteenth century armament
(a) Breech-loading cannon. The chamber containing the powder charge was held in place by an iron wedge that was hammered in tight.
(b) A falconet.
(c) A hand gun, the sort of weapon that would be fired through holes in the bulwarks.
45. A fifteenth century breech-loading cannon recovered in 1847 from a wreck off the Danish island of Anholt. The gun is mounted on an oak stock.
(a) The complete gun. The main barrel, or hall, seems to be about 8ft long and the overall length of gun and stock about 14ft.
(b) The main barrel. It does not seem to be of bar-and-hoop construction and may be made of a rolled sheet of iron, reinforced with iron rings shrunk on to it, as one of the *Mary Rose*'s guns is made.
(c) The chamber that held the powder charge. It was usual to give each gun several chambers, which could be loaded in advance so that a rapid fire could be kept up.
(d) Another view of the gun.

recorded but one may have been a spare. Only the big ships had 'wheels'.

There are no references to buntlines, clew-lines or martnets, at any rate under those names, in the inventories. Martnets were nevertheless in use, whatever their name, for they can be seen on the 'kraeck' main-sail.

Some mainsails had an unfamiliar piece of gear called a 'stryks'. It was an important piece because in the next century the huge *Henry Grace à Dieu* had '8 principal men to the stryks of the mainsail'. The word occurs only in the Henry VII and Henry VIII inventories. It is not in dictionaries of mediaeval English and no similar word in a nautical context has been found in German or Dutch dictionaries. Stryks seems to be connected with the common Germanic root meaning to stretch and, more distantly, to hoist. That the stryks was a tackle for hoisting the main yard is unlikely, for tyes and a jeer were doing that job. The word's basic meaning, to stretch, suggests that it may have been a tackle for stretching the sail by holding its foot down. Tackles for that purpose were in use on Continental ships in the fifteenth and early sixteenth centuries. One may be seen on the Portuguese carrack depicted in Chapter 2. The existence of such a tackle on English ships in the early sixteenth century is implied by the way the centre of the mainsail on the ship in some contemporary paintings is pulled in. Inventories sometimes list one 'strykrope' and sometimes two. The second one, if not just a spare, might be for the bonnet, which also had its holding tackle.

Other items of gear, of unknown purpose and nature, are the 'tailing ropes' of the mainsail. They are found at both the beginning and the end of the century. On the *Holigost* there were '12 small ropes for tailropes and brails' and on the *Sovereign* in 1495-7 six 'tayling ropes' are recorded. None of Henry VII's other ships had tailing ropes and they do not occur in the inventories of the next century.

There were also things called 'trepgatelynes' and 'tragetes', which may have been alternative names for a single item. All we know about them is that the *Holigost*'s pair had two pulleys each. Whatever tragetes or trepgates were they remained in use until at least 1531.

The final piece of sail gear is the bonnet, which was a broad strip of canvas that was laced to the bottom of the sail to increase its propulsive power. The bonnet's lashing is described in Chapter 3. Ships might set two or even three bonnets on the mainsail.

ARMAMENT

The English are believed to have used guns on ships for the first time at the Battle of Sluys in 1340, but for more than a century afterwards the effective missile armament of warships (and merchantmen) was arrows and javelins supplemented by stones and heavy iron rods flung from the tops. In the fifteenth century guns are recorded on ships from the reigns of Henry IV and Henry V but they were probably small and few in number. In 1410-12 the *Christopher* had three iron guns with stocks and five chambers, and at the same date the *Marie of the Tower* had an iron gun with two chambers and a brass gun with one. All these guns, therefore, were breech-loaders. Among the *Carake*'s equipment was '1 vice for the spryngole'. A century later a vice was a screw-in chamber for a breech-loading gun[24].

Guns were in general use by the middle of the century, for an English ship in 1466-7 had 'xj gonnys grete and small'[25] and the 'kraeck' has eight in her after-castle and another in her top. The Warwick Roll ships have three and in one instance four guns on each side of the waist. The guns have foresights like land cannon of the time. Foresights disappeared when recoiling cannon, firing through ports, came into use because the sight was liable to catch on the upper edge of the port. The Warwick ships' armaments are probably only token ones because on Henry VII's ships, only a few years after the supposed date of the drawings, guns were plentiful. In 1485 the *Grace Dieu* had 21 guns and the *Mary of the Tower* 58. Ten years later the *Sovereign*'s armament was: on the forecastle deck, 16 iron serpentines; in the forecastle, 24 iron serpentines; in the waist, 20 stone guns (ie guns firing a stone shot); in the somercastle (under the half-deck), 20 iron serpentines, 1 brass serpentine and 11 stone guns; in the stern (ie firing astern), 4 serpentines;

46. A late fifteenth or early sixteenth century breech-loader in the Tøjhus Museum, Copenhagen. The bed is 11ft long, the barrel 5ft 9in long with a 6in bore, and the chamber 22in long (although it may not belong to the gun).
47. The gun from the wreck in the Cattewater, Plymouth. It is very like the Anholt gun although the wreck is now thought to be from the sixteenth century. The Cattewater gun is a little more than 6ft in overall length.

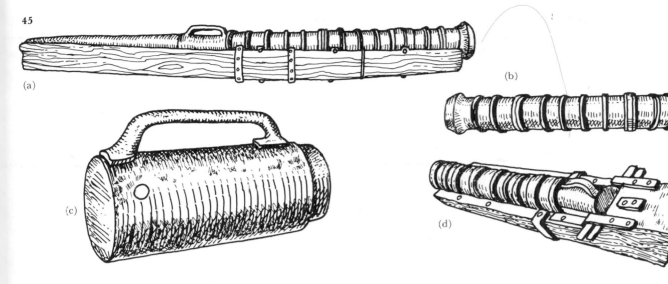

in the deck over the somercastle, 25 iron serpentines; and on the poop, 20 more. Only totals are given for the *Regent*'s guns: 30 brass serpentines and 195 of iron. All the guns on both ships were breech-loaders, for their chambers are listed.

The presence of so many guns on the two ships implies that most of them were small 'man-killers' rather than 'ship-smashers' – but some guns carried in ships in the second half of the fifteenth century were certainly capable of firing a large shot. The huge portholes on the Hastings Manuscript ship, even when allowance has been made for exaggeration, indicate the presence of large calibre guns such as those shown on board some of the Warwick Roll ships. The pictorial evidence has been confirmed by the recovery of some guns, said to be mid-fifteenth century, from a wreck off the Danish island of Anholt[26]. At least one of the guns had a bore of about 10in and a barrel length of over 10ft. Some more evidence is provided by the *Sovereign*'s inventory, which lists 200 iron 'dice' 1½in square. Only a gun of a fairly large calibre could fire a charge of such shot. Furthermore, we know from other sources that stone guns fired a large shot and were likely to be the biggest guns, which would account for their being in the *Sovereign*'s waist and somer-castle. Contemporary records say little about the construction, shape and size of ships' guns. It is practically certain, however, that the early iron guns were made by the bar-and-hoop method but the brass (which means bronze) guns would probably be cast. How the guns were mounted is almost as obscure as their shapes and sizes. The Anholt gun has a stock like those on the Cattewater gun and on some of the *Mary Rose* guns, a method of mounting that lasted until at least the middle of the next century. Guns mounted in that way are to be

seen on the big Warwick Roll carrack for their muzzles are close to the deck and poke out through the bulwarks. On some of the other ships the guns' muzzles are over the top of the bulwarks and therefore must be 3ft or so above the deck. Swivel mountings for guns of the size implied by the drawings are unlikely yet there is no evidence that wheeled carriages were in use in the 1480s on board ship. That is, however, an 'argument from silence' for land guns were mounted on two- and four-wheeled carriages at that time. It is, therefore, by no means impossible that some such carriage had been adapted for sea service. Another possibility is that the guns were mounted on some sort of trestle. Improbable though it seems, trestle gun mountings were in use on English ships, and no doubt on others, as late as the beginning of the seventeenth century though the description of their construction is regrettably vague. The smaller guns were swivel-mounted, a method that must have been devised well before 1470 and which lasted until the early 1800s.

SUPPORT CRAFT AND BOATS
The previous sections have been concerned with the big ships but the ordinary patrol work of the naval forces was not done by the giants of the fleet in the Middle Ages any more than it is at the present day. For that work a variety of small craft were used. We know their names – 'balingers', 'barks', 'barges', 'crayers' and 'hoys' are some of them – but little else. What is known about small merchantmen will be found in *English Merchant Shipping 1460-1540* by Dorothy Burwash. It is usefully supplemented by some of WA's drawings which show the deck layout and other details. Many of the support craft in wartime would be commandeered merchantmen, but support craft were sometimes built specifically for naval

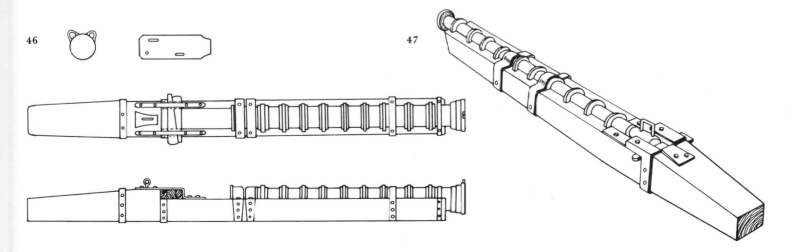

service. The great *Grace Dieu* of 1418 had two consorts, the balingers *Falconer* and *Valentine*, the first being of 80 tons and the *Valentine* a little more. Another of Henry V's big ships, the *Jesus*, of 1000 tons, had a balinger for a consort that was known at first as the *Follower* and later as the *Little Jesus*. The appearance of balingers can only be guessed at. They were oared craft, for the *Valentine* had 48 oars (which probably includes some spares) and the *Falconer* had 38. Perhaps they rowed 40 and 30 oars respectively. Of their hull shape we know little. As oared ships they would be fairly low-built and this is confirmed by an account of an unsuccessful attack by a squadron of English balingers on a French carrack in 1416. The carrack was said to have been higher than the English ships by the height of a lance – perhaps 12ft. Balingers were probably clinker-built and one, in 1400, had a 'castle' of which the location is not given. In 1410 the balinger *Gabriel* had a bowsprit, one mast, one yard, a sail with two bonnets, two backstays and two forestays among her gear[4]. A little later the *Holigost's* balinger had a mizzenmast but another, at the same time, seems to have been single-masted.

By 1422 mizzenmasts were a normal part of a balinger's rig but there is no mention of a foremast. A foresail, though not a foremast, is recorded from 1438. The absence of a foremast has been interpreted to mean that balingers had only two masts, a mainmast with a square sail and a lateen mizzen, and a spritsail set under the bowsprit – a primitive ketch rig. It is an ingenious hypothesis but in view of the disorganised state of Henry VI's fleet in the 1430s it is as least as likely that the foremast was simply missing. Barges were similar to balingers in rig and were also oared craft. Some were fighting ships and others, like the *Nicholas of the Tower* at the beginning of the century, acted as Royal yachts.

From the 1430s until the end of the century there is a gap in the English records so far as support craft are concerned and even the naval accounts of Henry VII tell us little about the appearance of his two new small ships *Sweepstake* and *Mary Fortune*. Both were oared vessels, the first having 60 'long oars' and the other one 80. As the totals would include the spares we cannot say how many oarports the ships had. The *Mary Fortune* had a forecastle but as it is mentioned in connection with repair work the absence of reference to one on the *Sweepstake* is not significant. Both ships were clinker-built and had three masts. An interesting feature about the rig of

these two ships is that they had bonaventure mizzenmasts but no mizzenmasts. This is not merely an interchange of names because other ships are listed as having mizzenmasts but not bonaventure masts, and the four-masters have both. As will be seen in the next chapter, some early Tudor ships are shown in pictures as having a mizzenmast right aft and over the sternpost. The late fifteenth century bonaventure mizzenmast was, presumably, similarly placed.

More is known about the fittings of fifteenth century boats than about their shapes. The big ships had a 'great boat' that would be towed astern and one or more runabout boats such as the 'joliwat' (various spellings are known) and the 'cock-boat'. All boats seem to have been double-ended but it is not clear from pictures whether they were clinker- or carvel-built. Those built for Henry VII's ships seem to have been clinker. If a boat shown in the Warwick Roll is typical there was considerable sheer to each end and the oars worked through holes in the top strake.

28

49. A drawing of a German carrack and ship's boat based on a manuscript illustration. Although this picture is dated about 1490, the ship belongs to an earlier age. Despite the original artist's shortcomings as a nautical draughtsman there is a lot of interesting detail shown: the hull appears to be carvel-planked, there are three wales, apparently made of two belts of timber, and the double-hook shape of the rudder irons is found on other ships. The centre ship has a pair of big guns on her broadside. The rigging, what there is of it, is reasonably accurate. Note the triple parrels, the shrouds set up with deadeyes to channels, and the ratlines. The ship is a four-master and the artist has done his best to show the mizzen lifts.

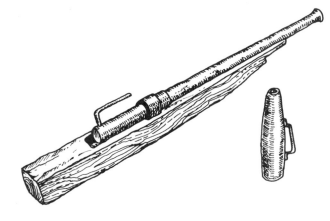

48. A small breech-loading swivel gun found in the Zuider Zee, believed to be from the seventeeth century but very like the gun in the 'kraeck's' mizzen top (1).

REFERENCES

Abbreviations
IJNA: International Journal of Nautical Archaeology
MM: The Mariner's Mirror, the Journal of the Society for Nautical Research
NRS: The Navy Records Society publications.

1 *The Pageant of the Birth, Life and Death of Richard Beauchamp, Earl of Warwick, KG*, a facsimile print of the original, which is in the British Library, London (Cottonian Mss, Julius E, IV), by Longmans (1914); the manuscript is usually known as the Warwick Roll
2 *The Naval Accounts and Inventories of the Reign of Henry VII NRS* Vol VIII (1896)
3 *The Cog of Bremen,* S Fliedner & R Pohl-Weber, Focke Museum, Hamburg, West Germany (1972); 'Nautical Archaeology in Germany', D Elmers, *IJNA* (1974) Vol 3, pp141–2; 'The anti-hogging hull of the cog of Bremen', R M Rose, *MM* (1977) Vol 63 p108
4 'The Accounts of John Starling', A H Moore, *MM* (1914) Vol IV p23 and p168
5 For hulks see *MM* (1972) Vol 58 pp103, 344–7, 395 and (1973) Vol 59 p103. Most of the information is about Tudor period hulks
6 'The Ship of the Renaissance', R M Nance, *MM* (1955) Vol 41 pp 180–192 and 281–295; 'More about the Ship of the Renaissance', Guilleux la Roërie, *MM* (1957) Vol 53 pp179–193

7 Alcetre's letter is printed in full in *English Historical Documents* Vol IV (1327–1485), Eyre and Spottiswood (1969). See also MM (1922) Vol VIII p376.

8 *MM* (1923) Vol IX p83 et seq

9 'Henry V's *Grace Dieu*', M W Prynne, *MM* (1968) Vol 54 pp115–128. This summarises what had been discovered up to then about the ship and gives the references to the original examination of the wreck. See also A McKee, Chapter 10 of *A History of Sea-faring from Underwater Archaeology*, G Bass (Editor)

10 'Clove Board', L G Carr Laughton, *MM* (1957) Vol 43 pp247–8

11 *The Florentine Galleys in the 15th Century*, M E Mallet, Oxford (1967); the *Grace Dieu* data are given in *MM* (1977) Vol 63 pp6–7

12 'The Building of the *Grace Dieu*, *Valentine* and *Falconer* at Southampton, 1416–20', Mrs Carpenter Turner, *MM* (1954) Vol 40 pp55–72; 'The Building of the *Holy Ghost of the Tower*, 1414–16', Mrs Carpenter Turner, *MM* (1954) Vol 40 pp270–281

13 'Italian Naval Architecture about 1445', R C Anderson, *MM* (1925) Vol XI pp135–163

14 R M Nance, *MM* (1924) Vol X p305

15 'Anchors and Accessories 1340–1640', J T Tinniswood, *MM* (1945) Vol 31 pp84–105

16 *A History of the Royal Navy*, (Chapter VII) Sir Harris Nicholas, London (1847)

17 'English Galleys 1272–1377', J T Tinniswood, *MM* (1949) Vol 35 pp299–301

18 *The Materials of Medieval Painting* D V Thompson, New York (1956)

19 *Middle English Sea Terms*, B Sandahl, Uppsala, Sweden; see: mizzen, topsail and topmast, spritsail, susters, dryngs, and robands, quoting E364/54 D (Public Records Office, London)

20 The relevant references are *MM* (1911) Vol 1 p251; (1913) Vol III p67 and p183; and (1932) Vol XVIII p193

21 For brass sheaves see L G Carr Laughton, *MM* (1933) Vol XX p117

22 'Two Tudor rigging puzzles', G F Howard, *MM* (1976) Vol 62 p191

23 R M Nance, *MM* (1920) Vol VI pp85–6

24 'Early Tudor ship guns', L G Carr Laughton, *MM* (1960) Vol 46 pp242–285

25 E101/55/3, Public Records Office, London. Quoted in Reference 18, p39

26 *National Museets Arbejdsmark*, Copenhagen (1974)

27 *Instruccion Nautica para Navegar*, Diego Garcia de Palacio, Mexico (1587), reprint by Ediciones Cultura Hispanica (1944)

GREAT GUNS & GALLEONS

The revolution in naval construction that began during the last 20 years of the fifteenth century continued in the first quarter of the next one and completed the transformation of the mediaeval carrack into a vessel that differed only in detail from the sailing warship of the succeeding centuries. The changes in hull form were brought about, to a great extent, by changes in armament. At the end of the fifteenth century English warships, like those of other States, carried large numbers of guns but most of them were comparatively small, quick-firing breech-loaders and only a few heavy-shotted pieces were mounted. The latter were on the maindeck in the waist and sometimes under the half-deck. By the end of the first decade of the sixteenth century big guns were being mounted on board in increasing numbers. Henry VIII's *Henry Grace à Dieu* of 1500 tons, which was built in 1514, had an armament of 186 guns of which at least 18 were heavy-shotted weapons. The change reflected a phase in the continual struggle between attack and defence, for the mediaeval warship was designed for fighting *al fresco* because archers and javelin men were the source of missiles, but as the use of guns spread open decks became a disadvantage and higher, closed structures were added at bow and stern. The new fore- and aftercastles were strong enough to withstand shot from small guns and gunners and soldiers could remain under cover and fire their own weapons until the time came to board the enemy ship. The counter-move to the 'castles' was to mount on board what were, in effect, siege guns. These were carried at first on the maindeck but early in the century a way to mount them on the lower deck was worked out, and before long all but the smaller warships carried their heaviest guns in this position.

At the same time that these changes were being made rigging was being stabilised. Although the biggest ships had four masts, the great majority had three; there is some evidence that a fourth mast was found to be unnecessary even on the big ships, and its use was discontinued after about 1550 until its revival in the last years of the century. Topsails came into general use, and the biggest vessels began to ship topgallants. The spritsail was a regular feature of the sail plan. The old mediaeval rigging was replaced in the first half of the century by a new order that remained basically the same until the end of the sailing era. In armament too, all the essentials of the classical naval gun complements were introduced: muzzle-loading cannon mounted on trunnions on wheeled carriages, long-range culverin-type guns, and very heavy-shotted guns for action at close quarters. At the time of her loss in 1545, *Mary Rose* had cannon that fired a 70lb ball.

50. The ships in this lively scene are English and from the early sixteenth century. Some are warships, or else heavily armed merchantmen, with guns on their lower decks. The ship in the top left hand corner has one of its port lids raised. Shipboard activities are pictured in a natural way, quite different from the rigidity of mediaeval pictures. On the ship in the middle of the picture some of the crew are stowing the spritsail yard on the forecastle and on the anchored ship there is a man astride the main yardarm, while another sailor is climbing up the main shrouds. Rigging is only sketched in but what is shown is realistically drawn. Note the great thickness of the main stays, the lead of the bowlines and the running rigging of the mizzen. Three boats are going about their business. The boat towing the ship seems to have its oars through holes in the uppermost strake and is rowed one man to an oar, but the lowest boat has the oars over the top of the strake and each man has a pair of oars. This boat has a dark gunwale strake, a light one below it and the hull below that is dark coloured. The uppermost boat has higher stem- and sternposts than the others but their rise may have been exaggerated. In fact, except for the excessive curvature of the hulls and being steered by a sweep instead of a rudder, these boats are like those of the eighteenth century. The picture is part of a Pilot's Guide that is bound up with a miscellaneous collection of material from the thirteenth to the sixteenth centuries known as the Hastings Manuscript, and has been erroneously dated to about 1450.

51

51. English ships off Dover, about 1530. Although the hulls are distorted and the rigging merely sketched in there are many points of interest about the ships. The centre one has a complete tier of lower deck guns but the ship to the right has them only on the after part and a single gunport, perhaps on the maindeck, towards the bows. The tillers come in to the maindeck. Note the mizzenmast perched right at the end of the poop. This seems to have been the usual position for most, if not all, of the century. It is difficult to understand how a mast so far back could be effectively supported. Perhaps that was why it was called a bonaventure or 'Good Luck' mast!

52. A highly imaginative scene known as 'The Embarkation of Henry VIII for France'. The picture, which is in Hampton Court, was painted several years after the event it depicts (1520) and cannot be taken as contemporary evidence for the appearance of the ships that were actually there, which were the *Great Bark* (400 tons), the *Less Bark* (160), the *Kateryn Pleasaunce* (100) and the *Mary and John* (tonnage unknown: she was an old ship). As all the ships in the picture are big ones the artist has obtained his inspiration from some of Henry's biggest vessels. The ship with four masts and painted sails is popularly said to be the *Henry Grace à Dieu* although she is the twin of the ship in the foreground to the left of the tower.

Despite the exaggerated tumblehome and the tremendous overhang of the sterns (a feature often found in early sixteenth century drawings) the picture does convey the general shape of the hulls – short and tubby, with lofty fore- and aftercastles, and carrying a heavy armament. The rigging, however, is quite unreliable. All the ships have square mizzens and even square mizzen topsails, neither of which are otherwise known before 1600 at the earliest. Lifts and braces do not correspond with the inventories and only one ship has a spritsail although they were in general use before 1500. (A close-up of the centre ship is reproduced in the colour section.)

52

In contrast to the problems of tracing the developments in previous centuries, it is possible to date the sixteenth century innovations fairly closely, for there is not only a wealth of reliable pictures but also a mass of documentary evidence of all sorts even though this has, as yet, only been partly evaluated. Britain is fortunate in having a well-catalogued collection of records, from the reigns of Henry VIII and his daughter Elizabeth I, that cover almost 4/5 of the century and these have been drawn on extensively in this chapter, although it must not be assumed from what is written in the succeeding sections that the English were the only or even the main innovators in naval matters during the sixteenth century. New ideas spread rapidly, and each maritime State adopted those that fitted the requirements of its own naval strategy and, indeed, developed them further. Whether the credit for introducing big guns on the lower deck of a warship belongs to the English is not certain but there is no doubt about another development: the building of nimble, weatherly ships devoid of the usual high structures at bow and stern and carrying a formidable armament of long range guns. These ships were the Elizabethan galleons that were the envy and despair of the Spaniards throughout the long war between Spain and England.

THE HULL

Two major structural changes were made in the first quarter of the century. The first was the abandonment of clinker planking for large ships. The last English warship of any size to be built that way was the *Great Galley* of 1515 and she was given carvel planking in 1523. Other ships were treated in the same way and the remains of one of them, possibly the *Sovereign*, were dug up in Woolwich in 1912. The frames had originally had 'steps' 53 in their outer faces to let them fit closely over clinker planks, but the steps had subsequently been cut almost all away so that carvel planks could be fastened to the frames. Clinker planking was still used on small vessels, as it has been down to the present century. The remains of a small clinker-built ship, believed to belong to the sixteenth century, were found in 1964 when a new sewer was being made at Rye, Sussex. The vessel has an inner 54 and an outer skin of planking, a most unusual arrangement[1]. The second change was the substitution of a flat stern, the square tuck, for the old round stern. The after end of the hull was cut away vertically (or nearly so) almost down to the waterline and the side planks of the hull were fastened to a U-shaped stern frame that was planked across diagonally. Below the waterline the planking curved inwards to the sternpost as before. It has been suggested that the flat stern was developed so that guns could be mounted low down to provide defensive fire against galleys. These had big guns at their bows and, being low-built craft, could fire heavy shot into the hull of an opponent at its waterline. Whilst sterns were the old-fashioned round ones they were the best place to attack because it was impossible to mount guns low enough to provide adequate counter-fire, and late fifteenth and early sixteenth century guns were not hung by trunnions and consequently could not be depressed. Therefore, the argument runs, the stern was made flat so that guns could be mounted near the waterline[2]. The introduction of the flat stern had another effect. It allowed the shipwright to make the aftercastle an integral part of the hull and to build its after end out into a series of overhanging counters.

A third change, and probably the most important factor influencing the future development of the

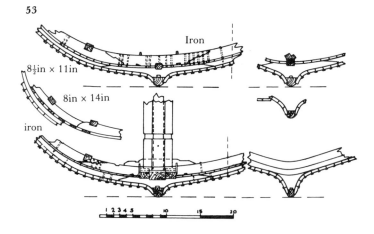

53

8½in × 11in

8in × 14in

iron

Iron

1 2 3 4 5   10   15   20

53. Remains of the ship exposed during excavations at Roff's Wharf, Woolwich. The ship had a beam of at least 45ft and a probable keel length of 115–120ft. The identity of this large ship is not certain but the balance of the evidence favours the *Sovereign* built in 1488, rebuilt in 1509 and laid up as worn out in 1521. The ship had originally been clinker-built but she had subsequently been given carvel planking and that operation involved cutting away the notches in the frames that allowed them to fit over the original clinker planking. As a result, the floor timbers were small for the size of the ship, so to give the hull the necessary strength riders were laid on the ceiling planks where they crossed the frames and longitudinal stringers were fitted. Thick battens were fastened over the seams on the outside. They may have been an original feature or a first-aid device to keep the ship watertight in her old age. The mainmast was made of a spindle of pine surrounded by thick baulks of oak and the whole bound together by bands of iron.
54. 'Double skin' clinker building.

warship, was the mounting of guns on the lower deck. Before the sixteenth century guns had been fired either over or through the waist rails, or through arched openings like big windows in the superstructure. When ships came to be armed with heavy battering cannon that sometimes weighed over two tons each, shipwrights were faced with a difficult problem. If the guns were to be mounted in any numbers on the main and upper decks they would have made the ship top-heavy or, at the very least, would have strained the hull. Moreover, because the early cannon could not be elevated or depressed their usefulness was restricted to smashing an opponent's upperworks instead of holing the waterline. According to tradition the solution was provided about 1500 by a Frenchman from Brest, Descharges by name, who cut gunports through the sides on the lower deck and fitted them with lids. As the story is told it misses the point of Descharges' achievement, which was not merely the cutting of lower deck ports, for those had been in use for a very long time as cargo ports and even for loading horses; what Descharges really did, it seems, was to work out how to place the ports without cutting the wales that provided so much of the longitudinal strength of a carvel-built hull. The gunports were at first only in the after end of the hull because the lower deck was too near the waterline amidships for ports to be cut there. As experi-

ence with stability was gained the height of the deck was progressively raised and ships were given ports in the forward end of the lower deck; and before very long a complete tier of guns was carried. When this came about is not definitely known. For English ships it seems to have been later than 1515 but well before 1546, when Anthony Anthony produced his pictures of Henry VIII's Navy.

The problem of the form of sixteenth century gun decks now presents itself[3]. It arises because the line of the gunports follows the sheer of the wales but these have so much sheer that if the decks sloped similarly it would have been difficult to work the guns safely at the higher ends, and yet if the deck was laid more or less level from bow to stern some of the ports would be too high for the guns' muzzles. The problem was solved, it is believed, by laying the lower deck and possibly the after part of the main deck also, in sections at different levels. Such a deck is in fact marked on one of the late sixteenth century plans of English ships in the manuscript known as the *Fragments of Ancient English Shipwrightry*.

One detail about decks remains to be mentioned and it is important because of the part it would play in attempting to reconstruct a hull profile: the height between successive decks. In a warship there would have to be sufficient headroom to allow a man to

55   *56*

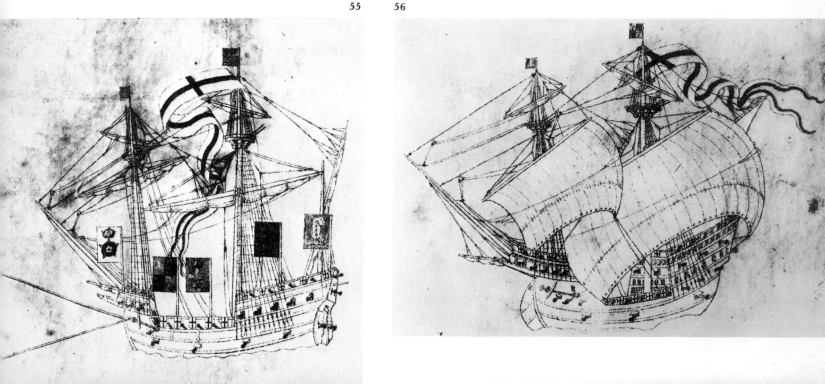

54

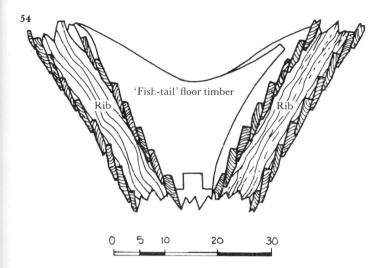

'Fish-tail' floor timber

Rib   Rib

0   5   10   20   30

move about quickly in the excitement of a fight and in the obscurity of the gunsmoke, without a risk of hitting his head against a beam. The specification for the *Mary Gonson*, which is believed to date from 1514, gives 5ft 9in and 5ft 10in as the clearances between deck and overhead beam. The forecastle (or, as it is called in the document, 'under the forecastle') was much loftier, for there was to be a distance of 6ft between the bitt-beam and the deck above. Since the bitt-beam would require adequate height above its deck there would have been about 10ft of headroom in the ship's forecastle. The loftiness of forecastle decks is borne out by contemporary pictures.

The changes described above were not of course the only ones. There was also a considerable reduction in the forward rake of the stem. Henry V's ship at Bayonne had a fore rake of more than half the length of the keel, but a century later the *Mary Gonson*'s fore rake was to be only slightly more than 1/3 of her keel and the rake of her sternpost 1/10. As the century progressed the extent of the fore rake was diminished, and by the end of the century fore rakes as short as 1/5 of the keel's length were being proposed, although the preferred proportion was about 3/10. The after rake of the later part of the century was between 1/16 and 1/20 of the keel length.

55–59. These ships are part of a large panoramic view of Calais and its environs about 1540 that was drawn by Thomas Pettyt and now forms part of the Cottonian Collection in the British Library. The ships may date from well before that time for their hulls correspond with what we know of the hull of the *Sovereign* of 1497 and with the specification for the *Mary Gonson* of 1514. Although the hulls are disproportionately small for the masts and sails they are well drawn and the ships have a seaworthy look about them. The pictures are partially coloured and are the earliest reliable evidence for the appearance of Tudor ships.

55. A heavily armed Royal ship. She has at least 40 broadside guns as well as 5 or 6 stern chasers and possibly other guns in the fore and after bulkheads in the waist to catch boarders in a crossfire. The rigging is carefully drawn, though not quite in proportion in parts, and the artist has not been too clear about the purpose of some of it. He may, indeed, have drawn the ship 'from life' at fairly close quarters. He has, for example, shown the deadeyes on the fore- and mainmasts but has not drawn any channels although such conspicuous objects, if they were on the ship, could hardly have escaped his notice. The mizzen shrouds have no deadeyes as was the case, sometimes, in the previous century. The muzzles of the guns in the waist and on the poop are over the bulwarks, so the guns must have been mounted well above the deck. The flags, which display the King's ancestry, are coloured: at the fore topmast head and the poop, a white ostrich feather on a green ground; at the main topmast and the waist, the Royal Standard; also in the waist, the fleur-de-lys in gold; and on the half-deck, the Portcullis in gold on a red ground. The long pennant is red on a white ground. The ribs of the tops are yellow and green and the barrels of the guns are painted a brassy yellow.

56. Another Royal ship, bigger than the previous one but with fewer guns on the lower deck. Three tiers of guns are in the aftercastle and two in the bulkhead overlooking the waist. The chevrons on the bulkhead and below the poop rail are green and white, the Tudor colours. A deck below them is a row of Tudor Roses. Other points of interest are the small hawsehole (still, however, high above the maindeck) and the bonnets attached to the fore and main courses. The holes along the foot of the bonnet are for lacing on a second one. If the wind grew too strong one or more of the bonnets would be taken off, so that the sail need not be reefed.

57. A different ship from the previous two. There are no waist rails and only two tiers of guns in the aftercastle, on the half-deck and the poop. The lowest stern guns seem to be on the same level as the broadside cannon, suggesting a flush deck. On the counter are the Tudor Rose and the fleur-de-lys with the Crown.

58. A ship like 57 but with differently shaped tops and a different topside in the waist. Across the stern are two rows of lights (windows) and the counter has the Tudor Rose and St George's Cross. The lowest stern guns are set lower down that those on the broadside, indicating a stepped deck there. This ship has riders on the lower part of the aftercastle.

59. There are some interesting differences between this ship and those shown in the preceding illustrations. There are more wales, the stern is narrower and the tiller comes into the half-deck. The only decoration is a shield with the St George Cross on the taffrail. It is possibly a Dutch- or Flemish-built ship like some shown in Breughel's pictures. The comparatively flat stern resembles those in Anthony's pictures.

57   58   59

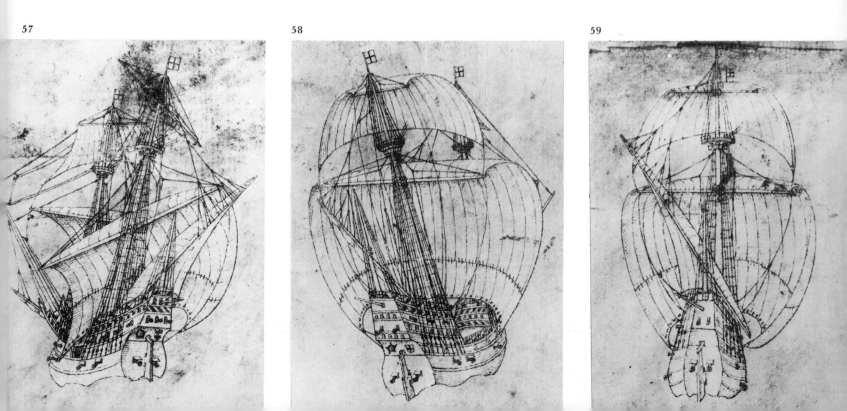

Other changes were, first, the piling up of deck upon deck at bow and stern and then, at any rate on Northern ships, a gradual reduction in height. At the end of the fifteenth century the *Sovereign* had only a half-deck and a poop above her maindeck and, probably, only a single deck at the bows. The *Mary Gonson* seems to have had a similar arrangement. The ships in the picture 52 showing Henry VIII's departure for France in 1520 have up to three levels in the forecastle and four aft, and the 63 huge Portuguese carrack, the *Santa Caterina do Monte Sinai* seems to have four and five respectively. Both pictures may have some artistic licence about them but no such doubts attach themselves to Anthony Anthony's magnificent collection of coloured drawings of the whole of Henry VIII's Navy, a collection presented to the King in 60 1546 and now known as the Anthony Roll. The very naivety of Anthony's style guarantees that he was trying to reproduce what he saw, and in any case Henry VIII knew too much about his ships to tolerate factual misrepresentation, whatever he may have thought about the draughtsmanship. Anthony gives the *Henry Grace à Dieu* four decks above her maindeck at the stern and three, and a kind of penthouse on top of all, at the bows. The *Henry Grace à Dieu* was an exceptionally big ship, but other ships are shown with similar piled up structures. As in previous centuries height gave advantage but when heavy guns were put on board as well as numerous smaller ones the weight of armament created stability problems as well as straining the hull. To overcome the

stability difficulties the upper structures were made as light as possible and the upper hull was narrowed. According to pictures the upperworks were sometimes, perhaps even usually, made of clinker work and, to give the light planking sufficient strength to carry guns and withstand the pull of the shrouds, exterior riders were fastened to the outside. In the second half of the century the English adopted 'stand-off' tactics and the high superstructures preferred by the 'grapple-and-board' school were discarded. The Spaniards and the Portuguese, however, retained them until the last years of the century.

Despite improvements in hull form and rig the carrack-type ship remained unwieldy and in a beam wind must have sailed like a haystack. Meanwhile, other types of hull were being tried and were to develop into the low-built galleons that in the hands of Elizabethan seamen would bring about far-reaching changes in the course of European history. The origin of these low-built hulls, and when they first appeared, is not known, nor have we any information about their proportions, but the vessels shown in the Anthony Roll have the look of a mature design about them. The startling thing about these new ships is their close resemblance in appearance to the later Elizabethan warships – the affinities can be seen at once by comparing the various contemporary pictures.

It is easier to describe the hulls of ships of the first 75 years of the century than to reconstruct their out-

60

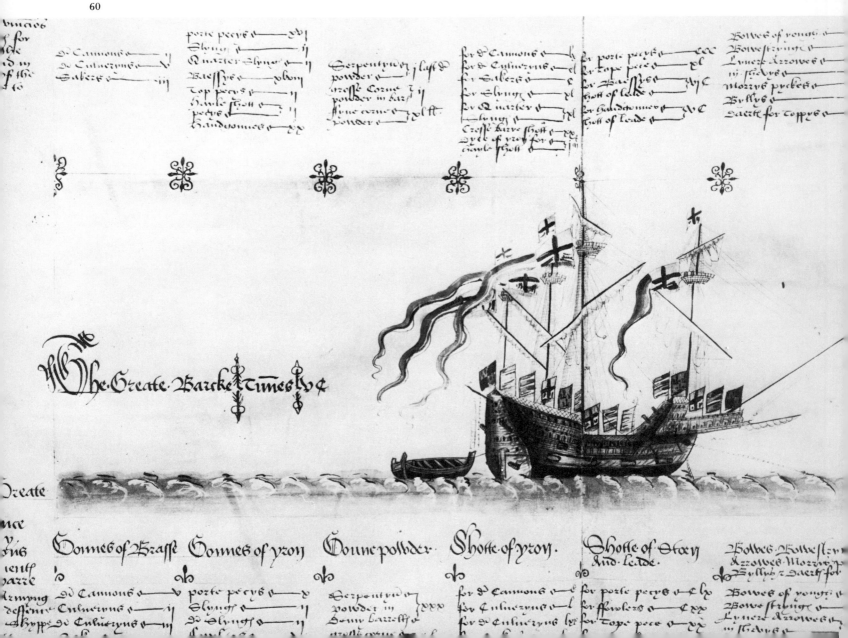

60. In 1545 Anthony Anthony, an officer in the Artillery, presented to Henry VIII two Rolls containing coloured drawings of every ship in the King's Navy. The title of the first Roll (spelling modernised) gives its scope: 'This is the first Roll declaring the number of the King's Majesty's own ships with every ship's name, with their tonnage and number of men. As also the ordnance, artillery, munitions and habiliment for war for the arming and defence of the said ships against their enemies upon the sea.' The first Roll is in the Pepysian Library, Cambridge, and the other one in the British Library, London. The pictures reproduced in this book are only a small part of the collection, which has never been published in full. The Roll is a treasure-house of information about the hulls of English warships in the 1540s (although the rigging, unfortunately, is merely sketched) and each drawing is an individual portrait. The *Great Bark* of 400 tons, built in 1512, is shown here. She has the typical fore- and after-castles of a carrack but the forestage has a much greater overhang than that of the *Henry Grace à Dieu* and the forecastle as a whole is a different shape, variations that inspire confidence in the reliability of Anthony's drawings so long as allowance is made for the naïvety of his style. Like her companion ships, the *Great Bark* has a comparatively flat stern that is quite different in appearance from the overhanging sterns of the ships in the painting of the 'Embarkation of Henry VIII' (see colour section). Although the *Great Bark* was only about one-third of the tonnage of the *Henry Grace à Dieu* she carried a formidable array of guns: 5 demi-cannon, 2 culverins, 3 demi-culverins, 2 sakers, 10 port-pieces, 2 slings, 2 half-slings, 6 fowlers, 30 bases and a top-piece (a swivel gun for the top).

61. Possible arrangements of the decks in an early Tudor warship. If a tracing of the exterior sheer is laid on the interior profile the gunports that follow the sheer of the wales will be found to fit the horizontal decks.

62. An engraving, by Peter Breughel the Elder, of a Flemish warship of about the middle of the sixteenth century or a little later. Although not strictly a 2-decker, the ship has guns on her main and lower decks and has 4 guns a side above the waist, on what must be a spar deck. The hull details are interesting and resemble some of those found on English ships in the second half of the century: a short and relatively low forecastle, a long beakhead, hawseholes on the lower deck and simple decoration. The numerous riders on the aftercastle, however, would not have been found on an English ship of that date. The

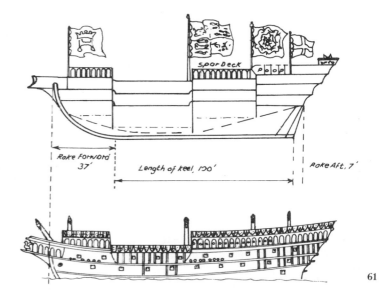

rigging is a curious mixture. Parts of it show careful observation, such as the chafing mat on the bowsprit to protect the foot of the foresail, the boomkin for the foretacks and the lead of the bowlines, but other essential parts–parrels, main topsail braces and mizzen lifts – are omitted or left incomplete.

63. A big four-masted Portuguese carrack, probably the *Santa Caterina do Monte Sinai,* of about 1520. In accordance with artistic convention the three carracks in the centre of the picture, and perhaps that on the right near the fort, are different views of the same ship. The enormous mainmast, typical of carracks, carries an immense mainyard and a hugh windbag of a sail that has two bonnets laced to its foot. The tackles holding back the central part of the sail are clearly drawn and the martnets for gathering in the sail for furling can be seen near the top of the mainsail. At this date and for long afterwards fore- and mainsails were lowered for furling; consequently there were no reef-points and no footropes to the yards, which the seamen had to straddle when they were putting the gaskets on the sail. The slender topmasts are lashed close to the lower mastheads and could not be lowered in bad weather. The carrack has the old-fashioned round stern but if the artist has rendered the run on the planking correctly it must have been very like the round stern introduced by the English in the next century. The roof-like framework over the waist is to support the nettings that served to keep out boarders and gave some protection from falling blocks and other debris in a fight.

64. The *Stora Krafvel* of 1534:

A. Keel	130ft	Midship breadth	40ft
B. Length 'in the middle of the ship'	174ft	Thickness of the sides (? each 3ft)	6ft
C. Aftercastle	34ft	H. Height above water	54ft
D. Midships	47ft	J. Draught	22ft
E. Foreships	58ft		
F. Forecastle	40ft		
G. Length, beakhead bulkhead to taffrail	179ft		

The dimensions are in either Swedish or Danzig feet, which were, respectively, 3% and 9% shorter than English feet.

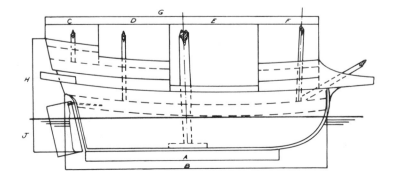

lines. Only one set of dimensions for English ships has come to light from that time, that for the *Mary Gonson,* a ship of 400 to 500 tons[5]. The dimensions of the contemporary *Henry Grace à Dieu* are not known but it has been suggested that she had a keel 125ft long, a beam of 41ft and an overall length on deck of 175ft[6]. A slightly later Swedish ship, the *Stora Krafvel*[7] of 1534, had similar dimensions and the *Mars,* another Swedish ship, built in the 1560s, measured as follows: length overall 211ft; keel 118ft; fore rake 30½ft; after rake 13½ft; length stem to sternpost 162ft; moulded beam 45½; height of sternpost 38ft; height of stem 46½ft; total height of stern 70½ft; length of beakhead 34ft; and rudder 40ft.

The history of ship development in England between the death of Henry VIII in 1547 and the accession of Elizabeth I in 1558 is still largely unknown but after 1558 there is copious documentation of all kinds, not only dry official records but also the letters and personal papers that show what men were thinking about ships and how to design them, even though theory did not go far beyond giving a formal basis to what was still traditional 'rule of thumb'. William Borough, example, who was Comptroller of the Navy from 1588 to 1596, set down as the best proportions for ships:

Shortest, broadest and deepest ships 2:1:1/2
Merchant and general purpose ships 2 to 2 1/4:1:11/24
Galleons and nimble ships of war 3:1:2/5
(The formula: Keel:Midship breadth:Depth in hold)

The proportions of the last group remained in favour, with small variations, right down to the end of the sailing warship era.

The most important source of information about the appearance of English ships in the last quarter of the century is the wonderful collection of coloured draughts, and the accompanying working memoranda,

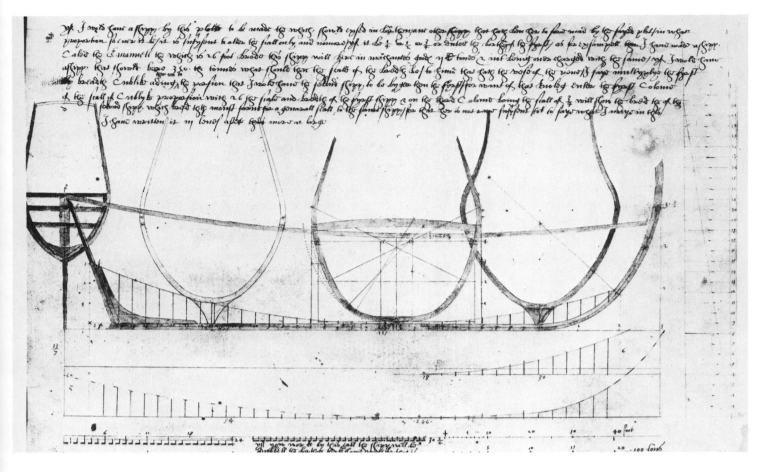

known as the *Fragments of Ancient English Shipwrightry*. The collection is believed to be the work of Matthew Baker, who was the principal shipwright in the later years of Elizabeth's reign. Its date is uncertain. A note written on one of the plans refers to a ship built in 1586 but the plan may of course have been drawn before that date or even a long time after it. Whether the plans are those of Royal ships, or whether they are of ships that may have been proposed but not built, is still debated. Current opinion inclines to the latter view. Whether that is right or not, the plans represent the sort of ships that, in the capable hands of English seamen, defeated the Armada and reduced the Spanish Navy to baffled helplessness. Some are especially interesting because they are the earliest examples of a Northern European ship's lines and sail plan. The hull sections show a feature that was characteristic of English ships (we cannot say whether other countries' ships also had it), namely, a distinct bulge or 'knuckle' in the curve of the side just above the water-line. This feature is to be found in the *Mary Gonson*'s hull and was still part of the design as late as 1670 (see Chapter 3). The manner in which this particular kind of hull section was produced is described in the early sevententh-century *Treatise on Shipbuilding*[8].

One English ship from the last quarter of the century differed from all the others. This was the *Ark Royal* (the Lord Admiral's flagship during the Armada campaign), which was described by him as being the best ship in the world. The *Ark Royal*'s hull form has not in fact been discovered but some basic data are known. Her keel/beam/depth in hold measurements were 100ft/37ft/15ft, her fore rake was $33\frac{1}{2}$ft and her after rake 6ft. When she was built the *Ark Royal* had a galleon beak, a single deck to her forecastle and open galleries at her stern. But what distinguished the *Ark Royal* from her companion ships was the unusual construction of her after part. There were two turrets, or rather half-turrets

65. The earliest known plan of an English ship, thought to date from the 1580s. The midship section, from which, together with the length of the keel, the rest of the hull lines could be developed, is formed from several arcs whose centres are marked 'X' on the plan. These lines and the sail plan (see colour section), also from the *Fragments of Ancient English Shipwrightry*, have been the basis for most of the models and 'replicas' of Elizabethan and early seventeenth century ships.

like those on Scottish castles, at her stern and her poop bulwarks were battlemented. There may have been another pair of turrets at the forward end of the poop, used for latrines.

Since stern galleries have been mentioned, it will be convenient to sketch their development on English ships, so far as it is known, at this point. They are first shown in the Anthony Roll of 1546 (on the *Greyhound*) but they were certainly not commonplace then nor for a long time afterwards. Although one picture, thought to be about 1570, has a stern gallery there is none on the ships shown attacking Smerwick Fort, and of the plans in the *Fragments of Ancient English Shipwrightry* some have galleries and others do not. As far as we know, English ships had only a single gallery until, at the earliest, the last years of the century. Continental fashion seems to have been much the same, but if pictures are reliable the gallery projected further aft than it did on English ships. On single-decked English ships the gallery was usually at about the level of the maindeck bulwarks, ie about half way between the maindeck and the half-deck. On two-decked ships the gallery was usually at the level of the upper deck but it was sometimes set between the upper and the lower deck, a position that seems surprisingly low and liable to damage in heavy seas. English galleries in the sixteenth century were open, that is to say they were either unroofed, or if there was a roof the sides of the galleries were open rails.

66

A final point of interest about the construction of English hulls is that at the beginning of the century planks were still quite short, probably only about 12ft long, and were made by splitting the tree trunks and shaping the wood with adzes. Later in the century sawn planks came into more general use, and these were probably longer though definite evidence has not yet come to light. When planks were short the part played by the wales in strengthening the hull, and the importance of not weakening them by cutting gunports through them, is easy to appreciate.

HULL FITTINGS AND INBOARD WORKS

Hawseholes. Until at least the late 1540s English ships had their hawseholes set high up in the forecastle, at a level, so far as can be made out from pictures, above the top of the bulwarks. The cable therefore came into the maindeck as it did in the previous century (see Chapter 1). The ships in the Anthony Roll have large hawseholes but this may be a mistake by the artist since more realistically drawn ships, of about the same time, have normal sizes hawseholes, with a flange round them to act as a rubbing piece. The hawseholes on Continental ships were similarly placed. About the middle of the century hawseholes were shifted down to the lower deck. It is likely that the change came about because the lower deck had been laid higher to accommodate the heavy guns.

Wales, fenders and riders. Throughout the century English warships had three principal wales on each side. One was just above the waterline, another was at the height (amidships) of the lower deck when it had been shifted up, and the third seem to have been at the level of the upper deck. The wales followed the sheer of the hull (in fact they determined it) but the decks did not coincide with them except amidships. Above the wales, along the sides of the upperworks, were longitudinal members like thin wales. The biggest ships may have had more wales and more longitudinals. Fenders are shown at the waists of some English ships of about 1540 but do not appear on any other of the Anthony Roll drawings nor on the plans from the *Fragments of Ancient English Shipwrightry,* so it is safe to say that they were not regular fittings in the sixteenth century. The well-known pictures of ships by Peter Breughel, however, show the hulls with several fenders. External riders, on the other hand, were common in the first half of the century. Their purpose was to strengthen the comparatively lightly built upperworks and to counteract the pull of the shrouds. English ships do not seem to have had riders after the 1560s but they were still to be seen on some Continental ships.

Channels. The history of sixteenth century channels is obscure and their appearance in pictures of English ships intermittent down to the end of the century. Channels are such conspicuous objects that their omission by the

66. A smaller ship than that in 65. The outline of the stepped lower deck is marked on the plan though whether the rise at the after end was really as close to the gun is doubtful. The black and white broken line below the arched openings in the aftercastle seems to mark the place for the stern gallery. The figurehead is reminiscent of the faces found on Italian Renaissance fountains and the scrollwork along the sides is an anticipation of eighteenth century fashions. The rigging details are interesting as they show the chains for the lower deadeyes (which are surprisingly close together) and the position of the fore and main channels; there are no mizzen channels and the shrouds are set up inboard. The mizzenmast is further forward than it had been throughout the century but is still quite a lot further aft than it was in the succeeding centuries.

67. The midship section of a ship being built—and a very big one, for if the scale is correct the extreme beam would have been nearly 48ft and thus wider than the *Sovereign of the Seas* of 1637. The hull's section has the narrow, pinched-in shape characteristic of many designs produced by the three-arc method. The section has the 'knuckle' at the point of maximum breadth that was a feature of English ships as early as 1514. The draughtsman has taken pains to show how the knees are fitted over the longitudinal stringers on the inside of the hull and has shown the stringers running aft to the outline of the stern. The diagonal struts served both to tie the hull together and to stiffen the decks against the weight and recoil of the guns. (Struts of that sort were in use on Danish ships as late as the 1640s.) The identity of such a large ship (assuming that the drawing is correctly to scale) is an interesting question. So big a ship would normally have some guns on the second deck above the keel and a full battery on the third deck. The pillars under the fourth deck suggest that it, too, was a gun-carrying deck. Was the ship intended to be a 3-decker? And if so, was the draught connected in some way with the *Prince Royal,* the first English 3-decker?

68. A model of an Elizabethan galleon in the Science Museum, London, based on the dimensions of the *Elizabeth Jonas* after her rebuild in 1597–8 (keel 100ft, beam 38ft, depth 18ft, fore rake 36ft and after rake 6ft), the lines and structural details being from the Baker *'Fragments'* and a list of the rigging of the Queen's ships in 1600. The shape of the hull and the style of its decoration, however, are more appropriate to the 1580s than about 1600 but none of the Queen's ships had a fore topgallant sail in 1588. On the other hand, if the ship is represented as after her rebuild in 1597–8 the decoration does not agree with contemporary accounts of the decoration of the *Elizabeth* and other ships. Furthermore, by 1613 the appearance of warships shows greater differences than would be expected to occur in such a short period of time.

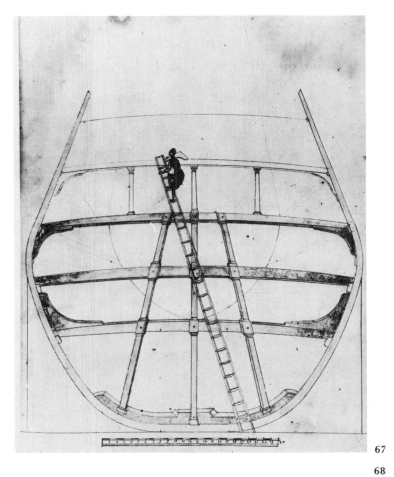

67

68

artists can hardly be carelessness. Even the plans in the *Fragments of Ancient English Shipwrightry* do not always have channels, although in these cases they may have been deliberately omitted because shipwrights would take them for granted as standard fittings. On the whole, however, the scanty evidence suggests that until at least the last quarter of the century projecting channels were the exception. A possible explanation is that when the topsides were narrowed in to counteract the weight of the guns the shrouds were found to clear the sides without the presence of a projecting shelf. Later, however, when the amount of tumblehome was reduced and when spar decks came into use, the need for channels was seen again. To judge from pictures of Continental ships, channels were a regular feature, but a late sixteenth century model of a Danish ship, in the Trinity House, Leith, has none.

Gunports were rectangular on main and lower decks but might be arched or even circular on higher ones. Only the lower ports had lids and on English ships these were always hinged at the top. The depiction of side-hinged port lids may not be 'artist's licence' because Spanish ships sometimes had such ports about the end of the century, but they must have been rare. The dimensions of two early English port lids are known. The *Mary Gonson*'s ports were to be 32in by 27in and a port lid found on the *Mary Rose* measures 28½in by 25½in by 4in.

71

69–71. Three engravings, by the Dutch artist Visscher, purporting to represent some of the English ships that took part in the Armada fighting. They are of little use as evidence because they were produced long after that struggle and at least two, the *White Bear* (71) and the *Golden Lion* (70), have a suspicious resemblance to similar drawings said to show Dutch ships. The so-called *Ark Royal* (69) lacks her distinguishing battlemented poop bulwarks, the oddly shaped turrets are probably figments of the artist's imagination though based on some account of her stern turrets, and the rigging is largely a meaningless jumble of lines. The *Golden Lion* is no better. She is unlikely to have had a lateen mizzen topsail or the dome-like structure attached to her quarter gallery.

Rudder and tiller. These were fitted in the sixteenth century in the same way as they had been in the preceding one, the introduction of the square tuck making no difference to the hanging of the rudder or to the fastening of the tiller to the rudder-head. The position of the tiller hole with respect to the decks is difficult to determine. At the beginning of the century it seems to have been on the maindeck but later on the tiller seems to have been on the deck above the maindeck. The matter is complicated by the existence in some ships of steps (changes in level) in the decks in the after parts. The only hard fact is that the tiller must have come in over the top of the sternpost. At some time in the century a lever device, known in English as a whipstaff, was adopted as a means of moving the tiller. The whipstaff allowed the helmsman to stand on a deck above the tiller and in all but the biggest ships would give him a view of the sails. The whipstaff allowed only a few degrees of swing to the rudder but that was enough when combined with manipulation of the sails.

Bulwarks and rails. Ships might have built-up bulwarks, rails, or a combination of both. Some might have none of those, or at any rate only low ones, for Sir Edward Etchvngham, writing in 1513 about a fight that his ship had been in, said that because the ship had no rails about the deck he had fixed a cable around it at breast height and had hung cloths, bedding and mattresses from the cable to hide the men[9]. It was the practice then and for long afterwards to hang cloths along the rails. The rails might be fixed to frame timbers carried up, to stanchions fixed to timber-heads or to supports fixed on the outside of the hull. Besides their bulwarks etc, ships might have protective nettings or timber lattices that reached from the top of the bulwarks or rails to a midline gangway running from forecastle to half-deck. Nets and lattices were sometimes fitted to the topmost decks at bow and stern. Pavesses remained in use until at least 1550 on English ships – and on Continental ships too, according to Breughel's drawings. Pavesses had fallen out of use by Queen Elizabeth I's time yet it is curious to find them on a plan from the last quarter of the century.

Bulkheads. As the fore- and aftercastles developed into multi-decked strongholds their bulkheads were pierced for cannon and hand-guns so that boarders in the waist could be caught in a cross-fire. There might be only a pair of guns at each end of the waist, or several on each of the decks. The huge archway into the forecastle that the older carracks had is still found in the sixteenth century but was replaced quite early on by a narrower one. This is always shown as open although some means of barricading it in a fight would be expected. The after bulkheads are not often shown in pictures but there must have been doorways opening on to each deck.

72

Hatchways and gratings. Evidence for these important features is conspicuously lacking before the last decade of the century. The main hatchway stood about half way between the forecastle bulkhead and the mainmast. According to early seventeenth century evidence there would be smaller hatchways and companionways in the forecastle deck and the quarterdeck but no contemporary evidence of them in the sixteenth century has come to light. The hatchways were covered with gratings to admit light and air below deck. By the end of the century, if not earlier, English ships had raised coamings round the main hatchway.

Belfry. The *Henry Grace à Dieu* had a great brass bell and another Royal ship, the *Gabriel Royal*, had a bell 'hanging in the deck', a phrase taken to mean that it was under the half-deck. On Drake's *Golden Hind*, according to a Spanish witness, the bell hung near the pump-dale (the trough that carried the pump-water to the scuppers). Nothing is known about *how* any of the bells were hung. The picture purporting to represent the *White Bear* of 1588 has a bell under a little porch at the fore end of the quarterdeck.

Stern lanterns. The absence of specific references to stern lanterns suggests that they were not regular fittings in the sixteenth century or at any rate until the second half of it. A French document of 1545[10], quoting the practice of the early part of the century, recommends hanging a flaming cresset over the stern at night unless the wind be aft and strong, when the fire risk would be too great, in which case a lantern was to be used. English

practice would have been similar. The only contemporary illustrations of English stern lanterns are those on the *Revenge* and on the rather exotic picture of a ship supposed to be the *Ark Royal* in the Armada fight.

Bitts. The old-fashioned bitt-beam was still used on English ships at the beginning of the century, for the *Mary Gonson* had one and its length is expressly stated to be 'between the timbers'. When exactly it was supplanted by the familiar bitts is not known.

Knights. If the *Henry Grace à Dieu*'s inventory reflects typical early sixteenth century practice each mast had several knights. This ship's mainmast had seven: a pair for the mainyard's lifts, one for each of the three jeer tackles and three spare (ie thin, not surplus). No contemporary pictures show the knights, but it may be assumed that their tops were carved in the fashion of the time.

Cleats, kevels and belaying pins. Where and how the running rigging was made fast is not stated in the records. Some would be fastened to convenient timberheads but there would not be enough of these for all the rigging. Belaying pins were probably in use by the end of the century, if not well before it. The *Mary Rose* has yielded part of a large kevel, of the sort called (later) a staghorn.

The wheel. Although this piece of gear was on the *Henry Grace à Dieu* and was to have been fitted to the *Mary Gonson* around 1514 nothing more is known about it other than what has been mentioned in the previous chapter. Neither wheels nor wheelropes are mentioned in the

71

69

73

72. Part of the Swedish *Elefanten* of 1559, a ship about the same size as the *Henry Grace à Dieu*. Interesting features of this fragment of the wreck are the floor timbers and lower futtocks made from natural crooks, and the thick planks (nos 5 and 7 from the bottom) like wales.

73. These pictures of mid-sixteenth century ships are based on drawings of ships embellishing a map of Ireland, made in 1567 by John Goghe, that is now in the Public Records Office, London. Note the unusual side-hinged port lids, the single-bladed sheerhooks on the main yardarms and the man on the fore-deck of the ship on the right, ready to release the grapnel hanging from the end of the bowsprit. The same ship has the lead of the mizzen sheet shown.

post-1550 inventories. The *Henry Grace à Dieu* had another and otherwise unknown piece of gear to her mainsail. This was a 'trin' and together with her two dryngs required 20 men. 'Trin' seems to be a word implying a wheel or other rotary device but whether it was the same thing as 'the wheel for to wind up the main-sail' is not known.

Capstans and windlasses. Sixteenth century capstans pose as many problems as those of the previous century. We do not even know, as a rule, how many a ship had until the last quarter of the century. The *Henry Grace à Dieu*'s inventory does not list capstans and although another source refers to her main capstan no others are mentioned. The *Mary Gonson* was to have two, a main capstan and one 'in the forecastel', which means that it was to stand on the forecastle deck. Two capstans, a main and a jeer capstan, was the normal quota at the end of the century.

74

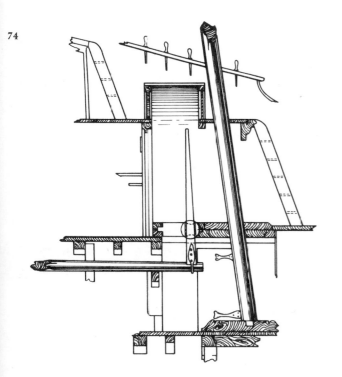

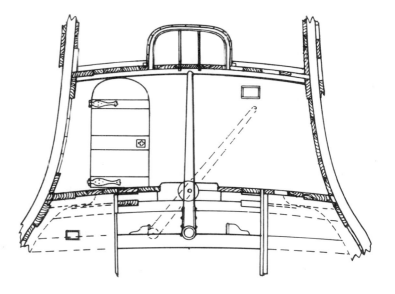

74. How the whipstaff worked. The helmsman could see through the front of the little hutch on the uppermost deck.

75

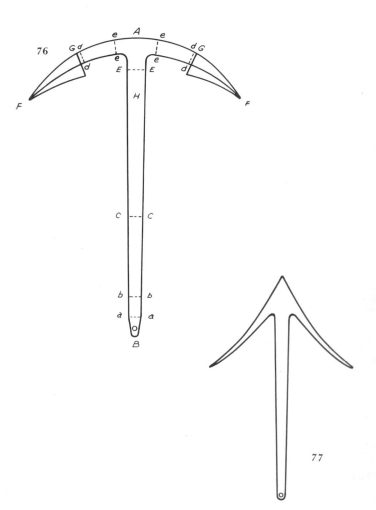

76

77

The location of the capstans is as uncertain as their number. For the main capstan the only guide to its placing is that it had to be on the same deck as the hawseholes so that, when they were on the maindeck (which was the upper deck in the fifteenth and sixteenth centuries), the capstan must have been there also. That is not the end of the matter, however, for if early sixteenth century capstans were placed as they were on the *Regent* the main capstan was under the half-deck and in that case there must have been some means by which the cable, or a messenger if one was used, could pass in and out of the half-deck. There is also, of course, the problem of the high hawseholes that has been discussed in Chapter 1. When the hawseholes were moved down to the lower deck the main capstan went there too, and according to early nineteenth century authorities it always stood just abaft the mainmast.

Nothing is known about the placing of the auxiliary capstans between the first and last quarters of the century. By then the jeer capstan stood in the waist between the hatchway and the forecastle bulkhead. In the last years of the century, however, the newest warships had their waist covered over and some evidence suggests that the jeer capstan stood on the new deck[11]. As no sixteenth century illustrations of capstans are known it must be assumed that they were like those of the seventeenth century. Windlasses were used only on small craft and boats, but nothing is known about their proportions or shape.

75. A remarkable picture of an English warship of the 1570s, with much carefully recorded detail and a few surprising omissions. The hinges on the gunport lids and the small hole for the lid's hoisting rope are examples of the first and the absence of deadeyes an example of the second, although the rigging is, on the whole, accurately reproduced. Note the futtock shrouds, the garlands fastening the topmasts to the lower mastheads, and the lead of the mainbraces. A few parts have been left unfinished, like the falls of the forebraces, and the cutting away of the right hand side of the picture has destroyed what would have shown us how the spritsail was rigged. The hull has been given too much sheer but is otherwise well proportioned. The underbody is white, indicating that it was coated with tallow and white lead instead of the pitch and tar used on Henry VIII's ships. The figurehead is striped and may be intended for a tiger despite its resemblance to a bear's head. If it is a tiger the ship is probably the *Swiftsure* of 450 tons, built in 1573. In 1585 she was armed with 2 cannon periers, 4 culverins, 8 demi-culverins, 8 sakers and 4 falcons, in addition to which she had 2 port-pieces, 6 fowlers and 8 bases.

76. A late sixteenth century anchor of 20cwt based on details in the *'Fragments'*. AB = 15ft; E–E = e–e = 10in; a–a, b–b, c–c, d–d = 7in; AF = 5ft = FH; FG = AG = 2ft 6in.

77. A reconstruction of the *Henry Grace à Dieu's* grapnel. Only two of the four arms are shown.

Pumps. The old-fashioned hand pump remained in use throughout the century but in the 1570s a chain pump was installed in English ships, and no doubt in those of other countries (although they were still not in use in the French Navy as late as the eighteenth century). The mechanism consisted of an endless chain of S-shaped iron links that had wooden blocks, called burrs, attached to them. The burrs were covered with rags and the chain, by anaology with later chain pumps, ran over a winch on deck and down a wooden duct, and after passing round a sheave at the bottom of the ship's well came up through another duct carrying water with it. At the top of the uptake duct the water was discharged into a transverse trough, called the pump-dale, that carried it to the scuppers. Whether the burrs were round or square is not known: probably the former. Apart from their greater rate of discharge, chain-pumps had the advantage of being independent of suction and free from trouble with leaking valves and they could therefore be placed on the maindeck instead of discharging on to a lower one. However since the water was under no pressure such pumps could not be used for activities like firefighting where a jet of water would be required.

Davits and catheads. Until the invention of catheads, anchors were still hoisted by a tackle from a davit. The date of the introduction of catheads is not known; they are not shown on drawings of English ships before the 1580s, they are absent from the early seventeenth (?) century model in the Ashmolean Museum and they are not shown on Breughel's ships. When so much is uncertain all that can be said is that anchors were probably hoisted with davits up to 1550 and possibly with catheads after 1580, but in between is anybody's guess.

Anchors and cables. As with fifteenth century ships we know the names of anchors, the number a ship carried and in some instances the sizes of the cables for them, but little about the size and shape of the anchors. According to a study by J T Tinniswood[12]:

1 An anchor's stock was 2 to 2½ times as long as its arm.
2 Flukes (palms) were equilaterally triangular, usually half as long as the arm but sometimes a little less.
3 Arms were usually arcs of circles but straight ones are to be found.
4 The angle between shank and arm was about 45° in the first half of the century and about 60° in the second.
5 The anchor stock was as long as, or a little longer than, the shank.
6 The diameter of the anchor ring was slightly less than half the arm's length.
7 There was sometimes a ring at the crown.

These proportions are confirmed by the *Fragments of Ancient English Shipwrightry* (folio 116), which gives the best proportions – in their writer's opinion – for an anchor of 20cwt. Unfortunately there is no satisfactory way, as yet, for working out the length of an anchor's shank, and therefore its other dimensions, from its weight. Did such a formula exist, the table of weights of anchors for every size of ship and boat that is preserved in the Public Records Office would be an invaluable guide to late sixteenth and early seventeenth century English anchors[13]. Continental ships' anchors may have been made to different proportions. Indeed, Spanish anchors were proverbially thin and so may others have been.

Besides their anchors, warships of the first half of the century carried grapnels. These were not only at the end of the bowsprit, as they were in the previous century, but in the case of the *Henry Grace à Dieu* there was a grapnel at each end of the mainyard, although these had been done away with by 1546. Grapnels are usually depicted with their arms curved like a fish-hook but the *Henry Grace à Dieu*'s bow grapnel and those of the *Mary Rose* and the *Jesus of Lubeck* have straight arms. Perhaps this shape made it easier for the grapnel to go through the deck planking of an enemy ship.

For most of the century information about cable sizes is scanty. In 1514 the biggest cables on the *Henry Grace à Dieu* were 17in in circumference, surprisingly small for a ship of 1500 tons. From that date until Queen Elizabeth's reign data are lacking. The document mentioned above in connection with anchor weights give a rule for cable sizes, stating that the best (ie the biggest) cable should be ½in in circumference for every foot of the ship's breadth. This proportion, however, may have been an ideal one or may have referred to older and perhaps less strong cables, for in 1588 the relation between beam and cable size on the Queen's ships was not so exact.

RELATIONSHIP BETWEEN BEAM AND CABLE SIZE 1588

Ship	Tonnage	Beam (ft)	Biggest cable (in)
Triumph	1100	40	18
Ark Royal	690	37	17
Rainbow	500	33½	15
Tiger	200	?	11
Marylon (=Merlin)	50	c14	7½

The sizes of the smaller cables were usually 1in less in circumference than the next highest.

DECORATION

Until the second half of the century the decoration of English ships could only be described as sober and restrained. At the very beginning of the century the bill for repainting the *Regent* and the *Mary Fortune* came to only £2 19s 10d and when the great *Henry Grace à Dieu* was built the only items that are known to have been painted are the tops, sails and images (whatever and wherever those were), although the accounts for her building record the use of red and white lead, yellow ochre, vermilion, crimson lake, brown and verdigris (a green), and varnish. The picture of the departure of Henry VIII for France shows the upperworks of some of the ships as gaily painted, but the scene was painted some years after the event and is unreliable in other respects. It is more significant that neither the ships drawn by Thomas Pettyt nor those of the Anthony Roll have much decoration. On the former vessels the diagonal stripes are green and so are the ribs of the tops. Anthony's picture of the *Henry Grace à Dieu* has the diagonal stripes on the hull painted a dull red but most of the hull above the main wale is a light brown, the colour of the wood. Other ships in the Roll are painted in a similar manner. Below the waterline the hulls are a dark brown, representing the colour of the tar and pitch with which the bottoms were coated. The decoration of Continental ships was much the same, judging from the numerous drawings of ships in an atlas compiled by the famous French pilot Le Testu about the middle of the century[14]. The hulls, for the most part, are brown or ochre above water and dark brown or black below the waterline. The upperworks have bands of yellow or red, blue, green and white.

Although ship decoration was restrained even as late as the 1560s it must have been more elaborate than in the first quarter of the century because painting

78

78. Some mid-sixteenth century ships based on the atlas of the French pilot, Guillaume le Testu.

79. The *Unicorn* (top) and the *Salamander* are the only ships in Henry VIII's fleet known to have had figures perched on their prows. Both ships were prizes, the former a Scottish ship, the other a French one. Not until nearly the end of the century do we have any evidence of similarly placed figureheads on English ships. (Drawings based on the Anthony Anthony Roll.)

and colouring red (the distinction is not known for sure) the *White Bear* in 1563 cost £20, equivalent perhaps to more than £2,000 today (1979). At about the same time the *Bonaventure*'s upperworks were black and white and at a later date the *Revenge* and the *Scout* were green and white. Other colours used on Elizabethan ships (not necessarily outside) were vermilion, russet, bice (a bluish green), brown, verdigris, green and aneral (an ashen grey). Some of the plans in the *Fragments of Ancient English Shipwrightry* show the first appearance of a new decorative motif, scrollwork based on plant tendrils. Although the idea did not catch on at the time it foretold the coming of the baroque decoration of the next century. As the sixteenth century closed the first definite signs of that extravagant but fascinating style appear. The bill for decorating the *Elizabeth* in 1598 was £180, accounted for by '. . . new painting and gilding with fine gold her beakhead on both sides with Her Majesty's Arms and supporters, for painting the forecastle, the cubbridge heads [the forecastle bulkheads] on the waist, the outside from stem to stern, for like painting both the galleries with Her Majesty's Arms and supporters on both sides, the stern new painted with divers devices and beasts gilt with fine gold; for new painting the captain's cabin, the somer deck [the half-deck] as well overhead as on the sides, the barbican, the dining room and the study'. At about the same time the *Rainbow* had a gilt figurehead and on her sides 'planets, rainbows and clouds', as well as the Royal Arms at three levels on her stern. The cost was £60. Decoration was not confined to painting and gilding. There were also carvings although, as far as our information goes, they were rare on English ships until the last quarter of the century. Like the ships of other countries, English ships had figureheads, but up to at least the middle of the century they were small and mounted on a spur at the fore end of the forestage. The smaller craft in the Anthony Roll have no figureheads at all but a ram-like projection similar to that on galleys. Two of Henry VIII's ships had mythical creatures perched on their ram beaks, but these particular vessels were prizes. In the second half of the century the figurehead had become an integral part of the end of the beak and, judging from the few examples known, often had some allegorical reference to the ship's name. When the *White Bear* was rebuilt in 1598 her carved decorations included '. . . an image of Jupiter sitting upon an eagle with the clouds, before the head of the ship £12; two side boards for the head with compartments and badges and frutiages £10; sixteen brackets going round the head at 12 shillings the piece; 28 pieces of spoil or artillery round the ship at 14 shillings the piece; the great piece of Neptune and the nymphs about him for the upright of the stern £6 10s'. Some of the decoration would have been painted but it is likely that the brackets and the Neptune were carved, at least in part. This is the earliest reference to the fashion of placing the figurehead on a little platform clear of the beakhead rails that had a vogue in the first part of the next century. Taken together with what is known of practice in the preceding decades, the novelty of the *White Bear*'s figurehead calls into question the practice of putting standing figures of deer on models and 'replicas' claimed to represent the *Golden Hind*. One other item of decoration remains to be mentioned: the *Henry Grace à Dieu* had a crowned orb on a little spritmast at the end of her bowsprit.

Warships had decorations along the bulwarks and round the tops. Until at least the middle of the century heraldically painted shields were hung along the rails as a protection for the crew, spaces being left for the

79

guns' muzzles. By the end of the century the shields had been replaced by decorated cloths. Top armings, as the cloths around the top were called, might also be 'a penny plain or tuppence coloured'.

By far the most decorative feature on sixteenth century English ships was the profusion of flags, banners and streamers. They denoted the rank and importance of the principal person(s) on board; they were intended to impress lesser mortals and foreigners; and on occasion they expressed *joie de vivre* as flags and streamers do at the present day. In addition, flags were beginning to be used for signalling. The profusion of flags great and small and the long streamers shown in pictures is confirmed by contemporary records. The *Henry Grace à Dieu* had two streamers for her mainmast 40 and 51yds long, one for the foremast 56yds long and a streamer for the mizzenmast 28yds long. Ten banners were each 3½yds long and eighteen were 3yds in length. The banners were fringed with silk, and both flags and banners were coloured and bore the Royal Arms and emblems. Similar flags were flown in the last quarter of the century. A manuscript in the British Library, entitled *Sizes of Streamers and Banners fit for the Queen's Ships*[15] lists streamers of 28 by 3yds, 24 by 3yds, 20 by 2yds 2ft, 18 by 2yds 2ft, and 15 by 2yds. Damask banners fringed and quartered (with coats of Arms) were 5 by 4½yds. Workaday flags were, of course, much simpler[16].

Sails were sometimes decorated in the sixteenth century but not to the degree implied by many popular pictures and stories. Only the most important ships, and these only on important occasions, would have their sails decorated with anything other than, at most, a simple emblem. What is shown in one of Visscher's pictures and on Barentsoen's ship, which is the basis for so many decorated sails on models and in pictures, is of very doubtful accuracy.

What was said in the previous chapter about paints applies just as much to the sixteenth century. Oil bound paints were still too dear to be used over large areas: oil, tar, pitch and sometimes varnish was the normal treatment. Even when oil paints were used they would be dull and lacking in gloss, the brilliant, high gloss finishes that are commonplace today being quite unknown. The reds, for example, would be like the 'red oxide' undercoat used on motor car bodies, and the green's like the patina on bronze or copper roofs. Blues were often made from another copper ore, azurite. Specimens of these minerals, and many others used for colouring, may be seen in any mineralogical museum. As for the style of decoration, books on Tudor architecture will show the English fashions and Renaissance paintings those of Continental countries.

BOWSPRITS – Sixteenth Century		
Date	Entry point	Probable position of heel
1500–1520	Outer end of forestage	At or near foremast, on deck below point of entry
1540s	**1** Outer end of forestage on its upper deck of	At or near foremast, on deck below point of entry
	2 Outer end of the forestage just below upper deck	By foremast, on deck under forecastle (main deck)
	3 On second forecastle deck	On main deck(?), passing to one side of foremast
	4 Outer end of forestage or beakhead	As above
	5 Upper end of forecastle	As above
1570 and after	Beakhead, at or just in front of beakhead bulkhead	On main deck in single-decked ships, lower deck in 2-deckers, passing to one side of foremast

80. Holbein's drawing of a small Flemish or German merchant ship of about 1530. It is a mixture of accurate observation (the mainstay's tackle and the way the lanyards are knotted, for example) and mere filling-in. Important parts of the rigging, such as braces and bowlines, are omitted altogether yet small details like the shape of the knees supporting the channels, and the fore part of the ship's boat, are accurately rendered. The anxiety of the boat's crew to get aboard is understandable! The figurehead is an unusual one and much larger than those shown in other contemporary pictures.

MASTS AND YARDS

The opening years of the sixteenth century were a period of experiment and development in rig about which we know little, yet the difference between the *Regent*'s rigging in 1497 and the *Henry Grace à Dieu*'s in 1514 is a measure of the progress made even though some of the latter ship's sails, such as her lateen mizzen topsail and topgallant sail, were more trouble than they were worth. The *Henry Grace à Dieu* was exceptional in the complexity of her rig, as befitted the biggest ship in Navy. The normal rig for all but the biggest ships consisted, for most of the century, of the spritsail, fore and main courses, fore and main topsails and one, but sometimes two, lateen mizzens. Stunsails may have been tried, for there is a reference in the accounts of the *Great Bark*, built in 1512, to '. . . 8 small masts at 6s 8d the pece ymploied in the *Great Bark* and other the Kynges shippes for steddyng sails . . .'[17]. At some time in the first half of the century old established gear like pollankers, dryngs, stryk ropes and the 'wheel for to wind up the mainsail' disappear and the new order of rigging, when it appears in the inventory made of Queen Elizabeth's ships after the Armada fight, is almost identical with seventeenth century practice.

The bowsprit. Throughout the century the bowsprit was a long spar that rose at between 30° and 40°, the angle being greater at the beginning of the century. According to pictures the visible part was about as long as the foremast above the deck. The housing of the bowsprit varied a good deal during the century, as the tabular summary of the English evidence shows. At the beginning of the next century the bowsprit lay on the starboard side of the foremast, so it probably did so earlier on. There is a reference to a spritmast on the bowsprit of the *Sweepstake* in 1514[18]. It is unlikely to have carried a sail and probably had an emblem such as the *Henry Grace à Dieu* carried at the end of her bowsprit.

MAST PROPORTIONS – Sixteenth Century

Date	Fore	Main	Mizzen	Aftermizzen
1500–1520	0.66	1	0.6	–
c1540	0.7	1	0.6	–
c1540	0.7	1	0.7	0.6
c1570	0.8	1	0.7	0.55
After 1585	0.9	1	0.67	0.44

Lower masts. Both the fore- and the mizzenmasts grew in proportion to the mainmast throughout the century but because there are no contemporary data available in any quantity before the 1580s the relative proportions before that date have to be deduced from pictures. The results are not as inaccurate as might be expected because although the heights of the masts are exaggerated the proportions of the masts' components are easy to set off on a drawing. Pictures, of course, only give the above-deck lengths of the lower masts and it is not really practical to work out the absolute proportions because of uncertainty as to where the fore- and mizzenmasts were stepped. For English ships the above-deck proportions are given in the table. For comparison, the absolute proportions of the masts of the ship used as the last example are 0.8:1:0.6:0.4. The plan is in the *Fragments of Ancient English Shipwrightry* which, in another place (folio 127) gives the proportionate sizes of the masts of a three-masted ship as fore 26, main 30, and

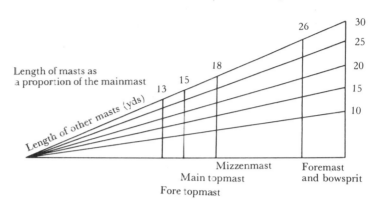

81. A scale for determining the proportionate sizes of masts for a given size of mainmast, based on the Baker '*Fragments*'.

mizzen 18, the ratio being 0.87:1:0.6. The accompanying diagram, which comes from the same source, is a scale for working out the sizes of masts.

As for the lengths of masts, all we know before the last quarter of the century is that the *Great Bark*, a ship of 400 tons built in 1512, had a mainmast 75ft long in 1531[19] but without knowing her dimensions no conclusions can be drawn about the relationship between keel and mast lengths. A Swedish ship, the *Stora Kraveln* had in 1532 (or thereabouts) a mainmast 126ft long and a keel of 130ft. The *Fragments of Ancient English Shipwrightry* has a formula that amounts to saying that the mainmast's length should be twice the sum of a ship's breadth and depth. A ship of 32ft beam and 16ft depth in hold would therefore have a 96ft mainmast.

Masts were thicker for a given length in the first half of the century than they were towards its end. The mainmast of the Woolwich wreck[20] was 52in in diameter well below deck level (and therefore wider at the partners). The mast of the *Great Bark* was 92in in circumference at the upper deck thus being 29in in diameter. A mast of the same length (75ft) would have had a diameter of only 24in at the end of the century. English ships were not the only ones with very thick masts. The *Stora Krafvel*'s mainmast was 5ft 8in thick at the bottom and 3ft 10in at the masthead[7]. A late sixteenth century manuscript in the British Library[21] contains a table of circumferences at the partners and at the mastheads for 25 masts ranging in length from 36 to 108ft. The examples in the table are a representative selection and show how the proportionate diameter of a mast increased with its length. The diameters of the mastheads were 2/3 of the diameters at the partners, and according to folio 127 of the *Fragments of Ancient English Shipwrightry* the diameters between partners and masthead should be: at the partners, 1; at 1/4 length, 0.99; at 1/2 length, 0.928; at 3/4, 0.83; and at the masthead, 0.6. (The figures in the original are fractions.)

MAST DIAMETERS – late Sixteenth Century

Length of mast (ft)	Diameter at the partners (in)	Ratio, diameter to length
36	7 2/3	1:58
48	12 2/3	1:46
60	18	1:40
72	23	1:38
84	28	1:36
96	33	1:35
108	38	1:34

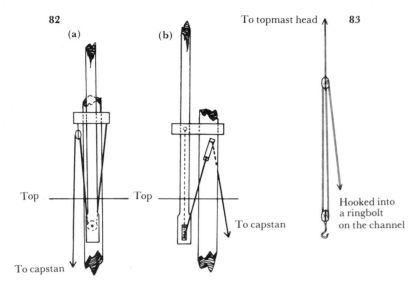

82

(a)   (b)   To topmast head   83

Top   Top

To capstan   To capstan

Hooked into
a ringbolt
on the channel

TOPMASTS AS FRACTIONS OF THE ABOVE-DECK LENGTH OF THEIR LOWER MASTS – Sixteenth Century		
Date	Fore	Main
1500–1520	0.4?	c0.6
c1530	0.5	?
c1540	0.6	0.5
c1570	0.6	0.6
After 1580	0.6	0.64

82. Alternative ways of hoisting topmasts. Both methods were in use in the early seventeenth century and therefore were probably used also in the previous century. (a) is the simplest and is probably the earliest: it is from Manwaring's *A Seaman's Dictionary* written in the 1620s. (b) is according to the *Treatise on Rigging*, an anonymous manuscript written about the same time.
83. Topmast tackles.

The available evidence is insufficient to fix the position of the mainmast with any exactness and the best that can be said is that the half way point between the transom and the stemhead will not be far out. The foremast's position was more variable. The earliest pictures show it as apparently over the stemhead but that is rather unlikely and probably it was immediately behind the stem. Later pictures show the mast well behind the stem. In the last quarter of the century the line of the foremast met the stem at about the waterline and was therefore well forward of the end of the keel. The extent varied, of course, with the amount of fore rake but was between 1/3 and 1/2 the distance between the keel's end and the line of the stemhead. The mizzenmast's position was more variable.

For most of the century, on English three-masted ships and on many Continental ones, the mizzenmast is shown as stepped only a little way short of the taffrail and almost vertically over the top of the sternpost. This was the position of the aftermizzen on four-masters, the main mizzen then standing about half way between the taffrail and the mainmast. By the end of the century the mizzenmast on three-masters had been moved forward somewhat and stood above the after end of the keel. The date at which it took up its familiar position between 1/3 and 1/2 of the distance from the taffrail to the mainmast has not yet been ascertained, but there is no doubt that throughout the sixteenth century the mizzen was much further aft than it was in subsequent centuries. The aftermizzen on four-masted ships was called the bonaventure mast and this seems to have been the name of a three-master's mizzen when it was right aft, for the *Mary Fortune* in 1497 had a bonaventure mast but no mizzen, whereas her four-masted contemporaries had main and bonaventure mizzens. Perhaps the name 'bonaventure' (Good Luck) was given because of the precarious position of the mast although it was probably because it was a 'fair weather' sail. The position of mast steps differed from one mast to another. Mainmasts were always stepped on the kelson but fore- and mizzenmasts were higher up. Foremasts may have stood on the lower deck or, if they were placed very far forward, on the maindeck. All that can be said about the mizzenmast is that it, and the aftermizzen, must have been on a deck above the tiller.

The size of mainmasts on big ships makes it almost certain that in most cases they would be built up. The Woolwich wreck's mast had a spindle of pine surrounded by baulks of oak, the whole being held together with iron hoops. Above the deck built-up masts were

strengthened with rope wooldings. In the seventeenth century these were made from 3in rope and there were 8–10 on the mainmast and 6–8 on foremasts. If big enough trees could be obtained lower masts were no doubt made of 'single sticks'. In 1531 the *Great Bark* had '. . . a new mainmast of spruce hounsyd and scarfyd with the same wood . . .' which does not suggest a built-up mast. Sixteenth century mastheads were short, for they did not stand above the top's rim, but in the second half of the century either the masthead was longer or the tops were shallower, for the masthead is visible. In one contemporary illustration the length of the foremast head is 1/14 of the above-deck length of its mast, the main masthead is just over 1/10 of its visible mast, the main mizzen's is 1/16 and the bonaventure mizzen's 1/12. Nothing is known about the shape of the mastheads. Probably they were the same shape as in the next century.

Tops and caps. As topmasts grew in size the principal function of the top changed from being a fighting platform to a support for the topmast's rigging. Throughout the century tops were circular in plan and more or less bowl shaped, with their sides flaring out evenly or in two steps. Sometimes the sides spread so widely that a man standing on the floor of the top could not have reached the rim without being off balance. Some tops were deep and others so shallow as to be almost like a saucer. As a rough rule, the later the top the simpler its shape. The construction is shown in a diagram in Chapter 3 but how the more exotic shapes were built up remains to be discovered. Half-tops (characteristic of galleys) are sometimes found on mizzenmasts. Lower mast tops were big structures. The ships in some early illustrations have tops whose width is about 1/4 to 1/5 of the above-deck length of the mainmast. They have perhaps been drawn too large but early sixteenth century tops certainly were big, for the *Great Elizabeth,* a ship of 900 tons, had at one time six single serpentines and two stone guns in her main top, and the *Henry Grace à Dieu* had 12 men in her main top. There was a brief vogue for tops on the topmast heads – these were called the topgallants – but none is recorded on English ships after the 1540s.

The early history of the masthead cap is obscure. Until means were devised for lowering topmasts whilst at sea, a device traditionally introduced into English ships by John Hawkyns in the 1570s, the topmast was either lashed to the lower masthead or fastened to it by an iron band known as a garland. The masthead cap may have been introduced at the same time as the lowerable topmast but it is quite possible that the cap came first and that the greater ease with which the topmasts could then be lowered suggested the idea of doing it at sea. Tops were still fitted with cranelines, as in the previous centuries.

Topmasts and topgallant masts. These spars, like Topsy in the story, 'just growed', as the accompanying table shows. The *Fragments of Ancient English Shipwrightry* states that a fore topmast should be 0.44 and the main topmast 0.52 of the *whole* length of the lower mast. Two mid-century Swedish ships had main topmasts just under half as long as the mainmasts[22]. Topmasts are shown on Henry VIII's big ships on both mizzen and bonaventure mizzenmasts, but the fashion did not last into the second half of the century for the apparent topmasts on Elizabethan ships were rarely used as such and served principally as flagstaffs. As for sizes, those in one illustration are about half the visible length of their lower masts. The *Fragments of Ancient English Shipwrightry* gives the length of a main mizzen topmast as 0.35 of the *main* lower mast.

Topgallant masts were carried only on the very biggest ships, such as the *Henry Grace à Dieu*. She had three, but only one, that on the maintopmast, was the normal complement. English ships in the second half of the century cannot have carried topgallant masts as regular fittings because there is no reference to their gear in the post-Armada inventories. Nevertheless, the *'Fragments'* gives the lengths of fore and main topgallant masts as 0.25 and 0.27 respectively of the length of the main lower mast and those on the spar and sail plan reproduced later are half the length of their topmasts. Perhaps topgallant masts were 'optional extras'. Topgallant masts were fastened to the topmast heads in the same way that topmasts were to the lower masts, and when topmasts were made lowerable topgallant masts had to be made so as well. When topmasts and topgallant masts were held by garlands they were fastened so closely against the lower spar that artists sometimes mistook the two parts for a single mast. When the caps came into use, however, the upper spar stood forward of the lower mast. The difference in appearance can be seen by comparing the various illustrations.

LOWER YARDS – Sixteenth Century

1. As a proportion of their above-deck lower mast

Yard	1600–1520	c1545	c1570	c1585
Fore	0.8–0.9	0.8	0.95	Nearly equal
Main	Equal	0.75–0.8	1.1(?)	1.2
Mizzen	1.4	(a) 2.0*	1.4	1.6
		(b) 1.25		
		(c) 1.3		
Bonaventure mizzen	–	–	0.8	0.7

2. As a proportion of the mainyard

Yard	1500-1520	c1540	c1570	c1585	After 1585
Spritsail	0.66–0.75	–	–	–	0.56–0.6
Fore	0.63	0.7	0.7	0.78	0.75
Mizzen	1.0	0.9	0.94	0.9	0.75
Bonaventure mizzen	–	–	0.5	0.57	0.56

*This is the proportion in the illustrations but it is almost certainly too big

---

Although the gear for hoisting the topmasts is, strictly speaking, running rigging, it is more convenient to refer to it here since we have no details of the sixteenth century arrangements which were, it must be assumed, the same as those of the early seventeenth century.

Yards. Before the 1580s the relative lengths of yards on English ships have to be worked out from pictures and must therefore be treated with caution because the artist may not have set off the lengths correctly and because, almost always, the yards are set at angles to the viewpoint. Except for the latest figures, therefore, the data in the tables must be taken as an approximation only. On the *Fragments of Ancient English Shipwrightry* plan the yards' lengths as proportions of their lower masts are fore, 0.9; main, 0.96; mizzen, 1.4 (?); bonaventure mizzen, 1.5 (?). The uncertainty about the last two figures arises because the location of the mast step is not known.

Actual dimensions, as distinct from proportions, are rare. The *Stora Krafvel*, which was the Swedish equivalent to the *Henry Grace à Dieu*, had a mainyard 102ft long and 8ft in maximum girth (= 2ft 7in in diameter), corresponding to a length:thickness ratio of 40:1. The mainyard was slightly less than the sum of half the keel's length (130ft) and the ship's breadth (40ft). The rule in the *Fragments of Ancient English Shipwrightry* is that the mainyard's length should be equal to half the length of the keel plus the ship's breadth 'within the timbers'. It is virtually the same formula as the Swedish one and may well represent an old tradition. The *'Fragments'* also give us the first set of dimensions for English yards (folio 81). A mainyard of 90ft should have a diameter at the middle of 22½in, which corresponds to a length:thickness ratio of 48:1. For other yards proportionate to a 90ft mainyard the maximum diameters are given as: spritsail yard 12⅞in, foreyard 16⅞in, fore topsail yard 5½in, and main topsail yard 7½in. The yardarms should be 1/3 to 1/2 the maximum thickness of the yard.

Some mainyards, in the first half of the century, were made of two overlapping pieces (as they had been in the previous century) but probably only the biggest ships had them for the new yard for the *Great Bark* (400 tons) in 1531 was made 'of spruce of one piece'. All other yards, including the lateen mizzenyards, seem to have been one-piece spars. No dimensions for mizzenyards are known but one picture shows the lower end of the main mizzenyard to be thicker than the upper end, as it was in the seventeenth and eighteenth centuries. Lateen mizzen topsail yards are sometimes shown in pictures but how often they were set is an open question. The lateen topgallants on the *Henry Grace à Dieu* were quite exceptional and, so far as we know, were not repeated. The possibility that some sort of stunsails (and therefore stunsail yards) were in use in the sixteenth century has already been mentioned but no illustration of them has come to light, so it may be that the words 'employed . . . for steadying sails' refer to something different from stunsails as we know them.

The only one of the numerous necessary yard fittings to be mentioned in the English records are the sheerhooks which were normally at the end of the mainyard although both the *Henry Grace à Dieu* and the *Jesus of Lubeck* had them on their foreyards also. The former ship had a grapnel at each end of her mainyard, so there must have been a block or a sheave there for the grapnel's chain although neither is listed in the ship's inventory.

Mast	Henry Grace à Dieu	Mary Rose	Gabriel Royal
TOPMAST AND TOPGALLANT MAST SHROUDS – early Sixteenth Century			
Fore topmast	12 shrouds, no deadeyes	?	8 shrouds, no deadeyes
Fore topgallant mast	8 shrouds, no deadeyes	None listed	None listed
Main topmast	14 shrouds, with deadeyes	10 shrouds, no deadeyes	None listed
Main topgallant mast	10 shrouds, with deadeyes	10 shrouds, no deadeyes	10 shrouds, no deadeyes
Mizzen topmast	10 shrouds, with deadeyes	8 shrouds, no deadeyes	6 shrouds, no deadeyes
Mizzen topgallant mast	6 shrouds, no deadeyes	None listed	None
Bonaventure mizzen topgallant mast	8 shrouds, no deadeyes	None	None

STANDING RIGGING

At some time in the first half of the century thorough-going changes were made to the rigging of English warships. The *Henry Grace à Dieu* and her consorts were rigged in 1514 in a manner that differed only in detail from the *Regent* in 1497, and even in 1531 the *Great Bark* was rigged in much the same way, but Elizabethan ships were rigged in the fashion of the early seventeenth century except for the absence of the spritsail topsail. The extent of the changes that were made is apparent if the inventory of the *Henry Grace à Dieu* is compared with the surveys made of the Queen's ships in 1588 and with the late sixteenth century list of 'The names of all the Ropes and Rigging of a Ship'. To avoid repetition of what has been written in Chapter 1, and in anticipation of the account of seventeenth century rigging, the sections that follow here will be concerned principally with items peculiar to the sixteenth century and which differ from later practice.

The bowsprit. No standing rigging, not even a gammon lashing, is recorded in any of the inventories nor is any shown in contemporary pictures. How the bowsprit was steadied remains unknown.

Lower masts. Tackles, shrouds and backstays were regular fittings throughout the century but many more of each were used at the beginning than at its end. The *Great Elizabeth* had 10 swifting tackles a side in 1509 and the *Henry Grace à Dieu* had 8. The latter ship had 20 shrouds on each side of her mainmast and the *Gabriel Royal,* a smaller ship, had 16 whereas by the 1580s 9 a side were sufficient. It was not only mainmasts that had so many shrouds. Eight shrouds to a foremast, each side, and six to a mizzen were normal on Henry VIII's warships but 6 and 4 are all that was thought necessary for a late Elizabethan ship. One reason for having so many shrouds on the early ships was probably a natural caution in dealing with a newly developed rig but there may have been another one. A lot of the rope on the early Tudor ships was English-made and it is possible, though unproven, that it was not as strong as the overseas material that was used later[23]. Fore and main shrouds were set up with deadeyes and lanyards but mizzen shrouds were sometimes set up with tackles, galley-fashion, and at others with deadeyes. Mizzen shrouds are shown in pictures as fastened outboard or inboard; probably the latter arrangement was used when the shrouds had tackles. Deadeyes were secured with chains. Three links seem to have been the normal number and on one picture they are drawn as ovals although that may be merely a convention. One of Breughel's drawings shows the uppermost link clinched through the lower deadeye but that is an unsound arrangement and it is more likely that the link went round the deadeye. The deadeyes were pearshaped and were set closer to one another than was the rule in later centuries. How the lanyard was fastened, at any rate on one ship, is shown in Holbein's drawing. The knot to prevent the end of the lanyard slipping is an interesting and convincing detail. 80

Topmasts and topgallant masts. The early sixteenth century English inventories list the shrouds to these spars in a puzzling manner, as shown in the table. As in the case of the *Regent*'s topmast shrouds (see Chapter 1) the question is whether the absence of deadeyes merely means that they were not recorded or whether some method of securing the shrouds without them was in use. The reigns of Henry VII and Henry VIII were times of experiment in rigging and it would be precipitate to dismiss the absence of deadeyes as careless stock-taking. By the last quarter of the century, however, topmast deadeyes were regular fittings. Until that time, pictures 55 show the topmast shrouds as fastened to the rims of the tops, but such an arrangement would not have been strong enough to hold any but the smallest of topmasts and it must be assumed that the ends of the shrouds were secured to the floor of the top. By 1570, and possibly well before that date, the lower deadeyes were fastened, by means of a rope called a puttock, or a puttock shroud, that went through a hole in the edge of the top's floor or through a slot in the floor's edge. The lower end of the puttock was attached, at first, to a convenient lower shroud but later the ends were taken to a wooden bar (the futtock staff) that was lashed to the shrouds. According to one contemporary picture, the bar is set at about 1/6 of the shrouds' length below the top.

The early topmasts and the topgallant masts seem to have had neither tackles nor backstays but the fore, main and mizzen topmasts on the *Stora Krafvel* in 1559 had tackles. In view of the rapid spread of new developments it is quite likely that English ships had topmast tackles at that time. No details have been found, although presumably they were like early seventeenth century tackles.

Stays. Fore and main lower masts always had stays and the mizzenmast had them on some ships but not on others, but the bonaventure mizzenmast did not have one until about the middle of the century. The absence of mizzen and bonaventure mizzen stays may have been due to the need to swing the mizzenyard when the ship tacked. Fore and main topmasts and topgallant masts had stays but it was unusual to find them on the mizzen topmast before the second half of the century. Where the stays were made fast has to be deduced from pictures. The evidence is listed in the accompanying table.

At the beginning of the century English ships had a mysterious fitting called a 'sherwyn' that had some connection with the mainstay[24]. The *Mary Rose* had one and a sherwyn was to have been fitted to the *Mary Gonson*. On the basis of two items in that ship's specification,

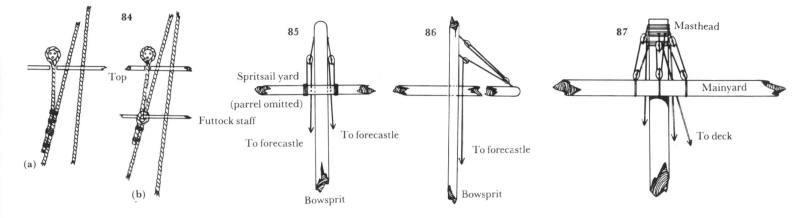

84. How puttock (futtock) shrouds were fastened. (a) is the earlier version.
85. Possible arrangement of spritsail halliards on the *Henry Grace à Dieu*.
86. Possible arrangement of spritsail yard lifts on the *Henry Grace à Dieu*.
87. Probable arrangement of the *Henry Grace à Dieu*'s main jeers.

namely, 'The forecastell fro the stem afterwards – 18½ foott; From the stem to the sherwyn – 8 footte', it has been argued that the mainstay was therefore set up beyond the stem, in the forestage. Such an arrangement is difficult to accept, for in the first place none of the representative contemporary pictures shows anything like such a set-up and secondly the outboard end of the forestage would have been a structurally weak place to fasten an important rope like the mainstay. In any case, the second entry does not necessarily mean that the sherwyn was forward of the stem. It could equally mean that it was aft of it, and that the mainstay would therefore be near the foremast as all the pictures show.

Some of the early lower stays were multiple. The *Great Elizabeth* had two mainstays, the *Gabriel Royal* had three and the *Henry Grace à Dieu* had four, each with a pair of deadeyes. The last ship also had a double forestay with a pair of deadeyes. Alternative ways of setting up the lower ends of the stays were blocks or hearts. No information is available about how the upper ends were fitted round the mastheads. They may have had just a large eye-splice that went over the lower rigging. Mizzenstays are rarely shown in pictures although we know from the inventories that they were not uncommon. When mizzenstays are shown in pictures their lower ends seem to be fastened near the mainmast. Nothing is known about how topmast and topgallant stays were rigged.

RUNNING RIGGING

Spritsail yard. For most of the century, if not for all of it, the spritsail yard was brought into the forestage when the sail had been furled. To be so, the yard seems to have been slung without a parrel, for none is listed in the inventories although the *Mary Rose* in 1514 had a spritsail yard truss. At the end of the century there was a 'horse or tye whereon the spritsail yard rideth'; this was probably a rope fastened under the bowsprit and along which the spritsail yard could be hauled in and out. On the *Henry Grace à Dieu* and the *Gabriel Royal* the spritsail yard had two halliards, each of which had a single pulley. The late-century list of rigging does not mention spritsail yard halliards but the 1588 survey of the Queen's ships has something called a 'false tye'. Spritsail lifts might be simple, with only a single pulley, or they might have two or even three pulleys. Spritsail braces are not listed in the English inventories before the last quarter of the century. The spritsail may therefore have been controlled only by the sheets.

FASTENINGS OF THE STAYS – Sixteenth Century					
Stay	1500–1520	c1530	c1545	c1570	After 1580
Fore	Half way along bowsprit	Half way along bowsprit	2/3 way along bowsprit	2/3 way along bowsprit	2/3 to 3/4 way along bowsprit
Main	Close to foremost	Close to foremost	At foremast	At foremast	At foremast
Mizzen	None	None	None	None?	At mainmast
Bonaventure mizzen	None	None	None	None	None?
Fore top-mast	None	None	Outer end of bowsprit	Bowsprit end	Bowsprit end
Main top-mast	Fore lower masthead	Fore lower masthead	Fore lower masthead	Fore lower masthead	Fore lower masthead
Mizzen topmast	None	None	None	Main shrouds	Main shrouds?
Bonaventure mizzen topmast	None	None	None	Main mizzen shrouds	None

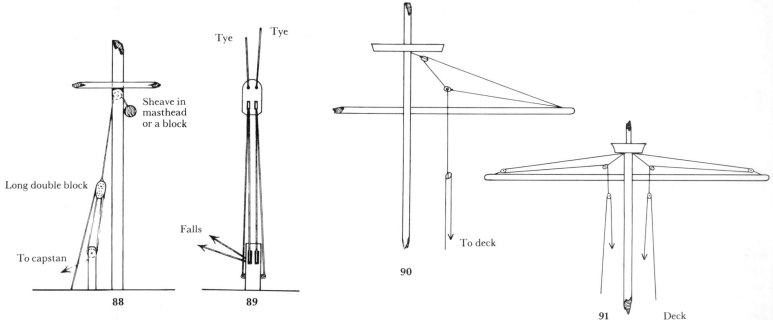

Fore- and mainyards. Tyes and halliards were used to hoist the yards and for the heaviest there were jeers as well. The enormous mainyard of the *Henry Grace à Dieu* had two tyes and three jeers but the smaller *Mary Rose* had one tye and one jeer and the *Gabriel Royal* managed with only a single tye. Seventy years later the *Ark Royal*'s fore- and mainyards each had a tye and a jeer.

The rigging of the tyes and halliards, according to the evidence of the inventories, was the subject of a good deal of experiment. The *Mary Rose*'s mainyard was hoisted by a tye and halliard as well as a jeer. As no ramhead is listed the tye and halliard was the simple sort. The *Great Bark* had two tyes and two halliards, whereas the *Gabriel Royal* had two tyes and two halliards as well as a ramhead. The arrangement on the *Henry Grace à Dieu* is more difficult to understand. Her foreyard had two tyes and a two-sheaved ramhead but no tyes are listed. The mainyard also had two tyes but neither halliards nor ramhead are listed in the inventory. The simplest explanation is that they were worn out; alternatively, the clerk or the copyist may have forgotten to put the rest in. Jeers present no difficulty apart from the question of how their falls were made fast – presumably to a cleat on the knight, each jeer having its own knight.

Lifts exhibit interesting variety. The simplest start under the top, run through the yardarm block and back to another block under the top, from which they go down to the deck. On the bigger ships the lift would have a tackle on its lower end. More elaborate arrangements were also known.

No sixteenth century description of the parrels, or the associated gear that held the yard to the mast, is known but it is obvious from the Henry VIII inventories that those of the early part of the century were similar to the arrangements on the *Regent* and the *Sovereign* at the end of the 1490s, that is to say they comprised parrels, trusses, truss-parrels and dryngs, and in some cases a breast-rope, which was a preventer binding round mast and yard for safety in the event of the parrel breaking. By the end of the century dryngs had gone and the number of trusses had been reduced. However, when so few facts are available it would be pointless to go into the possibilities, and any discussion of the construction of parrels etc is better left until the seventeenth century arrangements are being dealt with. But before leaving the topic there is one feature of the main parrel of the *Henry Grace à Dieu* that deserves mention. It is the single pulley to wind up the parrel, and is the first known example of the knaveline that served to stop the parrel

94. The usual arrangement of lower lifts in the late sixteenth century. The lift may have started from the masthead instead of from the stay collar as in the seventeenth century.
95. The *Henry Grace à Dieu*'s knaveline. The fifteenth century trepgate line or tregete may have been something similar.
96. Possible arrangement for hoisting the main mizzenyard of the *Henry Grace à Dieu*.
97. The *Henry Grace à Dieu*'s bonaventure mizzenyard was hoisted by tyes and halliards.
98. Mizzen lifts of the *Henry Grace à Dieu*.
(a) Single blocks.
(b) Deadeyes.

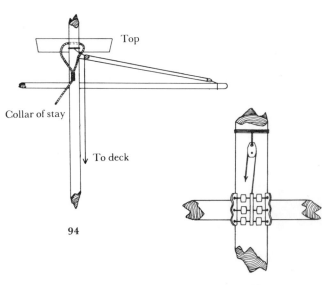

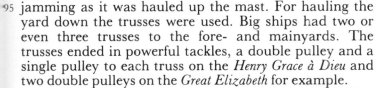

88. Hoisting the *Mary Rose's* mainyard with a tye and halliard.
89. The *Gabriel Royal's* 2 tyes, 2 halliards and ramhead.
90–93. The rigging of the lifts in 55–59 seems to have baffled the artist, as well it might, and it is difficult to understand what the arrangement really was. 90–93 are possible versions but they do not explain how the pendant of the lead-block from the masthead (if that is what the block is) could vary in length as it appears to do on some of the pictures.
90. Lifts as in illustration 57.
91. Main lifts as shown in illustrations 56 and 59.
92. Main lifts as shown in illustration 55.
93. Alternative arrangement of main lifts.

95 jamming as it was hauled up the mast. For hauling the yard down the trusses were used. Big ships had two or even three trusses to the fore- and mainyards. The trusses ended in powerful tackles, a double pulley and a single pulley to each truss on the *Henry Grace à Dieu* and two double pulleys on the *Great Elizabeth* for example.

The rigging of the braces was straightforward. According to one illustration mainbraces started well back on the poop and after running through a pendant block from the yardarm came back to a place near their starting point where they were, presumably, made fast to a convenient timber-head or to a large cleat. In the second half of the century the mainbraces started at the uppermost corner of the poop and returned to the poop bulwarks a little way forward of their starting point. The early lead of the forebraces is not known and two versions may have been used in the second half of the 75 century. In the *Swiftsure* (?) picture the forebraces start from the mainstay and come back to it, after which they would be led down to the deck, but other ships appear to have their forebraces starting at the after end of the waist and returning there. However, it would be unwise to accept what the pictures show as being completely authentic because the ships in point have their sails furled and the artist may have drawn the sheets apparently coming from the yardarms.

Those mysterious pieces of gear, stodyngs (one of the various spellings) and tregetes (trepgates), make their last appearances, the first in the 1514 inventories and the other one in 1531. Stodyngs appear twice in the list of the *Henry Grace à Dieu's* gear, once as part of the mainmast's rigging, when they seem to be some sort of backstay and the second time as 'stodyngs to the foreyard . . . 2'. Perhaps in that case they were preventer braces. Two tregetes were among the mainyard's gear on the *Great Bark* in 1531[19].

Mizzenyards. With the possible exception of the last few years of the century English ships of the 1500s had only lateen yards on their mizzenmasts, and in practice only one yard to a mast after the Henrician experiments with lateen topsails and topgallants, although lateen mizzen topsails remained 'on strength' until the beginning of the seventeenth century. Mizzenyards were hoisted by tye and halliard in one form or another, for a good deal of variety is shown in the early records. A single tye and a single halliard might be used, as on the *Mary Rose* in 1514, but the *Great Bark* in 1531 had a tye and two halliards. The *Henry Grace à Dieu* is recorded as having two tyes, two halliards and a ramhead to her main mizzen but only one tye with two halliards and no ramhead for the bonaventure mizzenmast.

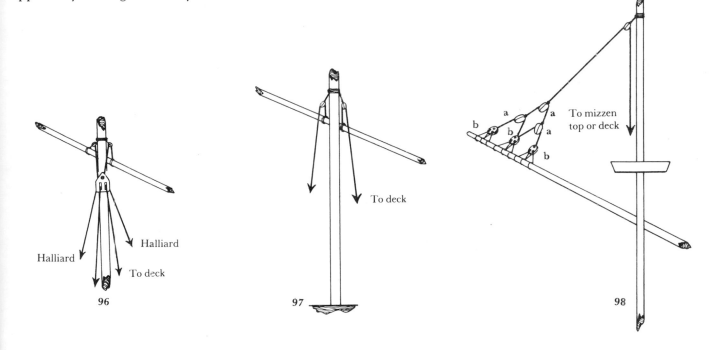

To mizzen top or deck

To deck

Halliard
Halliard
To deck

96 **97** **98**

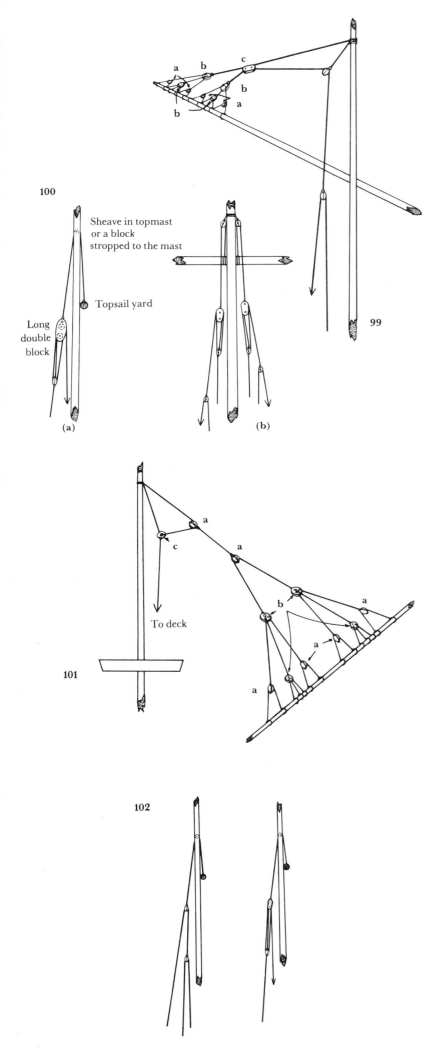

100

Sheave in topmast
or a block
stropped to the mast

Topsail yard

Long
double
block

99

(a)   (b)

101

To deck

102

It is curious that the mizzen- and bonaventure mizzenyards are sometimes, apparently, without a parrel although there is a truss. If the absence of a parrel really means that one was not used the implication is that the yard was set 'flying'.

The mizzen lifts display quite early on the penchant for complexity that is such a characteristic feature of seventeenth century rigging but because we have to rely on pictures for details, except in the *Henry Grace à Dieu*'s case, it is not always possible to work out how the lifts were set up. At first, the lifts seem to have been taken to the mizzen masthead but by the 1530s at the latest they had been moved to the main topmast head. The mizzen lifts on the ships in Thomas Pettyt's drawing are not properly set off and would jam before the yard was fully topped up. Bonaventure mizzenyards 55 were at first without lifts but the later ones were rigged 57 like the mizzenyard. The lifts went to the main mizzen 58 topmast head and then, probably, to the mizzen top. The 59 lateen mizzen topsails and topgallant sails, judging from their gear, had lifts like the lower lateen yards.

Topsail and topgallant yards. These yards were hoisted with tyes and halliards but, unfortunately, details are scarce in the inventories and in pictures the vital parts are either invisible or difficult to distinguish. As usual, the *Henry Grace à Dieu* presents a puzzle, for her main topsail yard was hoisted with a single tye and a halliard but her fore topsail had two halliards, each of which had a double and two single pulleys but no tye. Main topsail halliards normally went down to the deck without any fuss, but the fore topsail halliards were taken to the forestay and set up there with a complex tackle. This had come into use by the 1540s and became increasingly elaborate as the century progressed. Topgallant yards were hoisted by a simple halliard and the falls copied those of the topsail halliard.

Topsail yards had parrels, and throughout the century the bigger yards had trusses also, although there is some slight evidence that they were falling into disuse on English ships by the last quarter of the century. According to early seventeenth century evidence, topsail yard parrels were smaller versions of those on the lower yards. Topgallant yard parrels were also simple ones and may even have been the old-fashioned rope ring. Another possibility is that the topgallant yards had no parrels and were set 'flying'.

Sixteenth century pictures are unsatisfactory sources for the lead of topsail yard braces. Sometimes the braces are omitted and at others they are drawn in a perfunctory manner. Some pictures have the mainbraces starting from the poop and returning there although on occasions they are so far forward that their tractive power would have been small. Another illustration shows

99. Possible interpretation of mizzen lifts as shown on one of the ships in illustration 121.
(a) Single blocks.
(b) 3-hole deadeyes.
(c) Long double block.
100. Possible arrangement of topsail halliards – (a) main; (b) fore – on the *Henry Grace à Dieu*.
101. Fore topsail halliard of the ship in 55 and 56.
(a) Single blocks.
(b) 3-hole deadeyes.
(c) Bullseye.
102. Possible rig of topsail and topgallant yard halliards in the late sixteenth century.
103–106. The main features of sixteenth century sails. 103 applies to courses, 104 to bonnets, 105 to topsails, and 106 to the lateen mizzen. (From the Spanish *Instruction Nautica* of 1587).

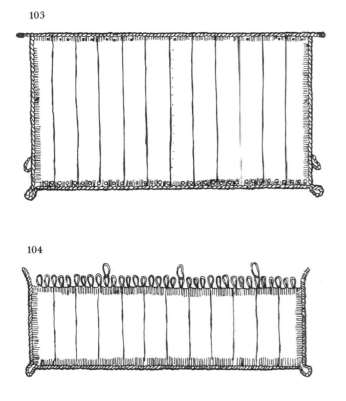

103

104

105

106

them starting from the foremost mizzen shroud a little below the futtock staff, and returning to the mizzen top. They may have been made fast there cr brought down to the deck. The lead of the early fore topsail braces has not been discovered but in the second half of the century they went to the main topmast stay and then, via leading blocks on the main stay, to a belaying point near the fore end of the waist. Main topgallant braces may have followed the pattern of the topsail braces but to the mizzen topmast or they may have gone to the upper end of the mizzenyard. Fore topgallant braces, at any rate the late ones, repeated the lead of the lower ones but to the main topgallant stay.

SAILS AND THEIR GEAR
Sails throughout the sixteenth century were huge wind bags, but whether they were really as balloon-like as earlier pictures show is open to argument, for artists certainly delighted in drawing the swelling curves of the great lower sails. More accurate ship portraits, especially those from the Dutch school, show that by the end of the century the bagginess, though still excessive to modern eyes, had been much reduced. Topsails were much narrower at the head than at the foot and were somewhat less baggy. Topgallant sails, when they appear in pictures, are smaller versions of the topsails. Two sail plans are known from the 1580s or thereabouts. One set is based on drawings in a Spanish book on navigation and shipbuilding published in 1587[25] and the other plan is from the *Fragments of Ancient English Shipwrightry*. Folio 115 of that document gives the relative areas of a ship's sails as ratios: mainsail:foresail 3:2; mainsail:spritsail 10:3; mainsail:fore topsail 10:3; mainsail:main topsail 12:7; mainsail:main mizzensail 3:1; mainsail:bonaventure mizzensail $6\frac{1}{3}$:1; and mainsail:main topgallant sail 25:1.

The main sheets started well aft and at about the level of the half-deck, and after running through the sheet-block at the clew of the mainsail came inboard through the ship's side near the starting point and a deck

higher up. The fore sheets started and finished at the after end of the waist. Fore and main topsail sheets went, of course, to the ends of the yards below but the subsequent leads are not known although the sheets must have come in to the centre of the yard and probably were then taken down to the foot of the mast. Topgallant sheets would be similarly treated. The spritsail sheets, no doubt, came in to the fore end of the forecastle and were made fast to timber-heads or belaying pins there.

The lateen mizzens were usually sheeted to an outligger, though not by any means invariably. When there was a bonaventure mizzen it was sheeted to the outligger and the main mizzen sheet was set up to the after end of the poop. How the lateen topsails and topgallant sails on the *Henry Grace à Dieu* were sheeted has not been satisfactorily explained. On Landström's interesting drawing of the ship[26] the upper lateen sails are sheeted to outliggers from the tops and the fore ends of the yards are held down by ropes (tacks) from the tops. Anthony's drawing of the ship, however, does not show any outliggers from the tops. Perhaps the upper lateens were sheeted to the end of the yard below. Furled lateen topsails are sometimes shown on pictures from the end of the century but there is no sign of sheets. Another curious fact is that mizzen tacks are hardly ever shown in pictures, an omission that is confirmed by their absence from the inventories. Mizzenyards are given braces in the inventories and these are, presumably, what were later called mizzen bowlines.

Bowlines were rigged in much the same way as they were in the next century but many pictures lack essential details beyond showing the bowlines going to the bowsprit. More carefully drawn pictures, such as those by Thomas Pettyt, show the fore bowlines going to a block on the forestay at about 1/4 of its length from the bowsprit, from there to a block or deadeye on the bowsprit, and then into the upper deck of the forecastle. The main bowlines are taken straight to a block, or blocks, on the bowsprit and then back to the forecastle. Fore topsail bowlines have a similar lead to the lower ones but go to

THE GUNS OF SOME OF HENRY VIII'S SHIPS 1509-1515

Ship & tonnage	Slings	Culverins	Curtows	Murderers	Great stone guns	Stone guns	Serpentines	Falcons	Cast pieces	Other guns
Christ (300)	3			8		15	26	2		
Gabriel Royal (700)	2	2	1	3	2	7	15	14		
Great Barbara (400)				10		2	19	8		
Great Elizabeth (900)	6			8	16	13	90			
Great Nicholas (400)	2			5		1	11		2	
Henry Grace a Dieu (1500)	1	2	1	18	16	8	126	6		5
John Baptist (400)	2			10			34	1	1	
Katherine Fortileza (700)	6		1	14		13	41	2		
Mary Rose (500)	2		5	6		26	33	5	2	
Peter Pomegranate (450)	3			11		6	61	2		
Katherine Galley (80)	2	1					6			
Rose Galley (80)	3			4		1	2			

The list as given here is a simplified version of the original[27] and the *Sovereign*'s armament has been omitted because it was almost the same as that given above. The 'Great' before the names of some ships does not refer to the standing of the person whose name the ship bears but to the existence of a smaller vessel with the same name, as for example the *Less Barbara* of only 150 tons.

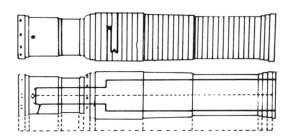

107. Two extremes of ordnance: a breech-loading gun from a late sixteenth century wreck off the Bahamas; and the huge bombard 'Mons Meg', now at Edinburgh Castle.

THE ARMAMENT OF HENRY VIII'S SHIPS c1540[29]

| | Brass Guns | | | | | | | | Iron Guns | | | | | |
Ship & tonnage	Cannon	Demi-cannon	Culverins	Demi-culverins	Sakers	Falcons	Falconets	Fowlers	Port-pieces	Double slings	Single slings	Fowlers	Double bases	Quarter slings
Lion (160)					1	2			7		2	2	2	20
Sweepstake (300)					5	2	1		9		2	2	8	16
Jennet (200)					1	1			6	2	3	4	6	21
Primrose (160)				2	3	1	1		10	6		2	17	10
Small Galley (400)	2	6		6	2				10	4	3		30	10
Great Galley (500)	5			2	4	2			12		2		50	10
Trinity Henry (80)		1		1	2	1			11		7	1		30
Mynyon (40)		2		1	4	2			9		6	2		33
Peter (450)	2	2	1		5			10	10		4	5		52
Mary Rose (500)	4	2		2	5	2			9		6	6		60

the fore topmast stay and from there are brought back to the foretop. Main topsail bowlines are taken to a pair of lead blocks on the maintopmast stay, then to pendant blocks below the foretop and down to the deck. Bowline bridles, the ropes that attached the bowlines to the sails, usually had three 'legs'. Of stryk ropes there is nothing to add to what has been written in Chapter 1.

Sail furling gear consisted of clewgarnets, martnets, brails and, at the beginning of the century, the 'wheel for to wind up the mainsail', but only the square sails have their furling gear recorded in the inventories and nothing is allocated to the mizzens. Except for the 'wheel' all this gear seems to have been rigged as it was early in the seventeenth century. It will therefore be dealt with in the next chapter.

One piece of sail-furling gear is not to be seen in contemporary pictures nor is it recorded in the inventories – the reef-points. They went out of use by the middle of the century at the very latest and may even have gone before it opened. Reef-points had become unnecessary when the practice of lowering the main- and foresails to reef them was adopted and they did not reappear until the 1660s.

The area of fore-, main- and mizzensails, and sometimes spritsails, was increased by lacing on one or more bonnets. How that was done is shown in the next chapter.

Deadeyes and blocks are rarely drawn with close attention to proportions and there is much that is uncertain about both the shape and the size of sixteenth century blocks. What little is known suggests that the older forms remained in use, as we know from the *Wasa* finds, but that blocks with the familiar shapes seen on 'Navy Board' models were used in increasing numbers. They would have been at least as big as those of the seventeenth century and may have been bigger. Some sixteenth century blocks in Sjöhistoriska Museet at Stockholm have the proportions:

Large single block 1 1/4:1:1/3
Small single block 1 1/3:1:1/3
Treble block 2:1:1 1/8
Snatch-block *c*1600 3 1/8:1:5/6
(The formula: Length:Breadth:Thickness)

ARMAMENT

In contrast to the well-documented history of the development of artillery on land, and of the *use* of guns at sea in the sixteenth century, it is not yet possible to give anything like a definitive account of the development of ships' guns despite the large amount of material preserved in State archives. The first systematic study of early English naval guns appeared in 1960[27] and even that, important though it is, hardly goes beyond sketching in the outlines. There is nothing as yet that is comparable to Michael Lewis' study of English and Spanish ship guns at the time of the Armada, but underwater archaeology is bringing about a significant widening of our knowledge of early guns and is providing a valuable supplement to the documentary sources.

The first stage of the revolution in the sailing warship's armament was the installing of guns as the main source of missiles, and it was completed by AD 1500. A few years later the second stage, which was to have far-reaching effects, began. This involved the mounting of heavy guns on the lower deck and within 20 years, at most, ships were carrying a powerful armament on two decks as well as a secondary one made up of numerous lighter guns in the upperworks. The new development did not take place at a stroke. The lower

deck, which was known as the orlop, was too near the waterline (except towards the stern) for gunports to be made on the broadside, and at first the guns were mounted only in the after part of the hull. As experience was gained the orlop was laid higher above the waterline and allowed guns to be mounted at the fore end as well. Finally, when stability problems had been overcome, a complete battery was installed and the steps to the three-decker could follow in orderly sequence. Once the way to carry heavy guns had been discovered development of 'ship-smashing' armament was rapid. The earliest comprehensive English gun list is for the *Sovereign* after her reconstruction in 1509[28].

THE *SOVEREIGN*'S GUNS 1509

Whole curtows of brass 4
Falcons of brass 2
Serpentines of brass 4
Great pieces (=guns) of iron 7
Serpentines of iron great and small 42
Half-curtows of brass 3
Culverins of brass 2
Culverins without a stock 1
Slings of iron 4
Stone guns for the top 2

As the gun revolution got into its stride the weak and usually small 'man-killers' were replaced by 'ship-smashers'. The extent of the change that took place between 1509 and 1546 is apparent from a comparison of the armament of the *Henry Grace à Dieu* at those dates, and between that of the *Peter Pomegranate* in 1509 and that of a similar sized ship, the *Great Bark,* in 1546.

For 20 years after Henry VIII's death in 1547 information about the armament of English ships is scanty, but what there is shows that his policy of fewer but more powerful guns had been carried on. One of Henry's ships, the *Jesus of Lubeck,* survived until 1568 when she was captured by the Spaniards at San Juan de Ulloa after a heroic fight. The inventory that her captors

---

ALTERATIONS IN GUN TYPES 1509–1546

Guns	Henry Grace à Dieu 1509	Henry Grace à Dieu 1546	Peter Pomegranate 1509	Great Bark 1546
Slings	1	4	3	2
Half-slings		2		2
Culverins	2	4		2
Demi-culverins		2		3
Curtows	1			
Murderers	18	11		
Great stone guns	16			
Cannons		4		
Demi-cannons		3		2
Assorted heavy guns	8			
Cannon-periers		2		
Port-pieces		14		10
Falcons	6	2	2	
Serpentines	126		61	
Small stone guns	8		6	
Other small guns	1		8	
Sakers		4		2
Fowlers		13		6
Bases		60		30
Top-pieces		2		1
Hail shot pieces		40		20

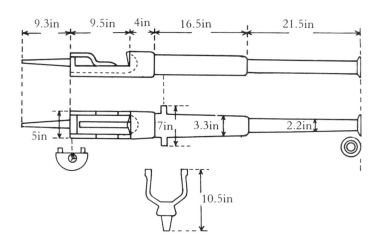

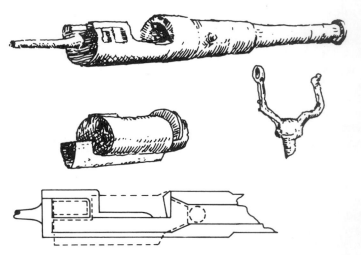

THE WYNTER ARMAMENT ESTABLISHMENT 1569

Ship & tonnage	Demi-cannon	Cannon-periers	Culverins	Demi-culverins	Sakers	Minions	Port-pieces	Fowlers	Bases	Falcons	Falconets
Elizabeth Jonas (855)	9	4	14	7	6	2	4	10	12	8	–
Triumph (955)	9	4	13	7	6	2	4	10	12	–	–
White Bear (915)	11	6	17	10	4	4	4	10	12	4	–
Victory (694)	6	4	12	8	2	–	6	10	12	4	–
Hope (520)	1	2	6	11	4	2	4	6	12	1	1
Mary Rose (596)	4	2	8	6	8	–	2	6	4	–	–
Nonpareil (446)	4	2	4	6	12	1	4	6	12	1	–
Lion (560)	4	4	6	8	6	–	2	6	12	2	–
Revenge (500)	2	4	10	6	10	–	2	4	6	2	–
Bonaventure (560)	4	2	6	8	6	2	4	6	12	2	–
Dreadnought (450)	–	2	4	10	6	–	2	8	8	2	–
Swiftsure (416)	–	2	4	8	8	–	2	6	8	4	–
Antelope (426)	–	2	2	6	6	2	4	4	10	2	–
Swallow (240?)	–	2	–	4	8	2	4	4	10	2	–
Foresight (306)	–	–	4	8	8	4	2	2	8	–	–
Aid	–	–	–	2	8	2	4	8	8	6	1
Bull (200)	–	–	–	6	8	2	–	4	4	1	–
Tiger (200)	–	–	–	6	10	2	–	4	4	2	–
Scout (120)	–	–	–	–	8	2	–	–	6	6	2
Achates (100)	–	–	–	–	2	4	–	–	4	10	–
Merlin (50)	–	–	–	–	–	–	–	2	2	6	2

108. Sketches and plans of a breech-loading swivel found on a site in Bridlington.

made of her guns has been analysed by Michael Lewis[30]. The working armament of the *Jesus* was: on the upper deck, 2 cannon periers of brass, 1 demi-cannon perier of iron, 3 demi-culverins of brass and 2 of iron, 1 brass falcon and 4 iron fowlers; and on the lower deck, 2 brass demi-culverins, 6 sakers of brass and 2 of iron, 1 brass falcon and 1 iron fowler. Below decks, in the hold, were 3 brass falcons, 2 iron periers, 10 iron fowlers and 24 robinets or bases of iron. The *Jesus'* companion ship, the *Swallow,* of 100 tons, also had a powerful armament but it is not always clear from the inventory what the guns were. The balance of probability seems to be 2 culverins on the quarterdeck, a demi-cannon perier, a fowler or sling, a saker and two falcons. The armaments of the two ships may have been unusually powerful for merchant ships, for the commander of the *Jesus,* John Hawkins, was well aware of the risks he ran in attempting to trade

with the Spanish colonies, and the disposition of the guns may have been an *ad hoc* one to meet the circumstances.

How to provide the most effective armament for warships was very much in the minds of the leading seamen of the second half of the century. Among the papers relating to the Spanish War of 1585-7 is one listing the different sorts of guns on the Queen's ships at the end of 1585 and the numbers necessary to bring the gun complements up to 'Sir William Wynter's proportion by him laid down in anno 1569 for the full furniture of the said ships'[31].

Much less is known about how the guns were distributed on board in the first half of the sixteenth century than about their numbers and kind. In his study of early Tudor ship armament L G Carr Laughton worked out the distribution at the time of the 1509-14 reorganisation of the Navy[32]. His arrangement, shown in the diagram, was based on the gun lists of the *Great Elizabeth* and the *Great Barbara,* which are given in the table, together with that of the *John the Baptist.*

DISTRIBUTION OF ARMAMENT 1509–14

Great Elizabeth

Forecastle (nether deck)	12	small serpentines of iron
Forecastle (middle deck)	8	stone guns of iron
Upper lop	2	great murderers of iron
Stern	2	great slings
Nether deck	16	great stone guns
	2	half slings of iron
	6	great murderers of iron
Nether deck in stern	3	single serpentines of iron
Middle deck	16	single serpentines of iron
Upper deck	2	half slings of iron
	6	single serpentines of brass
	6	single serpentines of iron
	1	stone gun
In the foretop	1	stone gun
In the mizzentop	1	stone gun

Other evidence states the ship had 8 serpentines and 8 smaller guns in her upper forecastle[33]

Great Barbara

Forecastle	6	serpentines of iron
Upper lop	2	murderers of iron
Waist	6	serpentines of iron
	2	double serpentines of iron
	1	single serpentine (of brass?)
Hull of ship	2	stone guns
	2	serpentines
Middle deck	2	murderers of iron
Barbican	2	murderers of iron
High deck (poop)	6	falconets of iron

John the Baptist

Forecastle	8	serpentines of iron
Upper lop	4	great guns of iron
Middle deck	2	slings of iron
Middle deck	2	slings of iron
	1	great gun of iron
Stern	4	serpentines of iron
	5	great guns of iron
Somercastle	18	double serpentines of iron
	4	single serpentines of iron
Upper deck	1	falcon of brass
Top guns of iron	1	

The document from which these details are taken lists the gun dispositions of several other Royal ships, including the *Mary Rose.*

109

109. Distribution of guns (solid lines show decks bearing guns).
(a) The overlop, or nether overlop, or upper lop.
(b) The somercastle, or nether deck, or barbican.
(c) The waist.
(d) The nether deck in the forecastle.
(b) (c) and (d) together are occasionally called the upper overlop.
(b) and (c) together are frequently called the nether deck.
(i) The breast of the ship.
second deck.
(f) The middle deck in the forecastle, or the upper forecastle.
(g) The highmost or highest deck, or the upper deck, or the deck; or (probably when shortened to a poop) the small deck.
(h) The upper deck in the forecastle (not in small ships).
(i) The breast of the ship
(j) This may have been called the cowbridge (or cubbridge) head, but the name occurs only once, and its precise use is not clear. Otherwise there seems to have been no name for this bulkhead, though it carried guns.
110. Recently discovered guns from Spanish Armada wrecks. Top to bottom, they are: a 50pdr from *La Trinidad Valencera*; a bronze demi-culverin from *El Gran Grifon* (muzzle only) restored to demonstrate the off-centre bore – in the summer of 1977 the rest of this gun was found and it proved to be longer, a full 12ft in fact; a long 6pdr from the *Trinidad;* a 4pdr from the same ship; and a 3pdr demi-saker from the *Grifon.*

GUN TYPES – early Sixteenth Century

SHORT Gun	Length in calibres	Bore (in)	Type	LONG Gun	Length in calibres	Bore (in)	Type
Bombard	Over 15	11–12	Breech-loader	Serpentine	30	Up to 8	Breech-loader
Curtow	10–15	6–10	Muzzle-loader	Sling	30	Up to ?	Breech-loader
Murderer	10–15	8–11	Breech-loader	Culverin	30–40	$4\frac{3}{4}$–$6\frac{3}{4}$	Muzzle-loader
Stone gun	5–10	6–12	Breech-loader	Basilisk	?	Up to 8	Breech-loader
Pot gun	Under 5	?	Muzzle-loader				

Probably because the later distribution of guns on the decks became standardised it is unusual to find it documented, a state of affairs that adds to the value of the list of guns proposed for a new ship (probably the *Warspite*) being built in 1595[11].

ARMAMENT FOR PROPOSED NEW SHIP 1595

For the sides on the lower overlop	16	culverins
For the stern and prow on the lower overlop	4	culverins
For the capstan deck on the sides	8	demi-culverins
For the stern and prow on the sides	4	demi-culverins
For the waist fore and aft	6	sakers
For the half-deck	2	sakers

What ships' guns looked like before the 1530s is far from clear. In general, they were shorter than land guns of the same calibre because of the need to accommodate them in a working space that was rarely 20ft long (ie half the ship's breadth) and might be as little as 10ft. Some slight evidence suggests that ports on opposite sides of the ship might be staggered to make more room but that could only be a partial solution to the problem because of the necessary presence of hatchways, pumps and other fittings down the middle of the decks. The fact that the early ship guns (in the sixteenth century) were of the built-up kind that became obsolete as cast, muzzle-loading cannon came into general use has resulted in all but a few examples being scrapped and our knowledge of ship guns of that sort has, until very recently, been confined almost entirely to those salved from the wreck of the *Mary Rose*. However, underwater discoveries are now producing an assortment of early guns mainly, so far, from sites in the Baltic. The latest discoveries from the *Mary Rose* have also thrown new light on the construction of the early guns but the overall picture nevertheless remains sketchy.

In his study of early English ship guns, L G Carr Laughton classified those of the first part of the century into two groups according to their length-to-calibre ratio. Short guns had lengths of between 5 and about 15 calibres and long guns were over 20 calibres

All the bigger breech-loaders were built-up guns but the swivels, made of brass (bronze), would be cast. Only the barrels of the breech-loaders were built up, the chamber that held the powder being cast or forged. Muzzle-loaders were much the same in appearance in the 1530s as they were 300 years later and were mounted on their carriages in the same way.

Guns from the second half of the century are better known[34] but it is a curious fact that dimensions of the surviving specimens are rarely to be found. The gun-list of the *Due Repulse* (777 tons built in 1596), gives some contemporary figures[11]:

Brass culverins $8\frac{1}{2}$ft long	16
Brass culverins 10ft long	4
Demi-culverins of iron $8\frac{1}{2}$ft long	16
Demi-culverins of iron 9ft long	4
Sakers $8\frac{1}{2}$ft long	8

110

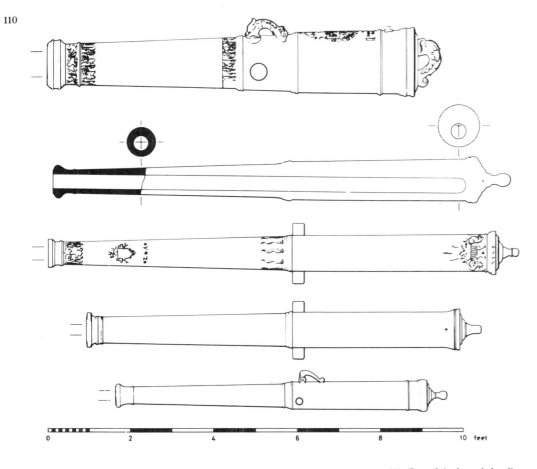

111. One of the breech-loading guns recovered from the *Mary Rose* in 1840. The trapezoidal shape of the gun's bed is unusual and the reason for it is not known. Most of the iron work that held the gun to its bed and the rings for the bed's lashings have rusted away.

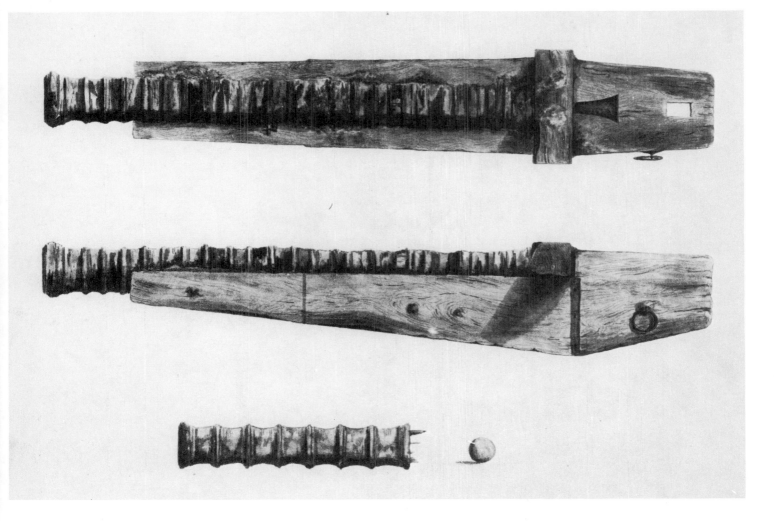

112

113

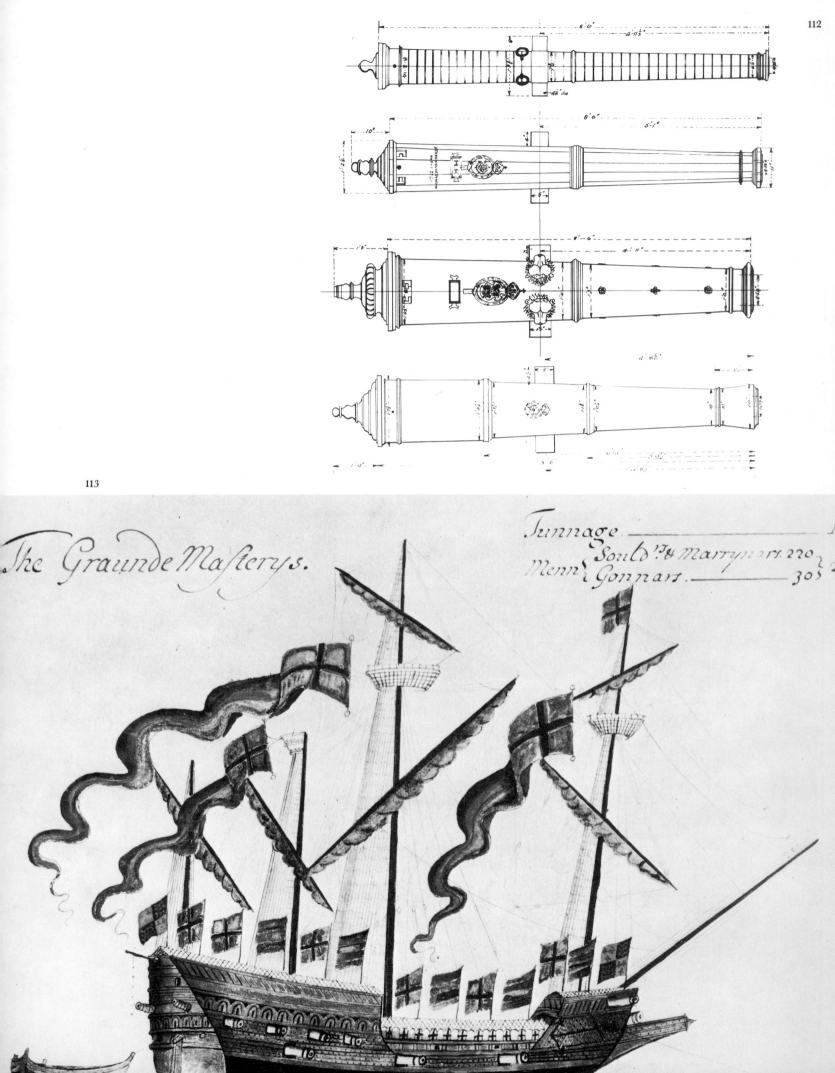

The Graunde Masterys.

Tunnage _____ 4,
Menn { Sould.rs & Marrynars. 220 } 305 2,
      { Gonnars. _____ 305

112. Sixteenth century English ordnance. From top to bottom, they are: an iron 'serpent' ascribed to the middle of the fifteenth century but probably from the end of the century or the early 1500s; a brass 'culverin bastard' recovered from the *Mary Rose* – the gun is twelve-sided; a brass 'cannon royal' also recovered from the *Mary Rose*; a brass culverin dated 1590.

113. The *Grand Mistress* (450 tons) and

114. The *Greyhound* (200 tons). These ships, both built in 1545, were members of a new class of fighting ship known to the English as galliasses. They were a new departure and quite different from the Mediterranean galleas (which was a large and strongly built galley) in both appearance and mode of propulsion, which was entirely by sail. The name galliass was probably given because of the new ships' low build and finer lines compared with the ponderous carracks designed for grapple-and-board tactics. Henry VIII's galliasses are, in fact, the prototypes of the Elizabethan galleons and reflect the growing belief of English seamen that gunfire at a distance, and not boarding, was the recipe for victory at sea. Anthony has taken care, as usual, to depict the individual characteristics of the ships. The *Grand Mistress* has a pair of 'catholes', for mooring cables, in her stern at maindeck level (and therefore the main capstan must have been on that deck), but the *Greyhound* does not have any and her boat is tied up to the stern gallery. This gallery is the earliest example so far known on an English ship. Both ships have diagonal planking on the sides of the forecastle. By analogy with Mediterranean ships the planking would be clinker but Anthony seems to show it as carvel like the hull planks, and his evidence should not be lightly disregarded. He has attempted to put in the rigging but has made a poor job of it. The ships are armed with fewer cannon than the older type of warship but the guns were probably more powerful. The stern guns of the *Grand Mistress* are the old-fashioned built-up sort but the broadside guns are cast weapons. Note the powerful bow gun, a feature of galley armament.

In the circumstances under which ship guns have been preserved or recovered the survival of the mountings is exceptional. In British waters a wheel-less carriage was found on the Cattewater wreck and several were brought up from the *Mary Rose*[35]. In the recent investigations of her wreck part of a two-wheeled carriage was found and the remains of gun-carriage wheels have been recovered from the Armada ship *La Trinidad Valencera* that was wrecked off the coast of Ireland in 1588[36]. Several wheel-less carriages have been recovered from wrecks in the Baltic, some very good examples being in the Royal Arsenal Museum at Copenhagen, and at least one example of a mid-century four-wheeled carriage has been found in Swedish waters[37].

The wheel-less bed was still very much the same as it had been in the previous century. Wheel-less carriages are usually thought of as being non-recoil mountings and that was, no doubt, generally the case[38]. But one of the *Mary Rose* carriages has a slot or channel, about 6in wide and nearly as deep, running the whole length of the underside of the bed. It suggests that the bed rested on, or fitted over, a squared timber but whether that was to allow the gun to recoil or to prevent it slewing round when it was fired is not known. This carriage has another peculiarity: in profile it is trapezoidal, the upper edge sloping down towards the front, so that the gun's muzzle is only a few inches above the bottom of the bed. Wheeled carriages were commonplace by 1514 on English ships and a distinction is made between 'trotil wheels', which were trucks, and other

114

115. The *Flower de Luce* (20 tons): one of the rowbarges, which were another of Henry VIII's attempts to combine sails and oars in a warship. Rowbarges were much longer for their beam than ordinary ships and may have had a keel of about 50ft and a beam of 10ft. There were 15 oars a side. On his picture of the *Flower de Luce* Anthony has put 2 guns in the after part of the ship, and a big bow-chaser, making 5 guns in all, but his list of guns gives the ship 1 demi-culverin and 1 saker, both of brass, and 7 bases, which are swivels.

116. Two pinnaces, the *Hare* and the *Trego Rennyger*. Both ships were of 20 tons. The *Trego* is probably either a foreign-built ship or named after a distinguished foreigner. Small craft were often used as despatch vessels, scouts or official yachts. The *Hare* has 1 saker and 12 bases as her principal armament, the other ship has only 12 bases.

117. The *Galie Subtile* (200 tons). Henry VIII had several true galleys in his Navy but this was the only Mediterranean-type galley to be built in England. Galleys of this sort were never successful in English waters although the English, the French and the Spaniards made more than one attempt to incorporate galleys in their 'Channel Fleets'.

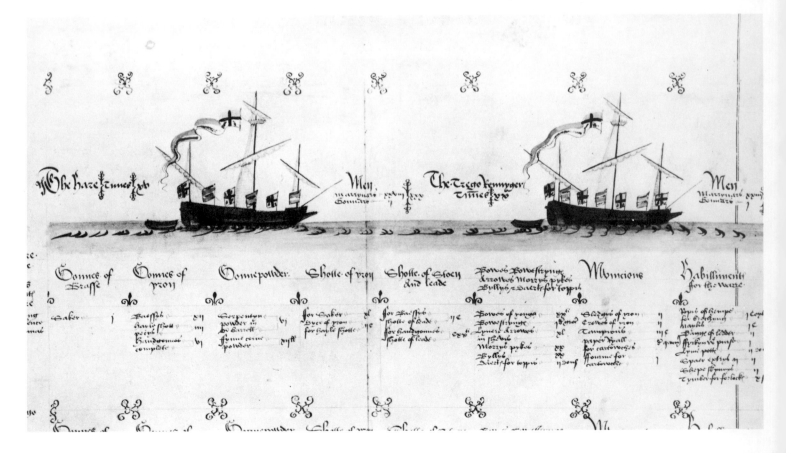

sorts of wheels. Some carriages had two wheels but those for the heaviest guns had four. The familiar step-sided carriage may have been in use as early as the 1530s if a Swedish example is correctly dated.

The adoption of the wheeled carriage on board ship may have been connected with the development of the practice of hanging the guns by trunnions cast integrally with the barrel. The early examples may have had a fixed elevation, because guns that have a pair of trunnions on each side are known and these might even be square in section, a type that survived into the seventeenth century. The earliest example of an English stepped carriage is shown on the Arms granted to Sir Francis Drake in 1581. Gun carriages of that type were remarkably small. At the end of the century a full cannon's carriage was only 5½ft long and a demi-cannon's 5ft. It was usual to paint the ship's name on English gun carriages, and it is as well to mention, though out of the proper place, that English ships at least, then and for a long time afterwards, did *not* have their names painted or carved on bow or stern.

SUPPORT CRAFT AND BOATS

The dividing line between capital ships and those with a secondary rôle to play is less easy to draw in the sixteenth century than in any of the succeeding ones partly because the whole century was a time of active experiment in ship design and armament and partly because of the prevalent practice of arming quite small vessels with heavy guns so that it was possible, at any rate in theory, for a small ship to damage a big one. The distinction problem is illustrated by the oar/sail hybrids that were given a long trial by Henry VIII. They were built to meet the threat posed by French galleys that could out-manoeuvre a vessel relying on sail alone and attack it at the most vulnerable part, the stern. Henry wished to have ships that could manoeuvre under oars, stand up to sail and carry a heavy, broadside armament. That the experiment failed, as it was bound to, is no discredit to Henry's shipwrights who were, like shipwrights elsewhere in Europe, trying to counter the agility of the galley but retain the robustness of the traditional sailing ship[39]. Henry's oar/sail hybrids ranged from little row-

117

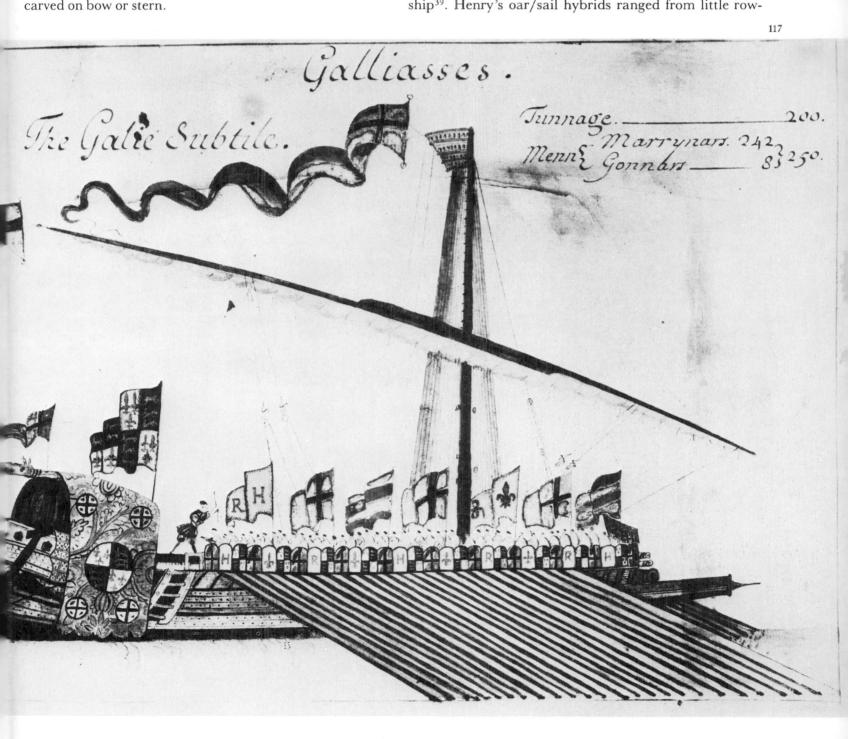

118. The *Tygar* (200 tons), one of the most interesting of sixteenth century English ships. She was built in 1545–6 at the same time as three other similar ships, the *Bull, Antelope* and *Hart.* All four had the same midship section and it was thought to be such an excellent one that the famous Elizabethan shipwright Matthew Baker preserved it among his papers. All four ships had long lives, the *Tygar* surviving in one form or another until at least 1603. The remarkable thing about this ship is her hull form. It has little sheer, an unusual thing then and for a long time afterwards, and she carries her guns on a flush maindeck, thus anticipating, by a couple of centuries, the frigate. Above the guns, as the pavesses show, there was a wide fighting gangway, or perhaps a whole deck. The oars, 20 a side, are on the lower deck.

119. This plan from the *Fragments of Ancient Shipwrightry* seems to be a design for a modified *Tygar.* It has the same low sheer, low forecastle and quarterdeck and the *Tygar's* ram-like beak. There are guns on the lower deck and on the maindeck in the waist. The ship would have been bigger and of finer lines than the *Tygar,* for the notes on the plan state that the keel was to be 104ft, the beam 26ft and the depth 11ft whereas the *Tygar's* dimensions were 75ft or thereabouts on the keel, 22ft beam and 11ft deep in the hold. The plan has 28 to 30 guns; the *Tygar* had 28 in 1585.

120. The midship section of the *Tygar, Greyhound, Bull* and *Hart.* From the midship section, the keel's length and the rakes fore and aft, a shipwright could develop the shape of the hull by the process described in the early seventeenth century manuscript known as *A Treatise on Shipbuilding.*

120

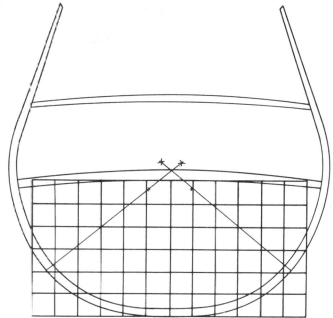

119

barges of 20 tons to the *Great Galley* of 500 tons. How her oars and armament were combined has not been discovered. The most interesting oared warship, in several ways, is the *Tygar.* She has her guns on a deck 118 above the oars, of which there were 20 a side, and above the guns is what might seem to be a high bulwark connecting poop and forecastle if it were not for the row of big pavesses right round the ship. Their position in relation to the guns implies a gangway along each side or even a deck between forecastle and poop. Another peculiarity of the *Tygar* is her slight sheer and the small rise to the wales, which suggest that she was flush-decked. One picture shows the *Tygar* in her mid-Elizabethan form. The oars have gone, her main battery 121 has been moved down to the level of the former oar-deck and her masts reduced to three, but she still has a long, lean look and bears a remarkable resemblance to the ship in the *'Fragments'* plan. Three other ships were built to the 119 same pattern as the *Tygar* and all four survived right to the end of the Queen's reign (1603). The others were the *Bull, Antelope* and *Hart* and it must have been the all-round excellence of the group that induced Matthew Baker to preserve a drawing of the midship section of the *Tygar* and to note on it that the other three had the same section. The *Bull's* dimensions in 1591 were: keel 80ft; beam 22ft; and depth in hold 11ft. The ship had a keel:beam ratio of $3\frac{2}{3}$:1 compared with the more usual $2\frac{1}{2}$:1. The dimensions may have been the original ones and as the *Bull* in 1546 had two more oars a side than the *Tygar* that ship would have been 4-5ft shorter.

At the other end of the scale were the row-barges like the *Flower de Luce* of 20 tons and the *Hare.* 115 Despite her small size the *Flower de Luce* carried a culverin, a saker and seven bases. Henry VIII's fleet also had a few true galleys but they were never anything but white elephants.

Oared sailing ships fell into disfavour in the second half of the century and the auxiliary work of the fleet was done by craft of which we know the names but little else: 'shallops', 'hoys', 'drumlers', 'plates', 'flyboats', 'pinnaces' and 'crompsters' as well as some 122

121

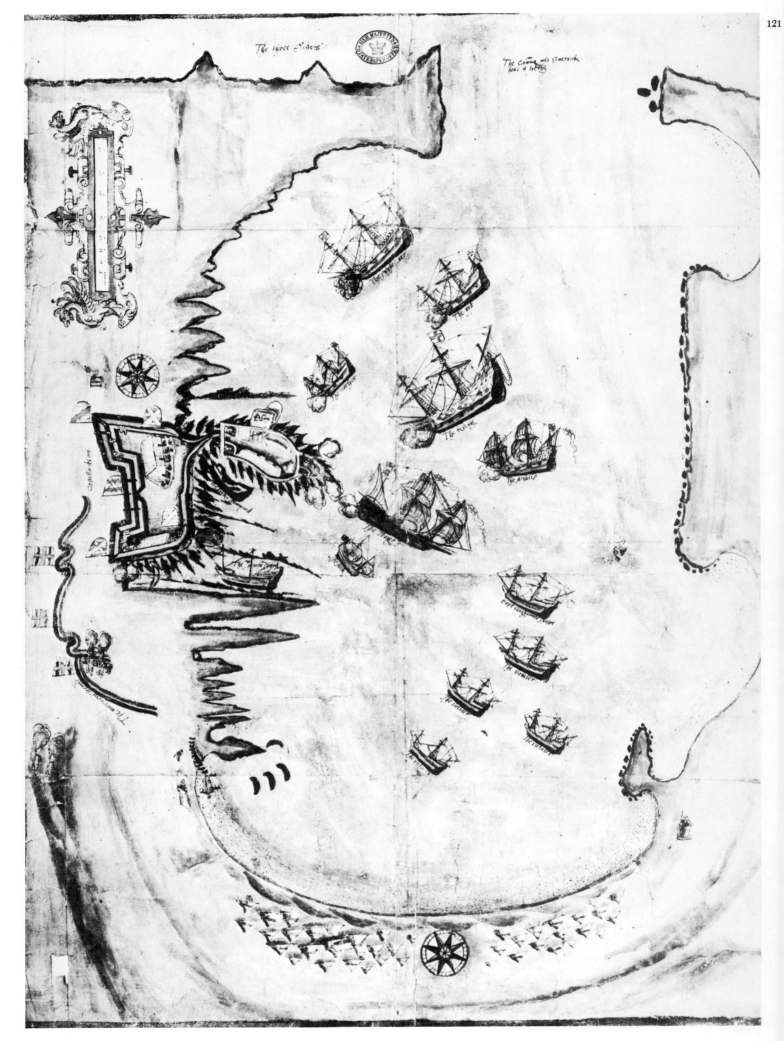

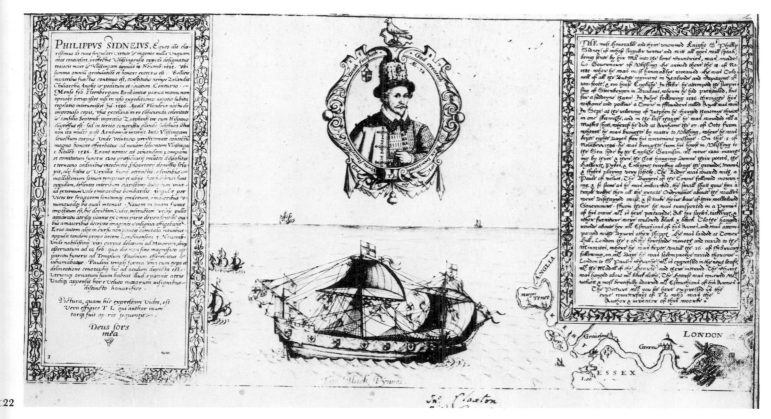

121. Ships attacking the Spaniards in Smerwick Fort, Ireland, in 1580. They are (top to bottom) the *Swiftsure*, *Marlyon*, *Ayd*, *Revenge* and *Tygar*. The other ships are merchantmen carrying stores and food. The little ship near the *Tygar* is an early example of what would later be called a brig. Despite the stylization of the drawing and the exaggeration of the size of some features such as gunports, the ships' pictures agree with what is known from other sources, for example the low, sleek look of the *Tygar*, the large size of the *Revenge* and the smallness of the *Marlyon*, a vessel of only about 50 tons. The painting on the *Revenge*'s poop resembles that on some of the plans in the '*Fragments*', but the broad band of lozenges on her broadside may be an arming cloth. Her stern lantern and the rope ladder are interesting items not often shown at the time.

122. The *Black Pinnace* that brought Sir Philip Sidney's body back from the Netherlands after he had been killed at Zutphen in 1586. The ship has the old-fashioned two-topsail rig and the mizzen perched right at the after end of the poop. Along her side at deck level is an arming-cloth with Coats of Arms, whilst over the maindeck an anti boarding net, or perhaps an awning, is suspended by 'crow's feet'. The rigging is carefully drawn and seems to be accurately rendered.

123. Two examples of the 'cromster' based on contemporary illustrations. Although small these vessels were heavily armed.

called 'frigates' – which seem to have had as many varieties as the name had spellings. One of the ships attacking Smerwick Fort, the *Marlyon*, is a pinnace. She would have been about 50ft on the keel, 17ft in beam and about 7ft deep in the hold. The crompster was a Dutch vessel that was sometimes used in the English Navy. Crompsters were beamy, shallow-draught ships designed for coastal and estuarine work but were nevertheless sometimes as big as 200 tons. They were fore-and-aft rigged, with a spritsail like a modern Thames barge. Crompsters carried a heavy armament and were the 'pocket battleships' of their day[40].

The last group of craft, boats, have been treated summarily by the inventories except in the case of the *Henry Grace à Dieu*'s 'great boat' which was really a small ship for it had four masts and carried an armament of 11 guns. The 'great boat's' 60 oars put it in much the same class as the *Sweepstake* of 1497. The Hastings Manuscript Pilot's Guide shows smaller boats that, except for their excessive curvature, appear to be very like those of the eighteenth century. If the drawing is reliable one boat's crew pulled two oars each and another's one per man. The Anthony Roll boats are drawn in a conventional style but, notwithstanding that, some interesting details can be made out. The boats are double-ended and have an upstanding sternpost as well as a stout stemhead. On each quarter is a strong timber, presumably for taking tow-ropes. Whether the boats were clinker- or carvel-planked cannot be made out. The *Henry Grace à Dieu*'s jolly-boat and cock-boat had only a single mast and sail. That may have been a survival of the mediaeval single squaresail rig but so little is known about the early history of the fore-and-aft rig and of lugsails that dogmatism is out of place.

Few dimensions of boats have turned up. In 1570 boats for the *Bull* and the *Tygar* were to be 25ft long, 8ft 8in in beam and 3ft 3in deep. The 'great boat' was always towed but the others were hoisted aboard by tackles on the main- and foremasts. Nothing is recorded about how they were stowed on deck.

RAST·V·TER·WAPEN·GHY·CHRISTEN·SCHAPEN·WILT·STRYT·BEGINNEN

124

REFERENCES

Abbreviations
IJNA: International Journal of Nautical Archaeology
MM: The Mariner's Mirror, the Journal of the Society for Nautical Research
NRS: The Navy Records Society publications.

1 'The Remains of two old vessels found at Rye, Sussex', H Lovegrove, *MM* (1964) Vol 50, pp115–22

2 'The Square Tuck and the Gun-deck', L G Carr Laughton, *MM* (1961) Vol 47, pp100–5

3 'The Development of the Capital Ship', G Robinson, *MM* (1921) Vol VII, p110

4 *Fragments of Ancient English Shipwrightry,* Pepysian Library, Magdalene College, Cambridge

5 'The *Mary Gonson*', R C Anderson, *MM* (1960) Vol 46, pp199–204

6 'The *Henry Grace a Dieu*', L G Carr Laughton, *MM* (1931) Vol XVII, p175; and R C Anderson, *MM* (1932) Vol XVIII, pp94 and 428

7 'The *Stora Krafvel* of 1532', R C Anderson, *MM* (1924) Vol X, pp388–9; and H Börjeson, *MM* (1928) Vol XIV, pp158–62; 'The *Stora Krafvel* of 1559', S Svensson, *MM* (1938) Vol XXIV

8 *A Treatise on Shipbuilding written about 1620–25,* W Salisbury (Editor), Society for Nautical Research Occasional Publications No 6, (1958)

9 *A History of the Administration of the Royal Navy 1509–1660,* M Oppenheim, p61, quoting Cottonian Mss Caligula D, vi, f 107 (British Library)

10 *Miscellany, NRS,* Vol 1 (1901)

11 The guns of the *Warspite* and *Due Repulse:* State Papers Domestic (Elizabeth CCLVIV/43 (Public Records Office), quoted in *The Successors of Drake* by Sir Julian Corbett

12 'Anchors and Accessories', J T Tinniswood, *MM* (1945) Vol 31, pp84–105

13 Oppenheim, p123, quoting State Papers Domestic CCLXXXVI f 36 and Add Mss 9336 f 10 (British Library)

14 'Guillaume Le Testu and his Work', J Sottas, *MM* (1912) Vol III, pp65–73

15 The Sizes of Streamers and Banners fit for the Queen's Ships: Harleian Mss 253/61 (British Library)

16 Flags of the Queen's Ships on the Cadiz Expedition, 1596, quoted in Reference 10 above; and *British Flags,* W G Perrin, Cambridge University Press (1922)

17 Chapter House Books, Vol VI, quoted in Reference 9 above, p54

18 Chapter House Books, Vol XII, f 510, quoted in Reference 9 above, p58

19 Cottonian Mss, Appendix XXVIII, I. Printed in *MM* (1919) Vol V, p21

20 'The Woolwich Ship', W Salisbury, *MM* (1961) Vol 47, pp81–93

124. This interesting model is said to be from the second half of the sixteenth century but it has several features more appropriate to the first half of that century. The ram-like spur on the stem and the figurehead perched on a projecting timber above the spur resemble those on the ships in the picture of Henry VIII's departure for France, as do the high fore- and aftercastles and the steeply rising bowsprit. Other ineresting features are the riders on the aftercastle's sides and the long main channels. The ship has a lateen mizzen topsail but the rigging has unfortunately disappeared. The chevron decoration, which is often regarded as typically English, may have been common to North European ships, for it has been found on French ships of about the middle of the century.

125. The plan of a Venetian merchantman, or 'cocca', of the beginning of the sixteenth century (the date is open to doubt) based on a contemporary model in the Museo Storico Navale, Venice. The hull with its low fore- and after-castles and backward raking stem resembles those of the ships in the Hastings Manuscript, although it is surprising to find a stern gallery at so early a date. A replica of the model is in the National Maritime Museum, Greenwich.

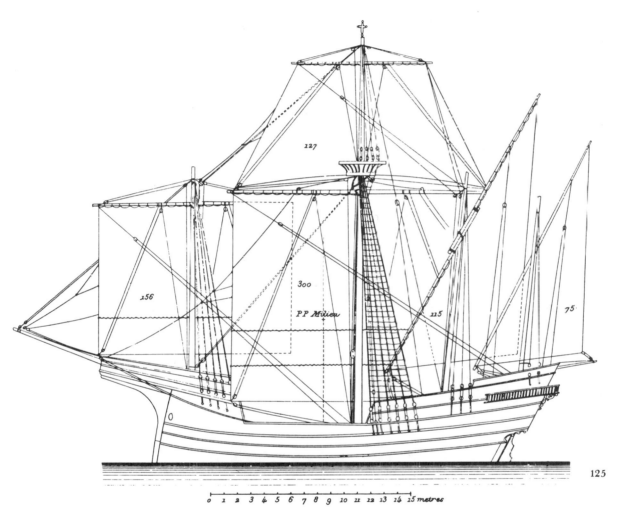

125

21 The Proportions and Sizes of Masts: Harleian Mss 253 ff 5, 6, 10b, 11 and 306 f 99 (British Library)
22 Reference 7 above and *MM* (1939) Vol XXXV pp297-99
23 'Two Tudor Rigging Puzzles', G F Howard, *MM* (1976) Vol 62, p190
24 'The Sherwyn', L G Carr Laughton, *MM* (1932) Vol XVIII, p326, quoting State Papers 1/230; E/36/13 f 55 and 1/9 f 233 (Public Records Office)
25 *Instruccion Nautica para Navegar*, Diego Garcia de Palacio, Mexico (1587), reprint by Ediciones Cultura Hispanica (1944)
26 *The Ship*, B Lanström, p116
27 'Early Tudor Ship Guns', L G Carr Laughton, *MM* (1960) Vol 46, pp242-285; should be read in conjunction with *The Gun*, Dudley Pope (1965) and *Guns at Sea*, P Padfield (1973)
28 Letters and Papers, Henry VIII, No 5721 f 229
29 Letters and Papers, Henry VIII, XV, 196; printed in *MM* (1920) Vol VI, p281
30 'The Guns of the *Jesus of Lubeck*', M Lewis, *MM* (1936) Vol XXII, p324 et seq
31 Quoted in *The Spanish War 1585-7, NRS*, Vol XI
32 State Papers Domestic 1/9 f 241 and E36/13 f 76 (Public Records Office)
33 Letters and Papers, Henry VIII, i, 5271, quoted Reference 9 above, p54

34 *Armada Guns*, M Lewis (1961)
35 *History Under the Sea*, Alexander McKee, London (1968)
36 *Full Fathom Five*, C Martin, London (1976)
37 In *Sjöhistoriska Museet*, Stockholm
38 'Old Naval Gun Carriages', J R Moody, *MM* (1952) Vol 38, pp301-11
39 See *Oared Fighting Ships*, R C Anderson (1962); 'Oared Vessels in the Elizabethan Navy', *MM* (1966) Vol 52, pp371-9; 'The Galliasses of the Wing', *MM* (1969) Vol 55, pp465-7, both by T Glasgow Jnr
40 'Crompsters', R M Nance, *MM* (1919) Vol V, pp46-51; 'The Crompster in Literature and Pictures', R H Boulind, *MM* (1968) Vol 54, pp3-17

126. The most famous ship of the seventeenth century, as depicted in the well-known engraving by J Payne. The care and accuracy with which every detail of hull and rigging is rendered in the picture make it the most complete record of the appearance of any ship of Charles I's reign. The *Sovereign of the Seas* was designed by Phineas Pett and built in 1637 by his son Peter.

PRÆGRANDIS ILLIVS ATQ CELEBERR. NAVIS SVB AVSPICIS CAROLI MAGN: BRIT: FRA: ET HIB: REGIS AN° 1637 EXSTRVCTÆ DELINEATIO EXPRESSISSIMA *Architectus Petro Pett*

SHIP OF THE LINE

As the sixteenth century saw the development of ship armament into something not very different from what it was three centuries later so, in the seventeenth century, hull and rig reached a state of development that would be altered only in detail for the rest of the sailing warship's history. Three-deckers became commonplace and rigging reached its maximum complexity – which is not the same thing as maximum efficiency. By the second half of the century staysails made their appearance and right at its end jibs came into use on big ships. Progress was not limited to the 2- and 3-deckers. The first steps were taken towards the development of the frigate and though, as it happened, they led into a cul-de-sac the idea would be revived successfully in a modified form in the next century. On small craft the fore-and-aft rig came into more general use and led to the development of the sloops, cutters and schooners that played an increasingly important part in the eighteenth and nineteenth centuries. Bomb ketches, which were small, strongly built ships that carried one or two mortars capable of hurling a large explosive shell, made their appearance and so did yachts. In short, the last traces of sixteenth century and earlier styles of build and rig disappeared and by 1700 only a few innovations remained to be developed during the course of the 160 years that were to follow.

The seventeenth century may be claimed, with justice, to be the most important in the whole history of the European sailing warship, for it was in that period that most of the major design problems were solved by the shipwrights of one country or another. Moreover, the solutions were not provided by simply following traditional rule of thumb methods. The second half of the century saw the beginning of the science of naval architecture and the study of the principles underlying the design of a hull and the working of the rigging. Parallel with that change in outlook went a development of the art of draughtsmanship that led, in its turn, to a more accurate laying out of the parts of a ship and less reliance on the eye of the Master Shipwright. The plans in the *Fragments of Ancient English Shipwrightry*, delightful though their appearance is, really give little information about the shape of the body of the ship, which would have to be drawn out by a method like that in the anonymous *Treatise on Shipbuilding* that was written about 1625[1]. Not all plans were as carefully drawn as those in the *'Fragments'* as some of the examples in this chapter show. The next stage was a plan combining a perspective view of the ship's hull with several cross-sections. By the 1660s, however, Pepys' friend Anthony Deane was producing the kind of detailed plan that remained in fashion for over two centuries.

Throughout the whole of the century shipbuilding was in a state of ferment in all the maritime States of Europe and especially in the Northern States and France. The diffusion of ideas was accelerated by the movements of shipwrights from one country to another, a movement reminiscent of the master masons of the Middle Ages. Dutchmen worked in Danish and Swedish dockyards, as did some English shipwrights, of whom the Sheldon family in Sweden are probably the most famous. Scottish shipwrights worked in Denmark. David Balfour was one, and Daniel Sinclair, who built the *Norske Löwe* in 1634 for Christian IV was another. The story of Czar Peter the Great working in the Dockyards at Deptford and Amsterdam is well known though less is known, at any rate in Western Europe, about the innovations that Peter subsequently introduced into the Russian Navy. The wars involving the English, the Dutch and the French in the second half of the century occupy so much of the central stage of European history that the ships of the Baltic Powers are all too often left in the wings. This

127. The sail plan of the French 2-decker *La Couronne* from Paris' monumental work *Souvenirs de Marine*. The drawing is based on a rather crude engraving in the seventeenth century *Hydrographie* by Georges Fournier and the accuracy of some of the rigging detail is dubious.

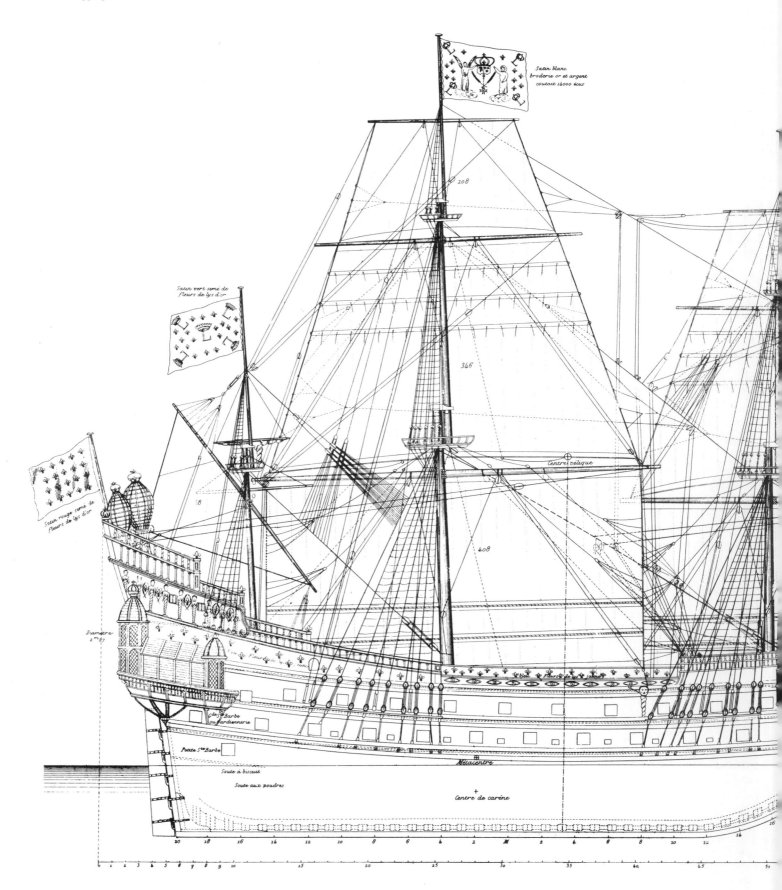

is a misleading situation, for the ships of Denmark and Sweden were every bit as advanced in design as those of England or the Netherlands. Of course, each country developed those features that seemed best fitted for the circumstances in which the ships were likely to be employed. English ships were noted for the robustness of their construction, a feature that stood them in good stead in the wars with the Dutch, whose ships, being of lighter construction, suffered more severely in the stand-up fights of the time. Dutch ships were as a rule smaller than the English ones and had flatter bottoms and shallower draught to enable them to sail in the shallow waters off the Dutch coasts. Danish and Swedish ships were sometimes built in the Dutch style but quite early in the century shipwrights in both countries developed their own style of hull. The efficacy of a warship was not by any means governed only by the form of the hull. A potent factor was the relation between hull size and number of guns. Spanish ships, for example, were usually bigger for a given gunpower than those of the other States whereas English ships were often so overloaded with guns that they were sluggish sailers although able to overpower the other ships when once at close quarters.

The seventeenth century might well be called the age of the 'prestige ship' for it was during that century that the fashion for building specially large, heavily armed and superabundantly decorated ships reached its peak. It was a belief firmly held by the kings of all the maritime States that royal dignity had to be upheld on the high seas by a ship of the largest possible size, carrying the heaviest armament and decorated regardless of cost or utility and, at times, of taste and even the stability of the ship. When Colbert, Louis IV's Minister, wrote 'Nothing is more impressive nor so befits the Majesty of the King than that his ships bear the finest ornament yet seen on the high seas' he was only stating what was the conviction of every king who had a fleet. Christian IV of Denmark had a 'prestige ship', the *Tre Kroner*, in the early 1600s, Gustavus Adolphus had the ill-fated *Wasa* built in 1628, and the famous *Sovereign of the Seas* was launched in 1637. The French, not to be outdone by mere islanders, built *La Couronne* in 1638.

In contrast to the two previous centuries, the seventeenth century provides plenty of reliable and detailed information about the build, rigging, armament and decoration of ships of almost every kind. Pictures by artists of the Dutch School of naturalistic painting are trustworthy evidence for ships' appearance – with one proviso. In the early part of the century, as remarked in Chapter 2, it was far from unusual for a Dutch ship to masquerade in a picture as, for example, an English one. There are grounds for suspecting, too, that an artist might have drawn on his imagination, at times, more than is usually supposed. Vroom's two paintings of the *Prince Royal,* in 1613 and 1623, agree with one another, 139 but on the other hand Willaerts' painting of the same ship in 1613 shows quite a different vessel[2]. The evidence of the draught of an early Jacobean 3-decker supports the 128 Vroom version[3].

Manuscripts and books on shipbuilding and rigging make their appearance, the earliest English one having been written about 1625, and after the middle of the century both sorts become plentiful. Several plans have survived from the first half of the century. The earliest English plan is that of the 3-decker just mentioned and is almost certainly connected with the *Prince Royal* of 1610. Another one is thought to represent the *Phoenix* of 1613[4] and a third, a plan of a pinnace, of a 223

128

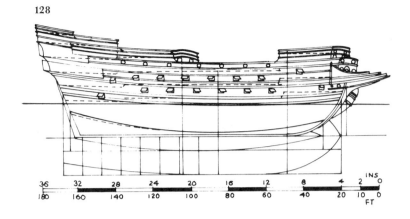

252 date after 1609, was found in the Danish State Archives[5]. That Archive contains a remarkable group of plans from about 1630 and in the Swedish State Archive is a rough 130 draft of a 2-decker of about 1615. After 1650 the number of plans from all the Northern European archives and museums increases rapidly.

Documentary and pictorial sources are reinforced, and in some cases contradicted by, a new one; the beautifully made contemporary models known in England as Navy Board or Dockyard models. Some are presentation models like the astonishing ivory model of the Danish *Norske Löwe* of 1634 at Copenhagen[6], others are models of projected ships, and yet others represent ships actually built. A fair number, however, do not seem to represent any particular ship. The oldest seventeenth century model is probably that of a Swedish 2-decker said to date from about 1600. It is probably a little older than a rather roughly made English model in the Ash- 132 molean Museum, Oxford. The oldest 'Navy Board' type model is that of the Swedish *Amaranthe* of 1654, a model that has much of its original rigging. In England the 133 earliest of the 'Navy Board' models is that of a 50–58 gun 134 ship of 1655, but if the series of English models starts late its numbers exceed those of other countries. Most of the models, fortunately, are still in Britain although a mag-nificent collection went to the USA in the 1920s and now forms the Henry Huddleston Rogers Collection at Annapolis. As the general appearance of 'Navy Board' models is well known there is no need to describe them, but it should be noted that the style of open framing shown when the bottom of the model is left unplanked does not always correspond with that used on a real ship[7]. The frames of the *Dartmouth*, wrecked in 1690, are quite close together[8].

Seventeenth century developments were not concerned only with the building and rigging of ships. The first steps were taken towards standardising the composition of fleets and their armament. Elizabethan seamen had proved that boarding or smash-and-grab tactics were of no avail in the face of a more nimble and weatherly ship, and good gunnery. Sixty years after the Armada the Anglo-Dutch sea fights showed that mixed fleets of warships and merchantmen were less effective than a fleet made up of warships only, and that below a certain size a ship, whether a warship or a merchant vessel, was asking for trouble if it joined in a mêlée where it might find itself opposed by a much more powerful ship. Naval tactics were slowly moving towards the adop-tion of the formal line of battle with its implicit expecta-tion that ships would be, as a general rule, opposed by vessels of much the same size and gunpower as them-selves. Even before the Anglo-Dutch wars it had become customary, in England, to grade warships in what later

128. A reconstruction of the draught of a Jacobean 3-decker from an incomplete plan in the National Maritime Museum. Mr W Salisbury, who carried out the reconstruction, believes that the plan is associated with the *Prince Royal*.

129. The bows and midship section of a Danish 2-decked ship of about 1630. The absence of holes for the gammon lashing means that it went under the stem knee. The diagonal struts in the hold are like those on the midship section in Baker's *'Fragments'* and are still in evidence in Edward Dummer's drawing of a late seventeenth century 1st Rate.

130. This drawing is based on a very crudely executed sketch in the Swedish Riksarkivet. It is dated at about 1615, and the ship measures about 80 Swedish feet on the keel.

131. Another plan from the Swedish Riksarkivet, but of a somewhat later ship (about 1660). It is an 18-gun pinnace of Dutch appearance, with a keel length of 62 Swedish feet.

132. The origin of this model, which has been in the Ashmolean Collection at Oxford since at least 1689, is unknown. Claims that it represents Sir Francis Drake's *Golden Hind* or that it is the model made by Phineas Pett in 1634 for the infant Prince Charles have little evidence to support them. There are indeed some sixteenth century features about the model, such as the overhanging poop, open stern and quarter galleries, absence of channels and figurehead, but there are other features more appropriate to the seventeenth century. The bowsprit has the remains of a knee for a spritsail topmast, there are two gammon lashings although gammonings are not recorded in the 1588 inventory of the Queen's ships, the foremast is farther aft than English ships had it in the sixteenth century and the mizzenmast is considerably further forward. There are also some peculiarities about the hull. The hawseholes are set very low and the fore end of the forecastle is a convex curve as it is on the *Prince Royal* according to Willaert's rather imaginative painting of that ship (in the National Maritime Museum). The bowsprit seems to be stepped on the ship's centreline, which was not the case in the sixteenth century so far as we know. The balance of evidence points to a ship of the first quarter of the seven-teenth century and perhaps a Continental one. As for the association with Prince Charles, it seems unlikely that such a crudely made model would have been given by such an important shipwright as Pett.

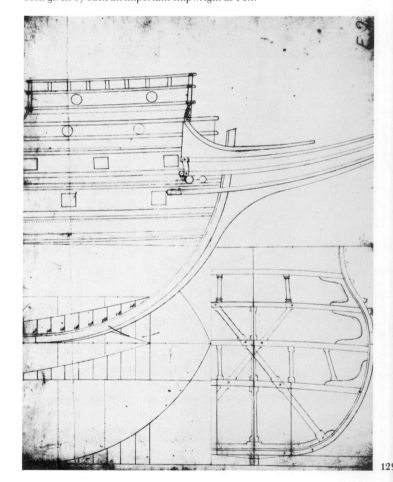

129

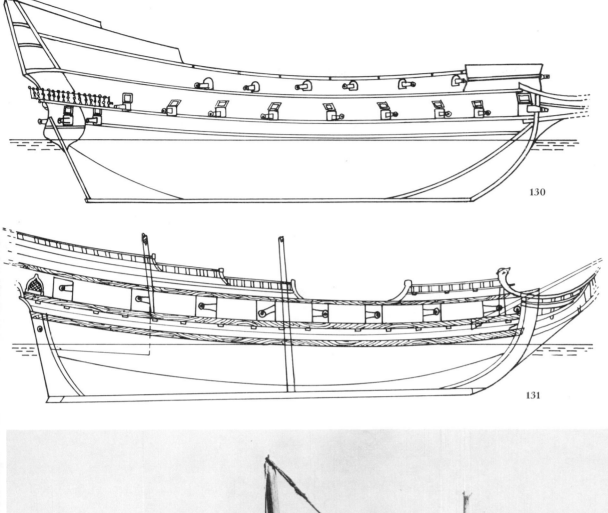

130

131

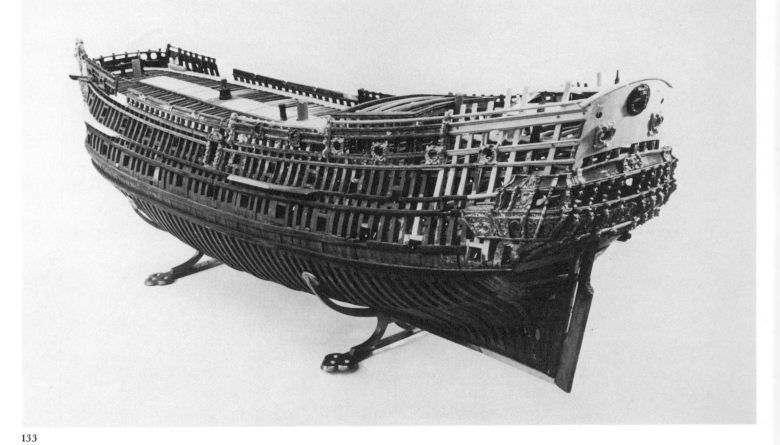

133

134

133. One of the earliest English 'Navy Board' models. It is of a 3-decker and is believed to have been taken to Sweden in 1659 by the famous shipwright Francis Sheldon, who founded a family of shipwrights in Swedish service. Note the ornate entry port, the old style of capstan and the circular ports for the chase guns. As the light coloured parts of the model show, it has suffered considerable damage.

134. A model of a 50–58 gun ship of 1655, the oldest 'Navy Board' model in England. It is similar to the Sheldon model of about the same date. The model is in the National Maritime Museum, Greenwich.

became known as Rates. James I's Navy was divided into four groups called Ranks. The first rank had ships of 44 to 55 guns, the second had those of 38 to 42 guns, the third rank's had 26 to 34 guns and the fourth rank contained all the smaller craft. This arrangement lasted until 1655 when the Navy was graded into six Rates according to the gun complements of the ships[9].

One source of knowledge about seventeenth century (and later) ships has not yet been mentioned. It is the remains of the ships themselves. A find on the scale of the *Wasa* is only likely to be repeated in the Baltic, but substantial remains have been discovered in many other places. In British waters the most important is without doubt that of the *Dartmouth,* a ship of 40 guns at the time she was wrecked off the island of Mull (Scotland) in 1690.

THE HULL

Throughout Elizabeth I's reign expert opinion about the best proportion for a warship had swayed between a keel:beam ratio of 2½:1 and about 3:1. Three ships built in the last 15 years of the sixteenth century, *Vanguard, Due Repulse* and *Warspite,* exemplify the different opinions. The question passed, unsettled, into the seventeenth century. The *Prince Royal* of 1610 (the first English 3-decker) had a keel:beam ratio of just over 2.4:1[11]. The anonymous writer of the *Treatise on Shipbuilding* recommended 2.5:1 and that was the keel:beam ratio of the famous *Sovereign of the Seas.* A Danish ship of about 1640 had a ratio of almost 4:1 but later ships, for example the *Hummeren,* a single-decker, and the *Dannebrog,* a 2-decker built in 1692, had keel:beam ratios of 3:1. In point of fact the question of the ideal proportion was never settled decisively. Over 100 years after the launch of the *Sovereign of the Seas,* the *Victory* was built with a keel three times her beam. Shortness of hull was the result of a necessary compromise. A longer hull could carry more guns and might make a faster ship but the tendency of the ends to droop increased with length, and a high length:breadth ratio reduced manoeuvrability compared with a shorter vessel of the same beam. Taking all the factors into account, seventeenth century shipwrights had little doubt that for big warships the keel:beam ratio should lie between 2.5:1 and 3:1, perhaps a little less, perhaps a little more. Keel length, however, is not a satisfactory measure of comparison in size between ships, except over a fairly short period and between ships of a similar build, because the length on the waterline (or the length of the later base line, the gun-deck) depended on the amount of fore and after rake. Of the two, only the fore rake played a significant part. At the beginning of the century it might be equal to the breadth on English ships, and was not normally less than three-quarters of it. Two ships of about 500 tons each, built in 1633, had fore rakes of 0.93 and 0.88 of their breadths (or approximately 0.3 of the keel's length)[10]. Forty years later the rake had diminished to 0.6 of the breadth and only 0.2 of the keel length. The fore rake became less still as the century went on. Foreign ships appear to have had similar proportions.

For the French *La Couronne* of 1638[12] the sum of the rakes was equal to one-third of the keel length; a Danish ship of 1613 and another of about 1640 had a fore rake of about 0.25 of the keel, and a third, built in 1692, had a rake of nearly 0.23 of the keel.

Another dimension that affects the comparison of hull shapes is their depth. What this term meant when the measurement was recorded depended on which method of measuring for tonnage was in use. The datum line for measuring the depth was a line between the sides of the ship at the point of its greatest breadth, and from the middle of that line the depth was measured. The uncertainty arises because the depth might be measured to the bottom of the keel, or to its top or, on other formulae, to the outside of the bottom plank. Whatever method was used, the depth, often referred to in English sources as the depth in hold, was somewhat less than half the breadth of the ship. The *Prince Royal* had a depth of 17ft and a breadth of 43½ft, a proportion of almost 0.4:1. The *Treatise on Shipbuilding* recommends 0.42:1 and that was the *Sovereign of the Seas'* proportion. One of Anthony Deane's draughts from the late 1660s has a depth that is 0.4 of the breadth[14].

From the lengths of keel, breadth and depth the lines of a ship were produced by geometrical methods. The procedure is described in the *Treatise on Shipbuilding* and a simplified account will be found in *Elizabethan Ship* by Gregory Robinson[14]. The key to the whole shape was the midship section and it is a measure of the importance that shipwrights attached to the shape of the midship section that when the design for the *Sovereign of the Seas* was submitted to Charles I the shipwrights concerned asked that the King would not disclose the plan to anyone. The method of drawing the midship section had been in use since Tudor times and probably, in one form or another, for much longer. When ships were short for their length and had only one, or at most two, gun-decks, the method produced satisfactory designs, but it failed when heavier armaments were put on board and when a third gun-deck was added, so that many ships had to have their stability increased by adding extra layers of planking at the waterline, and in some cases by stripping off the planking and 'padding out' the frames. The reason for the instability was that the geometrical method used by English shipwrights – and the various refinements did not alter the shape of the section significantly – produced a midship section, and consequently an entire hull, that had an insufficient proportion below the waterline and therefore inadequate displacement. It was not until the second half of the century that a way was devised for calculating, even if only roughly, the volume of a hull from its plan. Anthony Deane is credited with being the first English shipwright to calculate the draught of water of a ship in advance of its launch. Thereafter, and with the help of improved methods of developing the lines, shipwrights were able to build more stable ships, although crank, or 'tender', ships crop up until the end of the sailing era and even after it. The degree to which the basic proportions of English ships changed during the first three-quarters of the century is shown in the table.

Better seaworthiness was gradually obtained. The bows were made bluffer so that the ship plunged less heavily, and the stern was broadened at the waterline. A reduction in the height of the superstructures aft improved working to windward. In the last quarter of the century the shape of the underbody of English ships was given a more rounded form, based almost on a semicircle, that provided more buoyancy. There is not suf-

KEEL:BEAM RATIOS – Late Sixteenth Century				
Ship	Built	Keel (ft)	Beam (ft)	Ratio
Vanguard	1586	108	32	3.38:1
Due Repulse	1596	105	37	2.83:1
Warspite	1596	90	36	2.5:1

BASIC PROPORTIONS OF ENGLISH SHIPS 1586–1670

Measurement	c1586*	c1620**	1637***	1670****
Main breadth as fraction of keel length (L)	L/3 – 2L/5	9/25 × L	11/30 × L	3/10 × L
Maximum breadth of upper deck as fraction of main breadth (B)	2/3 × B	2/3 × B	2/3 × B	2/3 × B (?)
Transom	4/9 × B	B/2 – 10/19 × B	3/5 × B	2/3 × B – 26/36 × B
Depth	B/2	3/7 × B	3/7 × B	3/7 × B
Point of maximum breadth from front of keel	Nearly L/3	L/3	L/3	L/3
Flat of floor	B/4 – B/3	2/7 × B	3/10 × B	3/10 × B – B/3
Sweep at runghead	B/4 – 3/10 × B	15/56 × B	22/93 × B	
Middle sweep	3/5 × B – 9/10 × B	3/5 × B	2/3 × B	5/9 × B
Sweep of breadth	B/4 – B/5	B/4	3/14 × B	7/36 × B
Sweep above breadth		B/4	3/10 × B	17/36 × B
Height of stem		3/4 × B – B		
Fore rake		3/4 × B – B	4/5 × B	3/4 × B
After rake		18° – 22°	10/52 × B	11/72 × B
Height of sternpost		2/3 × B		3/4 × B

*From Baker. Approximate date.
**From *Treatise on Shipbuilding*. Approximate date.
****Sovereign of the Seas*
****From Deane.

ficient material to enable the changes in hull form to be plotted in any detail before 1660 but after that date the 'Navy Board' models, if their lines were taken off, would provide a very interesting comparative series, especially in cases where a plan of the ship also exists.

There was a steady growth in the size of warships. The biggest of Queen Elizabeth's ships had a keel of 110ft, that of the *Prince Royal* built in 1610 was 115ft long and the *Sovereign of the Seas'* keel was 126ft. For comparison, Nelson's *Victory* has a keel 150ft long. The chief development was not in mere size, notwithstanding that the *Sovereign of the Seas* had nearly twice the tonnage of the biggest Elizabethan ship, but in gun-carrying decks. By the end of the 1500s the biggest ships had a full tier of guns on their lower deck and nearly a complete one on the upper deck. In addition, some of the latest ships had either broad gangways or a spar deck over the waist and carried guns there. The spar decks were soon planked over and the way was open for the true 3-decker, a ship armed with a full battery of guns on each of her complete decks. The first English 3-decker was the *Prince Royal* of 1200 tons, built by Phineas Pett in 1610. Design and construction of the ship, and its builder's character too, were subjected to fierce but on the whole unsuccessful criticism, and it is interesting to find that as part of Pett's defence of his work he was able to show that he had followed the traditions of the previous reign. In other words, the *Prince Royal* was not a departure from an established style, as the Elizabethan galleon was from the carrack, but an elaboration of an existing type.

The process of covering the waist with a spar deck or gangway was repeated on both the *Prince Royal* and the *Sovereign of the Seas* but no guns were mounted there, so that neither ship was a 4-decker in the sense that the *Santissima Trinidad* of Nelson's day was.

The increase in the number of gun-decks was accompanied by a reduction in sheer, a reduction that continued until, in the nineteenth century, the profile of the hull was almost flat. Reducing the sheer, and with it the sheer of the wales, allowed the gun-decks to be laid flush because it was possible to place the gunports without cutting the wales to a dangerous extent. The *Prince Royal* had 'broken' or 'stepped' decks to avoid that, although the breaks were only in the after parts, but the *Sovereign of the Seas* had three flush gun-decks. From then onwards only small English ships had breaks in their decks, but for a different reason: to provide sufficient headroom at the ends where the floors rose up.

An increase in the number of decks and guns, and even in size, was not the feature that would have caught the eye of an old seaman who had fought against the Armada if he had been taken to see a ship of 1650. After all, he would have heard from his grandfather about the huge *Henry Grace à Dieu* and he might even have seen, at low tide, the remains of the great *Grace Dieu* of 1418. What the old man would probably have commented on, favourably or otherwise, would have been the new-fangled stern and the mass of decoration. For at some time in the first half of the seventeenth century English shipwrights adopted the 'round tuck' in place of the old flat stern, and this new feature distinguished English ships from those of Continental fleets throughout the greater part of the century. Some European States retained the 'flat tuck' even into the eighteenth century. The new stern was not just a reversion to the fifteenth century one, which was a development of the double-ended hull. In the new round tuck only the lowest strakes of planking came in to the sternpost and the rest were brought round and up to the transom. The flat part of the stern now began about 10ft above the waterline instead of below it, and consequently there was a smoother flow of water to the rudder and less drag. When the new style of stern was introduced is not known with any certainty. The *Prince Royal* had the old stern but the *Convertine* may have had the round tuck in 1618. The *Soevereign of the Seas* had a square tuck in 1637 yet, on the other hand, one picture shows the ship with a square tuck but with the planks curved as though it was a round one. With so much uncertainty the best that can be said is that square tucks were the rule up to about 1620 and

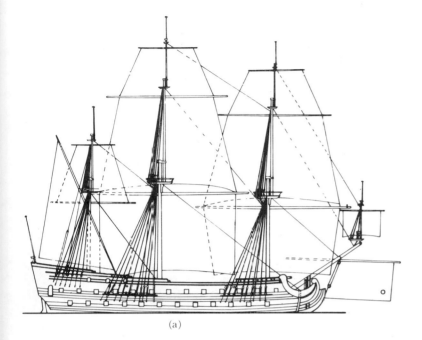

(a)

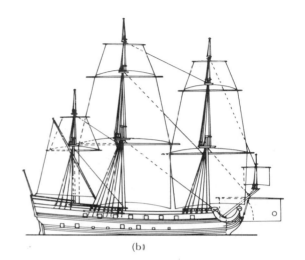

(b)

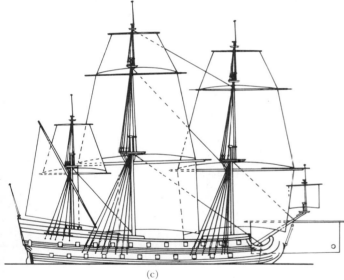

(c)

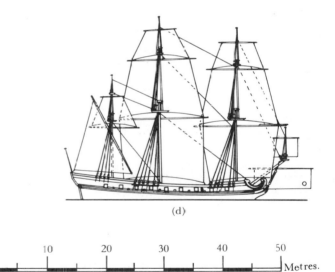

(d)

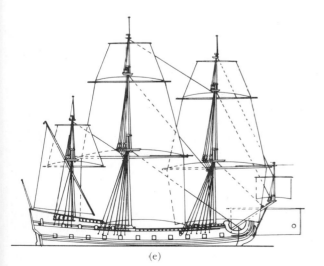

(e)

0   10   20   30   40   50

Metres.

135. Comparative profiles of French ships from the end of the seventeenth century. They are:

(a) *Le Fendant* – 2nd Rate, Second Order (60 guns), built at Le Havre in 1700
(b) An unicentified 3rd Rate, First Order (48 guns)
(c) *Le Capricieux* – 4th Rate (34 guns) built at Dunkerque in 1689
(d) An unicentified 5th Rate (24 guns)
(e) An unidentified 'frigate' (16 guns)

The French rating system was introduced in 1661, when the first three 'Rangs' were further subdivided into 'Ordres'. The rates were later altered as ships grew bigger but at this time there was no 6th Rate. Ships larger than those shown here were rated 2nd Rate, First Order up to 70 guns, and 1st Rate over that number.

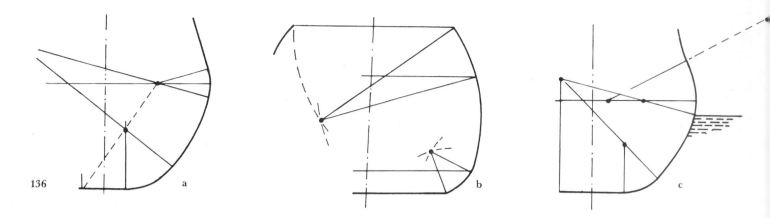

136

a   b   c

round tucks after 1640, although yachts and some other small ships were built with square tucks until the early eighteenth century and occasionally even later.

It is likely that the round tuck led to a change in the way the rudder-head was fitted. Ever since the sternpost rudder had come into use on big ships the rudder-head had been outside the ship and the tiller brought inboard through a rectangular opening in the stern. As the opening had to be wide enough to allow the tiller to swing it was difficult to keep water out in rough weather. At some time before the 1660s, however, it was realised that if the rudder-head was taken up through the counter a smaller opening would suffice and a canvas jacket could be fitted over it. Evidence for the date of this innovation is scanty and its adoption, at any rate on English ships, was slow. The *Royal Katherine* had an inboard rudder-head in 1664 but the old style is found on 'Navy Board' models of later ships.

The complexity of the stern's superstructure developed rapidly during the first quarter of the century. The Elizabethan stern was basically two flat surfaces, the upper one projecting slightly over the lower, to which it was joined by a curved counter. Across the stern and along the quarters ran a gallery a little above the level of the upper deck. At the beginning of the century two galleries were usual on big ships, the lower one being at the lower deck's level, but the *Prince Royal* had three. Swedish and Danish ships appear to have had one or two galleries. On English ships the first steps towards closing in the galleries were taken soon after 1600, if not earlier – the early English pinnace shown in the illustration has her side galleries partly roofed. When there were two galleries it seems likely, however, that only one was roofed. On the *Prince Royal* the middle gallery was closed in all round but the upper and lower ones were left open. The next step in the sequence of development was to close in all the stern galleries and the greater part of the side ones. The whole matter of the development of stern and quarter galleries is one of great complexity, however, because it is closely bound up with the contemporary fashions in decoration and is ripe for a new examination of the evidence, especially that relating to Continental ships which had sterns and galleries constructed differently from those on English ships.

The fore end of the seventeenth century ship also underwent changes in shape, but to a lesser extent than the stern did. Three areas were involved: the entry (the fore part of the hull in the water), the beakhead bulkhead, and the beak itself. The bluffer entry has already been mentioned. The shape of the beakhead bulkhead was governed by the construction of the bows. The hull timbers were cut off at a level corresponding to the deck above the lowest gun-deck, and above that level

the forecastle was closed off by a bulkhead that ran right across the bow. The bulkhead was usually flat, to allow forward fire, but sometimes the lower part of the bulkhead was convex and the upper part flat. At least one door gave access to the head and it was usually in the centre of the bulkhead, for the bowsprit, until after 1670, was stepped to starboard of the centreline. The door might be flanked by gunports and sometimes had a porch over it, and on 2-decked ships there was sometimes a pair of gunports in the upper part of the beakhead bulkhead. The contemporary draught of a Jacobean 3-decker has two doors and two circular gunports in the upper part of the bulkhead. On the *Prince Royal,* the upper part of the bulkhead was set back to leave a platform in front of it at the level of the spardeck. Generally speaking, the later beakhead bulkheads were flat but there is an interesting exception: the *Royal Charles* of 1673 had two semi-circular galleries on her bulkhead at the level of the ship's upper deck.

The beak itself underwent a good deal of change. In the late sixteenth century it had been long and narrow and continued the line of the wales, a form which was carried over into Stuart times and lasted until at least 1650. A similar style of beakhead is found on Dutch, Danish and Swedish ships and seems to have lasted longer than it did on English vessels. At the end of the sixteenth century English beakheads were shallow and had a flat cross-section but in about 1600 that was changed to a V-shaped trough. Then, about 40 years later, the beak began to turn upwards. The change in slope was accompanied by, and may have been a consequence of, a shortening of the head knee, and the net effect of the two changes was to give the beak a modified V-section. By 1655 the new form was the normal one. During the remainder of the century the head knee was made stouter and the fore rake was reduced, the knee being rounded up more and more until its upper part was almost vertical. Like the stern, the beak and the beakhead bulkhead were vehicles for exuberant adornment, a subject which will be considered in the section on decoration.

There was little structural change in the sides of ships. The degree of inward slope, or tumblehome, remained much the same although some countries' ships, for example Dutch ones, had more than English ships. On the latter, the topsides were usually concave, though some shipwrights made them flat (but not vertical). One feature that *did* change was the arrangement of the wales. As they did in the sixteenth century — and probably ever since they were first fitted — these longitudinal stiffeners ran from stem to stern in arcs of concentric circles. The lowest wale started at the transom across the top of the sternpost, sloped down to reach the waterline a little

252

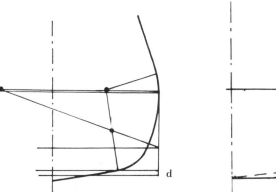
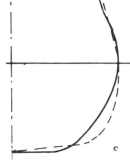

136. Methods of laying out the 'midships bend'.
(a) Traditional English fashion found in Matthew Baker, formed of three 'sweeps' (still being used in the early seventeenth century).
(b) As given by Furttenbach, 1629.
(c) Deane's method, from his 'Doctrine', 1670.
(d) Typical Dutch fashion, as given by Witsen (1671).
(e) Comparison of typical English (solid line) and Dutch sections.

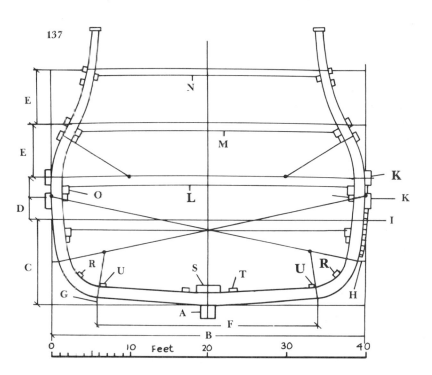

137. Dimensions of three ships built at Gothenburg, Sweden, 1633–4

	Göta Ark 72 guns (1634)	Jupiter 36 guns (1633)	Göteborg 32 guns (1633)
A. Keel Depth	22in	20in	16in
Width	23in	22in	19in
Length	130ft	106ft	91ft
Length from stempost to sternpost	168ft	138ft	120ft
B. Breadth within plank	40ft	33ft	27ft
C. Height from top of keel to upper side of hold beams	11ft	15ft	13ft
D. From hold beams to beams of lower deck	5½ft	15ft	13ft
E. Height between decks	7ft	7½ft	6¼ft
F. Breadth of floor	28½ft	24½ft	18ft
G. Rise of floor	11in	10in	7in
H. Hänger vid nagelen*	11in	10in	9in
Wing Transom	23½ft	17ft	15ft
From lower edge of sterm to keel	17ft	14ft	12ft
Thickness of floor timbers	15in	14in	11in
Thickness of 2nd and 3rd futtocks	11in	9in	7in
I. Thickness of planking	5in	4in	3in
K. Wales Width	36in	27in	18in
Thickness	9in	8in	7in
Lower deck beams	15in	14in	12in
M. Middle deck beams	12in	11in	9in
N. Upper deck beams	10in		
O. Clamps to lower deck: upper	9in	7in	5in
P. Clamps to lower deck: lower	6in	4½in	3½in
R. Thickstuff over floor heads	6in	4½in	3½in
S. Kelson Thickness	11in	9in	7in
Breadth	3ft	2½ft	2ft
T. Sleeper beams, nearest kelson	6in	4½in	3½in
U. Other sleeper beams in hold	4in	3in	2½in
Distance between deck beams	4ft	4ft	4ft

*Hänger vid nagelen – to hang at the nail. A similar phrase 'to overhang the nail' occurs in Mainwaring's The Seaman's Dictionary. The meaning is uncertain but seems to refer to the amount that the ship's side at its level of greatest breadth overhangs the side at the waterline or at some pre-determined point lower down.

138. A reconstructed midship section for the Prince Royal as suggested by Mr W Salisbury.

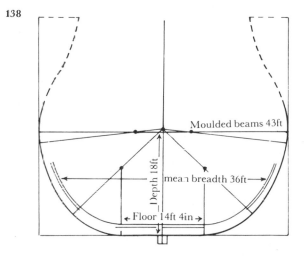

forward of the point of greatest breadth, and then rose up again as it went towards the stem. Wales were usually placed 3ft apart but the spacing might be altered to avoid cutting a gunport through a wale. The lowest wale was the broadest and thickest. Pictures sometimes show a wale below what would normally be the lowest one; this may indeed be an extra wale but is perhaps an example of girdling, ie fastening a belt of thick timber round the hull at the waterline to improve the stability. The *Sovereign of the Seas* had her wales arranged in pairs, a fashion that became standard on English ships. Foreign ships also had their wales in pairs, but as a rule the members of a pair were rather wider apart than on English ships.

Gunports were usually square but rectangular ones were not uncommon, and the size of ports varied somewhat with the calibre of the gun. The *Treatise on Shipbuilding* recommends 30in square for a ship of 550 tons but the guns' calibres are not stated. The *Leopard*, of 515 tons and built in 1634, had ports 28in high and 26in wide. The *Sovereign of the Seas'* lower deck ports were 32in square and those on the middle and upper decks 30 and 28in respectively. The uppermost gunports and those in the beakhead bulkhead were sometimes circular. Pictorial evidence for apparently round ports has to be treated with caution because square ports sometimes had circular wreaths round them and these give an appearance of circularity to the port.

139. The first English 3-decker, built by Phineas Pett and launched in 1610, the *Prince Royal* was 111ft on the keel, 43ft broad within the plank and 18ft deep in hold. At 1200 tons the *Prince Royal* was 200 tons bigger than the next biggest ship. Vroom's painting 'The Arrival of the Elector Palatine at Flushing in 1613' shows her with less sheer aft than either the *Repulse* or the *Red Lion*. The outline of her hull foreshadows that of the *Soverign of the Seas*. The *Prince Royal* differed in having a step or fall at the after end of her middle deck whereas the *Soverign of the Seas* had three flush decks. The shape of the hull in Vroom's picture agrees with the plan of an early Jacobean 3-decker that is in the National Maritime Museum but Vroom has given his ship a 'bonaventure crossjack yard' which is not in the 1611 inventory. Parts of the rigging are incomplete: for example, there are no braces to the fore and main topsail yards, or to the mizzen topsail yard, nor are the fore- and mainbraces shown. The absence of braces to the bonaventure mizzen topsail yard, however, agrees with the 1611 inventory, the yard being controlled by the sheets of the topsail.

140. One of the last ships to be built in Queen Elizabeth's reign, the *Repulse* accompanied the *Prince Royal* to Flushing in 1613 and this detail from Vroom's painting shows her approaching the port. The *Repulse* had been rebuilt in 1610, so the picture would be expected to show here in her modernised form. Whether it does is open to doubt. The shape of the stern galleries and the great sheer of the poop are reminiscent of Dutch ships' sterns. Of more relevance are the differences between the rigging as shown in the picture and what is recorded for the *Repulse* in the 1611 inventory. According to that the *Repulse* had a crossjack yard, a mizzen topsail yard and a bonaventure mizzenmast with lateen yard and topsail yard. There should also be a spritsail topmast but the end of the bowsprit is 'off the picture'. None the less, one would expect to see some of the spritsail topsail's rigging coming back to the beakhead. On the other hand, as the picture was not painted until about 1625 Vroom may have given the *Repulse* a later style of rig, when the bonaventure mizzen had fallen out of use.

139

141

141. One of the older Elizabethan warships, the *Red Lion* was rebuilt in 1609. Her ornate painting and gilding may have been put on for her visit to Flushing in company with the *Prince Royal* whose quarter can be seen on the right centre. As in the case of the *Repulse's* picture there are some peculiarities about the *Red Lion*. She has only three masts yet according to the 1611 inventory the *Red Lion* had a bonaventure mizzenmast. In fact, the forward position of the mizzenmast in the picture would be more appropriate to a 4-masted ship. There is no spritsail topmast though there was one in 1611. The fore topgallant mast is missing, but perhaps it had been sent down. In short, interesting though the picture is, it is doubtful evidence for the appearance of a famous English warship in 1613.

142. A drawing of the stern of a 3rd Rate of about 1634 by W van de Velde the Elder – an early example of the English 'round tuck' stern. The extraordinary feature about the stern is that the ends of the planks that run up to the transom are shown as clinker-work. Another peculiarity is the distinctly Dutch appearance of the stern, notwithstanding the English Royal Arms and the monogram 'CR'. There is also a hint of clinker planking on the side of the poop. (The Dutch-built *L'Esprit* was captured from the French in the Texel in 1627. She became the *St Esprit*.)

The information about hull form in the first half of the century that is given by models and draughts has been supplemented by the discovery of contracts and other specifications for building ships. The earliest, and probably the most important, is a contract drawn up in 1613 by Christian IV of Denmark for a ship to be built in North Germany. The ship was to be 90ft long on the keel, have a beam of 30ft and to have a depth in hold of 10ft. She was to have only a single gun-deck (to carry 16 broadside guns, 18pdrs), but a spar deck was to be over the waist. The amount of detail about structure and rigging makes this contract the most informative document before the middle of the century. It has been published, in translation, in the *Mariner's Mirror* for 1928[15]. The earliest English specifications are for the *Leopard* and the *Swallow* (478 tons) built in 1634[9] and the *Sovereign of the Seas*. As the *Leopard* and the *Swallow* were almost the same size only the former ship's dimensions are given in the relevant table, together with the original and final measurements for the *Sovereign of the Seas*. The *Leopard*, with a floor 0.4 of the breadth, was a fuller bodied ship than the *Sovereign of the Seas* with a floor 0.28 of the breadth. The *Leopard's* dimensions are very like those of the Danish ship in the 1613 contract. The next English specification is for the *Foresight* of 1649[16]. Although not so detailed as the Danish one it has a great deal of interesting material in it, and so has a Dutch contract of 1664. Both documents have been published in the *Mariner's Mirror*.

142

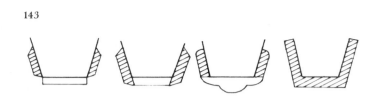

143

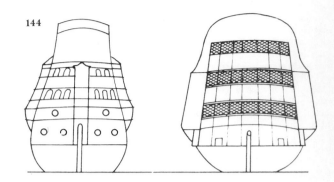

144

143. Stern and quarter galleries (shaded parts are closed in). Left to right they are: *Sovereign of the Seas,* 1637; *St Michael,* 1669 (lower and upper galleries); an 80-gun ship of 1695.
144. The general development in the shapes of sterns can be seen in this comparison of the *Sovereign of the Seas,* 1637 (left) and a 90-gun ship of 1680.

SPECIFICATIONS FOR *LEOPARD* (1634) and *SOVEREIGN OF THE SEAS* (1637)

	Leopard		Sovereign of the Seas			
			Original proposals			
	ft	in	ft	in	ft	in
Keel	95	0	127	0	126	0
Depth from diameter of breadth to top of keel	12	4	18	9	?	
Breadth within plank	33	0	46	2	46	6
Breadth at transom	–		28	0	28	0
Depth from diameter of breadth to lower edge of keel	–		21	3	–	
Depth in hold from lower edge of beam to seeling	–		–		17	0
Swimming line from bottom of keel	12	9	18	9	19	6
Height of diameter of breadth above waterline	–		–		2	0
Flat of floor	13	0	13	0	14	0
Sweep at runghead	–		–		11	0
Sweep to right of mould (futtock sweep)	–		–		31	0
Sweep between waterline and diameter of breadth	–		–		10	0
Sweep above breadth	–		–		14	0
Depth of keel	1	7	2	6	?	
Keel and dead-rising	–		2	6	?	
Rake of stem	30	6	38	0	37	6
Rake of sternpost	4	3	8	0	9	0
Height of tuck at fashion piece			16	0	17	0
Height of way forward			14	0		
Height of lowest port above waterline			5	0	5	0
Height of port sills above deck	2	1			2	0
Height of ports (first tier)	2	4	2	8		
Height of ports (second tier)			2	6		
Height of ports (third tier)			2	4		
Width of ports	2	2	As heights			
Distance between ports	8	6 and	10	0	'Some 9ft 0in,	
	9	0			some more'	
Lower edge of port from line of greatest breadth	5	0				
Height between decks (1st)	6	6	7	6	7	6
Height between decks (2nd)			7	3	7	6
Distance from diameter of breadth to top of waist	13	6				

OUTBOARD HULL FITTINGS

Anchors and their gear. By the seventeenth century the cathead was established as the normal means for getting the anchor on board. Its early form was a square baulk of timber projecting at an angle of rather more than 45° to the keel and having a slight upward slope. The cathead's arm was long enough for the anchor to clear the side of the ship. A strong bracket, reaching down as far as the lower rail of the head, supported the cathead. On the *Prince Royal* the bracket's lower end sloped forwards but on the *Sovereign of the Seas* it was almost vertical. For most of the first half of the century the catheads were set well below the upper deck of the forecastle and were sometimes at the level of the upper deck and sometimes at the level of the upper deck bulwarks. After 1660 at the latest on English ships, the catheads were placed on the upper deck of the forecastle and the supporting bracket brought round to fair in with the lower rail, with which it was, in the end, combined. At the outer end of the cathead were two and sometimes three sheaves for the tackle. In addition to catheads, fish davits were used but as they are rarely shown in pictures or fitted to models little can be said about them. A model in the National Maritime Museum, Greenwich, has a pair of fish davits in place. They are straight, square sectioned timbers, sheaved at their outer ends and having the inboard ends held in an iron stirrup fixed to the forecastle deck. Anchors and cables are not strictly speaking fittings but it is convenient to treat them as such. Ships normally carried 7 anchors: one sheet anchor, four bowers, one

145. This splendid model of the *Prince,* a 100-gun ship built in 1670, is one of the finest models of English 1st Rates, and is one of the very few that have been identified beyond doubt. The *Prince's* dimensions were: keel 131ft, breadth 45ft 9in and depth in hold 19ft. The draught was 19ft 6in, corresponding to a burthen of 1463 tons. The arament was twenty-six 42pdrs on the lower deck, twenty-eight 18pdrs on the middle deck and twenty-eight 9pdrs on the upper deck. On the quarterdeck were ten sakers (6pdrs), with four more on the forecastle. On the poop were four 3pdrs. The model's rigging is modern and is exactly to the proportions laid down for a 1st Rate in Sir Anthony Deane's *A Doctrine of Naval Architecture* of 1670.

146

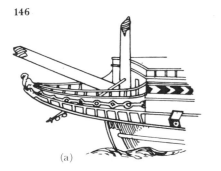

(a)

(c)

(b) ⊔ ⊔ ∪ ∨

(d)

146. The beakhead.
(a) Late sixteenth century.
(b) Changes in cross-section (left to right: about 1580, about 1600, mid-seventeenth century).
(c) *Prince*, 1670.
(d) *Royal Charles*, 1673.
147. The bows of the *Prince*. Equestrian figureheads were restricted at this date to ships named after members of the Royal Family. This photograph and 145 show the excessive lengths to which decoration was taken in the second half of the seventeenth century.

stream anchor and one kedge. The basic proportions of English anchors in the first quarter of the century are given in the accompanying drawing, but if pictures may be relied upon there was no fixed standard. The stock is sometimes shown as significantly longer than the shank and in other instances it is shorter. The length-of-arms:shank ratio also varied. The size of cables was determined, in theory, by the rule that the sheet cable should be $\frac{1}{2}$in in diameter for each foot of beam and cables for each of the other sorts of anchors, in descending order of size, were to be 1in less, eg if the sheet cable was 15in the bower anchors had 14in ones and so on. In practice this rule was not adhered to, and it may well have been out of date, for the *Sovereign of the Seas,* with a beam of 46$\frac{1}{2}$ft, had her biggest cable only 20in in circumference and the small *Lion's Whelps* of 25ft beam had 10in sheet cables. The contract for the Danish ship specifies a 14in sheet cable for a beam of 30ft.

Having dealt with cables it is appropriate to deal with the hawseholes. These were on the lower deck but what rule governed how many a ship ought to have is not known. In the first half of the century even small ships might have a pair on each side while bigger vessels had only one. Later, and as a very rough guide, single-decked ships had single hawseholes but 2- and 3-deckers had a pair on each side. The hawseholes had a surrounding piece of thick wood, known as a bolster, to take the chafe of the cable.

The last item connected with anchors is the band of protective planking known as an anchor lining or billboard. It was fixed to the side of the ship where the anchor's flukes were likely to catch as it was hauled up. It was just thick enough to level up the space between the wales, and at the top a thick, angular piece of wood was fitted to bring the anchor clear of the channel. Despite its obvious usefulness the anchor lining did not appear until the last quarter of the century. They are not on the model of the *St Michael* of 1669, but a model of a 90-gun ship of 1675 has a rudimentary form of lining. By 1691 the fully developed sort were in use.

Channels. On the early single- and 2-deckers the fore and main channels were on the wale above the uppermost tier of guns, and if there was a pair of wales then on the upper of the two, the chains going to the lower member of the pair. Mizzen channels were placed a deck higher than the others. When the first 3-deckers were built the fore and main channels remained in their traditional place, which now became the wale immediately *below* the uppermost tier of guns. The position of the *Prince Royal*'s mizzen channels is not easy to make out on her picture but they may have been about the level of her spar deck. The *Sovereign of the Seas* had the main and mizzen channels on the upper of her middle pair of wales and the mizzen channels a deck higher, an arrangement which remained standard English practice for the rest of the century. Continental practice was different. As early as 1626 the French had the fore and main channels on the wale above the upper deck guns and the mizzen a deck higher; on Dutch ships it was usual to put the fore and main channels on the second wale above the lower deck and guns. In consequence, as the wale sheered up and it crossed the line of ports on the upper deck, the main channel had to be cut to give the guns clear fire. It was not until nearly the end of the century that Dutch channels were set above the upper deck guns on 2-deckers. Danish practice was similar but the channels were set higher up, so that there was no need to cut them.

English channels, and probably those of other countries' ships, had curved iron brackets on their undersides to anchor them more securely to the ship's side. The lengths of the channels taken up by the deadeyes was about 2/5 of the vertical height of the trestletrees above the deck for the mainmast, about 1/3 of it on the foremast for the fore channels, and between 1/2 the spread of the main deadeyes and 1/2 that of the deadeyes on the fore channel for the mizzen channels. Channels projected beyond the end deadeyes by an amount roughly equal to half the space between a pair of deadeyes. As far as possible this spacing was kept even but it

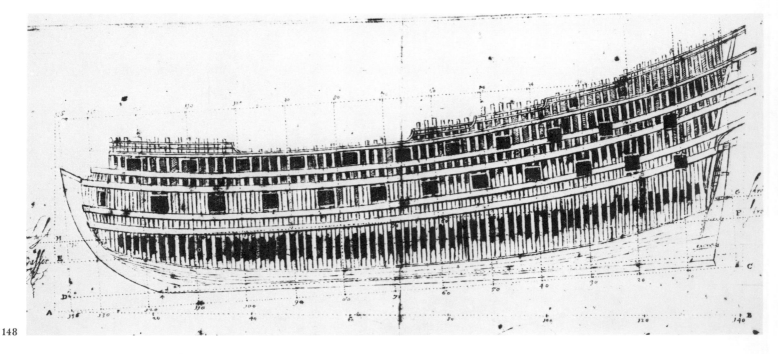

148

148. A Dutch plan of a 46-gun ship of the second half of the seventeenth century, by Johannes Sturckenburgh. The ship was to be 136ft (Amsterdam feet) on the gun-deck. The plan shows the ship as though on the launching ways. The comparatively light construction of the hull above the main deck explains why Dutch ships often suffered severely in fights with English ships of the same force.

149. The interior of the ship shown in 148. This time the ship has been drawn as she would be in the water. The draught astern is about 15in more than at the bow. The hull shows several differences from those of English ships. The decks sheer up towards the stern to a greater degree than English decks; the mizzenmast is stepped on the keel whereas the English often stepped it on the maindeck; there are large carved heads at the corners of the forecastle. Note that the draught is drawn freehand, a feature of Dutch plans into the eighteenth century.

150. The longitudinal section and deck plan of a 3rd Rate from Anthony Deane's *A Doctrine of Naval Architecture* (1670) which forms an interesting comparison with the Dutch plans in the two previous illustrations. The hull has a high sheer but the decks have only sufficient to make the water drain away quickly. Among the many interesting features on the plan are: double riding bitts on the lowerdeck; a double-barrelled capstan in the waist and a single-barrelled one, on the lower deck, between the main- and mizzenmasts. Both have the old-fashioned barrel head with a few bar holes. The curved companionway ladders are a feature not usually seen on contemporary models. The ship has her bowsprit stepped to starboard of the foremast and therefore on the same side of the stemhead. The mizzenmast is stepped on the keel although it was not at all unusual at that date to step it on the lower deck.

151. An anchor of about 1600 as reconstructed by J T Tinniswood based on a combination of pictorial evidence and Mainwaring's dictionary. The angle of the arm is 60°. The fluke CD is half the arm AC, and the shank is three times a fluke, plus half the beam CE; the thickness of the shank is 1/11 of the length at the centre.

149

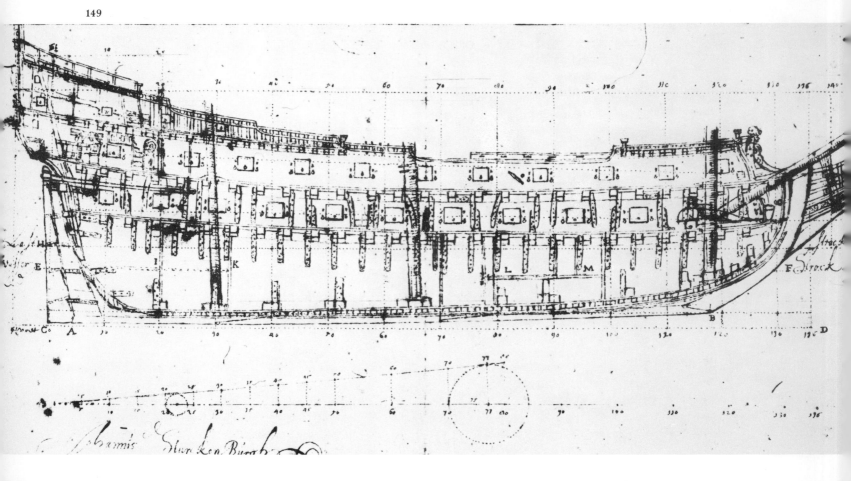

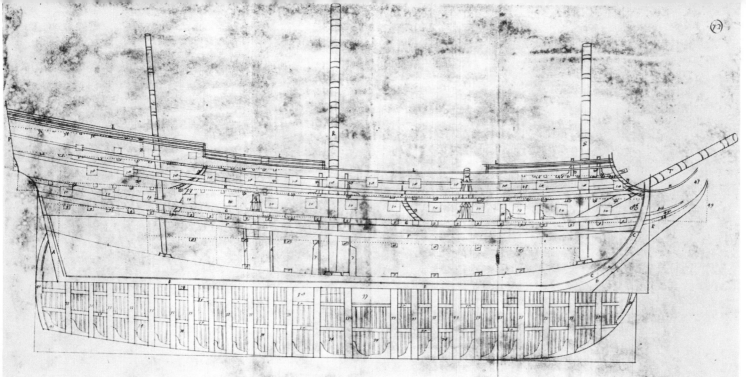

150

152. This model represents a ship of the largest class of Dutch men-of-war (of about 1665), and corresponds to a vessel with a gun-deck length of 154 English feet and an extreme breadth of 42ft. There are ports for 76 guns but it is likely that only 70 were carried. The hull has the shallow draught typical of Dutch ships of that period. Other features that distinguish the ship from contemporary English ones are the clinker planking of the topsides and the paucity of windows in the quarter galleries. The model is an accurate half-size copy of a contemporary model that was in the Hohenzollern Museum, Berlin. The masts and yards have the same proportions as the original model's and the rigging was added by the late Dr R C Anderson according to contemporary data.

151

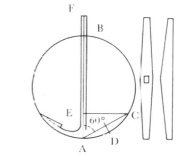

152

had of course to be modified whenever there was risk of damage from gun blast. A channel's width had to be enough to keep the shrouds clear of the side, whilst its thickness was usually half that of the wale to which it was fastened.

Fenders (skids). About the middle of the century the practice of fitting a pair of vertical riders to the outside of the hull, in the waist, began. It was a peculiarly English practice and was not found on Continental ships until the next century and then mostly on French ships. The purpose of the riders was to provide a sort of tramway up which the boats could be hoisted without their catching on the wales. The riders stretched from the bulwark rail to the upper of the lowest pair of wales and were well separated, one being amidships and the other about 1/3 of the gun-deck's length from the stem. Next, a third rider was fitted, about 3ft forward of the aftermost of the original pair. Finally, before the end of the century, a fourth one had been added, about midway between the foremost rider and the pair, an arrangement that lasted until the abolition of fenders in the nineteenth century. Notwithstanding the convenience of the fenders, their general adoption was slow according to the evidence of models, for it is not until after the 1670s that fenders can be regarded as regular fittings.

Entry ports. Until the advent of the 3-decker, entry to a ship was by clambering up some sort of ladder on the ship's side. The addition of the third deck made such a mode of entry inconvenient in the extreme and danger-ous when the ship was rolling. By 1610 someone had hit on the idea of making a door on the middle deck. The *Prince Royal*'s entry port (the earliest recorded) was on the port side. The *Sovereign of the Seas* had her entry port on the port side, just in front of the main channels, and it was, as would be expected on that ship, an ornate affair. The early entry ports did not project from the side but after a while a canopy was built over the doorway and a small platform in front of the port made entry easier. The entry port was reached by a flight of wooden steps, like cleats, nailed to the side, but for important visitors a gangway was probably rigged. The history of entry ports is still obscure. Only one seems to have been fitted, and on the port side, until at least the 1660s, for the earliest example of a port on the starboard side is on a model of the *Royal James* of 1671. From the middle of the 1670s the 3-deckers had two entry ports, and at the end of the century some of the 80-gun 2-deckers had an entry port on each side. Like skids, entry ports seem to have been peculiar to English ships.

Scuppers. These useful fittings are rarely shown on plans or in pictures, nor are they often found on models. They seem to have been about 3in or a little more in diameter and might be either lead tubes or blocks of wood bored through and lined with leather or lead. On the *Dartmouth* the lead scuppers were inclined at 25°. Scuppers were set in the lowest part of the deck and seem

154

153. A 70-gun ship of the late 1690s, smaller than the *Prince* and less richly decorated. The upper deck ports are hinged at their top edges.

154. The entry port of the *Prince* and other broadside details. The vertically hinged port lids are an interesting detail not shown on the Van de Velde drawing (172). Those on the middle-deck port abaft the entry port may have been fitted there because an ordinary, top-hinged lid would have fouled the lanyards of the deadeyes.

155. The forecastle of the *Prince*. The ornate structure in the middle of the bulk-head is the belfry. In the background is the enormous lashing for the end of the mainstay. The capstan is the old-fashioned sort in which the bars go right through the barrel. The lowest bar is so low down that men would not be able to exert their full strength on it.

156. The mainmast and the quarterdeck bulkhead of the *Prince*. The bitts still have the elaborately carved heads that gave the earlier 'knights' their name.

155

156

157. English belfries: *St Andrew*, 1670 (top) and *Mordaunt*, 1682.

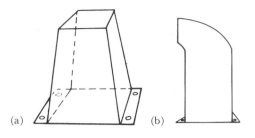

158. Galley chimneys.
(a) Early eighteenth, and therefore probably in use in the late seventeenth century.
(b) About 1692.
(c) Yacht, 1690.
(d) Yacht, about 1690.

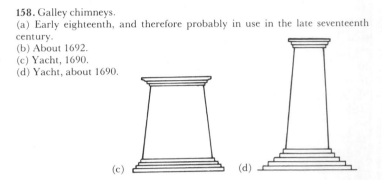

to have been about six in number. The outside orifice was covered by a leather flap valve or had a short length of leather hose attached, to stop sea water rushing back when the ship heeled.

Port lids. The gunport lids on Dutch ships and those from the Baltic States were curved to match the high degree of tumblehome of the sides of the hull, whereas on English ships, except perhaps at the beginning of the century, the port lids were flat. The differences in decoration will be referred to later.

INBOARD HULL FITTINGS

Bulkheads. Until the 1650s it was usual for the forecastle, half-deck and quarterdeck bulkheads to have up to three semi-circular bays, and these had openings for small cannon and hand-guns, but under the Commonwealth the bays were abolished and the bulkheads built flat. However, because cabins were built against the ends of the bulkheads their shape is still apparently bayed. For example, a model of the *Prince* of 1670 has two cabins (with a belfry between them) on the forecastle bulkhead. Similar structures were built against the half-deck and quarterdeck bulkheads, as many 'Navy Board' models show.

Belfry. When precisely the belfry was removed from its traditional site on the break of the half-deck to the fore part of the ship is not certain, although it seems to have been soon after 1660. The new belfry was a small, open-sided cabin that stood close to the forecastle bulkhead on big ships. Others had only an arch that stood above the forecastle bulkhead. Belfry and arches were made in different patterns and were decorated like the rest of the ship. To judge from the evidence of models, belfries seem to have been something of an English speciality for they are not shown on Dutch ships and little evidence for them on others has yet come to light.

Gratings and hatchways. The raised coamings in which the gratings were set, and which might be pierced for musketry, that were in vogue in Elizabethan times gave way to the familiar sort in which the gratings were only a few inches above the deck, a change that reflected the diminished need to make every possible provision for repelling boarders. The main hatchway was between the forecastle bulkhead and the mainmast and there were other hatchways and gratings in the half-deck and on the forecastle.

Galley chimneys. Like scuppers, these prosaic but essential features are not often seen on models or in pictures, nor on plans. For the early part of the century, this is because the cook-room was below decks in the fore part of the hold, although some means of taking the smoke away would be expected. By the end of the century (the date is uncertain) the cook-room had been moved to the forecastle and the galley chimney became a familiar feature.

Capstans and windlasses. As ships became bigger and carried heavier anchors as well as needing larger and therefore heavier spars, the old-fashioned capstan with its few bars was unable to provide enough power. The solution to the problem was found by Sir Samuel Morland, who invented the drum-headed (mushroom-headed) capstan at some time between 1660 and 1680. The earliest example on an English model, however, dates from 1695. Ships had several capstans, at least one, the main capstan, being on the lower deck to bring in the cable. A Danish ship of 1613 was to have both her capstans on the lower deck. A draught of an English 1st Rate of about 1680 shows three capstans (all drum-headed), one on the lower deck abaft the mainmast, another on the middle deck in the waist, and the third on the upper deck a little abaft the forecastle bulkhead. A Swedish plan of about the same date has a different arrangement. The main capstan has two superimposed barrels, one on the lower deck and the other under the half-deck. The other capstan is on the lower deck about midway between the fore- and mainmasts. All the capstans are the old, narrow-headed sort.

Windlasses were used only on the smaller English warships and on boats that were used for weighing anchors. The barrel might be round or octagonal, tapered a little towards each end, and fixed either between a pair of stout posts or else between blocks of wood fastened to the vessel's side. Round the barrel were fixed one or two toothed bands of iron to engage the pawl(s). These were also made of iron and were sometimes ornate. A model of a yacht (in the National Maritime Museum) has pawls that have gilded figures of recumbent dogs on their upper sides. Windlasses were certainly used on quite large Swedish ships, however, for a big one has been recovered from the wreck of the *Gröne Jägeren*, built in 1652.

Pumps. Both hand- and chain-pumps were like those of the preceding century.

Knights and bitts. Until about 1670 the knights on English ships remained as separate posts. One stood a little abaft the fore- and mainmasts, but the mizzen-knight was in front of its mast. Dimensionally, knights were about 2/3 of their mast's diameter in width and slightly less fore and aft. Fore- and mainknights each had three or four sheaves in their upper end and a strong eye-bolt just below the axle of the sheaves, whereas the mizzenknight had only two sheaves. In front of the fore- and mainmasts were smaller knights for the topsail sheets. Each mast had a pair of them, and each had only a single sheave. About 1660 the knights were connected by a cross-bar and became the familiar bitts. A little later the knight abaft the mast was replaced by a second pair of bitts with a cross-bar, but the mizzenmast never had

bitts during the seventeenth century. On the more ornately decorated ships the tops of the knights were carved into heads but many were simply trimmed to a finial. Where the knights and bitts stood, ie upon which deck, at different times during the century is not easy to say. On most ships at the beginning of the century the knights stood on the open deck although they might be covered by the spar deck when the ship had one. When a third true deck was added the mainknights remained on their original deck, which became the middle deck, and the foreknights were put under the forecastle deck. This arrangement was not a rigid one, for some models have their mainknights, or their bitts, on the upper deck and the foreknights/bitts either in the forecastle or up in the open on the forecastle deck.

159. Capstans (not to scale).
(a) 1660–1670.
(b) About 1670.
(c) Late seventeenth century.

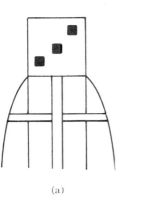
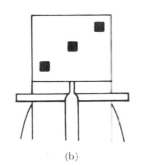
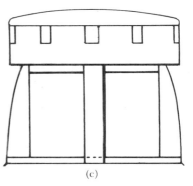

(a)　　　　(b)　　　　(c)

160. A double capstan recovered from the wreck of a large Swedish warship of about 1600. It is 4.25m high.
161. A windlass from the wreck of the Swedish *Gröne Jägaren* built in 1652. It is about 5m long and 0.5m in diameter.

160

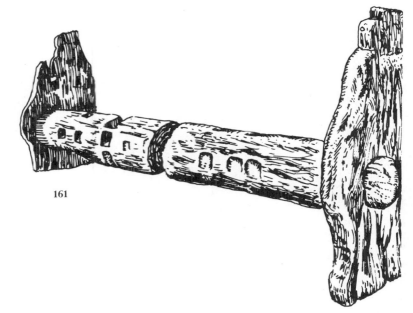

161

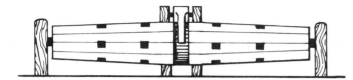

162. A simple windlass (from an English yacht).
163. Various styles of seventeenth century stern lanterns. When there is a 3-armed bracket two of the stays go to the taffrail at the level of the poop, and the third lower down.

In addition to the knights and bitts there were kevels fixed to the inside of the bulwarks, and also large cleats with a sheave in them. Dutch ships, and probably English ones too, had small knights fixed at convenient places along the inside of the bulwarks.

Lanterns. How many lanterns a ship carried is often uncertain. In Vroom's picture of the *Prince Royal* only one appears but it is known from other sources that lanterns were placed at the after ends of the quarter galleries. The other ships in the picture, the *Repulse* and the *Golden Lion,* also have only a single lantern. The *Sovereign of the Seas,* in keeping with her importance, had seven stern lanterns. The biggest stood on the poop and there was one on the first and third domes of each of her quarter galleries, but where the other two stood is not known. After the middle of the century stern lanterns always stood on the poop, one in the middle of the taff-rail and one at each end. Lanterns were also carried, on occasions, in the main-top; a model of a ship of 1685, in the National Maritime Museum, has one.

The shape of lanterns underwent several changes during the century. The early ones were poly-hedral and straight-sided. The *Merhonour*'s stern lantern, in 1622, was 7-sided with seven 'cartrooses' (presumably the window frames), each of the seven faces being separated from its neighbours by carved terms. As there were seven carved fishes as well these may have radiated from the centre of the roof to the edges. The lantern was crowned by a lion and the whole thing was gilded with fine gold[17]. The early lanterns were of great size. Those on the *Repulse* and the *Red Lion* were 4ft or more in height and on top of that was a domed roof. The main lantern of the *Sovereign of the Seas* was quite big, for Pepys recorded in 1660 that ten people stood in it at once. About the middle of the century globular lanterns came into fashion and held the field for some 40 years until they were displaced by a more or less standardised hexagonal form. The globular lanterns seem to have had light chambers about 4ft across. An interesting feature of some lanterns on 'Navy Board' models is that the light is not shown all round. The National Maritime Museum's model of the *Boyne* does not show a light forwards, and the same arrangement occurs on a model of a 40–50 gun ship of 1695. What provided the light in ships' lanterns is uncertain – there is evidence for big candles, but the shape of the bases of some lanterns suggests that oil (whale or colza, perhaps) was used[20].

DECORATION

The fashion for carving, painting and gilding that started in the last years of Queen Elizabeth's reign spread like an epidemic through the Navy as the baroque style was taken up enthusiastically by the English in the seventeenth century. It was given extra impetus by the general belief (among kings) that the appearance of a warship reflected the dignity and importance of the Monarch. The Stuart kings subscribed to this opinion so whole-heartedly that by the 1660s practically every part of the hull above water was painted, gilded or carved and some-times all three. Not only the stern and its associated galleries and the head, but all the minor inboard and outboard works such as belfry, bulkheads, rails, upper gunports and even hawseholes were treated in this way. Nor was profuse and expensive decoration confined to big ships, for yachts had their share. Dutch and French ships were as lavishly decorated as English ones though none matched the *Sovereign of the Seas,* which represents the most extensively and expensively decorated ship ever built. With the exception of the *Wasa,* Danish and Swedish ships were less extravagantly adorned, not perhaps from choice so much as the lack of money. Pictures, plans and models provide accurate information about ship decoration in increasing volume from about 1620 onwards and those sources are supplemented by actual examples: the mass of carved work from the *Wasa,* figureheads, and in Britain a State shallop built in 1689 for Queen Mary[21].

A good deal of source material has been reproduced in the numerous books about sailing ships, so that the general outline of ship decoration can be seen without too much difficulty, but to cover every aspect of the subject in a single chapter is impossible and there-fore, in the sections that follow, only the major features and the principal changes that affected them will be touched on.

The broadside. The excerpts from the accounts for decorating some of Queen Elizabeth's ships in 1598 are evidence that the simple geometric style of ship painting was giving way to, if it had not already been replaced by, a very different style. There is not sufficient evidence to show how general this style was but there is certainly nothing to show that it was exceptional. The two most important ships of the first half of the century, as befitted their rôles as 'prestige ships', had a different style of decoration. Both the *Prince Royal* and the *Sovereign of the Seas* had their sides above the middle deck divided into large panels, each of which enclosed carvings and paint-ings. The details of the former ship's decoration, as shown in Vroom's painting of her at Flushing, are confirmed by contemporary documents but it may have been a specially ornate one for the occasion. The evidence from the first half of the century is too scanty to be specific about decorative details but for the second half the 'Navy Board' models are proof that so far as the broadside was concerned, decoration was anything but lavish. A model of a 40–44 gun ship in the National Maritime Museum has pale blue topsides with scroll-work in gilt[22]. The model of the *St Michael* of 1669 has black topsides and so does the model of a 90-gun ship of 1675, but the model of a 94-gun ship of about 1670 has black topsides with trophies of arms and other military equipment in gilt[23]. Examples with red topsides are known. The lower part of the broadside on models, and as depicted in paintings, is usually shown as plain wood, which on a real ship would be treated with turpentine or varnish, except for the black wales. This was not invariably the case, however, for there is some evidence that a ship's side might be painted black as far up as the upper deck ports, and there is a reference that suggests that the *London* had her broadside painted in black and yellow bands[18].

The most conspicuous features of the broadside were the carved wreaths around the upper deck ports. The wreaths might be circular (which was the most common shape), square, or square with rounded corners. They were gilded or painted in 'gold colour'. Occasionally upper gunports had lion masks round them, the gun firing out of the open mouth. Port lids

themselves were not decorated on the outside but sometimes the inside face was painted or had a carving attached. The decoration, of course, was intended to be seen when the lid was raised.

The head. The sites for decoration on this part were the figurehead, the beak, and the beakhead bulkhead with the catheads. Only the most important ships had elaborate figureheads, the others having a lion in some form placed at the end of the beak and incorporated in its structure. The *Prince Royal*'s figurehead was in a new style. The beak rails ended in a scroll on which stood a huge helmeted head wearing a golden crown, and in front of the scroll was a small platform on which St George, on horseback, was fighting the Dragon. The Saint had only got as far as raising his sword and the

164–168. The almost photographic attention to detail in Van de Velde drawings makes them a fruitful source for the study of seventeenth century ships. This series not only illustrates the differences in the design and ship decoration favoured by the major naval powers, but also spans developments over most of the century.

164. The *Constant Reformation*, a 60-gun ship built in 1619 but not drawn until 1648. The quarter galleries with their flat ends resemble those on the *Repulse* (140) and the *Red Lion* (141). The lower deck has a 'fall' just before the aftermost gun. There is an entry port on the middle deck amidships and a box-like structure forward of the quarter gallery which is probably a latrine. The numerous timberheads would be used for belaying the running rigging.

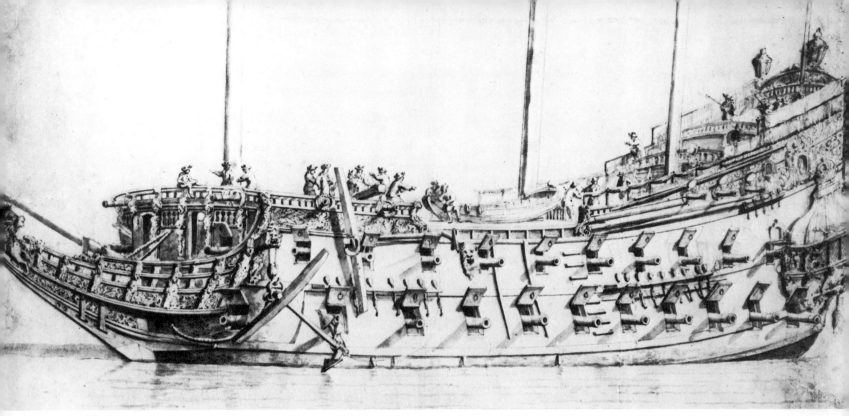

165

165. A Danish 2-decker, the *Hannibal* of 1646. The high sheer and the ogee roof of the quarter gallery indicate Dutch influence. The boat stowed on the spar deck is typically Dutch. The large mask on the broadside in the waist is the chess-tree by which the maintack was led inboard. The chase guns in the beakhead bulkhead are surprisingly low down. One would expect their blast to remove the upper head rails.

166. The *Eendracht*, 72 guns, built in 1653 and blown up in action in 1665 was one of the most famous Dutch ships of the period. The beakhead bulkhead and the topsides of the quarterdeck and poop are clinker-work. Other interesting features are the door in the beakhead bulkhead and the scuppers just above the waterline. They cannot have been of much use when the ship was heeled over. In contrast to English ships of the same period the *Eendracht* has high bulwarks on the quarterdeck and poop.

167

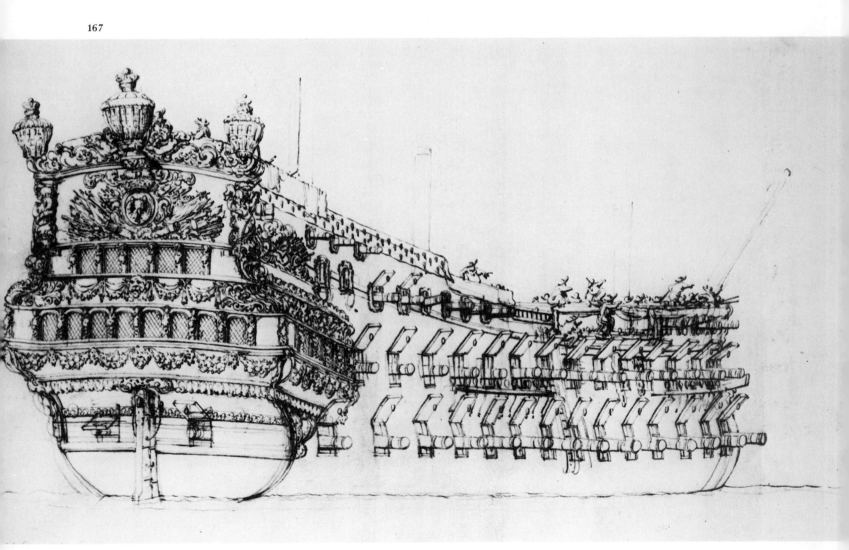

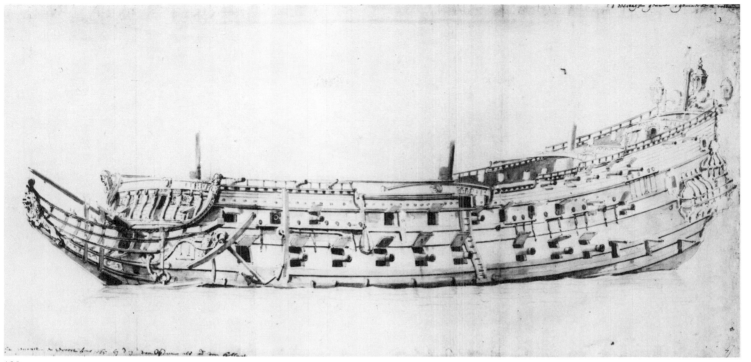

166

167. The *Superbe*, a large French 2-decker built in 1668 as the *Vermandois* (70 guns). The fore and main channels are just below the upper deck guns. There are no mizzen channels.

168. An unidentified Spanish 2-decker. The stern with its two projecting galleries is quite different from those of English and Dutch ships. At the fore end of the lower gallery is an entering ladder.

168

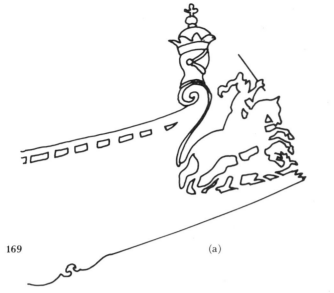

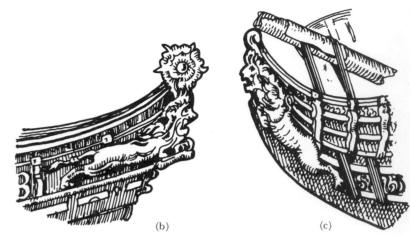

169 (a) (b) (c)

Dragon was making a promising attempt to bite the fore part of the horse. On a draught of a single-decked ship thought to be the *Phoenix* of 1613, the same theme occurs in a more advanced state. The Saint has put his sword through the Dragon's throat and is trying to push the unfortunate beast overboard, a fate likely to befall both combatants in a spell of heavy weather. On the *Sovereign of the Seas* the figurehead stood a little further back and was secured to the end of the beak. It was 'King Edgar trampling on seven kings', a style that Oliver Cromwell imitated on the *Naseby,* for her figurehead was 'Oliver on horseback trampling six nations underfoot: a Scot, Irishman, Dutchman, Frenchman, Spaniard and English, as was easily made out by their several habits. A Fame held a laurel over his insulting head: the words God with us'. When Charles II was restored to the Throne this figurehead was removed and burned and the ship renamed the *Royal Charles.* Its new figurehead was a Neptune. No picture of either figurehead is known.

As a general rule, equestrian heads were to be found only on big ships named after members of the Royal Family, but except for the *Prince Royal* and the *Sovereign of the Seas* there is not much known about equestrian figureheads before the Restoration in 1660. By this date the rounding up of the beak made the horse and rider look as though they were clambering up the back of the stemhead. Other big ships had allegorical figures. The *St Michael* of 1669, for example, had Jupiter in a chariot drawn by a double-headed eagle. For the majority of English ships, however, a lion sufficed. He came in a variety of breeds and his stance was governed by the slope of the beak: on the *Repulse* in 1613 the lion appears to be rushing out from among the head timbers and balancing a huge Tudor Rose on his head. When the stem was rounded up the lion assumed a more or less upright stance and is often shown clutching the top of the stemhead whilst he glares over it. Crowned lions were not uncommon in the first half of the century and were usual after 1660, and after that date they are often accompanied by a cherub on either side. A lion was, in fact, the most common seventeenth century figurehead and the Dutch used no other figure. Lions were popular with the Danes and the Swedes, and also with the Spaniards but not, apparently, with the French. English lions were commonly gilded, even when a ship was called the *Red Lion,* but Dutch lions were usually red with gilded manes.

The head rails and their supporting timbers were decorated and the spaces between the rails and frame timbers panelled on the earlier ships. On the *Prince Royal* the panels bore emblems proclaiming Prince Henry's distinguished ancestry: the Feathers, the Antelope and other Royal badges. The long, low beak of the early seventeenth century must have been a water trap in a seaway, and when the new, steeper stemhead was adopted the sides were left much more open.

The front of the forecastle, the beakhead bulkhead, offered an extensive background for decoration. The *Sovereign of the Seas* had six full length figures there representing the Virtues in the Classical style standing on carved pedestals. Between the figures was scrollwork. The gunports in the bulkhead had wreaths round them and the lower ones were fitted with carved lids. The beakhead bulkhead carried elaborate carving until the restricting order of 1703, and the usual pattern was similar to that of the *Sovereign of the Seas:* six allegorical figures with carvings in between them. Carvings were to be found in two other places in the head, the stemhead and the catheads. One pinnace had a plumed head on top of the stempost but this was not general practice on English ships judging from the few known examples of stempost carvings. Helmeted heads were to be seen on Dutch and Danish ships but at the corners of the forecastle. The *Red Lion* (1613) may have had a crouching lion although in the picture the animal appears to be on the lower end of the bowsprit. One, perhaps two, human figures were placed on the *Sovereign of the Seas'* stempost and the *Prince* of 1670 had a crouching lion. Soon after that date the bowsprit was shifted to the centreline of the ship and the carvings disappeared. After a while, a timber was brought up on each side of the stem to steady the bowsprit. The timbers became known as knightheads and had an appropriate figure carved on their tops.

Catheads and their brackets were also decorated. Carving was at first restricted to the outer end of the cathead and was usually a lion's mask. The sides of the cathead were painted and later the brackets were carved. This carving was sometimes quite elaborate, as on the *Sovereign of the Seas,* which had whole figures of lions (though a picture by van de Velde has human figures). Other ships had human figures in the Classical style under the catheads. This style, it should be remembered, changed during the century and what was popular during James I's reign (1603–25) was unfashionable by the reign of James II (1685–88).

169

169

253

169. Seventeenth century figureheads.
(a) *Prince Royal*.
(b) *Red Lion*.
(c) *Victory*, 1665.
(d) 70-gun ship of about 1670.
170. The *St Michael* of 90 guns, an English 1st Rate built in 1669. Because the English had deeper water at the approaches to their harbours they could build bigger ships than the Dutch, factors that were in their favour in their wars with the Dutch. Note the Jupiter figurehead.

(d)

170

172

171. The stern of the *Prince* of 1670. Unlike the Dutch stern (173) this one is a mass of windows. The many small panes of glass (or sometimes mica) that made up the windows are represented on the model by dotted rectangles inside the window frames.

172. A drawing of the stern of the *Prince* by W Van de Velde that generally confirms the accuracy of the model. However, in some respects the drawing differs from the model, for example in the decoration between the Feathers on the quarter and the mizzen channels, in the cabin windows at the fore end of the poop and in the ornate entry port. These differences may be due to model and drawing having been made at different dates, alterations having been made to the ship meanwhile. (The original drawing is in the Rijksmuseum, Amsterdam.)

173. The stern of the *Hollandia*, 82 guns, of 1664. The *Hollandia* was one of the biggest Dutch warships but was only a 2-decker. She was the flagship of the famous Admiral de Ruyter. The *Hollandia's* stern differs from those of English ships in the absence of windows and galleries, and in the excessive use of larger than life figures. An interesting feature of the poop is the clinker planking of the topsides.

173

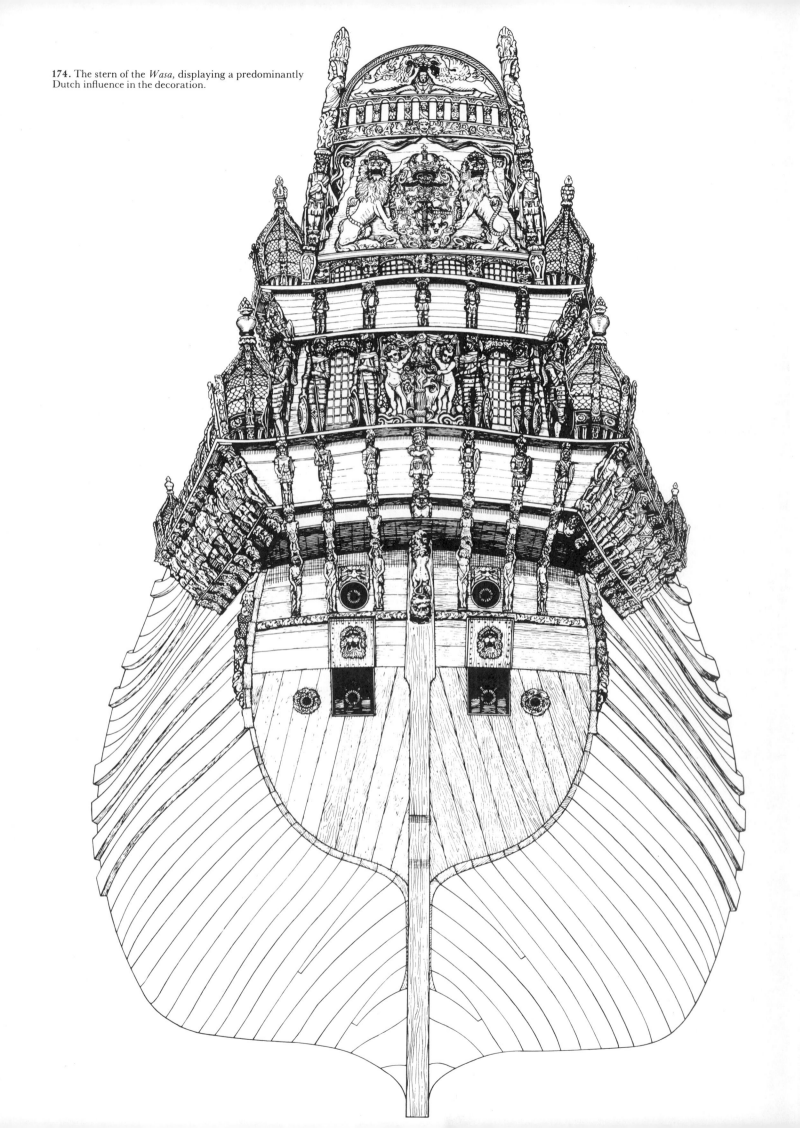

174. The stern of the *Wasa*, displaying a predominantly Dutch influence in the decoration.

Quarter galleries and stern. Not only were these the most extensively and most ornately decorated parts of the ship but they underwent more changes in structure and style of ornament than either the head or the broadside. Moreover, the sterns and galleries of foreign ships were often quite different from those of English ships and were decorated in a different manner. Ships' sterns, in fact, constitute a form of Baroque art that has not yet been fully explored. The only comprehensive English study of the subject is L G Carr Laughton's *Old Ships Figureheads and Sterns*, originally published in 1927. The elaboration of stern decoration on English ships began early in the century. The *Prince Royal*'s stern was still basically that in vogue during the sixteenth century, namely two flat surfaces, the upper one projecting slightly over the lower, both these and the sides of the galleries being profusely decorated with the Royal Arms and the emblems of the Prince's ancestry. Carved work, though plentiful, was not yet the most conspicuous feature of the stern. On the *Sovereign of the Seas*, in contrast, the stern was a mass of gilded carving from the lower deck upwards. Horizontal bands of heraldic emblems and figures in the Classical style alternated with rows of windows, the bands being linked together by carved pilasters. The Royal Arms stood over the rudder-head and at the top of the taffrail a group made up of a winged Victory and a pair of Sea Gods presided over the whole scheme. This ship, as is well known, was exceptional in the opulence of her decoration, but even comparatively small ships had a great deal of carved work on their sterns and quarter galleries and the amount increased

with the years. Nor were the ships of other countries any less decorated, although there were interesting differences to be seen between, for example, the sterns of Dutch and French ships and those of English vessels. The Dutch preferred, on the whole, to keep the upper part of the stern (the part above the level of the maindeck) free of windows and used the flat expanse as a surface to be covered with carvings or paintings. The *Gouda* of 1670 had a painting of a seaport on her taffrail and the *Hollandia* of 1664 had a coat of arms. Another Dutch ship (but possibly a Danish one) had an elephant there[24]. The fashion was not exclusively Dutch, for a Danish ship of 1680 had a large coat of arms on its taffrail and a French vessel of 1668 had a painting of a Roman ship. On the whole, however, French sterns were similar in general layout to English ones having rows of windows separated by galleries, and profuse carving. A feature more common on foreign than on English ships was the presence of larger than life-size figures at the corners of the stern (the quarters). Some were enormous and must have added undesirable stresses to the stern's framework as the ship rolled.

A minor feature remains to be mentioned although it is not strictly decoration. French ships,

175. The *Konung Karl*, a 90-gun ship built at Karlskrona, Sweden, in 1683. The ornate stern and open galleries resemble those of contemporary French ships. The head is very low, on a level with the lower deck. The figurehead represents Karl XI on horseback. There is a large entry port on the starboard side and presumably another one on the port side.

175

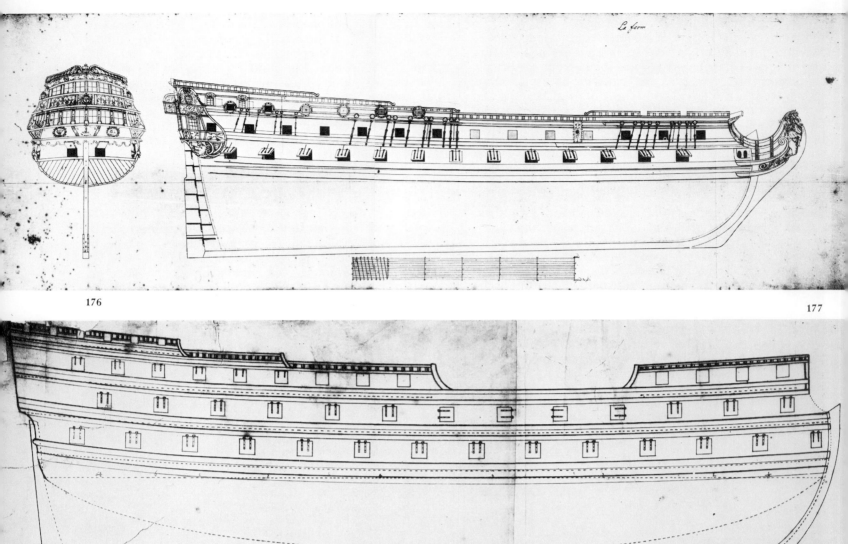

176

177

176. An original draught of *La Ferme*, a French 70-gun ship built in the 1690s. Like many of Louis XIV's warships, the sheer runs 'down hill' towards the bow without any rise forward. Note the name in a small plaque on the counter.

177. The Danish 2-decker *Dannebrog* of 1692. She has vertically hinged port lids on the upper deck in the waist. The stern is quite different from English or Dutch sterns.
178. The Danish 2-decker *Christianus Quintus* of 1665. Gun-deck length 146ft and breadth 38ft.

178

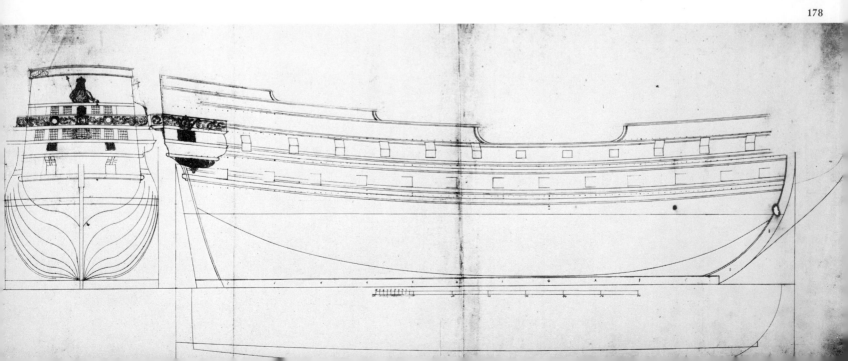

according to contemporary drawings, carried their names on panels fixed to the lowest stern gallery but the ships of other countries do not seem to have had them there or anywhere else.

Inboard works. Within the limited areas available, the inboard bulkheads and other structural features were as highly decorated as the head and stern and it is probably true to say that only the gun carriages were not carved, although they were painted. The bulkheads were adorned with carved pilasters and with vertical brackets with half- or full-figures on them. The belfry was treated in a similar manner. There were also carved balusters to the stairways from the quarterdeck. In addition, the flat surfaces of the panelled work might be painted.

Paintwork was used more extensively in the seventeenth than in previous centuries. Its use has, perhaps, been overlooked because of the fame (or notoriety) of the gilding on the *Prince Royal* and the *Sovereign of the Seas* and the lack of contemporary plans showing how a ship was to be painted. The earliest English example of a painting contract is that for the *Henry* and the *London* in 1655, according to which 'The figure of their head to be gilded with the two figures upon the galleries, and the arms upon the upright of the stern. Their heads [ie the ships' heads], sterns, galleries, rails, brackets and ports, their sides, timberheads and planksheers all to be primed and blacked as well as ever hath been used in the Navy, and painted gold colour proper to the carved work in oil, in form and manner as the *Resolution*. Their great cabins and staterooms to be walnut tree colour in oil, grained and revailed, and what is proper to be gilded to be laid gold colour suitable to the *Naseby* [ie like the *Naseby*'s decoration]. Their roundhouses and other cabins to be stone colour and green ... their half-decks, cuddy and forecastle to be of wanescote or other colour according to the direction of the master shipwright. Their bulkhead cabins upon their decks and quarter-decks, bitts, knight-heads, brackets and other things usual to be primed and painted as without board'[19].

There is a great deal of interest in this contract. Perhaps the most surprising feature is the extent of black painting to be done. It might be supposed that this reflected the serious views of life taken by the Puritans did the contract not include the phrase 'as well as ever hath been used in the Navy' nor refer to the *Resolution*'s decoration as a pattern, for she was the former *Prince Royal* (though in her rebuilt form) and one of the principal ships in the Navy. As the contract reads it suggests that much of the outside of the ships was to be black. Another interesting reference is to the use of 'gold colour' for gilding instead of gold leaf. Gold colour was produced by painting wood-tar, or a yellowish brown varnish, over a white ground and resembled the golden yellow decoration on English long-case clocks of the late eighteenth and early nineteenth century. It is likely that the use of this gold

colour gave rise to the popular belief that seventeenth century ships carried extensive true gilded work, a belief that seems to be reflected in the extensive use of gold paint on modern models of seventeenth century ships and in the restoration of contemporary ones. Although oil paints are mentioned without any special comment they were not bright and highly glossy materials such as present day paints, for the mode of preparation of neither the pigments nor the oils used was capable of producing the high purity materials on which brightness of shade depends. The shades, by present day standards, were distinctly dull. Some of the 'paints' used for inside work were really size-bound distempers and would have had a matt or 'eggshell' surface when dry.

MASTS AND YARDS

Contemporary books and manuscripts, accurate delineation of rigging by artists of the Dutch School and their followers, and models with their original rigging more or less intact allow the changes that took place during the seventeenth century to be followed in something like complete detail. The changes can be summed up quite shortly. For the masts, they were the introduction of the spritsail topmast at the end of the bowsprit, the abolition of the after- or bonaventure mizzen, and the carrying of fore and main topgallant masts as part of the regular establishment. New sails that appeared were the square mizzen topsail, staysails and, just at the end of the century, the jib on big ships. Stunsails became regular gear but their early history is still obscure.

The growing awareness of the Navy's importance is reflected in the number of documents that give the sizes of masts, yards and rigging for ships of every sort but because the seventeenth century was not an age of standardised products two very similar ships could, and did, have different sized masts and rigging. In the sections that follow an attempt is made to give an overall picture and lay down general principles. For the minutiae of rigging it will be necessary to consult some of the specialised sources listed in the bibliography.

Lower masts and bowspirit. The length of the main lower mast was the yardstick by which the lengths of the other masts were determined. Its length could be calculated in several ways: as a fraction of the keel length, as a multiple of the breadth or from one formula or another involving both keel length and breadth. One suspects, however, that some of these formulae were early examples of 'blinding with science'. From the length of the lower mainmast those of the fore- and mizzenmasts and the bowsprit were calculated by established formulae. Some typical proportions are given in the table, which has been compiled from several sources of which the main ones are *Seventeenth Century Rigging* by R C Anderson and *The Masting and Rigging of English Ships of War 1625–1860* by J Lees[25].

TYPICAL PROPORTIONS OF LOWER MASTS – Seventeeth Century							
	1600	1613	1618	1640	1655	1670	1684
Main lower mast as multiple of beam	2.38–2.7	2.4	2.43	2.4	2.5	2.3	2.3
Foremast as fraction of mainmast	0.9–0.93	0.8			0.89	0.9	0.9
Mizzenmast as fraction of the mainmast	0.73–0.76	*	*	*	*	0.67	0.67
Bonaventure mizzenmast as fraction of mainmast	0.58						
Main masthead as fraction of mainmast	0.067		0.067			0.11	0.11–0.125
Fore masthead as fraction of main masthead		0.8				0.9	

The proportion of the mizzen masthead was between 0.6 and 0.7 of main masthead.
*Length depended upon where mast was stepped.

179

179. Dutch warships – a grisaille of 1654 by W Van de Velde the Elder. The extraordinary accuracy with which the hull and rigging is rendered makes Van de Velde pictures, like the drawings, a first class source of information about ships of the seventeenth century.

180

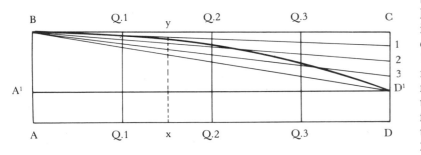

180. A scale for determining the intermediate diameters of masts and yards taken from *Shipbuilding Unveiled* by William Sutherland, 1727. AD represents the length of the mast from the partners to the masthead and AB and CD represent the diameter of the mast at the partners and AA' and DD' its diameter at the masthead. Q.1, Q.2 and Q.3 are the quarters of the length and 1, 2 and 3 represent the quarters of CD' (which is the difference between the maximum diameter of the mast and its diameter at the masthead). B is joined by straight lines to 1, 2, 3 and D' and a smooth curve is drawn from B to D' through the points of intersection of Q.1 and B-1, Q.2 to B-2, and Q.3 with B-3. To obtain the proportionate diameter at any point along AD a perpendicular is drawn from AD to the curve BD'. The ratio of the length of the perpendicular, eg XY, to AB gives the diameter of the mast at that point. The intermediate diameters of yards may be found in the same way, AB representing the maximum diameter of the yard and DD' its diameter at the yardarm.

The uncertainty about the mizzenmast's length arises because it was sometimes stepped in the hold and sometimes on the lower deck. In practice, its length had to be enough to bring the mizzen cap to a level about half way up the fore masthead. The bonaventure mast disappeared after 1625 but lingered on in the rigging lists until about 1640. The length of the foremast is not a ready measure of its height above deck because as the fore end of the keel was extended forward the mast's heel was brought lower down. The above-deck length did increase, nonetheless, for in about 1600 the foremast's cap was about level with the main trestletrees but by 1670 it had reached a point about half way up the main masthead. In this connection it should be noted, when reconstructing a rigging plan, that the height of the main trestletrees above the keel is greater than their distance from the mast's foot because the mainmast stood on a thick step that might be as much as 4ft on a big ship and 2ft on a small one. The figures given in the table are all for big ships; the mainmasts of small ships were significantly longer in proportion to the breadth. The *Lion's Whelps*, of 185 tons, had mainmasts that were 3 times the beam (which was 25ft).

It is often stated that a mainmast's diameter at the partners was 1/36 of its length but that is true only up to the 1660s, and after that it was 15/16in per yard of length or just over 1/38. For small ships the proportion was 1/48. The foremast's diameter was 15/16 of the mainmast's for most of the century but in about 1700 it was increased to the same as the mainmast. The mizzenmast's thickness was 15/16in per yard except possibly during the first quarter of the century, when it was stated by one writer to be 1in per yard (1/36)[26]. Masts tapered

181

towards both ends from the partners. Taking the diameter at the partners as 1, it was 3/4 at the hounds of the fore- and mainmasts and 2/3 at the masthead. The heel was about 2/3 of the maximum diameter. The mizzenmast tapered rather more, to 1/2 the maximum diameter. All the masts tapered in arcs of circles and a scale, one of many, is given here for working out the diameters at different points along the mast.

The position of the mainmast varied a little. It may have been just in front of the mid-point of the keel at the beginning of the century, but by the middle of the century it was near the mid-point of the gun-deck and therefore well before the middle of the keel. Later, the mast was moved back until it was abaft the gun-deck's mid-point (about 1/25 of the deck's length). In the foremast's case there was an apparent and an actual movement backwards. The first was a result of extending the fore end of the keel, which brought the waterline further forward, but there was also a definite shift aft until, about 1700, the foremast was one-third of the way between the end of the keel and the stemhead. The mizzenmast of 3-masted ships had been moved forward from its old position at the after end of the poop by 1613, and possibly even before 1600, to one about half way between the taffrail and the mainmast. Then it was moved backwards slightly, to a position about 0.4 of the

distance between the taffrail and the mainmast. The bonaventure mizzen on 4-masters kept its traditional place close to the taffrail but no definite rule has been found for the main mizzen. A little nearer to the bonaventure mizzen then to the mainmast seems to be the usual position.

Masts were given some degree of rake. The foremast usually leaned slightly forwards although instances of it being vertical are known; the mainmast leaned backwards up to as much as 1/25 of its length, but like the foremast it was sometimes vertical. The mizzenmast always sloped backwards and to a slightly greater degree than the mainmast.

Mastheads were cut square in section. At the hounds the square was the inscribed one corresponding to the mast's diameter there and from the hounds to the top of the mast the masthead was tapered, the port and starboard sides being parallel but the other two converging. Below the hounds were two thick brackets that supported the trestletrees and if the yard was hoisted by tyes (on English ships) the brackets had a sheave for the tye.

The lower parts of the fore- and mainmasts, but not mizzenmasts, were strengthened by rope wooldings and iron bands. The *Sovereign of the Seas* had more than a dozen wooldings on her mainmast but 8 to 10 was the usual number in the second half of the century. Foremasts had 6 to 8. Wooldings on big ships were made of 3in rope and enough turns were put on to make a band about equal in depth to the mast's diameter. Above and below each woolding was an iron band.

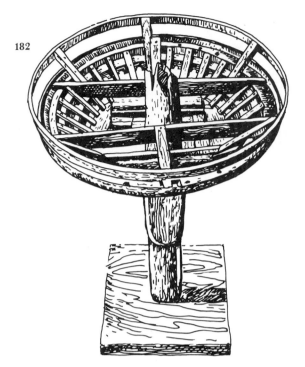

182. A model of a Swedish circular top of about 1600.

183. A gull's eye view of a shipyard, one of the illustrations in A C Raalamb's *Skeps Byggerij* of 1693. On the left (fig 8) a ship is being hove down so that the bottom can be repaired. The operation is shown in progress at the top right hand corner. Just below (fig 7) another ship is shown hove down alongside the sheer-hulk, a sort of floating crane used to put in or remove masts from a ship. Near the top centre, and halfway down the left hand side, ships are being constructed in the Dutch manner, in which the bottom planks are set in place before the frames are erected.

LENGTHS OF BOWSPRITS – Seventeenth Century		
Date	Proportion of foremast	Proportion of mainmast
1600	0.9–1.0	0.8–0.92
1627	1.0	0.8
1684	0.74	0.67

The long bowsprits shown in pictures were not figments of the artists' imaginations. They were long, sometimes as long as the foremast, as the accompanying table shows. The maximum thickness of bowsprits was 1/36 of the length in 1627 but thereafter it was 15/16in per yard of length. The outer end of the bowsprit was one-half of the maximum diameter and the taper between the two points was an arc of a circle. Bowsprits were fixed at an angle of 20° to 24° to the horizontal in the early years but the angle had increased to 30° by the 1670s, and as the stem knee was rounded up the angle increased to about 35° by 1700. What made bowsprits seem so long was the amount of their length that was outboard. At the beginning of the century about 3/4 was visible but by 1650 it had been reduced to 2/3 and 20 years later to almost 3/5. Bowsprits were woolded. The first was between the stemhead and the gammoning, there was one about 10ft from the outer end of the bowsprit and 3 or 4 between that one and the gammoning. Until the 1670s English ships had their bowsprits to one side of the stem, probably always on the starboard side, but after that date the bowsprit was moved to the centreline and bedded on top of the stemhead.

183

Tops and caps. The foundation of a top on the lower masts, and on topmast heads if tops were carried there as they sometimes were in the first 30 to 40 years of the century, was a pair of fore and aft supports, the trestletrees, that were fastened, one on each side of the mast, at the hounds. The crosstrees were fixed, in slots, across and at right angles to the trestletrees. The fore crosstree was sufficiently far forward to allow the topmast to be lowered but the after one was close to the masthead. Early seventeenth century tops were bowl-shaped and deep, and had a complex framework, but they were gradually replaced by saucer-like tops and then by flat ones, until by 1700 the rim of the top was only about 9in high. In action, cloth screens were fixed round the rims of tops, presumably on wood or iron stanchions set in the rim. In the floor of a top was a hole through which the shrouds passed and by which access was gained to the top (the later 'lubber's hole'). The hole was usually square and about 1/3 to 2/5 of the diameter of the top, and its centre was slightly forward of the centre of the top's floor. Tops were circular in plan on English ships until the 1690s, when the after edge of the mizzen top was made straight to allow the yard to be topped higher. A few years later fore and main tops were made in the same way. Continental ships' tops seem to have been circular throughout. Pictures of early tops show them as small compared with tops from about 1650 onwards; for the bowl-shaped tops this may be true but on English warships from about 1640, at least, the main top's width was between 1/3 and 2/5 of the ship's breadth. A list of the sizes of tops for each Rate of ship in 1664 has rather larger dimensions – the widths given in the list are presumably those of the floors of the tops but the flare of the sides would have made the overall widths appreciably bigger. When actual dimensions of tops are not available the floor's diameter can usually be taken as 7/6 of the length of the trestletrees. On the mainmast these were 0.3 to 0.36 of the beam for big ships and 0.25 for small ones. Another way of reckoning the trestletrees' lengths was to make them equal to, or slightly longer than, the masthead. The depth of trestletrees was sometimes taken as 1/13 of their length and by other writers as 1/2 the thickness of the mast at the hounds. Trestletrees were narrower than they were deep, about 7/8 or 9/10, or, alternatively, the width was 1/2 the thickness of the masthead at the cap. As a rule, crosstrees were slightly shorter than trestletrees, and had the same depth but only half the width. Both had the same tapered shape.

The top at the end of the bowsprit was made in the same way as those on lower masts but the trestletrees were fastened to a knee that stood at the end of the bowsprit. Crosstrees were set on top of the trestletrees and the floor of the top was built up as before. There is a remarkable statement in an anonymous treatise on rigging written about 1620–25 that the crosstrees on the bowsprit were made of *iron*[1]. No other instance of this is known. Bowsprit tops were never bowl-shaped but in early pictures they are shown as saucer-like. Later, like other tops, they were made flatter but in plan they were always circular. The knee on the bowsprit, around which the top was constructed, stood a little way inboard from the end of the bowsprit until about 1670, when it was moved outwards to be flush with the end of the spar. The upright arm of the knee was about 1/2 the length of the main masthead and the part on the bowsprit was as long, or a little longer. In thickness the knee was about 1/2 the main masthead's thickness. It is not certain that all classes of ships had bowsprit tops. There is slight but

definite evidence from the last decade or so of the century that sometimes there was no top and the spritsail topmast shrouds were taken to a kind of small channel shaped like a letter B, and, later still, to bolts in the bowsprit.

Masthead caps do not present any difficulties. English caps were always oblong, their length, breadth and depth usually being 1/2, 3/11 and 3/14 of the masthead's length. The centre of the square hole for the lower masthead was at 1/3 of the long axis of the cap; the hole for the topmast was circular and its centre was at 1/4 of the length of the cap from the fore end. All the edges of the cap were rounded off. Continental ships' caps were quite a different shape and several variations are known. The grooves in the tops of the caps were to take the topsail tyes.

Topmasts. The shape of a topmast differed from that of a lower mast in two respects. The heel of the topmast, the part below the masthead cap through which the topmast passed, was usually cut square to a section that was slightly wider than the diameter of the topmast at the point at which it passed through the cap. The length of the squared section is uncertain because although (on models) its top end usually comes about 1/4 of the way up the lower masthead the extent to which the heel protruded below the trestletrees varied. For most of the century it was equal to about twice the depth of the trestletrees. The lower end might be left square, or it might have the edges rounded off. In the heel were sheaves for one, or two, top-ropes.

The heels of topmasts were not invariably square-sectioned. A plan by the Swedish naval architect Raalamb shows a topmast with a round heel and a circular cross-section[27]. The other difference between topmasts and lower masts was in the shape of the upper end. Instead of having cheeks or bibs to support the trestletrees the upper part of the mast was shaped to leave a slightly wider part on which a ledge was cut to hold the trestletrees. Above that part the masthead was made in the normal shape, and between the heel and the masthead the topmast tapered in the same way that lower masts did. Spritsail topmasts were smaller versions of topmasts but differed in lacking a sheave for the top-rope, which was not required on the spritsail topmast. The heel of the mast rested on the bowsprit until about 1670, when its site was moved forward to place the mast's heel just beyond the bowsprit's end. The mast then rested on a fid as topmasts did. The lengths of topmasts as fractions of the main lower mast's length are shown in the table.

LENGTHS OF TOPMASTS – Seventeenth Century			
	About 1600	About 1620–50	1650–1700
Spritsail topmast	*	0.15–0.20	0.15–0.20
Fore topmast	0.38–0.44	0.45	0.54
Main topmast	0.45–0.52	0.50	0.60–0.67
Main mizzen topmast	0.28	0.33	0.30–0.35
Bonaventure mizzen topmast	0.21–0.24	0.25	–

*There is no spritsail topmast in the rigging list for the Queen's ships in 1600 but its gear is recorded in 1611. The bonaventure mizzenmast had disappeared by 1625 or thereabouts.

184. English and Dutch mastheads.

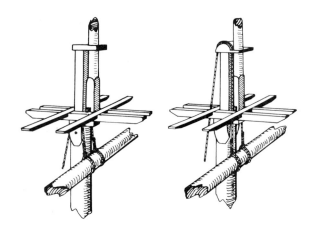

185. Dutch and French mast caps in development, sixteenth to eighteenth century.

The diameters of topmasts at the lower mast cap, expressed as fractions of the lower mast's maximum diameter were: fore topmast 0.45–0.54; main topmast 0.5–0.6; and main mizzen topmast 0.3–0.36. The diameter of the bonaventure mizzen topmast is not known. Spritsail topmasts were 15/16in wide for every yard of length. The diameters of topmasts just below the hounds was usually 3/4 of what it was at the lower cap.

Topgallant masts. Only the fore- and mainmasts had topgallant masts and those only on the big ships. The lower ends of the masts were like the heels of topmasts and had sheaves for the top-rope. They were smaller versions of the topmasts and, except in the early years of the century when the upper parts may have acted as flagstaffs, topgallant masts were fitted with trestletrees and crosstrees. Their lengths as fractions of their respective topmast's lengths are shown in the table.

LENGTHS OF TOPGALLANT MASTS
– Seventeenth Century

	About 1600	1620	About 1650	1670	1700
Fore	0.50–0.67	0.40	0.50	0.42	0.50
Main	0.52	0.40	0.50	0.42	0.50

Flagstaffs were like small topgallant masts except that their upper ends had a truck instead of trestletrees etc. Trucks might be flattened spheres, like present day ones, or globular, or they might have a conical spike on top of the truck. The length of flagstaffs was very variable and no general rule seems to have been in force. On a random selection of models and pictures the lengths of flagstaffs works out, as a proportion of the respective topmasts, as: spritmast 0.5–0.55; foremast 0.24–0.55; mainmast 0.2–0.5; and mizzenmast 0.4–0.75. On the whole, Continental ships had shorter flagstaffs than English ships but there is too little evidence available yet to be certain.

Topmast tops, trestletrees and caps. The depiction of tops at the heads of the fore and main topmasts (and on the mizzen topmast also on the *Sovereign of the Seas*) is confirmed for English ships by the 1640 list of tops' sizes. By 1664, however, only the lower masts had tops. Topgallants, to give them their proper name, were constructed in the same way as the lower tops but were only

half as wide. Topgallants were replaced by trestletrees and crosstrees, and the number of the latter was always the same as the number of topgallant (or flagstaff) shrouds. In 1675 topmast trestletrees' dimensions were given as multiples of the diameter of the topmast head, ie length 5, width 4/7, and depth 1 diameter less ½in. Other sources suggest that the topmast trestletrees should be 2/5 of those on the lower masts. Crosstrees were slightly longer than the trestletrees, 5½ diameters of the topmast head, and they had the same breadth but were only half as deep. The outer thirds of the crosstrees were curved. When a ship had a topgallant mast the crosstrees were set with their ends curving aft. If there were three topgallant shrouds the two after crosstrees were set right against the masthead, one fore and one aft, but the foremost one was sufficiently far forward to allow the topgallant mast to be lowered. When there were only two shrouds the middle crosstree was left off. Flagstaffs also required shrouds, usually two, and for these the foremost crosstree curved forwards and the other one aft.

Only one example is known of tops on the topgallant masts: the *Sovereign of the Seas* had them on all three masts.

All ships had flagstaffs whether or not they had topgallant masts, and the flagstaffs were set up like masts. If topgallant trestletrees were present on a ship their proportions were based on the topgallant mast in the same way that lower tops were based on the lower masts. A hybrid form of top, called a half-top, was in use on some Swedish ships at the end of the century. Caps on topmast and topgallant mastheads were the same shape as lower mast caps and were similarly proportioned to their respective masts.

Yards. At about the beginning of the century three new sails, and of course their yards, came into use. They were the spritsail topsail, the crossjack (mizzen course) and the square mizzen topsail. The mizzen course had only a short run for its money and disappeared by the 1620s but its yard was retained to spread the square mizzen topsail. This, and the spritsail topsail, soon established themselves as standard items. At about the same time that the new sails were brought into use the lateen mizzen topsail and the bonaventure mizzen became obsolete. The lateen topsail was never anything but a fair weather sail and we know no more about its use in the early seventeenth century than in earlier times. It was officially abolished in 1618 but had fallen into desuetude long before that date. The bonaventure mizzen probably disappeared before 1625 although its official existence was prolonged until 1640.

All the 'square' yards had the same shape: round in section and tapering towards the ends. Towards the end of the century, however, the lower yards on English ships had their central part, for a distance about equal to the width of the top, made octagonal. Topsail yards were short compared with lower yards until about the middle of the century, after which they were gradually increased in length until, by 1700, topsail yards were twice as long as they were at the beginning of the century. The growth in length coincided with the re-introduction of reefing, although which came first has not been settled. Certainly, reefing topsails would have been impracticable with the old, short topsail yards.

The lengths of lower yards could be calculated in several ways, all of them ultimately connected with either the keel's length or the maximum breadth of the ship, but no single rule based on one or other of those dimensions was in use. The length of the mainyard, which was the usual standard for the lower yards, was sometimes expressed as a fraction of the keel's length and sometimes as a fraction of the main lower mast, this in turn being calculated from the keel's length or the breadth and sometimes from a combination of both. The relationship between mainyard length and keel length varied but, except for a few examples at the beginning of the century, may be summed up by saying that in 1600 the mainyard was 0.8 of the keel's length, in 1627 it was 0.83 and between 1650 and 1700 it ranged from 0.8 to 0.95. The later figures do not give the complete picture, however, because during the second half of the century keels were made longer for a given gun-deck length, so that a ship of, say, 1680 would have had a longer mainyard than one of 1650 although the gun-decks were the same length. Moreover, since the lengths of the upper yards were often calculated from that of the mainyard, an increase in its length meant an increase in the lengths of the other yards. In practice, the use of different bases for calculating the lengths of yards makes a comparison of their sizes at different times during the century a matter of some difficulty. In the accompanying table the data given in four contemporary documents have been standardised as a fraction of either the mainmast's or the mainyard's length.

According to the scanty evidence, English yards in the first half of the century were 3/4in in thickness for every yard of length (1/48). In the second half, however, the thickness was 5/8in for every yard (nearly 1/58). On Dutch ships the yards were 1/44 of their length in thickness and on French ones 1/48. Yards tapered towards their ends in arcs of circles. What the degree of taper was before 1684 is not known but a manuscript of that date gives the proportionate diameters as: first quarter 23/24; second quarter 6/7; third quarter 2/3; and yardarm 1/3. Yards had an assortment of cleats and chocks to keep the various ropes in place. Unfortunately, although these fittings often seem to be so obviously useful they are not mentioned in contemporary accounts of masts and yards. The absence of reference may, of course, merely reflect the writers' beliefs that such obvious items did not need mentioning and the cleats and chocks may have been in use long before the first documentary reference to them. There were chocks at the ends of the yardarms to stop the braces etc slipping off the yards as early as 1623, but

chocks on the inner side, to stop the ropes slipping inwards, are not recorded on English ships before the 1690s although they were in use on Swedish ships at that date, apparently as normal fittings. The position of the inner chocks was governed by the length of the yardarm, which was 1/25 of the yard's length except on the cross-jack and spritsail yards, which had yardarms 1/20 of the yard's length. Yardarms towards the end of the century may have been longer, at any rate those on the topsail yards, which had reached 1/12 of the yard-length by 1720. On the middle part of the yard there were cleats to hold the tye, jeer-blocks and parrel-rope in place, and at the end of the century (and possibly long before) a kind of short jackstay was fitted to the fore side of the lower yards and the robands were fastened to it instead of being taken round the yard. Continental ships had similar arrangements. Lateen yards differed from 'square' yards in having the lower half thicker than the upper half, which had the same proportions as a 'square' yard.

	Middle	1st quarter	2nd quarter	3rd quarter	End
LATEEN YARD TAPER — Seventeenth Century					
Upper half	1	23/24	6/7	2/3	1/3
Lower half	1	29/30	11/12	3/4	1/2

As well as their normal sails, seventeenth century ships had some stunsails, though how many is not known with any certainty. English ships had fore and main stunsails in about 1625 and Dutch ships a few years later (always remembering that the first record of an innovation is not necessarily the date of its first appearance) but they are not found in rigging lists before about 1650. The introduction of upper stunsails is even less well attested but they were in use in the last quarter of the century on the fore and main topsail yards. The uncertainty about the number of stunsails extends to how they were spread. The scanty evidence points to the early stunsails being triangular, with the foot spread by a boom. At the beginning this may have been merely lashed to the yard but towards the end of the century a figure-of-eight iron strap was fitted to the yardarm. On big ships there was a similar one about 1/3 of the way from the yardarm to the mast but on small vessels the inner end of the boom was lashed to the yard. As a general rule, stunsail booms were fixed on the fore side of the yard but Dutch ships had them on the after side. Towards the end of the century lower stunsail booms were one-half the length of the corresponding yard on big ships and three-quarters on small ones. Those for topsail stunsails were 0.54 and 0.35. In diameter, lower booms were about 1/72 to 1/75 of their length but the upper ones were 1/52.

186. Topmast heels and topropes.

187. The rigging plan of the *Royal Louis* of 1692, from Paris' *Souvenirs de Marine*.

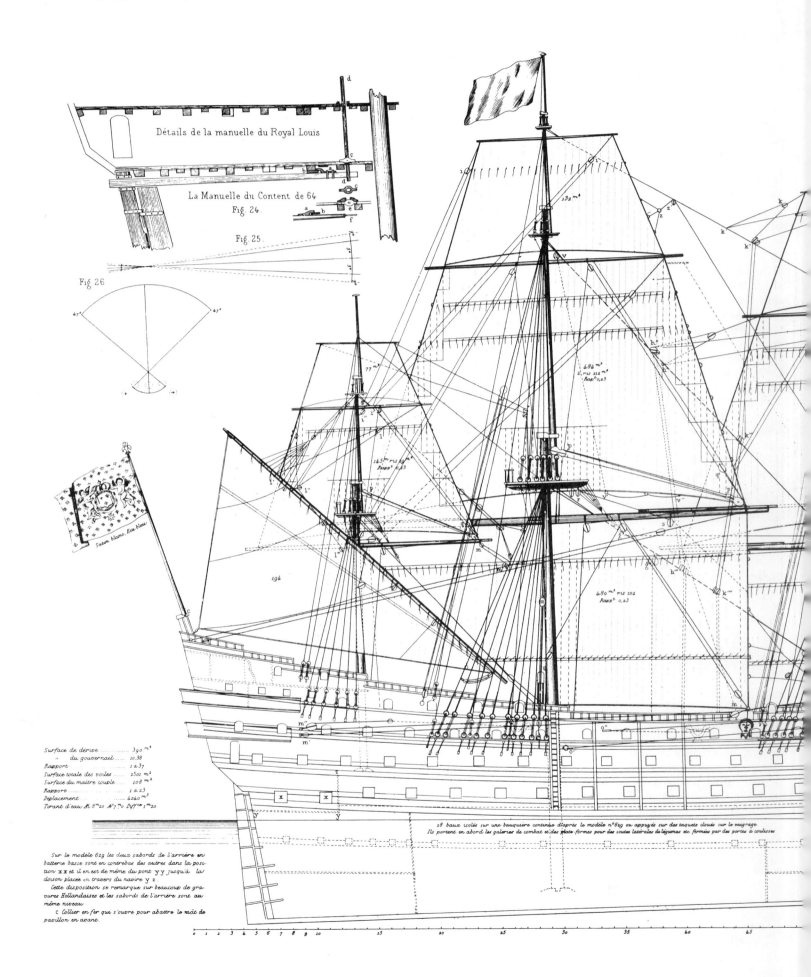

Détails de la manuelle du Royal Louis

La Manuelle du Content de 64
Fig. 24.

Fig. 25.

Fig 26.

Saten blanc. Ecu bleu.

Surface de dérive .... 390 m²
"   du gouvernail ... 10,38
Rapport .... 1 a 37
Surface totale des voiles ...... 2501 m²
Surface du maître couple ...... 108 m²
Rapport .... 1 a 23
Déplacement .... 6260 m³
Tirant d'eau Ar 8m20 Av 7m0 Diff^{ce} 1m20

Sur le modèle 629 les deux sabords de l'arrière en
batterie basse sont en contrebas des autres dans la position xx et il en est de même du pont yy jusqu'à la
cloison placée en travers du navire y z
   Cette disposition se remarque sur beaucoup de gra-
vures Hollandaises et les sabords de l'arrière sont au
même niveau
   c Collier en fer qui s'ouvre pour abattre le mât de
pavillon en avant.

18 baux isolés sur une bauquière contenus d'après le modèle n°629 ou appuyés sur des taquets cloués sur le vaigrage
Ils portent en abord les galeries de combat et des plates-formes pour des soutes latérales de légumes etc formées par des portes à coulisses

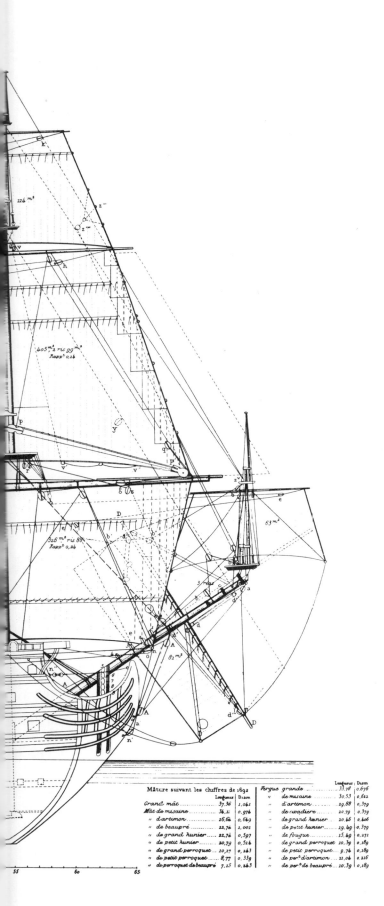

Mâture suivant les chiffres de 1692			Vergue grande 33,78	0,676
	Longueur	Diam	de misaine 30,53	0,612
Grand mât	37,36	1,041	d'artimon 29,88	0,379
Mât de misaine	34,1	0,976	de civadière 20,79	0,379
" d'artimon	26,60	0,649	de grand hunier . 20,45	0,406
" de beaupré	23,74	1,001	de petit hunier ... 19,69	0,379
" de petit hunier	22,74	0,597	de fougue 15,49	0,271
" de petit hunier	20,79	0,514	de grand perroquet 10,39	0,189
" de grand perroquet ...	10,17	0,263	de petit perroquet 9,76	0,189
" de petit perroquet ...	8,77	0,339	de per° d'artimon .. 11,06	0,216
" de perroquet de beaupré	7,13	0,263	de per° de beaupré 10,39	0,189

STANDING RIGGING

By 1600 standing and running rigging had reached a stage from which future development, except when new gear such as fore-and-aft sails was introduced, would consist for the most part of simplification (such as removal of the excessively complicated crowsfeet), the deletion of obsolete gear and standardisation. It had, in fact, reached a point of complexity at which to describe the rigging of even a small ship in complete detail would be impracticable in a book of this size, and consequently only the broad outlines will be sketched in. For fuller information one or other of the specialist books listed in the bibliography should be consulted.

Bowsprit. An English treatise on rigging written about 1625 states that the bowsprit was *gammed* to the ship's head, woolded to the foremast and bolted to the deck. It is not known when the gammoning first came into use. It is not shown on pictures of sixteenth century ships (though that is not conclusive evidence) but the *Prince Royal* had one in 1613. A date about the beginning of the century seems likely for two reasons. Firstly, the shifting of the foremast further aft would have lessened the effectiveness of the bowsprit/foremast lashing and, secondly, the spritsail topsail at the end of the bowsprit would exert a significant sideways force when the sail was set on a wind. At all events, the gammoning and the spritsail topsail appear in the records at about the same time. It is a curious fact, nevertheless, that the gammoning, under that name, does not appear in many seventeenth century inventories. It may be that it was regarded as a standard fastening rather than a piece of rigging, but more significantly Anthony Deane's key list to the rigging of a 1st Rate in 1670 has the gammon lashing listed as a bowsprit woolding and that may have been the case with the earlier inventories.

Throughout the century most English ships had a pair of lashings but Dutch ships sometimes had only one, as did some French and Swedish vessels. The earliest English gammonings were no more than 1/4 of the way from the stemhead to the outer end of the beak but as the knee was turned up more and more the lashing was moved along until finally it came close to the back of the figurehead. At first, the gammoning went round the bowsprit and under the knee of the head, a practice followed on some Dutch ships as late as the 1650s. On English ships, by 1630, the lashings were passed through a hole in the head knee, below the lower cheek, and with minor variations this remained the practice for the rest of the century. The gammoning was made of thick rope, usually right-handed, with a circumference of between 2/5 to 3/8 of the mainmast's diameter. On the bowsprit a group of chocks, usually one on top and two on each side, kept the lashing from slipping down the spar.

The introduction of jibs increased the sideways stress on the bowsprit and brought about an upwards one as well. To counter the upward pull a stay, the bobstay, was rigged between a point about half way along the bowsprit and the cutwater 2 to 3ft above the waterline. The bobstay had appeared on French ships by 1680 but the earliest English example is dated to 1701. English bobstays consisted of a long collar of strong rope fastened to the bowsprit and a similar one that passed through a hole in the cutwater. Each collar had a deadeye seized in the bight, and between the deadeyes a lanyard was passed. It started and finished at the bowsprit deadeye.

Lower masts. All lower masts were set up with tackles, shrouds and stays (including backstays), and on the mainmasts there was, in addition, hoisting tackle.

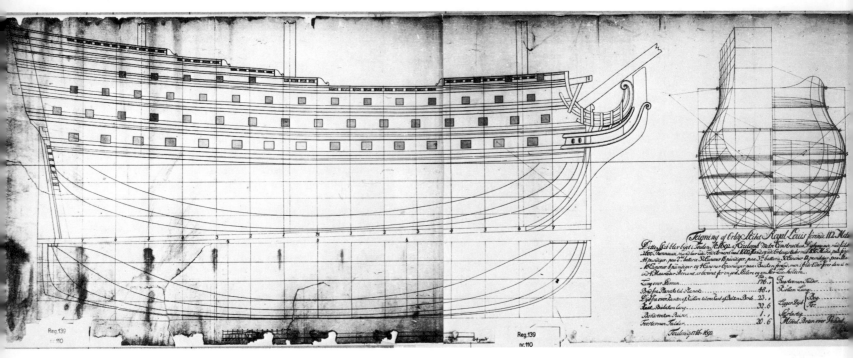

188. An original sheer draught of the *Royal Louis,* which reveals many detail differences from the Paris reconstruction – even the most highly regarded works must be treated with caution when not based on unimpeachable primary sources.

Tackles. Except on small ships each mast had a pair of tackles on each side and their pendants were the first rigging to go over the masthead. On English ships, until about 1655, the tackles were all the pendant-and-whip sort but after that date the mizzenmast had burton tackles. When there were two tackles a side the pendants were doubled over the masthead, but if there was only one the two pendants were 'cut spliced' over the mast-head. The lower ends of the pendant carried single or double blocks – these were sometimes fiddle-blocks – according to the complexity of the tackle. The tackle runners started from an eye- or ringbolt on the channel and the fall was belayed, presumably, to a timber-head or a kevel on the inside of the bulwarks. Tackle pendants were usually the same size as the corresponding shrouds, the runners being 2/3 and the falls 1/3 of the shrouds. If fiddle-blocks were used, they were as long as the mast was thick, but ordinary blocks were normally about 3/5 of the mast's diameter.

Shrouds. These went on over the tackles and their number, naturally, depended on the size of the ship, but within those limits there was little difference in the number of shrouds at the beginning and at the end of the century. The bonaventure mast seems to have had 4 or 5 shrouds but the evidence is too slight for dogmatism.

Shrouds were put on in pairs, each pair made by doubling a rope in the middle and putting a seizing on to it to make a loop big enough to go over the masthead. The foremost starboard pair went over first, then the foremost port pair, and so on. If there was an odd

number of shrouds the last ones were 'cut spliced' over the masthead. Fore and main shrouds were always set up with deadeyes and lanyards and, except on small ships, so were the mizzen shrouds. Small vessels, however, at the beginning of the century, sometimes had their mizzen shrouds set up with tackles, like a galley's shrouds. The bonaventure mizzen shrouds were usually set up with tackles.

The size (circumference) of main shrouds was about 1/4 of the mainmast's diameter, a little more at the beginning of the century, a little less in the second half. Taking the main shroud's size as 1, the approximate sizes of the other lower shrouds are as given in the table.

SIZES OF SHROUDS – Seventeenth Century			
	Fore	Mizzen	Bonaventure mizzen
1611	0.9	6.7	0.6
1640	0.85–0.9	0.55–0.67	–
1685	0.87–0.9	0.6	–

The deadeyes were, roughly, half the diameter of their mast. Down to 1640, at least, English deadeyes were asymmetric and shaped like a short, fat pear in outline but the cross-section was a short, broad ellipse. The pointed end of the deadeye was uppermost on the shroud deadeyes but was set downwards on the lower ones. The lower deadeyes were spaced as evenly along the channels as the gunports would allow, the foremost deadeye being placed just abreast of the after side of the mast. For one-third of the century, or more, all lower deadeyes were fastened to iron straps, known as plates, but from about 1640 to 1655 English ships had their deadeyes attached to 3-link iron chains, then after the later date plates came back into use. With Continental ships, on the other hand, chains were preferred. Whether chains or plates were used, all lower deadeyes had iron strops that were formed into a loop at the bottom, into which loop a hook on the chain or plate was fitted. The usual distance between the two rows of deadeyes was two diameters, or about the width of the respective mast.

No details of how mizzen and bonaventure shrouds were set up with tackles are available. Probably they were like masthead tackles.

TYPICAL NUMBERS OF SHROUDS – Seventeenth Century			
	Foremast	Mainmast	Mizzenmast
About 1618	8	10	5–6
After 1650	7–8	8–10	4–6
Small ships	4–5	5–6	3

Stays. If a ship had backstays that were set up with tackles, as some did at the beginning of the century (when they were known as swifters), their pendants went over the shrouds and then were set up like the other tackles. Of the other fore- and aft stays, the mainstay was the most important, for if it failed the mainmast was likely to fall and bring down the fore- and mizzenmasts with it. The importance of the mainstay is shown by its size: its circumference in the first quarter of the century was somewhat more than half the mainmast's diameter, although it was later standardised at one-half. The upper end of the stay went *over* the tackle pendants and shrouds. At one time the stay's loop may have been made by long-splicing the end into the main part, ie it was a variant of an eye-splice, but the usual way was to make a small eye in the end of the stay, pass it up between the crosstrees and round the masthead, and then to pass the rest of the stay through the eye. To stop the loop tightening round the masthead a special stopper, called a mouse, was worked on the stay. The lower end of the stay was set up with deadeyes and lanyards for most of the century but towards its end the deadeyes were replaced

by hearts. The lower deadeye, or heart, was seized into a long collar that passed on both sides of the foremast and went through a hole in the small knee that stood above the stem. The upper member of the pair was, of course, fastened to the lower end of the mainstay. The deadeyes that were used had five holes. On ships other than English ones in the second half of the century it was usual to set up the mainstay with a pair of 3-sheaved blocks. The forestay was set up in a similar manner but its lower end went to the bowsprit. At first, the collar was as far from the beakhead bulkhead as the upper end of the stay was above the forecastle deck, but later the collar was moved nearer so that its distance from the bulkhead was about 5/6 of the upper end's height. The mizzenstay was set up to a collar on the mainmast, 8–10ft above the deck. If there was a bonaventure mizzenstay, as there was on the *Prince Royal*, it was set up in a similar manner to the mizzenstay but to the mizzenmast. The sizes of the stays at different times during the century, when expressed as fractions of the mainstay's size, varied a little and, as a general rule, were proportionately thicker on the big ships. The examples have been taken from

189

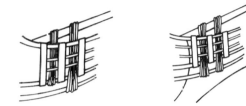

189. Seventeenth century development in bowsprit gammoning.
190. The rigging plan of a 1st Rate, from Anthony Deane's *A Doctrine of Naval Architecture*, 1670. The diagram on the left hand side of the plan shows the spread of the upper and lower shrouds on the mainmast.

190

191. Garnet tackle.

Main stay

contemporary rigging lists, the actual proportions being rounded to the nearest simple fraction.

The last piece of rigging to go over the main masthead was the pendant for the hoisting tackle. Two forms of the tackle were used, of which the earlier one was the garnet. In that tackle there was a single block on the end of the pendant and over the block went a runner with a 4-part fall. The pendant was seized to the mainstay so that the single block was over the hatchway. When the tackle was not in use the lower end was made fast to the mainstay or to the forecastle rail. In the other form of hoisting tackle, the 'winding tackle', the pendant had a double- or a treble-block (which might be a fiddle-

192. A plate from Raalamb's *Skeps Byggerij* of 1691 showing many rigging details.

block) and the tackle fall ran between the upper block and a similar one with a hook attached to it. The winding tackle was held over the hatch either by a guy from the fore masthead or one from near the foot of the foremast.

Topmasts and topgallant masts. These were set up with tackles, shrouds and stays like the lower masts. Fore- and mainmasts had a single tackle a side; so did the mizzen topmast until about the middle of the century, after which it had no tackles. Topmast tackle pendants were either eye-spliced or joined by a 'cut splice'. The early tackles were simple burton tackles but in the last decade of the century more complex versions came into use.

Topmasts had half as many shrouds as their lower masts. The shrouds were fitted over the masthead in a similar way and had deadeyes on their lower ends. The lower deadeyes were fastened to short iron straps (the puttock plates) that went through the edge of the top and were connected to the lower shrouds by short lengths of rope (the futtock shrouds). This arrangement was later simplified by combining the deadeye's iron strop with the puttock plate. The lower ends of the futtock shrouds were secured to a wooden bar, the futtock staff. The effect of fastening the futtock shrouds in that way was to pull the lower shrouds outwards and to counteract that pull a special tackle, the catharpin, was rigged between the futtock staves by fastening a single-sheave

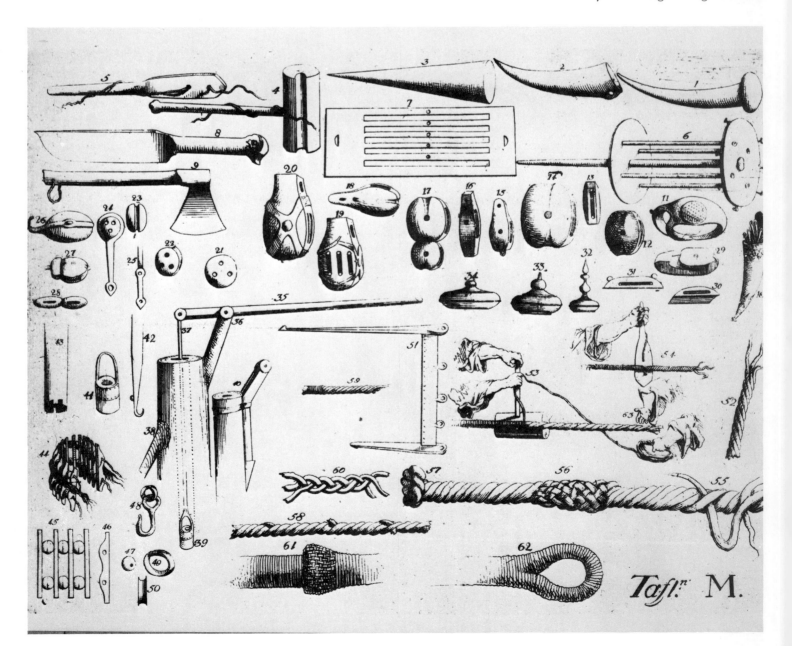

Tafl.ⁿ M.

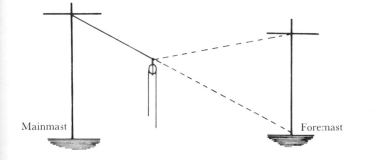

193. Alternative arrangements of winding tackle.

Mainmast · Foremast

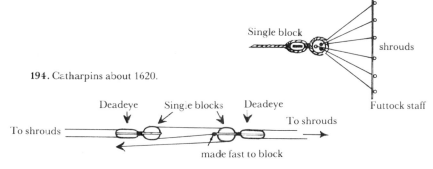

Single block · shrouds · Futtock staff

194. Catharpins about 1620.

Deadeye · Single blocks · Deadeye

To shrouds · To shrouds

made fast to block

block to each of two 3-hole deadeyes. Through each hole in the deadeyes ran a short length of rope, the ends of which were fastened to a pair of adjoining shrouds, so that each deadeye was connected to 6 shrouds. Next, a rope was taken from one block, run through the other block and taken back to the first one. After running through that one the rope was made fast between the opposite block and its deadeye.

Over the topmast shrouds went backstays. On English ships, until about 1640, there was only one a side on the fore and main topmasts and none on the mizzen. The number of backstays then increased until by the 1670s the fore and main topmasts had three on each side and the mizzen topmast had one. There were two sorts of backstay, running and standing. Running backstays were pendant-and-whip tackles that started from a timber-head or a rail near the after end of the rigging, and were belayed there. Standing backstays were known as early as 1611 but they were not at all common before the middle of the century. From then onwards the running backstays were gradually replaced by the standing kind although for a long time the big ships, at least, might have both sorts. Standing backstays were set up like shrouds, with deadeyes. As a general rule topmast backstays were as thick as the corresponding shrouds but occasionally they were a little bigger.

The upper ends of the topmast stays were fitted in the same way as the lower stays but the mode of attaching the lower end varied from one mast to another. The main topmast stay went through a block that was fastened either to the foremast head or to the forestay collar above the top, and then down towards the deck. Just below the lead-block a fiddle-block was attached to the end of the stay and a tackle rigged between it and a single block hooked to an eyebolt in the deck close to the foremast. Variants of those arrangements are known. In one, the lead-block hung below the top from a short pendant, and in another, of about 1620, the lower end of the stay was set up in the foretop with deadeyes. The fore topmast stay went to the end of the bowsprit, where it was set up with a tackle until the 1670s and afterwards either by a tackle or with deadeyes. When tackles were used the fall was, as a rule, hitched to the gammoning or to the forestay collar, but it was sometimes brought inboard.

The mizzen topmast stay, for reasons not known to us now, ended in a pair of complex tackles, one of which was attached to the aftermost main shroud on the port side and the other to the starboard. This elaborate system lingered on, at any rate in pictures and on some models, until the end of the century, but contemporary rigging lists make clear that after 1650 the mizzen topmast stay might be set up in the maintop, either with deadeyes or with a block and tackle like the main topmast stay.

The spritsail topmast was set up with shrouds and a backstay. About 1625 there were three shrouds a side and they were set up like the other topmast shrouds except that the puttocks were fastened to crosstrees on the bowsprit which were, according to an anonymous treatise on rigging, sometimes made of iron, although most spritmast crosstrees were made of wood. Later in the century the puttocks were fastened directly to the bowsprit. The spritsail topmast backstay was taken to the forestay via an elaborate tackle that was often a 'Bosun's Special'. Towards the end of the century, when fore staysails came into use, the tackle was shifted to the fore topmast stay. The following proportions summarise English practice with regard to the sizes of topmast stays but there were, of course, variations:

Fore topmast stay: 5/4 of the foretopmast shrouds
Main topmast stay: 5/4 of the main topmast shrouds
Mizzen topmast stay: Equal to mizzen topmast shrouds
Bonaventure mizzen topmast stay: Equal to bonaventure mizzen topmast shrouds
Spritsail topsail backstay: As fore topmast shrouds.

Two other pieces of rigging apply to the topmasts. The first one is not, strictly speaking, standing rigging. It is the top-rope, the gear used to raise and lower the topmasts, and its simplest form has already been described in Chapter 2. As topmasts grew bigger other arrangements came into use, some of them having two top-ropes, which was a common Continental fashion. A good many variants on the theme have been noticed. Some English ships had two ropes to the main topmast but only one on the fore topmast; others had two for each topmast. The top-ropes were almost as thick as the lower shrouds and had tackle-falls half their own thickness. The mizzen topmast did not have permanently rigged top-ropes, these being set up only as occasion demanded. The other piece of rigging was a device to keep the topsail from chafing against the stay. Ropes passed to and fro between a series of holes in the fore rim of the top and others that were bored edge to edge through a narrow, elliptical piece of wood known as a euphroe. The latter was fastened to the stay by a tackle made up of two single blocks. So far as is known, this device came into use about the middle of the century.

Topgallant masts. The rigging of these spars was a simpler version of the topmasts'. Only the biggest ships had topgallant tackles and then only one a side. There were two topgallant shrouds on each side, with three on the biggest ships. The shrouds were set up with deadeyes, the lower ones being fastened direct to the futtock staves by rope puttocks that went through holes at the ends of the crosstrees. If there was a topgallant top, as was fitted to some ships at the beginning of the century, the topgallant shrouds seem to have been fastened to the

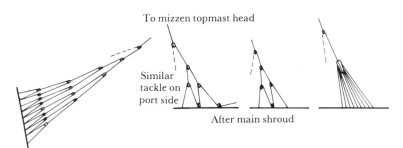

To mizzen topmast head

Similar tackle on port side

After main shroud

195. Mizzen topmast backstays.

top's rim (or perhaps taken down inside the top to the crosstrees). Backstays were simple pendant-and-whip tackles until about 1640, after which, for about 30 years, they seem to have been omitted. When re-introduced, the topgallant backstays were set up with deadeyes. Topgallant stays had only a long eye at their upper end. The main topgallant stay usually went to a block at the fore topmast head and was either made fast in the foretop or else had a tackle on its end, the fall of which was presumably made fast near the foot of the mast. The fore topgallant stay went to the outer end of the bowsprit until the spritsail topmast was adopted and then it was taken to a block at the spritsail topmast's head, went down to another block at the foot of the mast and might then be made fast to one of the spritsail topmast trestle-trees or be taken inboard along the bowsprit to the forecastle.

Flagstaffs. These had their shrouds set up directly to the topgallant crosstrees and the stays were taken to the same places as the topgallant stays.

Ratlines were rigged on all shrouds except those of the topgallant masts (and even these sometimes had them). On fore and main shrouds the ratlines stopped at the penultimate shroud on each side but on the mizzenmast and the topmasts they were taken right across the whole set. The distance between ratlines is uncertain but seems to have been about 16in. In thickness, lower ratlines were usually $1\frac{1}{2}$in rope, those on the topmasts were 1in, and any on the topgallant shrouds were made of $\frac{3}{4}$in rope. Seventeenth century ratlines seem to have had their ends hitched round the shroud, and on the intermediate shrouds, with clove hitches. The end hitches would have had the rope ends lashed to the standing part. The futtock shrouds also had ratlines.

RUNNING RIGGING

Spritsail yard. Except, perhaps, in the early years of the century the spritsail yard was rigged permanently outboard, and until about 1640 it had a parrel like a topsail yard's, but after that date the yard was usually hung by a sling. The normal position for the spritsail yard was just in front of the forestay collar, and whether hung by a

parrel or by a sling it had a tye and a halliard, or even, in the early years of the century, a halliard only, and that had its fall made fast to the gammoning. After 1640 a more powerful tackle was in use. The spritsail yard was steadied by a pair of lifts that went from the yardarms to blocks at the bowsprit's end, from where they came in to the range, a pinrail across the after end of the beak. The coming of the spritsail topmast complicated the arrangement and for a while the spritsail yard's lifts acted as sheets for the spritsail topsail. Later, they were taken to a pair of blocks on the cap that held the spritsail topmast. In about 1620 a tackle was rigged on their ends and the falls brought to the gammoning but they were afterwards taken to the forecastle rail via the long, multiple-sheave lead-block on the gammoning. Later still, the spritsail yard was given standing lifts that were set up to the bowsprit with deadeyes. These standing lifts served as lifelines for men going out on the spritsail yard, and at the end of the century, and perhaps before, they had knots (manrope knots?) worked on them.

The spritsail braces were simple for most of the century. Each brace started at the forestay, ran through a pendant block at the spritsail yardarm and went back to a lead-block on the forestay below the starting point of the brace. From there the brace went down to another lead-block in the head and inboard to the forecastle rail. After 1690 a more complex arrangement came into use – spritsail yard to pendant block on the forestay, back through pendant block from yardarm and up to lead-blocks at each end of the trestletrees, and then down to the bulwarks just abaft the forecastle bulkhead via a lead-block on the mainstay.

In size, the spritsail halliards, lifts and brace pendants were a little less than half the thickness of the fore shrouds, and the braces were 2/3 the thickness of the lifts. These are, of course, only generalisations and a study of contemporary lists shows that there were variations in the proportions from time to time.

Spritsail topsail yard. The parrel was like that of a topgallant yard, with two rows of trucks; the halliard had a single tye and a tackle with two single blocks, the lower one being fastened to the spritsail top. The tackle fall was belayed in the top, sometimes to the lower block. A manuscript of about 1620 has the tackle starting at the crosstrees and the fall made fast there. The early lifts started at the masthead, ran through a block at the yardarm and back to another block at the masthead, from which it was taken down to the spritsail top and made fast there. After about 1630 the upper blocks were shifted to the cap that held the flagstaff. The braces started at the forestay and went first through single blocks on short pendants from the yardarm, and from those to the forecastle via lead-blocks on the forestay and the long block on the gammoning.

199

198

200

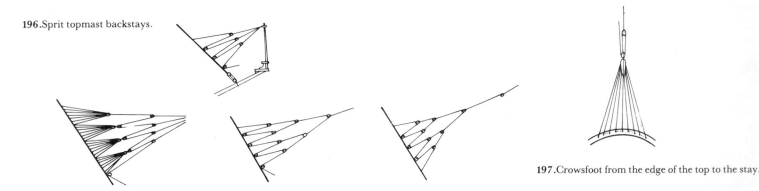

196. Sprit topmast backstays.

197. Crowsfoot from the edge of the top to the stay.

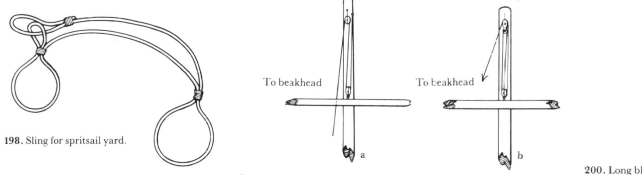

198. Sling for spritsail yard.

To beakhead

To beakhead

a

b

199. Spritsail halliard.

200. Long block on gammoning.

Lower yards. Until about the middle of the century there was a good deal of variety in the way the fore- and mainyards were hoisted. Tyes and halliards, and jeers, were optional ways and sometimes both were used together. According to the rigging list for 1611 foreyards had tyes and jeers but the mainyard had tyes only. The use of jeers increased during the first half of the century and by the 1640s all but the smallest ships had both tyes and jeers. After 1650 tyes gradually went out of use, until by the 1670s jeers were the normal way of hoisting the lower yards except on some of the small ships.

When tyes and halliards were used the tye had one of its ends hitched round the yard a little off-centre. The tye was then passed through a sheave in the hound on the same side (or a block in the early years), through the ramhead and back to the yard via the other hound, or block, and the end made fast to the yard. The halliard started from an eyebolt in the side of the knight and passed to and fro between the sheaves in the ramhead and those in the knight – usually three in each – and was made fast to the knight. If this was below deck the halliard passed through a scuttle or grating over the knight.

Jeers worked on a different principle. The simplest form had a block on the yard, at the centre, and another below the top. This block might be on a short pendant. The jeer fall started from the opposite side of the masthead to the pendant block and passed successively through the yard block and that on the masthead, after which it went down to the capstan via a lead-block at the foot of the mast. Naturally enough, variations on the scheme were tried at different times, and these are shown in the illustrations.

The lateen mizzenyard, like the fore- and mainyards, might be hoisted by a tye and halliard, or by jeers, or by both. But because the lateen yard had to be shifted so that it was always on the lee side of the mast the arrangement of the hoisting gear differed from that on the other yards. The tye went over a sheave in the masthead below the top *from aft forwards,* and had a block on its lower end. At first, the block was a single one and the halliard ran between it and the 2-sheaved knight (which stood in front of the mast), the second sheave acting as a lead-block. The end of the halliard was belayed round the head of the knight. As yards became bigger the upper block was given two sheaves and the knight sometimes had three. When jeers were introduced, in the 1640s, probably as an adjunct to the tye, they were the simple sort described above but when tyes were abolished more complex jeers came into use. On the biggest ships a treble block hung from the masthead and there was a double block on the yard. Smaller ships had one sheave less in each block. By the 1680s however, the 3-and-2 arrangement was standard on all but the smallest ships. In 1611 the mizzen tye was 9/10 the size

of the mizzen shrouds and the halliard as thick, or even thicker, than the mizzen shrouds. The jeer-blocks were normally about 1½ diameters of the yard in length.

Crossjack yard. From as early as 1620 this yard was held permanently aloft and consequently it had no hoisting gear. Instead, the yard was hung by a sling that passed round the masthead and the trestletrees and through a block on the yard. Instead of a parrel a rope strop was taken round the yard and the ends seized together behind the mast.

The other lower yards were held to their yards by *parrels* and *trusses.* Contemporary accounts of these important pieces of gear leave much to be desired as to the way they were rigged. The most succinct description is given in the anonymous *Treatise on Rigging:* the parrel fastens the yard to the mast and the truss serves to heave down the yard. The parrel consisted of a rope that went, loosely, round mast and yard three times and had the vertical riders (the ribs or sisters) threaded on it alternately with wooden balls known as trucks. Finally, the parrel-rope went round the outside of the ribs, in grooves, and was fastened to the yard. Later parrels had the end of the rope attached to a tackle so that the parrel could be tightened or slacked off. The truss-rope was fastened to the middle of the yard with a timber hitch and went down to the foot of the mast, to a lead-block, from which it was taken to the capstan. On 2-decked or 3-decked ships the mainyard's truss went to the deck below the upper deck and that belonging to the foremast to the upper deck, passing through the forecastle deck. On some models from the second half of the century the parrel has a rope that seems to be some sort of a preventer rope in case the parrel-rope should give way, but how it was rigged has not been ascertained. The rigging of the later truss is not clear, either. It may, in fact, have been found unnecessary once a means of slackening and tightening the parrel had been set up. Parrels had a small tackle, the knaveline, rigged between the top of the midmost rib of the parrel and the underside of the top. The tackle served to pull up the parrel so that the ribs did not jam, or catch on the wooldings, whilst the yard was being hoisted.

The mizzenyard's parrel had a different arrangement so that the yard could be swung round the mast. The parrel-rope was doubled and had a 2-hole deadeye seized in the bight. The usual ribs and trucks were then threaded on the rope and the parrel passed round the mast and the yard. The two ends of the parrel-rope were passed through the holes in the deadeye and fastened together. Into the bight so formed a thimble was seized, and a tackle attached to it. By heaving on the tackle the yard could be held against the mast; conversely, slacking off the tackle would allow the yard to be swung round.

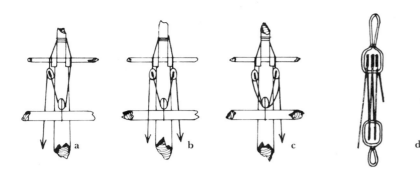

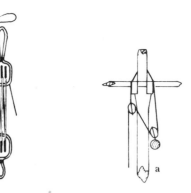

201. Jeers: (a) about 1620; (b) about 1640; (c) about 1660 and (d) about 1700.

202. Mizzen jeer: (a) early form and (b) later arrangement.

As to sizes of parrels, the ribs were slightly longer than the maximum thickness of the mast and the trucks were 1/5 of it. Big ships had 9 ribs and 3 rows of trucks; small vessels had 6 and 2. In 1611 fore and main parrel-ropes were 4/5 of the size of the shrouds and the truss-rope 1/2 to 3/5. After about 1650 the proportions were 3/5 for the parrel-rope but the truss-rope sizes are not usually given in the inventories, their place being taken by breast-ropes. The early mizzen parrel-ropes were about half the thickness of the mizzen shrouds but by the middle of the century they were as thick, and sometimes thicker, the change no doubt reflecting the proportionately bigger size of the sail.

Lifts. Until about 1660 lifts on the fore- and mainyards started from the stay collar, went through a single block at the yardarm, back to a single block on a pendant from the masthead above the top (though the block was *below* the top) and so to the deck. After that date the lift started from the strop of the masthead block but the arrangement otherwise remained the same until the end of the century, when the end of the lift was made fast to an eyebolt on the mast cap and the pendant of the block was shortened so that the block came above the top.

204   The lower lift-block was always fastened to the upper end of the topsail sheet block. These blocks were about equal in length to the maximum thickness of the yard and the lift-blocks were about 2/3. The history of 205 the crossjack lifts is obscure. The *Treatise on Rigging* says that there were no crossjack lifts yet they are included in the 1611 inventory and crossjack lifts are shown on the *Prince Royal*. By 1640 lifts were regular fittings and set up

like those on the fore- and mainyards but if a ship had no crossjack lifts the mizzen topsail sheets took their place. By the 1670s crossjack lifts were being replaced by standing lifts set up with deadeyes. The upper deadeyes were on a short span of rope clove-hitched over the mizzen cap. The lower ones were on long pendants fastened to the yard about 2–3ft in from its end.

The lateen yard needed only one lift. While the mizzen topmast remained short the lift went to the main topmast head but between 1620 and 1630 the lead was altered to the mizzen topmast head, an arrangement that lasted until some time about 1660, when the mizzen lift fell out of use (although it continued to appear on models, and perhaps on ships as an 'optional extra'). The mizzen lift was one of those pieces of gear on which any bosun worth his 'salt horse' was expected to let himself go. Some examples are shown in the illustrations. When there was a bonaventure mizzenyard its lift went, at first, to the mainmizzen topmast head but afterwards, as on the *Prince Royal*, to the bonaventure mizzen topmast head.

Braces. At the ends of the yards were pendants carrying single blocks, the pendants being about 1/6 to 1/4 of the length of the yard. The forebraces started from the mainstay, ran through the pendant-blocks and returned to lead-blocks on the stay from which the falls went down to the deck and were made fast to the bulwarks, possibly via other lead-blocks on the deck or the lower part of the bulwarks. The starting point of the braces was, at first, about 2/5 of the way up the stay, with the lead-blocks a little lower, but by the 1670s both had been moved to

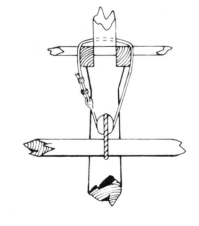

203. Sling of crossjack yard (top) and mizzen parrel.

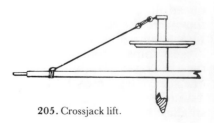

Lift block

Topsail sheet block

204. Lower yard lift block.

205. Crossjack lift.

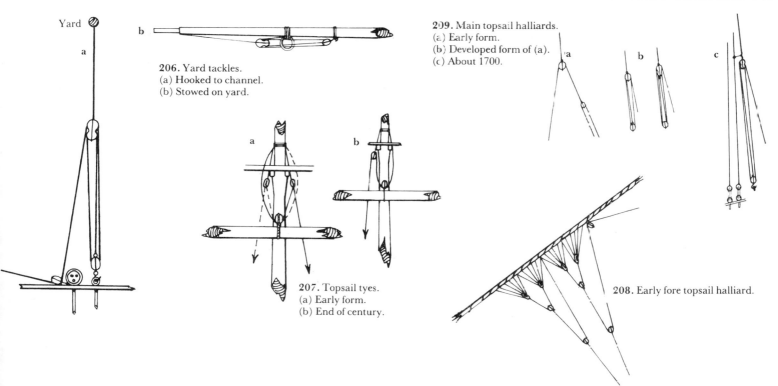

206. Yard tackles.
(a) Hooked to channel.
(b) Stowed on yard.

207. Topsail tyes.
(a) Early form.
(b) End of century.

208. Early fore topsail halliard.

209. Main topsail halliards.
(a) Early form.
(b) Developed form of (a).
(c) About 1700.

about the halfway point and towards the century's end were higher up again. The mainbraces started from the after end of the hull and came back to convenient belaying points nearby. In the 1620s the mainbrace was said to start from the aftermost timber-head and was made fast to the one in front of it. Later on, the mainbraces started from ringbolts in the side at about the level of the upper deck and returned via either a lead-block on the rail or a sheave in the bulwarks, or even just a block of wood with a hole in it. The hauling parts were taken sufficiently far forward to give a convenient length for pulling and were then belayed to large cleats on the bulwarks.

Crossjack braces, for most of the century, started at the aftermost main shrouds, went through pendant-blocks from the yardarms and then were taken *forwards* to lead-blocks on the main shrouds below the braces' starting points. The braces then ran down to the deck and were belayed to either a timber-head or a cleat on the bulwarks, possibly via a lead-block on the shrouds or a shroud truck. The *Treatise on Rigging*, however, states that the crossjack braces were single ropes from the yard-arms to the aftermost timbers of the poop, an arrangement which evidently proved unsatisfactory although it was tried again about 1670, equally unsuccessfully. Brace-blocks were, roughly speaking, 2/3 of the diameter of their yard, brace pendants were 1/2 the thickness of the shrouds and the falls were usually 1in less in thickness than the pendants.

The lateen yard did not have braces in the normal sense of the term but its lower end was controlled by a pair of ropes known as bowlines. The simple form used on small ships consisted of single ropes that went from the lower end of the yard to blocks on the aftermost main shrouds and then to the bulwarks and made fast. Bigger ships had a pair of blocks on the yardarm and the bowlines started at the main shrouds. After passing through the yardarm blocks the bowlines returned to lead-blocks on the shrouds and went down to the deck.

Yard tackles. In the last twenty years of the seventeenth century English ships, and probably those of other countries, had tackles fitted to their yardarms for hoisting the boats in and out. On English ships a fiddle-block

was fastened to the lower end of a pendant – which was about 18ft long – from the yardarm; the tackle-fall ran between it and a single block (from which the fall started) and then through a lead-block lashed to the first deadeye abaft the foremost mast-tackle and brought inboard through a convenient port. There was a hook on the strop of the lower block, and when one tackle was to be used the opposite one was hooked into a ringbolt on the channel to take the strain off the lift on the hoisting side. When not required, the tackles were hauled up and lashed to their yards.

Footropes. These are not running gear, of course, but it seems more appropriate to deal with them in this section than in isolation under standing rigging. Footropes are first recorded on English ships in 1640 and on the main-yard only. Some 30 years elapsed before they appeared on the foreyard, and a little later footropes are recorded for all but the crossjack and the mizzen. As, until quite recent times, innovations were often in use well before their existence is acknowledged in official publications, it may be safely taken for granted that footropes, which were called 'horses', were in use before the dates given above, although little is known about how the early footropes were rigged. Towards the end of the century, the arrangement was that the lower footropes were made fast inboard with deadeyes, but on the upper yards the inboard ends were merely fastened to the parrel. A remarkable feature of the early footropes is that there were no stirrups although these may have appeared by the end of the century. The thickest footropes were made of 5in rope and the smallest of $2\frac{1}{2}$in.

Topsail and topgallant yards. Broadly speaking, topsail yards were hoisted by simpler versions of the lower yards' gear: tyes and halliards for most of the century and then, as the topsail yards were made bigger, something like a jeer. On big ships there might be a pair of tyes to each topsail yard. The treatment of the halliards depended on which mast they belonged to. The fore topmast halliard went to the mainstay, to which it was sometimes set up with a complex crowsfoot, an example of which can be seen on the *Prince Royal*. The precise arrangement of these crowsfeet tackles has been a matter of dispute but the arrangements shown in the

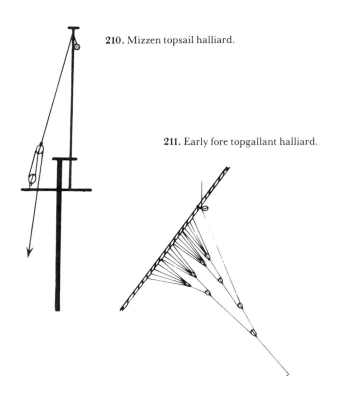

210. Mizzen topsail halliard.

211. Early fore topgallant halliard.

212. A rigging diagram from Raalamb's *Skeps Byggerij* of 1691. Just astern of the central ship a small drawing shows a ship with a triangular stunsail set from its main topsail yard, and to the left of that ship is another vessel with a jib and two triangular staysails.

illustrations are at any rate possible, although it is only fair to add that some authorities assert that the tackle is a fore topmast backstay. It is likely, however, that most ships used ordinary tackles of more or less complexity. The main topsail yard had a simple tye-and-halliard with a tackle appropriate to the size of the topsail yard. The tackle falls of the fore topsail yard were made fast to the starboard bulwarks (the tackle having started on the port side) just abaft the forecastle bulkhead. The main topsail tackle started on the starboard side and was belayed to the port side at the fore end of the quarter-deck.

Towards the end of the century a new arrangement came into use. A block was fastened to the centre of the yard and the tye ran through the block and a tye-block on each side of the masthead below the top. On the ends of the tyes were the usual tackles. Several variations of the arrangement are known, for details of which specialist rigging books should be consulted.

Mizzen topsail yards were hoisted by a tye only at first, but this was supplanted by a simple halliard, an arrangement that was in use until nearly 1700, when the system used on the fore and main topsail yards was substituted for it. Tyes were between $1\frac{1}{4}$ and $1\frac{1}{2}$ times as thick as the corresponding shrouds, and the halliards were about the same thickness as the shrouds. Tye blocks were about as long as the yard was thick.

Topgallant yards were hoisted in the same way as topsail yards but because they were smaller the gear was simpler. Parrels and trusses were made up of a rope looped round the yard to one side of the centre after

213. The sail plan of the *Wasa* reconstructed from a spare suit of sails found in her sailroom when she was raised.

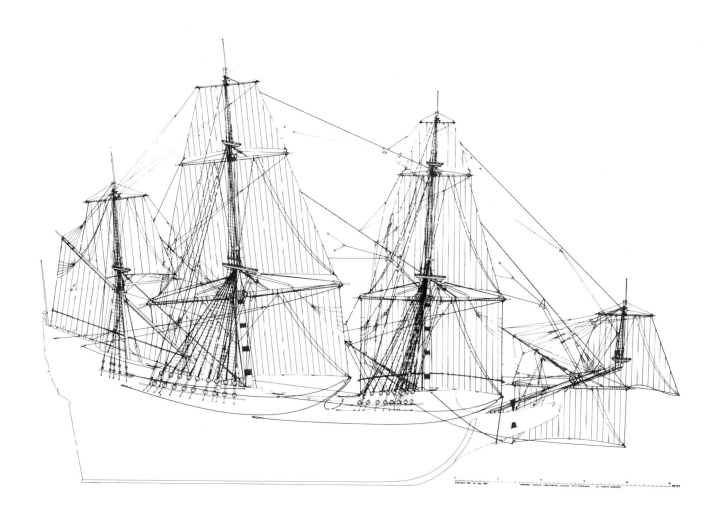

which sufficient ribs and trucks were threaded on to make the parrel. The two ends of the rope then went round the mast and over the yard, in opposite directions and on the opposite side of the centre. The rope was then taken backwards and forwards over the notches in the trucks and round the yard on either side of the mast until there were several turns round mast and yard. The ends of the parrel-rope were fastened either to each other or to one of the turns. Topsail yards had trusses until sometime about 1625 but not afterwards. Topgallant yards did not have trusses.

Topsail and topgallant lifts. When there was no topgallant yard the topsail lifts started at the topmast cap, where they might be fastened to an eyebolt on the cap or hitched through holes in the cap, or else fastened to a span of rope clove-hitched over the cap. The lifts ran through yardarm blocks, back to blocks at the topmast head and then to the top to be made fast. An alternative arrangement took the fall of the lift through a hole in the top and down to the bulwarks. When there were topgallant sails the topsail yard's lifts acted as topgallant sheets. Early topsail lifts were about 2/3 the size of the corresponding shrouds but in the second half of the century the proportion was about half.

Topsail and topgallant braces. Fore topsail braces started from the main topmast stay, went to a pendant-block from the fore topsail yard and back to a lead-block on the stay, from which they passed to the deck via another lead-block on the mainstay and were belayed to the bulwarks about midway along the waist. Main topsail braces were arranged differently. In the earlier form the brace began at the mizzen masthead, ran through the usual pendant-block from the yardarm and returned to a block on the foremost mizzen shroud. The rope then went forward to a block on the aftermost main shroud, about half way up, and from there down to the deck to be belayed near the main shrouds. About 1660 the starting point of the brace was shifted to below the crossjack yard. Two other variations were used. In one, the brace started from the mizzen shrouds just below the futtock staff but was otherwise as in the earlier form. In the other arrangement the brace started from a span of rope that was clove-hitched round the mast below the crossjack yard and then ran as before.

Mizzen topsail braces began near the upper end of the lateen yard. After passing through the pendant-blocks on the mizzen topsail yard they returned to a couple of lead-blocks on the lateen yard a little below the braces' starting point and from there went to the corners of the poop.

Fore and main topgallant braces were rigged in the same way as topsail braces but of course a stage higher up, being based on the main topmast stay and the mizzen topmast. Only the *Sovereign of the Seas* is known to have had mizzen topgallant braces, and these went to the lateen yard. As to sizes, early brace pendants were about

3/4 of the corresponding shrouds and the braces 1/2 to 2/3. Later braces were nearer to 1/2 the shrouds in thickness.

Blocks and deadeyes. The large size of some blocks will have been apparent from the proportions given in the preceding sections, and this is a feature of seventeenth century rigging that needs underlining, for blocks (and deadeyes) were indeed big. Tye blocks on 1st Rates were up to 30in long and proportionately wide, and tackle blocks were as much as 36in long. As a rough generalisation seventeenth century blocks were something like twice as big for a given size of ship as they were in the early nineteenth century. Deadeyes, as a rule, were about half as wide as their mast was thick and thus might be as much as 18in in diameter. But size was not the only way in which seventeenth century blocks and deadeyes differed from those on ships of the late eighteenth and early nineteenth centuries. Some of the old-fashioned fifteenth and sixteenth century shapes remained in use well into the 1600s. Just when English ships gave up using these kinds is not known for the earliest 'Navy Board' model with original rigging dates from 1692, but documentary evidence and actual examples show that Danish and Swedish ships had blocks of the old types as late as the third quarter of the century.

Deadeyes also differed in shape from those of later times. The early seventeenth century deadeyes were longer than they were wide, almost heart-shaped at the beginning of the century but gradually increasing in width until by the second half of it, at any rate on English ships, deadeyes were circular. The older form may have remained in use longer than is generally believed, for a deadeye from a Danish ship that sank in 1658 is 13in by 12in by 5in. Deadeyes, on the whole, seem to have been between 1/3 and just under 1/2 as thick as they were wide and at their edges they had to be sufficiently thick to allow for the groove that held the shroud.

Except for the examples from the *Dartmouth* (wrecked in 1690) no English seventeenth century blocks are known, but the Baltic has yielded examples from ships of many other countries. Unfortunately, their dimensions are difficult to find. Some mid-century blocks from Danish ships have measurements as detailed in the accompanying table.

SAILS

Seventeenth century sails were still made with a great deal of bagginess though less than was customary in the preceding centuries, and they were still fitted with bonnets well after the middle of the century. Sails were fastened to their yards with robands, hauled up by martnets and clewgarnets in the first half of the century and later by clewlines, leechlines, buntlines and reef-

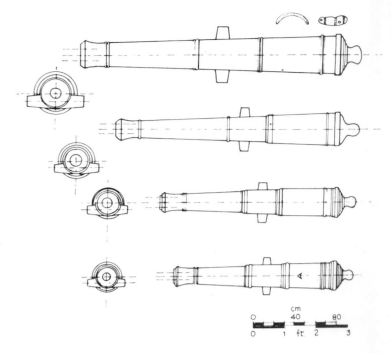

214. The guns of the *Dartmouth*. From the top they are: 9pdr demi-culverin (no 13) showing lead apron vent cover; 6pdr (no 18); saker-drake (no 17); 3pdr (no 10).

tackles. The last came into use, however, some 20 years after reefing had been reintroduced. The history of reefing between its disappearance on the bigger ships about the beginning of the sixteenth century and its reappearance 150 years or so later has yet to be worked out. All that we know is that in about 1655 English ships were given reef-points on their fore and main topsails. By 1680 the fore and main topsails had two bands of reef-points and the mizzen topsail may have had one band. At about the same time, fore and main courses were given a single band of reef-points and their introduction led to the abandoning of the time-honoured bonnet. English ships do not seem to have had topgallant reefs but they are shown on a drawing of a Swedish ship of about 1690. New sails – stunsails, staysails and jibs – appeared in that sequence. The earliest English stunsails date from about 1625, when they were said to be set on either side of the fore and main courses, but it is not until the 1650s that stunsails appear in the official inventories. Main topmast stunsails had appeared by 1675 and on the fore topmast by 1685, if not earlier. Seventeenth century stunsails were almost certainly triangular, for no stunsail yards appear in the inventories and the Swedish drawing just mentioned shows them as three-cornered, the lower edge being spread by a boom.

SIZES OF BLOCKS (DANISH) – mid Seventeenth Century					
Block	Length (in)	Breadth (in)	Thickness (in)	Sheave hole (in)	Sheave (in)
Single	$18\frac{1}{2}$	12	6	$12 \times 2\frac{3}{4}$	$9 \times 2\frac{1}{4}$
Single	$16\frac{1}{2}$	12	5	$11\frac{1}{2} \times 1\frac{3}{4}$	$8\frac{1}{2} \times 1\frac{3}{8}$ (pin 2)
Single	$8\frac{1}{2}$	6	$3\frac{1}{4}$	$6\frac{1}{4} \times 1\frac{1}{2}$	Missing (pin 1)
Single	$13\frac{1}{2}$	9	$5\frac{1}{2}$	$11 \times 1\frac{3}{4}$	$9\frac{1}{2} \times 1\frac{7}{8}$ (pin $1\frac{3}{4}$)
Treble	26	$15\frac{1}{2}$	16	$17 \times 1\frac{3}{4}$ outer	Missing (pin $1\frac{3}{4}$)
				$17 \times 3\frac{1}{4}$ inner	Missing (pin $1\frac{3}{4}$)
Topsail sheet	$27\frac{1}{2}$	$10\frac{1}{2}$	$6\frac{1}{2}$	$10\frac{1}{2} \times 1\frac{1}{2}$ upper	Missing (thickness 2)
				$13\frac{1}{2} \times 2\frac{1}{2}$ lower	Missing (thickness 2)

All the above blocks had deep scores on each face for the strop. The scores on the treble block were 8in long and $3\frac{1}{4}$in wide. Blocks subject to the greatest strain were bound with iron straps fixed diagonally across the cheeks of the block.

ARMAMENT OF ENGLISH SHIPS c1622

Ship & tonnage	Cannon-periers	Demi-cannon	Culverins	Demi-culverins	Sakers	Falcons	Port-pieces	Fowlers
Prince Royal (1200)	2	6	12	18	13	—	4	—
White Bear (915)	2	6	12	18	9	—	4	—
Merhonour (800)	2	6	12	12	8	—	4	—
Anne Royal (800)	2	5	12	13	8	—	4	—
Victory (656)	2	2	16	12	4	2	—	4
Swiftsure (694)	2	2	16	12	4	2	—	4
Constant Reformation (564)	2	2	16	12	4	2	4	—
St George (671)	2	2	16	12	4	2	2	2
St Andrew (671)	2	2	16	12	4	2	—	4
Triumph (692)	2	2	14	12	4	2	—	4
Defiance (700)	2	2	14	12	4	2	4	—
Repulse (700)	2	2	14	12	4	2	—	4

The distribution of the *Prince Royal's* armament was: 2 cannon-periers, 6 demi-cannon, 12 culverins on the lower deck; 18 demi-culverins on the middle deck and 13 sakers and 4 port-pieces on the upper deck. The much smaller *White Bear* and *Merhonour* had almost the same armament, which suggests that they were over-gunned for their tonnage, a persistent malpractice throughought the century.

Staysails had appeared on English ships by 1633 and a fore topmast staysail was in use by 1655. Within ten years of that date a ship might have main and mizzen staysails and fore and main topsail staysails. By 1690 mizzen topmast and main topgallant staysails were in use as well. The final addition to the seventeenth century sail plan was the jib, a triangular sail set between the fore topmast head and a spar lashed to the bowsprit and projecting well beyond the spritsail top. The new spar was the jibboom and at first was merely lashed to the bowsprit. The job was set 'flying', ie it was attached only to ropes from its corners and was not attached to a stay.

The running gear of the sails was, necessarily, elaborate and complicated and as this book is not designed to be a 'Rigger's Manual' the sails' rigging will not be described because excellent accounts of it are to be found in the many authoritative and readily obtainable specialist publications.

ARMAMENT

When James I ascended the throne in 1603 ship armament was settling into something like the pattern it would retain until the supercession of the wooden ship armed with muzzle-loading guns. The resemblance can be seen in the inventory of the guns carried by 11 of the biggest Royal ships about 1622. Omitting the old fashioned cannon-periers, which were obsolete by that date, and the port-pieces, the principal guns were demi-cannon (32pdr), culverin (18pdr) and demi-culverin (9pdr), and most were muzzle loaders. Breech loaders continued in use but except for the obsolescent port-pieces and fowlers they were small calibre pieces and swivels mounted along the bulwarks and perhaps behind the bulkheads in the waist.

GUNS CARRIED BY *SOVEREIGN OF THE SEAS*

Position	Number and type	Length (ft)
Lower tier		
Luffs, sides and quarters	20 cannon drakes*	9
Stern chasers	4 demi-cannon drakes	12½
Fore chasers	2 demi-cannon drakes	11½
Bows abaft the chase	2 demi-cannon drakes	10
Middle tier		
Luffs, sides and quarters	24 culverin drakes	8½
Fore chasers	2 culverins	11½
After chasers	4 culverins	11½
Upper tier		
Sides	24 demi-culverin drakes	8½
Fore chase	2 demi-culverins	10
After chase	2 demi-culverins	10
Forecastle	8 demi-culverin drakes	9
Half-deck	6 demi-culverin drakes	9
Quarterdeck	2 demi-culverin drakes	5½
Bulkhead abaft the forecastle	2 culverin drakes	5½

*Drakes were lighter in weight and shorter than ordinary guns of equal calibre. According to a treatise written in 1672, a demi-cannon drake with a bore diameter of 6½in had a length of 16 diameters (8ft 6in); a 5½in culverin drake was also 16 diameters (7ft 4in); a 4½in demi-culverin drake was again 16 diameters (6ft); and a 3½in saker drake was 18 diameters (5ft 3in). In comparison, the respective ordinary guns were 11ft, 11ft 6in, 8ft 1½in and 5ft 7in in length. A peculiarity of drakes was that their bores were tapered. Why this was so is not clear, for it meant that a greater proportion of the powder's energy was wasted than in an ordinary gun and the accuracy was probably lessened because of the greater 'wobble' of the shot as it passed along the barrel. Drakes were unpopular with sea-gunners because they recoiled more violently than full-weight guns and got hotter in action.

GUN ALLOCATION 1655

Rate	Cannon-drakes	Demi-cannon	Culverins	Demi-culverins	Sakers	Total
1st	19	9	28	30	5	91
2nd	—	6	30	24	4	64
3rd	—	4	22	26	8	60
4th	—	—	24	6	8	38
5th	—	—	—	18	4	22
6th	—	—	—	—	8	8

Information about the distribution of guns on board Charles I's ships is scanty, the most detailed list being that for the *Sovereign of the Seas*. The information about gun distribution on ships during the Commonwealth (1649–1660) has not yet been gathered into a corpus, but the examples given in the tables illustrate the steady movement towards a standard armament.

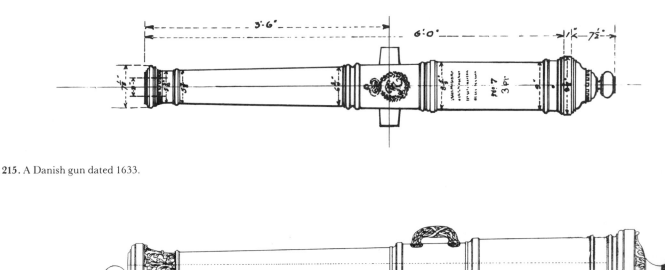

215. A Danish gun dated 1633.

216. An early seventeenth century Danish gun.

Except in minor details seventeenth century guns were like those of the previous century in appearance and, like those, might be made of brass (ie gunmetal) or iron. A characteristic feature of many of the guns was a pair of loops on the upper side of the barrel at about its centre of gravity. The loops were known as 'dolphins', were used to hold the lifting tackle when the gun was being hoisted about and were often in the shape of the mythical heraldic dolphin. Guns on the whole were not extensively decorated except on the most important ships. The *Sovereign of the Seas'* guns had the Rose and Crown, the Sceptre and Trident, and the Anchor and Cable to signify England's claim to the Dominion of the Narrow Seas. Below the Rose and Crown was the inscription 'Carolus Edgari sceptrum stabilivit aquarum' – a sentiment that other rulers were inclined to disagree with.

OFFICIAL 'GUN ESTABLISHMENT' 1677

Rate	Lower deck	Middle deck	Upper deck	Quarterdeck and forecastle
1st	26 cannon (42pdrs)	28 culverins (18pdrs)	44 sakers (5pdrs)	–
2nd	26 demi-cannon (32pdrs)	26 culverins	32 sakers	–
3rd	26 demi-cannon	–	24 12pdrs and 16 sakers	–

A little later the armament of the 2nd Rates was altered to 26 6pdrs on the upper deck, 10 on the quarterdeck and 2 3pdrs on the poop.

All the principal guns were mounted on wheeled carriages that superficially resemble those familiar to visitors to the *Victory* and other historic ships but which were, in fact, constructed in a different manner. The seventeenth century carriage was made up of two side pieces, the cheeks or brackets, fastened to a thick and rectangular wooden bed. Between the cheeks and directly below the place for the trunnions was a piece

GUNS CARRIED BY *LONDON* (2nd Rate) 1656

Lower tier	12 demi-cannon, 12 culverins
Middle tier	12 culverins, 12 demi-culverins
Forecastle	6 demi-culverins
Waist	4 demi-culverins
Quarterdeck	6 demi-culverins

217. French iron guns of 1680 (drawn by Jean Boudriot). The first French Establishment for iron guns was fixed in 1674 and included only the following calibres (with their lengths) from muzzle ring to base ring: 18pdr (2.72m), (2.56m), 8pdr (2.40m), 6pdr (2.24m), 4pdr (1.76m). The drawings represent guns of this Establishment.

218. French bronze guns of 1689 (drawn by Jean Boudriot). The 36pdr is 3.00m long from muzzle ring to base ring. Bronze guns were gradually replaced by iron guns in the 1690s and 1700s, a new Establishment of iron guns being introduced in 1690, which included all calibres: 36pdr (3.20-3.04m), 24pdr (3.04m), 18pdr (2.88m), 12pdr (2.72m), 8pdr (2.56m), 6pdr (2.24m), 4pdr (1.92m). Although proportions were altered in 1721, 1733 and 1758, the lengths remained constant until shortened by a new Establishment in 1766.

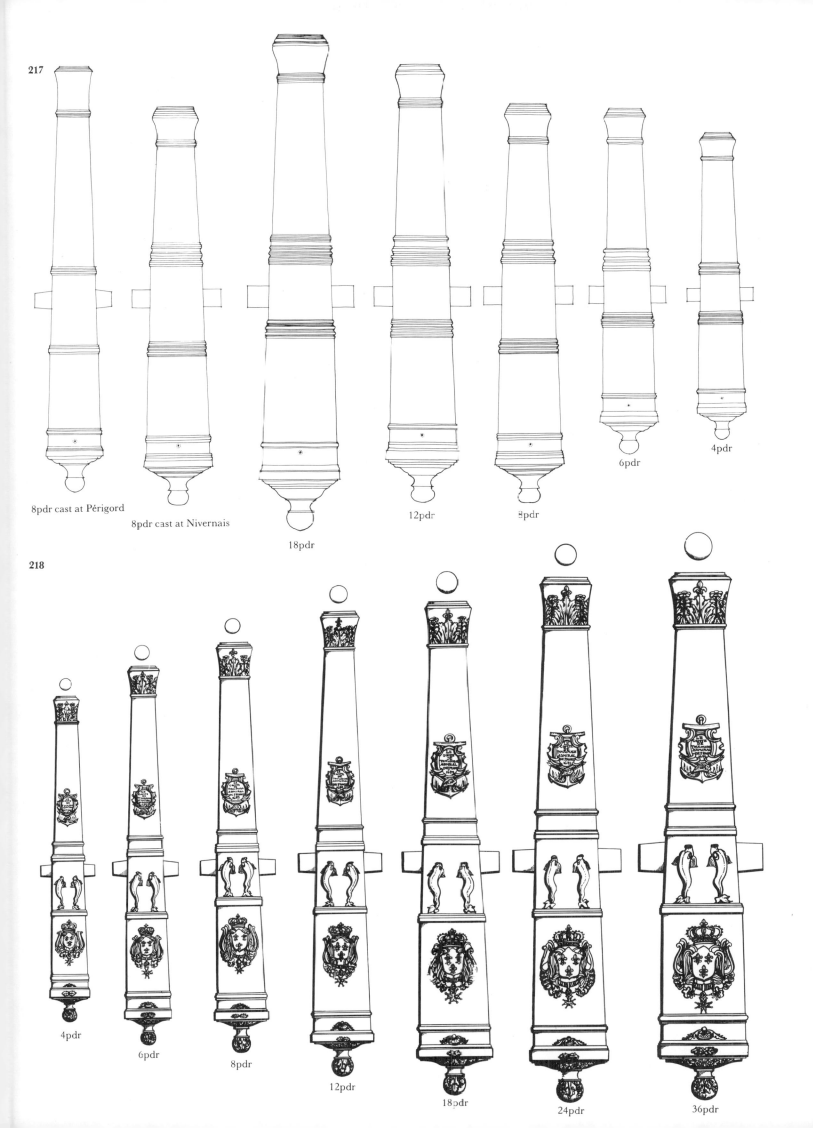

217

8pdr cast at Périgord

8pdr cast at Nivernais

18pdr

12pdr

8pdr

6pdr

4pdr

218

4pdr

6pdr

8pdr

12pdr

18pdr

24pdr

36pdr

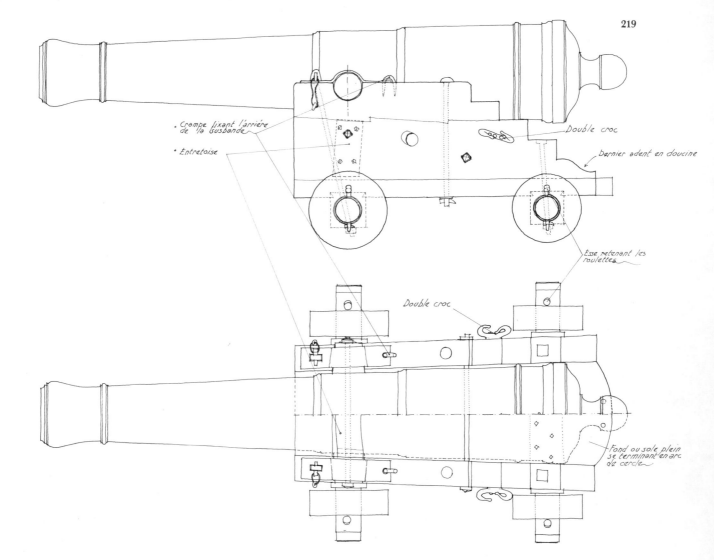

219

Crampe fixant l'arrière
de la busbande

Entretoise

Double croc

Dernier adent en doucine

Esse retenant les
roulettes

Double croc

Fond ou sole plein
se terminant en arc
de cercle

200

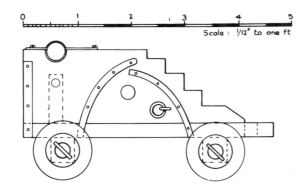

0   1   2   3   4   5
Scale : 1/12" to one ft

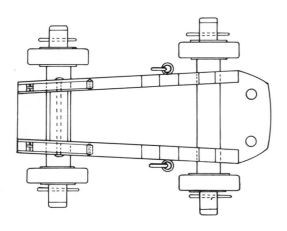

219. The standard pattern of French gun carriage from 1674 to 1758 (drawn by Jean Boudriot). This version for the 36pdr is 1.92m overall.

220. Plan of a Danish 8pdr gun carriage of about 1675, from measurements taken at the Tøhus Museum, Copenhagen. The scale of the drawing is 1:12. The principal dimensions of the carriage are given below in English inches, with the Old Danish equivalents (12 old Danish inches were equal to $12\frac{3}{4}$ English inches). The measurements are probably accurate only to the nearest $\frac{1}{4}$in, and in some parts only $\frac{1}{2}$in, because of damage to the carriage.

Length overall	57in ($4\frac{1}{2}$ Danish ft)
Height of top of carriage from floor	$28\frac{1}{2}$in ($2\frac{1}{4}$ Danish ft)
Height of sides of carriage above bottom of bed	20in ($1\frac{2}{3}$ Danish ft)
Distance between centres of axles	$33\frac{1}{2}$in ($2\frac{2}{3}$ Danish ft)
Axle trees	$5\frac{1}{2}$in square ($5\frac{1}{4}$ Danish in)
Diameter of axles	4in ($3\frac{3}{4}$ Danish in)
Height of transom piece above bed	10in ($9\frac{1}{2}$ Danish in)
Diameter of trucks	$13\frac{1}{2}$+ ($12\frac{1}{4}$–$12\frac{1}{2}$ Danish in)

221. A seventeenth century gun-tackle.

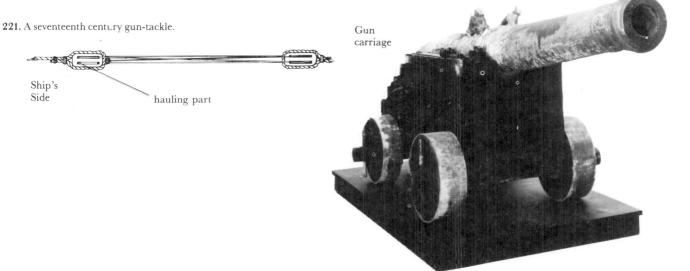

Ship's Side

hauling part

Gun carriage

222. A gun and carriage recovered from the *Wasa*.

of timber that was bolted to the cheeks and to the bed. Beneath the bed were the axletrees that carried the thick, solid wooden wheels called the trucks. These were usually reinforced by a pair of iron straps running across their face at right angles to the grain of the wood and might also have iron tyres pinned to their rims. The fore trucks were usually a little bigger than the rear pair. The latter were sometimes replaced by a pair of semi-circular blocks of wood, the friction between the blocks and the deck helping to damp down the gun's recoil.

GUNS CARRIED BY *DARTMOUTH* (5th Rate)

	1684	1687*
Lower deck	18 demi-culverins	16 demi-culverin drakes
Upper deck	10 sakers	16 sakers
Quarterdeck	4 minions	4 minions

*In 1690, when wrecked in the Sound of Mull, *Dartmouth* was carrying an armament more mixed still and containing saker-drakes and 3pdrs. This reflects the demands made on the Ordnance Department by the needs of the Navy for fitting out ships against French attacks – no doubt many old fashioned guns were brought back into service.

GUNS CARRIED BY *PEMBROKE, PORTSMOUTH* AND *MILFORD* (5th Rates)*

	Demi-culverins	8pdrs	6pdrs	3pdrs
Pembroke	4	–	6	8
Portsmouth	–	4	20	8
Milford	22	–	–	10

*Dating from about the same time as the *Dartmouth*.
The demi-culverins were 8ft long, the 6pdrs 7ft and the 3pdrs 5ft.

The gun's trunnions rested in semi-circular recesses in the upper edges of the cheeks and the recesses were often lined with iron. To prevent the gun jumping off the carriage metal straps were fixed over the tops of the trunnions. The breech of the gun was raised or lowered by moving beneath it a wooden wedge that rested on a strong piece of timber laid across a pair of the 'steps' at the rear of the carriage. Gun carriages seem surprisingly small for the size of their guns. A cannon about 12ft long and weighing over 3 tons had a carriage 5½ft long overall, and a demi-cannon's carriage was 5ft long. A Danish carriage for an 8pdr gun and dated to 1675 is 4ft 10in long and 2ft 10in high. English carriages were probably about the same height, for an English writer in about 1625 stated that the lower sill of a gun-port should be 20in above the deck and the muzzle of the gun 'near a foot' above the sill. If the phrase referred to the centre of the bore the top of the carriage would have been 2ft 8in or so above the deck. Guns were run out by tackles attached to the sides of the carriage and it would be natural to assume that these were the sort known as gun-tackles that were in use in the 1580s had not the English seaman Sir Henry Mainwaring stated that the tackles had double blocks[26]. So perhaps there was as yet no standard tackle. The gun's recoil was checked by a breeching rope that passed through holes in the sides of the carriage. The practice of securing the breeching rope to the cascabel of the gun does not seem to have been in use in the seventeenth century, or if it was, only in the last decade. To run the gun back without firing it, a tackle was rigged between the tail of the carriage and ringbolt in the deck close to the centreline of the ship.

220

221

223. A drawing based on a draught in the Admiralty Collection thought to represent the *Phoenix* of 1613. Its general resemblance to the ships in the following three illustrations is obvious.

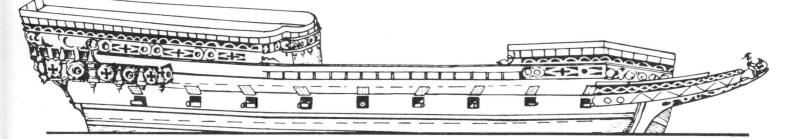

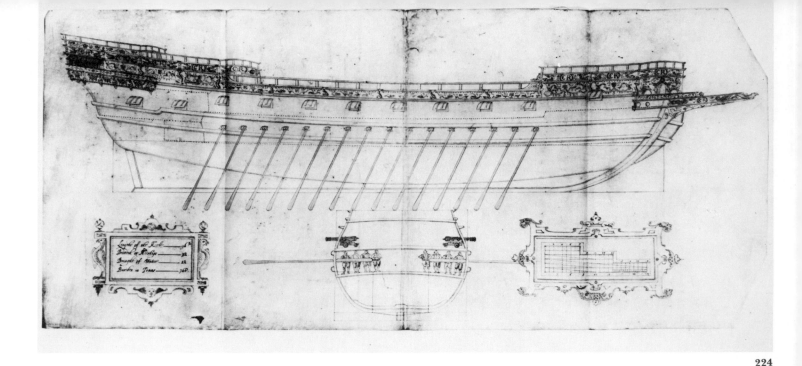

224. A design for a frigate or a pinnace of about 1625. But for the 'CR' monogram (Charles I) it would be tempting to date the plan to near the beginning of the century because of its resemblance to the early draught thought to be the English ship *Phoenix* and to one of the draughts in the *Fragments of Ancient English Shipwrightry*. The design is probably for a fast ship to deal with the pirates and privateers that infested the Channel and adjoining seas at that time. The plan is in the National Maritime Museum.

225. A single-decked ship of Dutch build. There are breaks (steps) in the decks fore and aft. The main battery is carried on the lower deck, the upper one preseumably having only light guns. Because of the great tumblehome of the sides the port lids are curved, and the nails show that they are made of two layers of plank. The decks follow the sheer at the after end.

226. A single-decked ship of about 1630. The flat bottom and shallow draught indicate Dutch influence. The fore rake is almost equal to the maximum breadth. The ship is flush decked and has much tumblehome above the main-deck. The main battery is carried on the lower deck.

227. The replica of the *Mayflower* under sail in April 1957.

228. A contemporary model of a Dutch pinnace of the mid-seventeenth century.

According to Robert Norton's book *The Gunner,* published in 1625, the breech-loading port-pieces and fowlers had a non-recoil carriage. The gun had a pair of square trunnions on each side that went into mortices in the bed. This had a pair of legs that were 'morticed before under the block of the carriage'. At the rear of the bed was a mortice or slot into which an upright post fitted and by means of a pulley, presumably on the post, the tail of the bed could be raised or lowered and it could be held in position by a pin through the post. When the gun was to be fired its muzzle 'lay upon the edge of the port and was triced with a rope about the muzzle'. There must also have been some sort of tackle for lifting the chamber into place, for the bigger port-pieces had chambers weighing several hundred-weights. Swivel guns were mounted in an iron stirrup set in a timber-head or a strong post, the wood of the mounting being bound with iron.

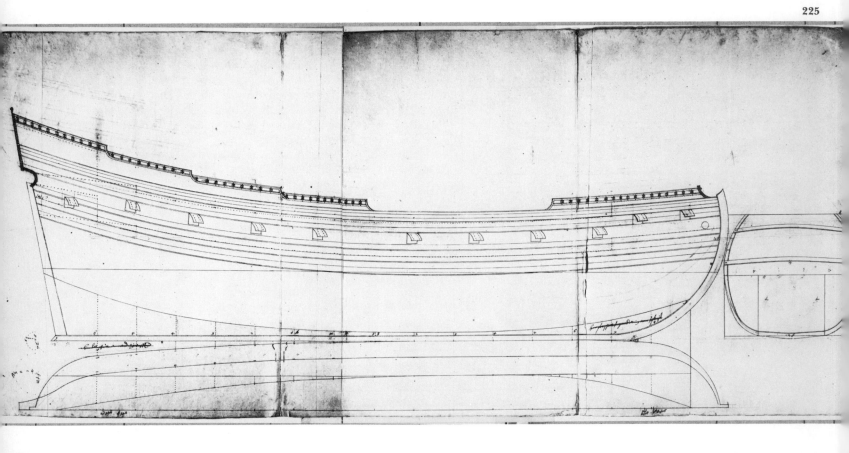

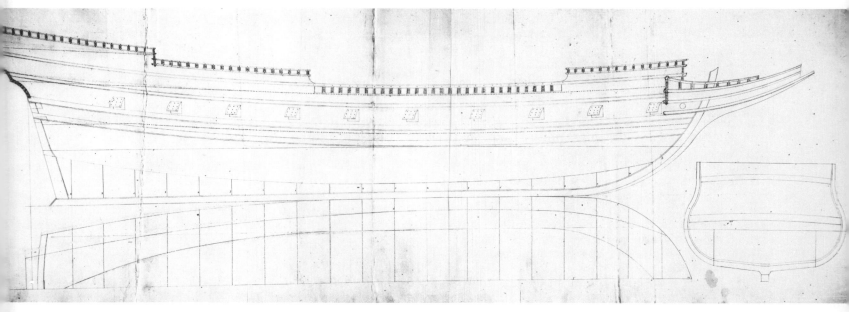

SUPPORT CRAFT

For more than half the seventeenth century a considerable part of the work of the English Navy, and probably that of the other Navies, was carried out, whenever an emergency arose, by hired merchantmen that acted as support ships, patrol craft and even took their place in the main battle fleets. During the decadence of the English Navy in the first thirty years of the century it was on hired merchantmen that fell the almost hopeless task of protecting English commerce from the pirates and privateers of all nations, including the English, that swarmed in the approaches to the Channel and Southern Ireland, and in the North Sea. Such police work was a task for which merchantmen, as a class, were ill-suited because by the nature of their build they were unlikely to be able to catch the fast and nimble ships used by pirates. Merchant ships played a more successful rôle in the battle fleets and gave a good account of themselves in the actions between the English and the Dutch in the First Dutch War (1652–4). Nevertheless, it was obvious by that time that the day when merchantmen could combat warships in a fleet action had passed and that henceforward the proper rôle for them would be as auxiliaries for support and patrol work, a rôle that they have played successfully down to the Second World War.

Little is known about the build of merchantmen from the beginning of the century. No plans are known and pictures by Dutch artists are not necessarily reliable evidence for the appearance of another country's ships. The biggest merchantmen, such as those that made the pioneering voyages to the East Indies were, practically speaking, warships, but what the smaller ones looked like is still very largely a matter of conjecture. The classic reconstruction of an early seventeenth century merchantmen is R C Anderson's model representing the *Mayflower*, which is based on some of the plans in the *Fragments of Ancient English Shipwrightry* on to which were grafted what is known about the ship's dimensions. The model has set the pattern for all subsequent models and 'replicas' of the ship, of which the best known is the 1957 version built to plans by the American naval architect W A Baker. In building that 'replica', however, several modifications had to be made to what would have been seventeenth century arrangements, in order to bring the ship into line with modern safety regulations. For example there are wooden staves across the shrouds at frequent intervals, footropes to the yards and a pair of

227

228

jaws to steady the mainyard against the mast instead of the old parrel. To judge from photographs the deadeyes and some of the blocks are not in agreement with what is known of seventeenth century shapes. One may doubt, too, whether a ship in 1620, and an old one at that, still had the decorations of a ship of 40 years or so earlier or, indeed, whether the ship had any decoration worth mentioning, for ship owners were not, and are not, given to spending money on old ships and would be unlikely to spend it to perpetuate an old style. It may also be remarked in passing, that the oft-repeated story that the barn at Jordans, in Buckinghamshire, is built from *Mayflower* timber has no foundation in fact[28].

Patrol by armed merchantmen having failed to curb the pirates, the next step was to build a squadron of small cruisers for the job. These were the 10 *Lion's Whelps* built in 1627 and called *First Whelp, Second Whelp* and so on. The *Whelps* were simply miniatures of the big warships in hull form and rig. Each was 62ft along the keel, 25ft in beam and 9ft deep in the hold, corresponding to a tonnage of 185. All had ports for oars, though just how many is not known. The *Whelps'* armament was a powerful one, originally made up of 4 culverins, 4 demi-culverins and 2 sakers, to which 2 demi-cannon were later added. The *Whelps* were not a success: their tubby hull and the weight of their armament spoiled their sailing qualities and most of the raiders, especially the Dunkirkers, could make rings round them. The Dunkirk ships had had a narrower beam and a shallower draught than the *Whelps*. One that was captured in 1636 and taken into the Navy was 63ft by 19ft by 9½ft and had a tonnage of 105 whereas the *Whelps* were 185 tons. Notwithstanding the failure of the *Whelps*, English shipwrights knew very well how to build 'nimble and forcible ships' as they were called, and could produce ships every bit as good as the Dunkirkers. The draught of one, designed in James I's reign, was found in the Danish State Archives[5]. The ship's dimensions were to be 68ft on the keel, 20ft beam and 8ft draught of water, corresponding to a tonnage of 114. The plan has ports for 18 broadside guns and there would probably be two more in the stern and perhaps a couple of bow-chasers on the forecastle. The ship was much the same size as the *Nicodemus* and was probably rigged in the same way. The Dutch produced a similar sort of ship which they called a *pinasschip*. Some were quite large, up to 75ft (Dutch units) on the keel and 24ft broad, and armed with 18 to 20 guns on the upper deck. The English also experimented with oar-and-sail hybrids. One, designed about 1625, was to be 96ft keel, 32ft beam and 14ft draught. There were 16 oars and 12 broadside ports a side. Whether the ship was ever built is not known[20].

The *Whelps* were succeeded by a different sort of warship, the frigate. Originally this was not the 'classical' frigate type but a small, fast sailing ship that had a higher keel:beam ratio than was usual at that time and perhaps other features of which we are now ignorant. Seventeenth century English frigates had keel:beam ratios of up to 4:1 and even as high as 4¾:1. They carried their main armament on the lower deck. These frigates were certainly not small ships, for the *Constant Warwick*, built in 1646 and often called the first English frigate, had a 90ft keel, 28ft beam and was 12ft deep in hold. Her tonnage was 379 and she carried 30 guns. Another frigate built in the same year, the *Adventure*, was 94ft by 27ft by 10ft and was armed with 38 guns. Both ships had a

229. The Dutch called ships of this sort pinnaces but they were near in function to the later frigates. This ship was to be 90ft from stem to stern and 24ft in beam. The mizzen channels are present. Note the four lower-deck scuppers, which appear to be bored-out blocks of wood. The reverse curve of the topsides at the bows is more pronounced than it was on English ships of the same period.

230. The frigate *Hummeren,* of 1665. The hull has a hull section the overall appearance of a Dutch pinnace, and a long beakhead reminiscent of ships of the early part of the century. The main battery is on the lower deck, where there are 8 sweep ports a side. Fore and main channels are shown but none for the mizzen shrouds. This draught is endorsed by King Frederick 'The ship shall be built at Glyckstad according to this model. Given at the castle of Kiobenhaffen the 5th of December 1664. Friderich'. Length between perpendiculars 106½ft. Armament 32 guns.

231. The English equivalent to the Dutch pinnace, a 36-gun ship of about 1660. Like the Dutch (228, 229), Danish (230) and French (232) examples, this ship had only one complete lower deck, a gap in the waist on the upper deck where no guns were mounted, and a small poop. This arrangement differentiates these ships from the later 'true frigate', which had two complete decks (with no guns on the lower deck).

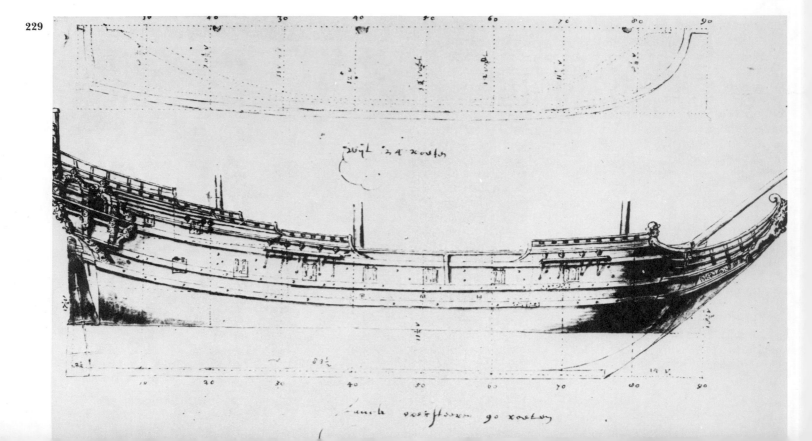

229

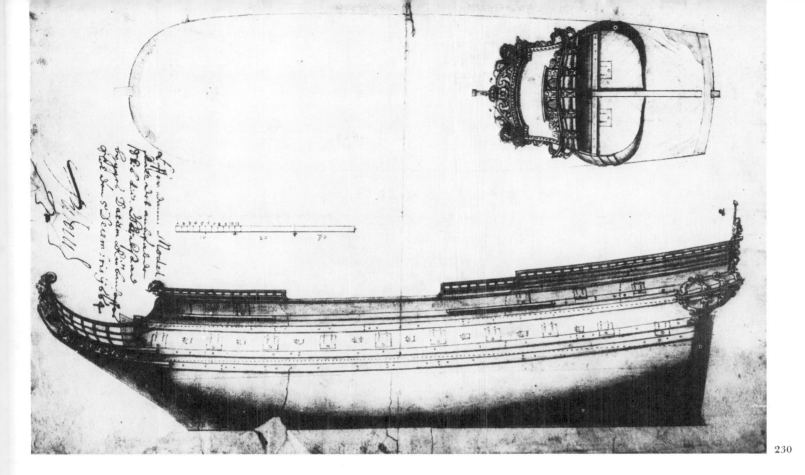

230

higher keel:beam ratio than was normal for ships of their time and had a shallower draught. The *Adventure* and at least two others of her class had oarports between the guns on the lower deck but whether the *Constant Warwick* did is not certain.

The type was a successful one but before long the ships were given more guns and converted into 2-deckers, a change that was said to have changed the *Constant Warwick* into 'a slug'. By the 1650s the name frigate had attached itself to other sorts of ship and came to mean either a faster-than-usual ship, rather as the name clipper did in the nineteenth century, or a ship that had a greater keel:beam ratio than was normal and was, so to

speak, frigate-built. Probably it was in that capacity that the *Naseby*, a 90-gun 1st Rate, was referred to as a frigate.

In the second half of the century the search for a fast and manoeuvrable warship led to the development of a class of oar-sail hybrids called galleys. These were not, of course, the traditional galleys but were either descendants of the 1625 type or a redevelopment of it. The type is exemplified by the design for the *Charles Galley* of 1676, which carried 20 guns on her upper deck and two more on each side beyond the oars on the lower deck. By the end of the century interest in oar-sail hybrids had waned although the idea survived and was resurrected from time to time in the eighteenth century.

231

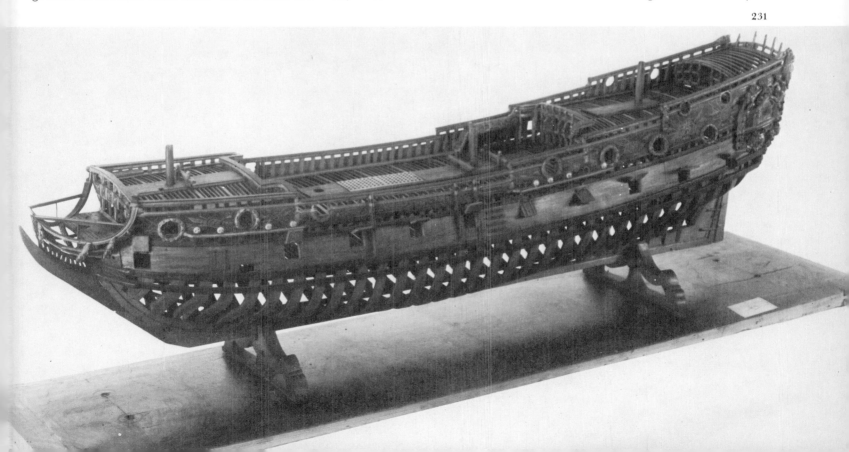

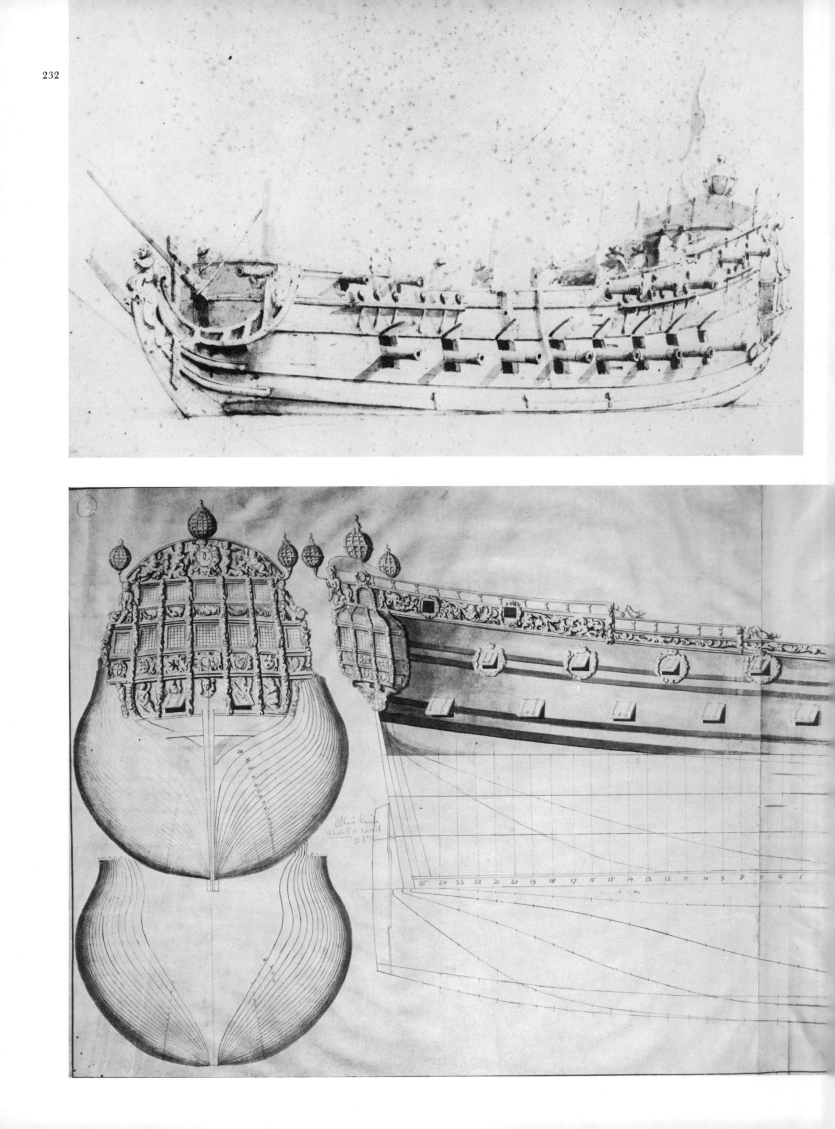

232. The 30-gun *Play*, a captured French ship formerly *Le Jeux* built in 1689 at Dunkerque. The high bulwarks of the quarterdeck and poop suggest Dutch influence. There are three scuppers admidships on the lower deck. The original Van de Velde drawing is in the National Maritime Museum.

233. It is not often that there is evidence against which to check Van de Velde drawings, but this original draught of the bow decorations of the *Jeux* confirms the accuracy of the previous drawing in most details. The figurehead of the child seems to have lost its garland, but this may reflect action damage during the ship's capture.

234. One of the Keltridge Collection of draughts of 1684 – a 4th Rate 'near the dimensions of the *Adventure*'. Nearly 40 years after her launch the *Adventure* was still being used as a model of excellence.

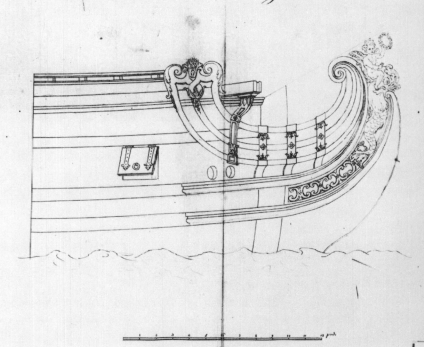

Proüe du Navire les Jeux.

233

234

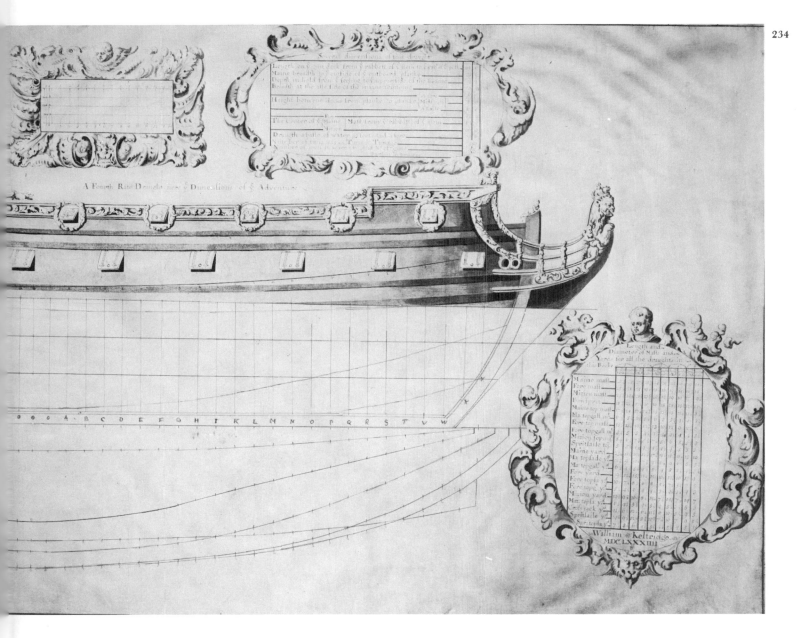

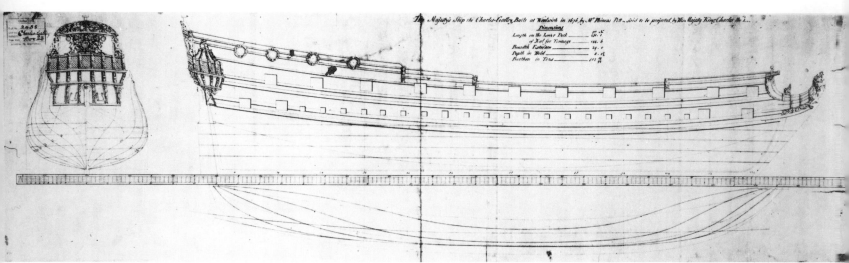

235

Frigates and oar-sail hybrids were not the only new types of warship to come into service in the seventeenth century, but except in the cases of yachts and bomb-vessels there is insufficient information yet to enable a reliable picture to be drawn. Yachts and bomb-vessels, in fact, were the two real innovations of the century insofar as the English navy was concerned because neither had any precedent in it. The development of the yacht, as a pleasure craft and a despatch vessel, began with the presentation of the *Mary* to Charles II, in 1660, by the Dutch. In her build and rig the *Mary* was a typical Dutch inland waterway and estuarine passenger boat, for she had been built for the Amsterdam Dutch East India Company. The *Mary*'s dimensions were: keel 52ft, beam 19ft, depth in hold 7ft 7in and draught 10ft. Being a shallow-draught boat she had the usual Dutch leeboards. The decoration was of a sumptuousness appropriate to a gift to a King. There was a Unicorn figurehead, gilded wreaths round the ports for the *Mary*'s 8 small guns and on the stern were the Royal Arms. The interior decoration was, naturally,

235. The *Charles Galley* of 1676. This ship is somewhat larger than the oar-and-sail pinnace (224) and has a keel:beam ratio of 3.93:1 compared with 3:1 on the earlier ship. There are 19 sweep ports a side. The larger port just under the beginning of the quarterdeck is a ballast port, and there are gunports near the bow and in the quarters.

236. 'The Prince's yacht and the State yacht leaving Moerdijk with Charles II, 1660' by W Van de Velde the Elder. This famous incident in the Restoration of Charles II is vividly described by Samuel Pepys in his Diary for 1660. The Prince's yacht is the *Mary*, given to him by the Dutch (right of centre). The State yacht is presumably the vessel on the left.

237. A Royal yacht of about 1674. The hull is contemporary and so are the mast, gaff and lower yard. The remainder of the rigging has been reconstructed from details in contemporary pictures. The model is thought to represent a projected design although its proportions are like those of the *Katherine* and *Portsmouth* of 1674. The model corresponds to a vessel 70ft long on the deck, 56ft keel, 20ft 4in beam and 8ft 1in deep, and is in the National Maritime Museum, Greenwich.

236

ornate and in the contemporary Dutch style. Under the English flag the *Mary* was gaff-rigged, with a mainsail and, probably, a foresail and fore staysail. She *may* have had a topsail[30]. A year later the Dutch gave Charles another, smaller yacht, the *Bezan*. She was 34ft on the keel, 14ft in breadth and 7ft in depth. Charles was so pleased with his yachts that he had several others built by English shipwrights, five of them being built between 1661 and 1663. The new yachts were designed to suit English coastal waters and were given less beam and a deeper draught than the Dutch vessels. The English yachts were a success and were soon put to good use as ancillary craft for naval service. They served another purpose, too. The King's desire for a fast and weatherly yacht, a desire that his brother James shared, encouraged shipwrights to study the newly emerging science of naval architecture and to apply its findings to the design of the yachts. Contrariwise, the sailing properties of the yachts provided data for further fruitful study as, indeed, yachting has to the present day. The rig of yachts, at first, was a single-masted gaff rig like the *Mary*'s but about 1682 the ketch rig was introduced. This was the 'square' ketch rig, which has been aptly described as a ship without a foremast.

No draughts of Caroline yachts have come to light up to now but a good deal is known about their external appearance from pictures by the van de Veldes and others, and from contemporary models in the National Maritime Museum, the reference numbers for the models being 1685–1, 1690–1, 1690–2 and 1690–3.

Yachts varied a great deal in size, from 24 tons (the *Deal*) to 180 tons. Like all other classes of ships yachts grew in size, as indicated in the table[31].

SIZES OF YACHTS 1660–1677				
Name	Built	Keel (ft)	Beam (ft)	Tons
Mary (I)	1660	52	19	100 (or 92)
Katherine	1661	49	19	94
Merlin	1666	53	19½	109
Saudadoes	1670	74	21½	180
Cleveland	1671	53½	19½	107
Portsmouth	1674	57	20½	133
Charles	1675	54	20½	120
Charlotte	1677	61	20½	143
Mary (II)	1677	66½	21½	155

Charles II kept an average of 15 yachts in service and they were employed on surveying and patrol work as well as in their services as transport for members of the Court and the Navy. Some took part in naval actions, one of them, the *Henrietta*, being sunk in action, whilst the *Katherine* was captured by the Dutch in 1673. The armaments the yachts carried were necessarily light. When the first *Mary* sank off Holyhead, Anglesey, in 1675, her armament included two 4pdrs, six 3pdrs and a

238. A draught of one of the first English bomb vessels, the *Mortar* of 1693. This vessel was ship-rigged, and measured 260 tons.

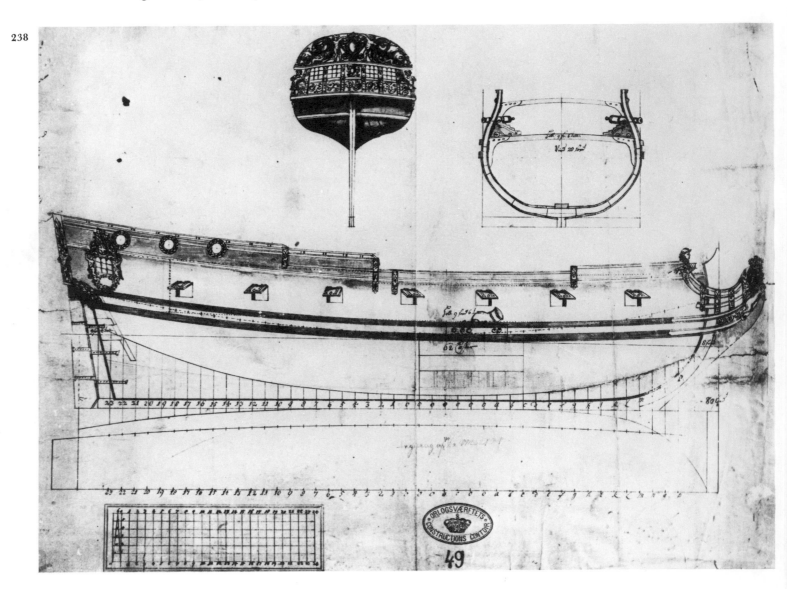

238

239

239. 'The Spanish Armada off the English coast' by C C van Wieringen. The scene represents the Spaniards throwing their horses overboard because food and water were exhausted. The picture was probably painted in the early 1600s and represents ships of that time. Note the carefully drawn boat at the stern of the central ship.

1½pdr. Three other guns noted when the wreck was discovered were removed clandestinely and have not since been traced. As the *Mary* was a comparatively small yacht the guns on the bigger yachts would be more powerful.

The other new type of warship, the bomb-vessel, appeared only in the last years of the century. Bomb-vessels were strongly-built craft, usually ketch-rigged, and carried a heavy mortar. They were used for attacking fortifications and other targets that were inaccessible by direct fire. Bomb-vessels appear to have been a French invention of about 1680 but like other newly invented weapons they were soon copied by other nations. The English had bomb-vessels by 1687 and the Danes soon afterwards. The early history of bomb-vessels is still obscure, however, and because they appeared so late in the seventeenth century a discussion of their development has been deferred to the next chapter.

BOATS

As with other aspects of the Navy's development in the seventeenth century, quantitative information about boats becomes more plentiful but interpreting the data is complicated by changes of name for established types of boats and by the use of the same name for different sorts of vessels. 'Pinnace' for example changes it meaning from a small ship to a ship's boat and for a while both meanings existed side by side. There is also a lack of reliable pictures of boats before the second half of the century. Notwithstanding these drawbacks, however, much more is known about seventeenth century boats than about those from any previous period[32].

The first dimensional evidence comes from the 1618 Commission of Inquiry into the administration of the Navy. The Commission noted that each of the ships in the two biggest Rates had a longboat, a pinnace and a skiff. The longboats were the biggest. The *Prince Royal*'s was 52ft 4in long, the *Assurance*'s 51ft 3in and that of the *Speedwell*, a 3rd Rate, was 40ft 6in. These boats were about half as long as the keels of the ships to which they belonged and as boats so long were too big to be hoisted aboard they had to be towed, to the detriment of their mother ship's sailing qualities. The Commission considered that the longboats were too big and recommended that the *Prince Royal*'s should be only 42ft long and the *Speedwell*'s 31ft. Those lengths are between 0.36 and 0.4 of the ships' keel lengths. Pinnaces were to be from 26 to 29ft long and jollywatts, which were to replace the skiffs, were to be from 17ft 6in to 19ft 8in. Another recommendation was that the length of longboats should be 3.5 to 3.8 beams, pinnaces 3.8 to 4 beams and jolly-watts 3.1 beams in length. Like so many good recommendations from Commissions, these were pigeon-holed. Nine years later another Commisssion reported the sizes of boats in use to be: longboats, as long as 52ft and as short as 21ft 3in; pinnaces, between 32ft 4in and 25ft; jollywatts, between 20ft and 14ft; a barge, 36ft 9in; and a shallop, 27ft. The longboats had a windlass and a davit, for use when weighing anchors. Pinnaces are clearly boats in this context, but at about the time the Commission was investigating, the Navy received two pinnaces, the *Henrietta* and the *Maria,* that were, equally clearly, small ships, for they were 52ft by 15ft by 6½ft and carried 6 guns apiece. It was expressly stated that they were to be carvel-built, which suggests that the other sort of pinnaces were clinker-planked. The Commission's report seems to have led, in time, to some standardisation of boat sizes, for in the 1650s 2nd Rates had a longboat, a pinnace and a skiff that were 35ft, 29ft and 20ft respectively whilst for 3rd Rates they were 33ft, 28ft and 20ft.

The appearance of English boats cannot be reconstructed with any exactitude because no contemporary plans have come to light, and although boats are often shown in pictures the natural emphasis on the picturesque leaves much detail invisible. Continental boats are better recorded, for several plans have been found. To judge from pictures English boats were like the Swedish ones.

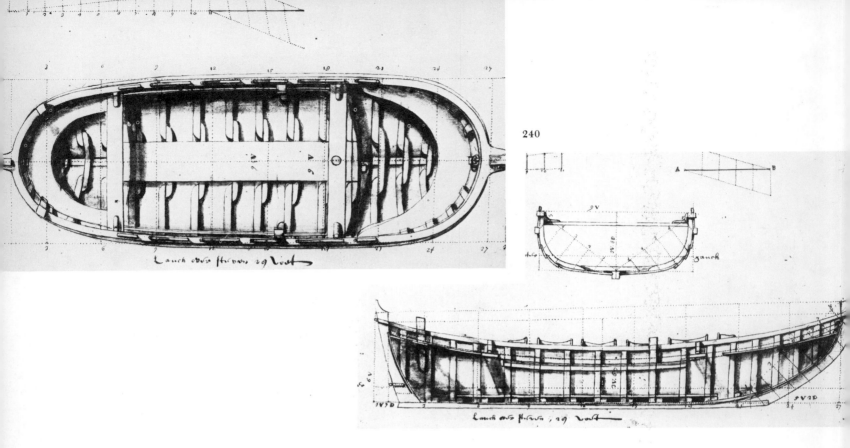

240

Boats were not decorated as lavishly as ships. English ones might have the stemhead black, the gunwale and the strake below it black and the rest of the hull above water brown (ie varnished or tarred wood), and the underbody is often shown white. Alternatively, the gunwale might be varnished, the strake below it painted 'gilt' and the one below that red. A boat of the last years of the century had the interiors of its stern panels painted blue and with floral patterns in gilt. It is unlikely, in fact, that there was any standard pattern for painting boats and each captain probably had his ship's boats painted to suit his fancy.

There is little to say about the stowing of the boats. Longboats, as already mentioned, were towed but the others were hoisted aboard and were presumably stowed one inside another.

REFERENCES

Abbreviations
IJNA: International Journal of Nautical Archaeology
MM: The Mariner's Mirror, the Journal of the Society for Nautical Research
MS: Model Shipwright
NRS: The Navy Records Society publications.

1 *A Treatise on Shipbuilding and a Treatise on Rigging written about 1620–25*, W Salisbury and R C Anderson (Editors), Society for Nautical Research (1958)
2 The picture is in the Queen's House, National Maritime Museum, London
3 'A Draught of a Jacobean 3-decker', W Salisbury, *MM* (1961) Vol 47 pp170–7
4 The plan believed to represent the *Phoenix* of 1613 is reproduced as Plate 1 of *Old Ship Figureheads and Sterns*, L G Carr Laughton, London (1925), but no Admiralty plan reference is given
5 'A "Royal Yacht" ', H C Bjerg, *MM* (1975) Vol 61 p94
6 The model is in the Rosenborg Palace, Copenhagen
7 On the framing of models see: R C Anderson, *MM* (1953) Vol 39 p139; W A Baker, *MM* (1954) Vol 40 pp80–1; R C Anderson, *MM* (1954) Vol 40 pp155–6; W Salisbury, *MM* (1954) Vol 40 pp156–9
8 'The *Dartmouth*, a British frigate wrecked off Mull, 1690. Pt 5: The ship', C M J Martin, *IJNA* (1978) Vol 7 pp29–58
9 *A History of the Administration of the Royal Navy 1509–1660*, M Oppenheim (1896), p207, quoting State Papers Domestic (James I), CLXI f 68, and p341, quoting State Papers Domestic (Commonwealth), CL f 170
10 Oppenheim, p259, quoting State Papers Domestic (Charles I), CCXXVIII f 63, 41.1

11 *The Autobiography of Phineas Pett, NRS* No 51
12 *Souvenirs de Marine Conservée: La Couronne*, Admiral Paris
13 *A Doctrine of Naval Architecture*, Sir Anthony Deane (1670), Pepysian Library, Magdalene College, Cambridge
14 *Elizabethan Ship*, Gregory Robinson, Longmans (1974)
15 'A Specification for a Danish ship of 1613', R C Anderson, *MM* (1932) Vol XVIII pp81–6; 'Danish Shipbuilding in 1613', Orlogskaptajn P Holck, translated by R C Anderson, *MM* (1932) Vol XVIII pp81–6; and 'Dutch Shipbuilding in 1664', Commander H Börjeson, translated by R C Anderson, *MM* (1928) Vol XIV pp158–62 ·
16 'A Collection of Shipbuilding Contracts', R C Anderson, *MM* (1955) Vol 41 pp48–52
17 *Old Ship Figureheads and Sterns*, L G Carr Laughton, London (1925), p142, quoting Declared Accounts 2659–61 (originals in the Public Records Office, London)
18 Carr Laughton, p265
19 Carr Laughton, p264
20 'The Lighting of Poop Lanterns', A McDermott, *MM* (1956) Vol 42 pp233–4
21 Now in the National Maritime Museum, London. See *State Barges*, Peter Norton, published by the National Maritime Museum
22 The Museum reference number is 1660–2
23 The Museum reference number is 1675–1
24 See *The Great Age of Sail*, Edita S A, Lausanne, p64
25 *Seventeenth Century Rigging*, R C Anderson, Percival Marshall (1955); *The Masting and Rigging of English Ships of War 1625–1860*, James Lees, Conway Maritime Press (1979)
26 'Seaman's Dictionary' in *The Life and Works of Sir Henry Manwayring, NRS* No 56 Vol 2
27 *Skepps Byggerij eller Adelig Öfnings*, A C Raalamb (1691), facsimile reprint by Sjöhistoriska Museet, Stockholm (1943)
28 The relevant references are: 'A *Mayflower* Model', R C Anderson, *MM* 1926) Vol XII p260; *The New Mayflower: Her Design and Construction*, W A Baker, Barre, Massachusetts; and 'The Jordans barn and the *Mayflower*', W Jorrocks, *MM* (1922) Vol VIII pp2, 81, 140, 237, 354
29 Now in the National Maritime Museum, London (Draught Room ref A192)
30 'The *Mary*: Charles II's yacht', P N Davies and P W J McBride, *IJNA* (1973) Vol 2 pp59–73
31 *Royal Yachts*, G P B Naish, published by the National Maritime Museum, London
32 *Boats of Men-of-War*, Commander W E May, published by the National Maritime Museum, London; 'Fittings for Wooden Warships. Part 2: Boats', Robert Gardiner, *MS* (1977) No 19 pp235–41.

241

242

240. A launch for a Dutch ship. The boat is 28ft overall and of 9½ft beam and is of shallow draught, clinker-built and with heavy frames made in three parts. The high sheer and the long, overhanging prow give the boat a resemblance to the boats in the Hastings Manuscript in Chapter 2. The boat had a single mast. Note the towing posts near the stern, which are like those shown on the boats in Anthony Anthony's drawings of Henry VIII's Navy.

241. This painting, by Botticelli, of a carrack of the second half of the fifteenth century is the most accurate known representation of the deck of a sailing ship of that time. Note the interesting capstan, and the end of the bitt-beam protruding well clear of the ship's side. It may have been used for catting the anchor.

242. The *Henry Grace à Dieu* in 1546, from the Anthony Anthony Roll. She has two complete gun-decks and each deck in the towering fore- and after-castles carries a heavy armament. The rigging is only a token representation but Anthony has taken pains to show some unusual features such as the mainyard made of two overlapping pieces, the sheerhooks on the fore and main yard-arms, the long bowsprit with a pointed grapnel hanging from a chain, and right at the end the crowned orb. The great length of the pennants is confirmed by the accounts and inventories of the ship. She is depicted here as she was after her rebuild in 1540 and differs from the vessel in the *Embarkation of Henry VIII'* painting (247) that is supposed to be the earlier *Henry Grace à Dieu*. The *Henry* was one of the biggest ships of her day and represents the ultimate development of the English carrack. Her armament comprised: (brass guns) 4 cannons, 3 demi-cannons, 14 culverins, 2 demi-culverins and 4 sakers; (iron guns) 3 falcons, 14 port-pieces, 14 slings, 2 half-slings, 8 fowlers, 60 bases, 2 top-pieces, 100 hand-guns and 40 hailshot pieces. ,

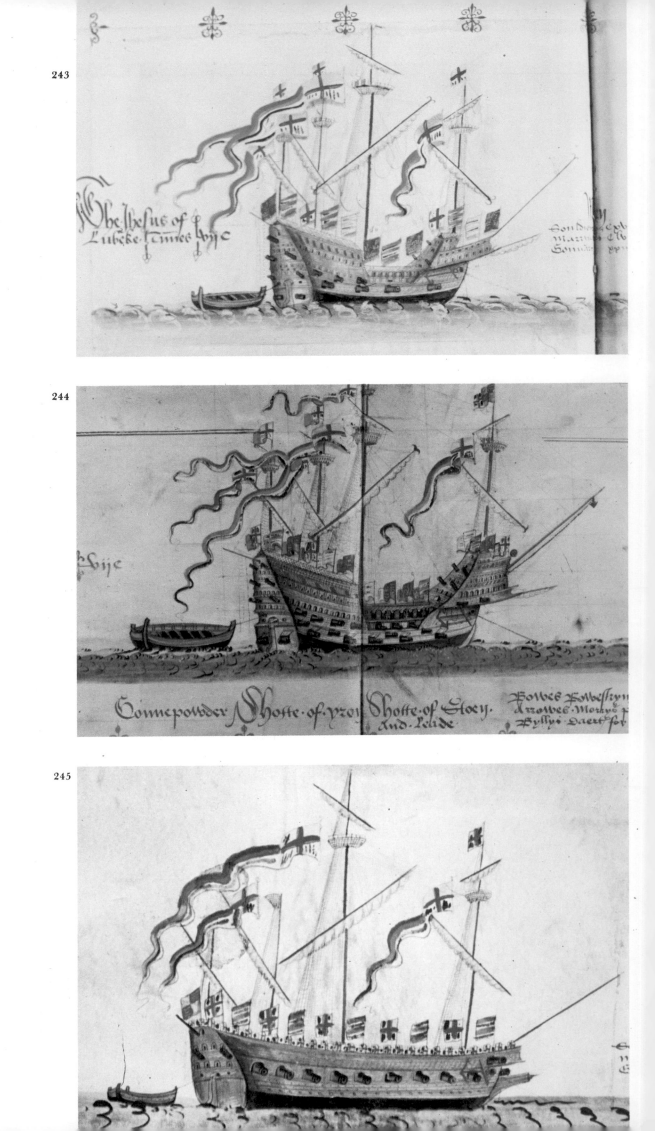

243

The Ihesus of
Lubeke tymes hije

244

hije

Gonnepowder Shotte of yron Shotte of Stoey
and Leide

245

243. As her name implies, the *Jesus of Lubeck* (700 tons) was a North German vessel that had been bought for Henry VIII's Navy. Anthony Anthony's picture shows the *Jesus* as she was in 1545, when her armament was: (brass guns) 2 cannon, 2 culverins and 2 sakers; (iron guns) 4 port-pieces, 10 slings, 4 fowlers, 12 bases, 2 top-pieces, 20 hailshot pieces and 20 hand-guns. A remarkable feature of the *Jesus* is the absence of gunport lids. As she is not the only ship in the Anthony Roll to be shown without them (the *Great Bark* and the *Matthew* have none except on the stern ports) perhaps the lids were hung inside the hull.

244. The *Mary Rose* (700 tons) was built in 1509 and had been extensively rebuilt before Anthony Anthony drew her picture in 1545. In that year she sank off Portsmouth whilst in action against the French. Although of the same tonnage as the *Jesus of Lubeck*, the *Mary Rose* was a bigger ship and carried a heavier armament. Anthony recorded it as: (brass guns 2 cannon, 2 demi-cannon, 2 culverins, 2 sakers and 1 falcon; (iron guns) 12 port-pieces, 2 slings, 2 half-slings, 2 quarter-slings, 6 fowlers, 30 bases, 2 top-pieces and 40 hailshot pieces. The *Mary Rose* had two counters above the rudder-head whereas the *Jesus* had only one.

245. The *Harte* (by Anthony Anthony), a very similar ship to the radical *Tyger* design (see 118). Like that ship, she had a long life, surviving until the end of the century.

246. The Anthony Anthony portrait of the 'galliass' *Greyhound* (see also 114).

247. Part of the large picture at Hampton Court known as 'The Embarkation of Henry VIII for France'. The picture was painted several years after the event (1520) and cannot be relied upon as contemporary evidence for the appearance of the ships that took part. The central ship is sometimes said to be the *Henry Grace à Dieu* but that ship was not present. Although the scene as depicted is imaginary it does convey something of the general appearance of Henry VIII's biggest ships: their short and tubby hulls with much tumble-home, the high 'castles' at bow and stern, and the heavy armament mounted low down in the hulls. The rigging, however, is unreliable. All the ships have square mizzens, and even square mizzen topsails, neither of which are otherwise known before the end of the six-ttenth century at the earliest. The lifts do not agree with what the inventories record and there are no braces to the upper yards.

248. The spar and sail plan for a ship with a keel of about 80ft from the Matthew Baker *'Fragments'*. The caps on the lower mast and topmast heads show that topmasts and topgallant masts could be lowered at sea. The mizzen-mast seems to have a pole flagstaff. The ship has a cathead, the first recorded example on an English ship. The lower deck guns are on two levels, the foremost and one of those at the after end being lower than the rest, ie the lower deck had a 'fall' or step at each end. The mast and sail plans are, however, later additions to the sheer draught and correspond with the dimensions given in a survey of the Royal Navy made in about 1600, whereas the decoration of the hull is more appropriate to the 1570s and 1580s. The draught has been variously identified, without reliable evidence, with the *Elizabeth Jonas*, the *Revenge* and the *Ark Royal*.

247

249. There are many features of interest in this draught (also from the (*Fragments*') beside the well-known comparison of the hull's shape with that of a fish. The foremast is stepped just in front of the beakhead bulkhead and rakes slightly forward. The mainmast is close to the half-deck bulkhead and appears to lean slightly backwards. The mizzenmast has been moved forward from its old position at the end of the poop and stands above the after end of the keel. There is a gangway, or perhaps a spar deck over the waist. The three large, semi-circular openings in the waist's bulwarks are an unusual feature. They are too big, too few and too high up to be oarports. They may be openings for swivel guns or large hand-guns. The door-like opening in the side abaft the main channel has sometimes been described as a door into a side gallery that would be placed there but not drawn in (as in French eighteenth century draughts), but it may be just a gunport. In the stern, at each side of the rudder-head, is a pair of small circular holes. They are the 'catholes' for the cables when the ship is moored by the stern. Note the peculiar construction of the fore and main channels: they are fastened to short, vertical riders on the side and stand clear of the hull.

250. This plan from the Baker *'Fragments'* is possibly a plan for an 'improved *Tygar'* (see also 118 and 119). The small circular openings between the gunports are too narrow for oars unless they were very narrow-bladed, and are probably for muskets.

248

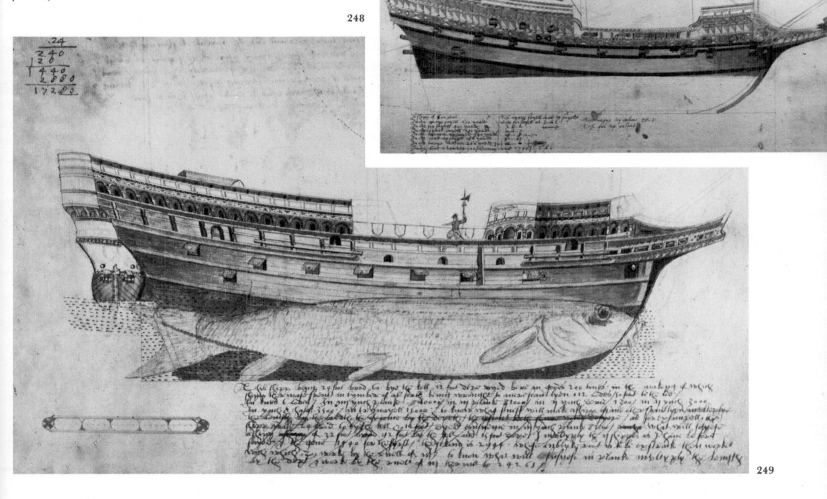

249

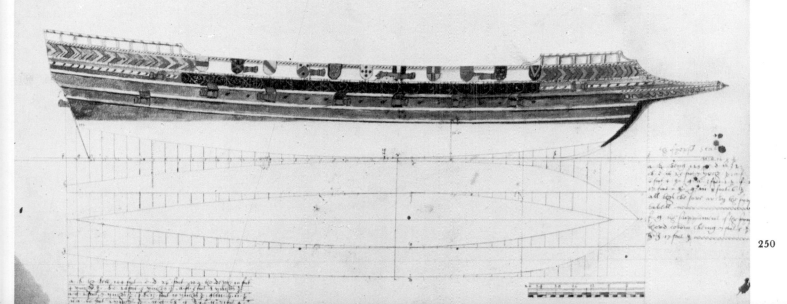

250

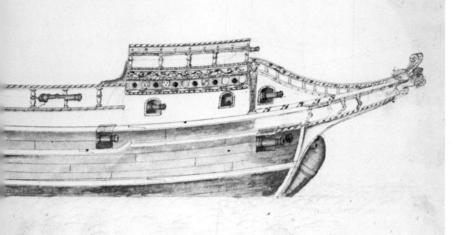

251. In this draught from the *'Fragments'* the resemblance of the ship's figure-head to the Lion of St Mark suggests that she may have been a Venetian ship of designed for sale to the Venetians. Features of particular interest are the short planks, the carefully marked scarphs of the wales, the carved brackets to the head rails and the statue at the corner of the forecastle. The decorative stanchions of the waist's bulwarks and the forecastle rails suggest that this was no ordinary ship. Note the gun on a stepped carriage in the waist and the faint outline of a similar carriage beneath the chase gun on the forecastle deck.

251

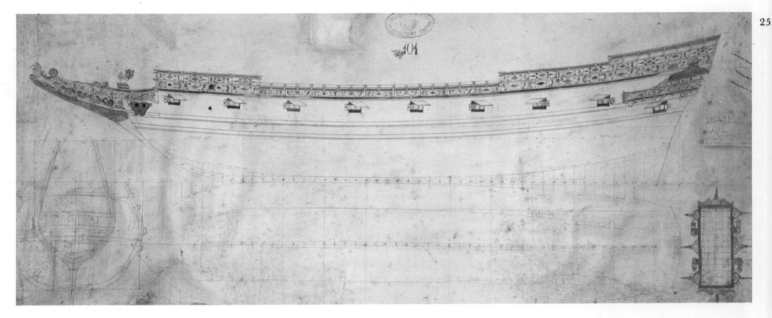

25

252. A Danish draught of an 18-gun 'pinnace' of the early seventeenth century. It has the joint arms of England and Scotland on the quarter galleries so can be no earlier than James I, but the resemblance to the draughts in the Matthew Baker *'Fragments'* is marked (see also 223–226).

253. An early seventeenth century Danish lion figurehead, although the colour is probably not original.

254. Abraham Willaerts' painting of a large Spanish warship at Naples was completed in 1669 but many of the features of the ship indicate a vessel of the first half of the century.

25

255

256

255. Willem van de Velde the Younger's fine study of the Battle of the Texel 1673. The centre ship is the Dutch *Gouden Leeuw* (the flagship of Cornelisz Tromp) and she is shown bearing down on the English *Royal Prince*.

256. The gilded equestrian figurehead of the *Prince* model (see also 147).

257. The stern of the *Mordaunt* 0f 48 guns. This ship was built in 1681 and purchased into the Royal Navy in 1683, It gives some idea of the degree of decoration during its most elaborate period.

258. The stern of a Stuart royal yacht of about 1690.

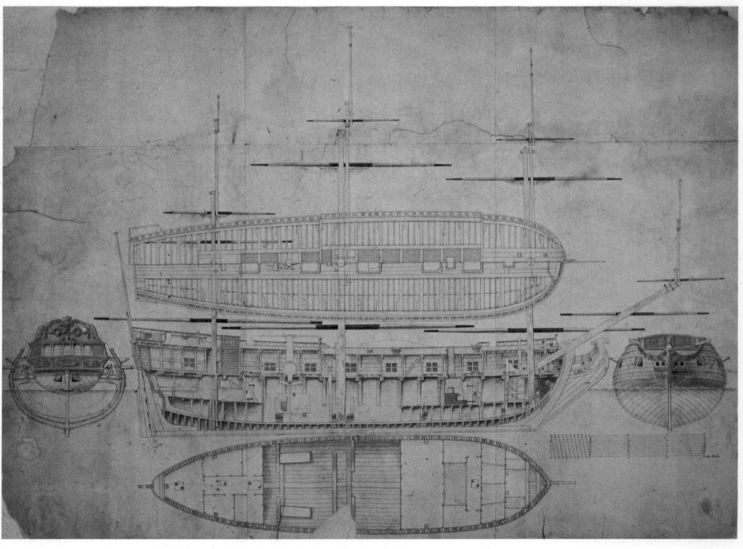

259. The stern of the *Soleil Royal,* 104 guns, built in 1690 (from a model in the Musée de la Marine, Paris).

260. A very colourful Danish composite draught of the sloop *Raae* of 1709. Plans like this are virtually non-existent in the British and French official collections until the nineteenth century – large numbers of ships and a high degree of standardisation meant that less time and effort could be spent on draughting.

261. The head of a 90-gun ship of 1703 showing the last flowering of Baroque gilded decoration in the Royal Navy.

262. A contemporary model of an English 50-gun ship built to the 1719 Establishment.

263. The head of a 60-gun ship of about 1730. This is an English model although the ship depicted may be Spanish.

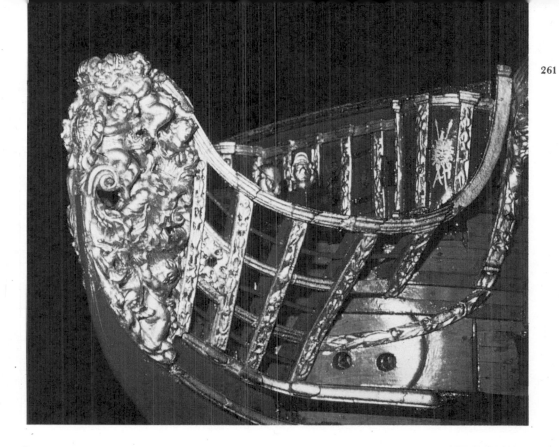

261

262

263

264. Part of the exceptionally detailed model of the bomb vessel *Granado* of 1742, built by Bob Lightley according to the 'Dockyard model' convention (with some exposed framing) from the original plans. It won the first National Maritime Museum modelmaking competition, and now resides in that museum.

265. Broadside detail of a 1745 Establishment 60-gun ship. This contemporary model was made by John Hancock of the Deptford Royal Dockyard.

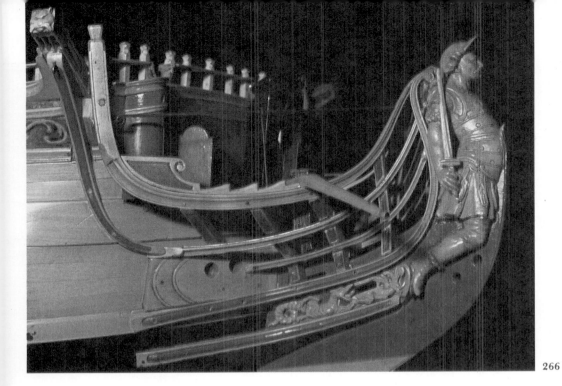

266

266. The bow of the *Achilles* of 60 guns (1757). The figurehead was one of the first with the very upright stance that became standard for the next half-century.

267. The famous United States frigate *Constitution*, of 1500 tons (English measurement) and 50 guns, currently preserved at Boston. The photograph shows her at sea for the bi-centennial celebrations of the Declaration of Independence. The large number of visitors on board the ship give an impression of the crowded decks of a warship.

267

268

268. De Loutherbourg's famous painting of the 'Glorious First of June' battle in 1794 is a very good reference for contemporary styles of ship decoration. The ship of the left is the British flagship *Queen Charlotte* which can be identified from the figurehead.

269. A contemporary model of a large 60-gun frigate of about 1813. These ships were designed as a counter to the American big frigates of the *Constitution* type.

270. A mortar at Pendennis Castle, Cornwall, dating from about 1830. Sea service mortars were mounted on similar beds. The bed is a modern reproduction made according to contemporary plans.

271. A nineteenth century coast defence gun at Pendennis Castle, mounted on a slide carriage. The front end of the lower carriage is pivoted but the rear end has a pair of trucks that run on iron rails. The carriage is a modern reproduction made to contemporary plans.

269

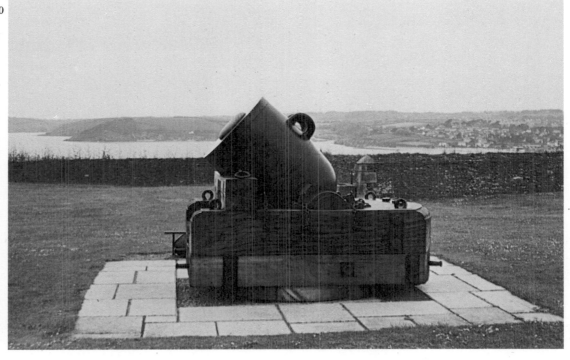

270

271

272. Lt Col Harold Wyllie's painting of the British frigate *Unicorn* as she will appear when restoration work has been completed. The ship, currently at Dundee, is a fine example of the last generation of sailing warships and includes all of Seppings' innovations, most noticeably the round stern.

FRIGATE & SLOOP

Shipbuilding development in the seventeenth century had been concentrated for the most part on the 'capital ships' of the time – the 2- and 3-deckers – and concentrated to such good effect that by 1700 most of the difficulties associated with building multi-decked vessels able to carry effectively a large number of heavy guns had been overcome so far as the knowledge and technology of the century permitted. Changes in the shape of the lower hull improved stability and additions to the sail plan conferred better sailing qualities. It can be said, as a general statement, that below the upper deck level an English ship's hull in 1700 differed only to a small degree (apart from size) from one of a ship of 1800. Much the same is true of rigging. The spritsail topsail disappeared and the lateen mizzen was gradually replaced by a gaffsail but, for the rest, changes in the sail plan were additions to the already existing order.

During the eighteenth century ships of every Navy grew in size and, concurrently, in gunpower, until the biggest ships reached the length beyond which drooping of the ends (hogging) became excessive. The 3-deckers were the most powerful class throughout the century and, indeed, until the end of the sailing warship era. (The *Santissima Trinidad* that fought at Trafalgar was nominally a 4-decker, but her quarterdeck and forecastle were joined to make the fourth deck.) A 3-decker was expensive to build, maintain and man, and it was not suitable for a great many of the tasks a Navy had to undertake. For these, a new class of powerful vessel was built, the 74-gun ships. The '74', as it was popularly known, was an excellent all-round warship, reasonably fast-sailing and powerful enough to form the backbone of battle fleets in the second half of the century. At the Battle of the First of June in 1794, 17 out of 26 British ships and 17 out of 25 French ones were '74's. At the Battle of the Nile in 1798, 8 out of the 12 French and all

13 of the British ships-of-the-line were 74-gun vessels. The '74' fascinated English writers on naval architecture and every book on the subject in the second half of the century, and into the nineteenth, has a '74' as the exemplar of what the author was writing about. The fascination did not vanish with the sailing warship, for what is, by far, the best study of an eighteenth century warship is Jean Boudriot's *Le Vaisseau de 74 Canons*[1].

What characterises ship development in the eighteenth century is not the slow improvement in the line-of-battle classes, but the rise in importance of auxiliary craft: the support vessels, scouts, convoy escorts and even exploration and survey ships that reflected European overseas expansion. These auxiliary craft ranged in size from 10-gun sloops of only a little over 100 tons to vessels not much smaller than the smallest ship-of-the-line. Of all support craft the most spectacular development was the frigate, a new class of ship that was, despite its name, different from the seventeenth century frigate. Many lesser known classes shared in the development: sloops, both square- and gaff-rigged, snows, brigs and schooners underwent improvement to meet the strains of the duties imposed on them in the long series of wars between all the European Navies.

THE HULL

Towards the end of the seventeenth century an important change was made to the shape of English ships' hulls. The age-old method of designing the midship section by fairing together three or more arcs of different radii was replaced by one that produced a midship section which was, below the line of maximum breadth, almost a semi-circle[2]. The new-style midship section was still produced by a geometrical process rather than from an understanding of the principles of

273

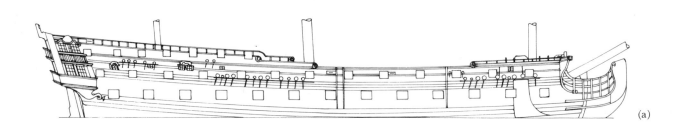

274

(a)

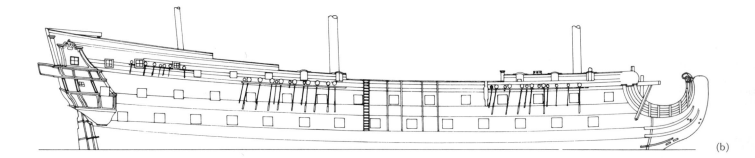

(b)

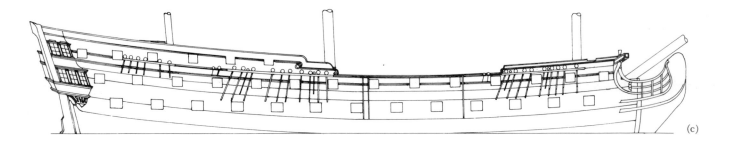

(c)

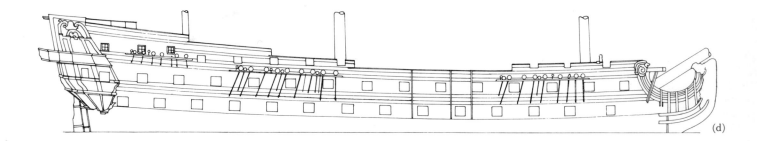

(d)

273. The classic eighteenth century line-of-battle ship, the '74'. This is a contemporary model of the *Egmont* of 1768, one of the first English 74-gun ships. The *Egmont* was designed by Sir Thomas Slade (who also designed the *Victory*) and was armed with twenty-eight 32pdrs on the lower deck, twenty-eight 18pdrs on the upper deck, fourteen 9pdrs on the quarterdeck and four on the forecastle. The figurehead represents the Earl of Egmont in his peerage robes. '74s' were the backbone of fleets for over half a century. They were big enough to stand in the line of battle but not so expensive to build and maintain as the 1st Rates. The low rails and bulwarks characteristic of English ships are very noticeable. Across the waist are the beams on which the spare spars and the boats were stowed.

274. Comparative profiles of 3rd Rates. The ships are:

(a) *Revenge*, an English 70-gun ship of 1065 tons, launched at Deptford in 1699. On a gun-deck length of 150ft, she carried 24pdrs and 9pdrs.

(b) *Terrible*, an English 74-gun ship of 1644 tons, launched at Toulon in 1739. On a gun-deck length of 164ft she carried a main battery of 32pdrs (French 36pdrs).

(c) The 1745 Establishment draught for English 70-gun ships. These ships were 160ft on the gun-deck and measured about 1450 tons. They were found to be too small for their main battery of 32pdrs, and were unsatisfactory in many ways. Some were completed as 64-gun ships, and were superseded by the new 74-gun ships from the mid-1750s.

(d) *Temeraire*, a French 74-gun ship of 1685 tons, launched at Toulon in 1749. She carried 32pdrs on a gun-deck length of 169ft.

(e) *Dragon*, one of the highly successful class of '74s' designed by Sir Thomas Slade (which included the *Egmont*). Of 1614 tons, she was launched at Deptford in 1760 and carried 32pdrs and 18pdrs on a gun-deck length of 168ft.

(f) *San Damsco*, a Spanish '74' captured by the English in 1797 at the Battle of St Vincent. She measured 1812 tons, with a gun-deck length of 176ft, and carried 32pdrs.

(g) *Bulwark*, an English '74' of 1925 tons, designed in 1796 although not launched until 1807. She carried 36pdrs on a gun-deck length of 183ft.

(h) *Hoche*, a French '74' 1901 tons, launched at Toulon in 1794. Her gun-deck, on which she carried 32pdrs, was 182ft long.

These profiles demonstrate not only the absolute growth in size during the century, but also the relative size of English and French or Spanish ships. Thus it can be seen that it is not true that English ships were *always* dramatically smaller than their contemporaries. During the period of the Establishments (before about 1750) English 3rd Rates were considerably smaller, but the early '74s' were as good as any French design, although still slightly lower tonnage. This disparity widened again during the 1780s and early 1790s but by 1800 the Royal Navy was again building '74s' that were the equal of Continental ships.

(*Drawings by John Roberts from originals in the National Maritime Museum*)

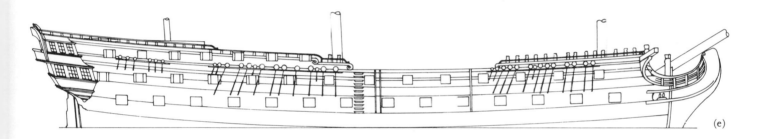

(e)

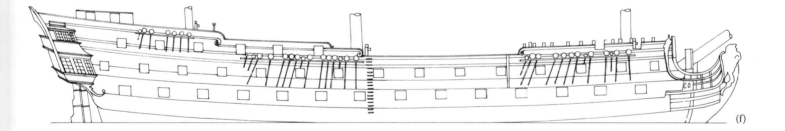

(f)

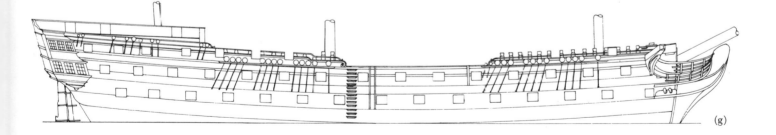

(g)

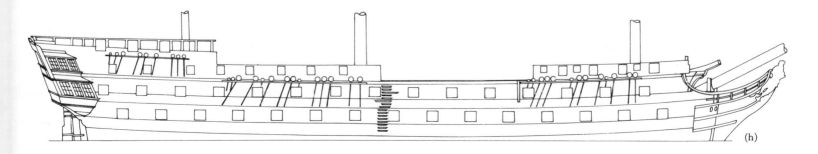

(h)

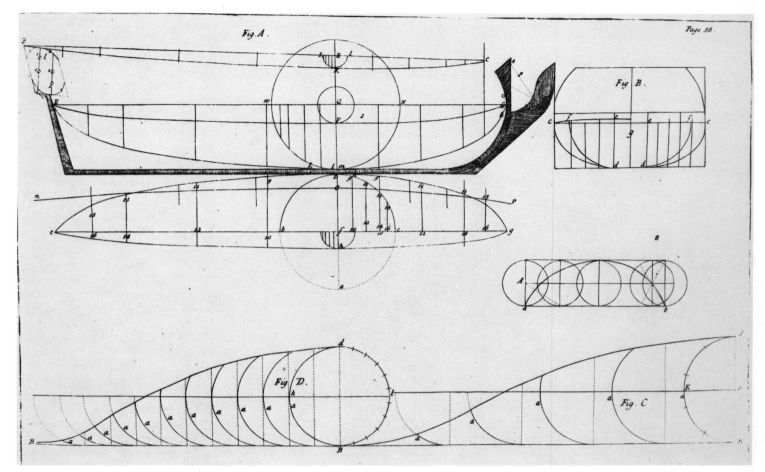

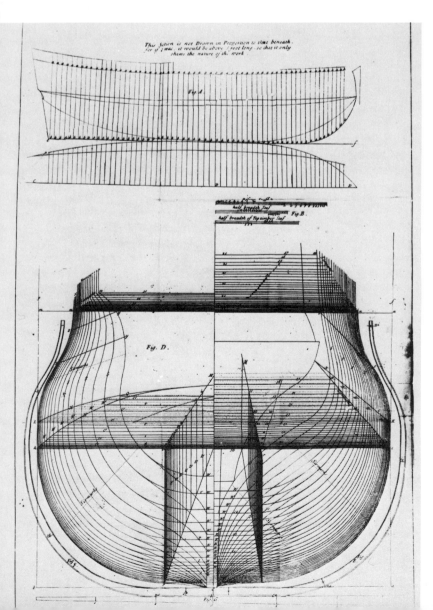

275. William Sutherland's system of developing cross-section, sheer, deck plan and camber of decks from circles.

276. A fully developed half-breadth plan from Sutherland's *Shipbuilder's Assistant*. If it is compared with seventeenth century methods (136) the increased fullness of the lower hull is apparent.

flotation, yet the change nevertheless led to the development of a fuller underbody and therefore greater buoyancy and better stability. Less is heard of crank ships, and girdling and 'furring' become rarer. Changes in hull form took place in the Continental navies' ships and particularly in France, where the underlying theories of naval architecture were being studied as a branch of science. The superiority of French designs has been exaggerated although, it is true, some French ships were very good. The apparent advantages were more often due to other factors: the habit of the English of overloading their ships with guns and the robustness of English construction that tended to make the ships sluggish but stood them in good stead in a fight at close quarters when the more lightly built French ships, like Dutch ships in the previous century, were more severely mauled. Moreover, the restrictions on ships' sizes laid down in the successive Establishments meant that English ships were usually smaller, for a given number of guns, than French or Spanish vessels. There were, of course, what may be called occupational differences between English ships and those of some other navies. Dutch ships were more flat-bottomed and had a shallower draught than English ships, and the same was true, though to a lesser degree, of Danish and Swedish ships which, like Dutch ships, had to sail in shallow waters.

Improvements in hull design went hand in hand with increase in size. The *Victory* of 1737, with 100 guns, was 400 tons larger than the *Sovereign of the Seas*, also of 100 guns but built a century earlier. By 1790 100-gun ships of 2300 tons were being built. The growth in size of support craft was proportionately greater. A 20-gun ship of 1745 was nearly as big as a 40-gun vessel of 40–50 years earlier and frigates built in 1800 were bigger at 1500 tons than seventeenth century 70-gun ships. The increase in size of all classes of ship was brought about by the ever-present demand for a more powerful armament and by the need to give warships the extra seaworthiness necessary for service in distant seas and, in the case of English ships, blockade duty and commerce protection. In the race for increased size English ships were hampered for a long time by the limits laid down in the several Establishments that were set up by the Admiralty in attempts to standardise the size of each class of warship. In the eighteenth century successive Establishments were laid down, in 1706, 1719, 1733, 1741 and 1745. The idea behind them was praiseworthy but, like so many regulations, the Establishments were often kept in force long after they had been overtaken by events abroad, and in consequence English shipwrights had to attempt to produce a ship equal in gunpower to enemy ships but with a smaller hull.

Changes in shape above the waterline are more conspicuous than those made to the underbody. During the century the beak was shortened and raised higher, sheer was reduced and the stern and its associated galleries altered in many significant details, so that a ship of, say, the 1733 Establishment differed in appearance from those built under earlier or later Establishment rules.

The head. By 1700 the transformation of the beak from a long, low and comparatively frail-looking structure to a short and sturdy one had been completed and no further changes, except in minor aspects, were made to the heads of big ships for nearly 100 years. On the smaller craft, however, some far-reaching changes were made, and these will be dealt with in the section on support craft.

The eighteenth century head consisted of a stout knee fixed to the stem and supported laterally by strong side knees – the cheeks. Above the cheeks were the head rails that curved steeply downwards before rising up to the back of the figurehead. The chief point to note about eighteenth century heads is their position *vis-à-vis* the ship's decks. At the beginning of the century, the head knee, where it butted against the stem, came up to about the level of the lower deck gunport sill and the two cheeks on each side were fastened to the lowest pair of wales. There were four rails to the head, the lowest point of the top rail coming midway between middle and upper deck levels. The bow timbers went up to the level of the middle deck in 3-decked ships, so that the platform in front of the beakhead bulkhead was higher than the head knee. To give the rails an adequate spread the cross section of the head was made like a flaring 'V'. This low head remained in use for some 50 years despite its being uncomfortably 'wet' in a seaway, although during that time some slight changes were made: an extra cheek on each side was added to the heads of 3-deckers, so that there was one cheek above and two below the hawse-holes; after about 1715 the bow timbers were taken to the upper deck level; and the head knee was shortened and given a backward rake to its upper part, which the hair

bracket, as the prolongation of the upper cheek was called, followed. As a result of the backward rake of the knee the figurehead assumed a 'stomach forwards' stance. After the middle of the century the head knee was raised a little higher. The fore side of the knee was given a distinctly concave curve from the waterline to the level of the top of the lower wale, then it turned upwards and rose nearly vertically for the rest of its length.

Throughout the eighteenth century the beakhead bulkhead on big ships was flat but had a semi-circular 'roundhouse' at each end that served as latrines for the crew. At first, the beakhead bulkhead was two decks deep and closed off the middle and upper decks, but when the bow timbers were taken to the upper deck the bulkhead was made only one deck deep, as it was on 2-deckers. The beakhead bulkhead was a source of weakness in a ship because it was too lightly constructed to offer protection against end-on fire. It was replaced by a fully built-up bow first of all in sloops, about 1732, and 25 years later in frigates, after being tried on the *Lyme* in 1748, but it was not until 1801 that the built-up or round bow was fitted to ships-of-the-line[3]. In other respects the head continued the tradition of the previous century although there were changes in the style of the figure-heads and the shapes of the rails that distinguish the ships of one decade from those of another.

A new piece of gear was fitted to the head in the eighteenth century. This was the boomkin that projected forwards at about 45° to the line of the keel. Boomkins are not often shown on models unless they are fully rigged and when this is the case it may be difficult to see how the inboard end is made fast. On big ships towards the end of the century the heels of the boomkins fitted against the knightheads (the strong timbers that held the bowsprit against lateral movement) and were bolted to them or to the framework of the head. The outer ends of the boomkins were steadied by guys or shrouds. One went from each boomkin to the cutwater and the other to the side of the bow. The early boomkins were straight but later they were made from naturally curved timber and were set with their outer ends pointing down. The boomkins were used to hold the foretacks as far forward as possible.

Wales. Quite early in the century the space between the members of the lowest pair of wales was filled in so that a solid belt of timber ran from one end of the ship to the other. It is likely that the practice began in the previous century but the first record of it on a new ship dates from 1717. Two years later a 3-decker had the lower pair of wales 'made solid'. The middle wales were the next to be filled in and by 1730 the upper ones were treated in the same way although exceptions to the general rule are found as late as the 1750s.

Gunport lids. Some changes were made in the port lids during the eighteenth century. In 1778 the Admiralty ordered that every other port on the gun-deck should have a small, hinged scuttle fitted to it, to allow ingress of light and·air. The scuttles were similar to the earlier oar-ports. Eleven years later the Order was amended to allow scuttles in every gun-deck port. Another innovation came in at the end of the century: the fitting of heavy stern-chase ports in two pieces, an upper and a lower one. Similar ports were in use on at least one Swedish ship (the *Adolf Frederick*, 1767), and Dutch ships sometimes had their broadside ports made in two parts. Even side-hinged ports may have been more common than models suggest, for a draught of the Danish 18-gun frigate *Bla Heyren* of 1756 shows 5 of the 8 broadside ports fitted with a pair of side-hinged lids each. French ships, and no

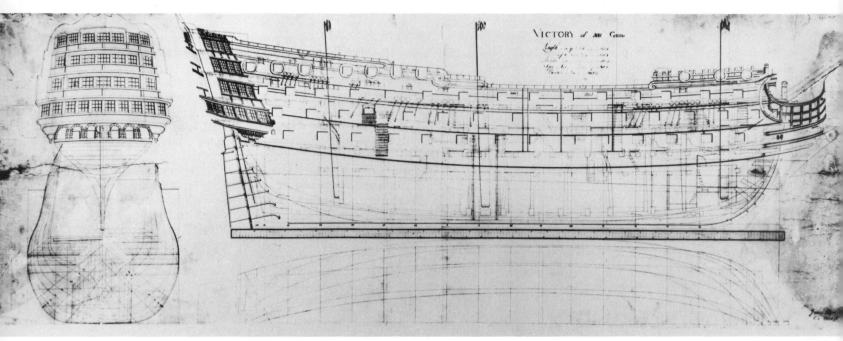

277. The *Victory* (100 guns) of 1737. The plan represents a ship built to the 1733 Establishment for a 100-gun ship. The *Victory* came to a tragic end in October 1744 when she was wrecked on the Casquets (Channel Islands) and Admiral Balchen and her crew of 1100 men were drowned. The *Victory* was a high-sided ship for her draught and this was believed to have made her lee-wardly and to have led to her loss.

278. A model of the *Victory*, which makes an interesting comparison with the draught. The height of the ship's side is apparent on this contemporary model. The awkward combination of spritsail topmast and jibboom remained on official rigging establishments until 1745 but the spritsail topmast was rarely to be seen at sea.

doubt those of other States, had scuttles in their port lids. The scuttles were not only for ventilation but allowed the gun to be loaded while the port lid was closed and the gun crew thus given some protection from musketry. To load the gun, the handle of the rammer was pushed out through the open scuttle.

Entry ports. Soon after the century opened entry ports on each side became normal on 3-deckers. Until somewhere about 1725 the entry port was between a pair of gunports but after that date it occupied the place of a gunport although there is evidence that once at sea a gun might be placed there. As the entry port was for the use of important visitors other members of the crew had to make use of the flight of broad, cleat-like steps that ran up the ship's side from the lowest wale to the bulwark rail in the waist.

Ballast ports were found only on ships that did not carry guns on their lower deck, or had only one or two at each end of it. The ports were amidships and resembled gunports but were a little smaller.

Bulwarks. The absence of robust screening for many of the deck crew was as much a feature of eighteenth century English ships as it had been of those of the seventeenth century. Although there were strong bulwarks in the waist most ships had, at most, only a low bulwark on the quarterdeck and none on the forecastle. The advantages of strong bulwarks were well understood, of course, but had to be weighed against the increase in leewardliness that they caused. For about half a century protection was provided in battle by stowing the crew's hammocks between nets supported by 'U'-

shaped iron stanchions set into the top of the rails. Useful and general though hammock barricades were, many commanding officers considered them to be insufficient in wartime and had solid bulwarks put up. These did not meet with official approval in peacetime and were taken down. The desire for something better than the hammocks gained force and by 1781 or thereabouts (roughly the same time as the carronade was adopted) frigates had built-up bulwarks on their quarterdecks, but 3-deckers did not get them until 1798. Forecastle bulwarks were first fitted to frigates in about 1800 but on bigger ships not until the early nineteenth century. French ships seem to have had quarterdeck bulwarks from the 1770s and added forecastle bulwarks soon afterwards. The ships of the Northern States were treated in the same way.

The stern. This is the most difficult part of the hull to deal with, for not only is the construction more complex than that of any other part but structure and decoration are intimately mixed. Moreover, the many changes in the details of the stern structure that were made during the century, and often at short intervals, make it impracticable to provide a comprehensive catalogue. What follows, therefore, is an outline only. 282 307

    Changes to the stern fall into two groups: those affecting the part below the transom, and the others, which apply to the structure above it. Below the transom the obvious change was an increase in breadth that gave the ship, it was said, a better seat on the water. The initial design of this broader stern was not a good one and many ships, those built to the 1745 Establish-

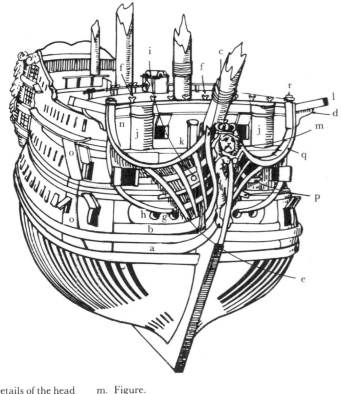

279. Details of the head.
a. Lower cheek.
b. Upper cheek.
c. Hair-bracket.
d. Cathead bracket.
e. Head timbers.
f. Timber-heads.
g. Hawseholes.
h. Bolsters.
i. Deadblock.
j. Round-houses.
k. Knightheads.
l. Cathead.
m. Figure.
n. Beakhead bulkhead.
o. Anchor lining.
p. Head rails.
q. Main rail.
r. Main rail head.
s. Fish davit cleat.
t. Galley funnel.
u. Belfry.
v. Foretack bumkin.
w. Bumkin cleats.
x. Berthing rail.

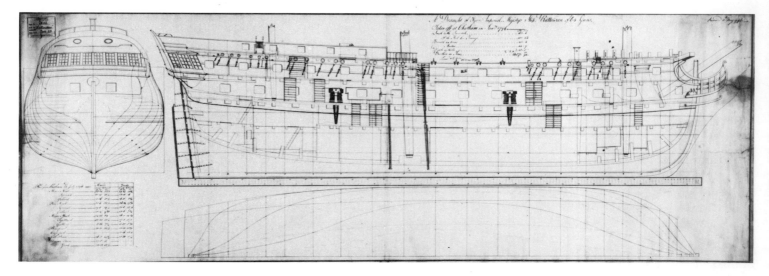

ment in particular, gained a reputation for poor response to the helm. A less noticeable change was the general adoption of the practice of taking the rudder-head up through the counter so that the whole of the tiller was inboard. The hole in the counter through which the tiller had formerly passed was reduced in size but still had to be large enough to allow the rudder to swing to its limit. Although the hole was covered with tarred canvas, called the rudder-coat, water could still come inboard in stormy weather in sufficient amounts to be dangerous to small vessels and an abominable nuisance in large ones. Above the transom the stern had superimposed galleries, sometimes open, sometimes closed in, that projected beyond the main structure of the stern. Associated with the galleries were rows of glazed windows (lights), sometimes running the whole width of the gallery but in other cases fitted only at the ends. There were considerable variations in the shape and extent of the galleries during the century, for details of which it will be necessary to study models and draughts of the period.

L G Carr Laughton has set down some broad generalisations about galleries:
1 Galleries always coincided with a deck.
2 There were as many rows of lights as there were complete gun-decks but the lights were always one deck higher. There were always, therefore, lights at quarterdeck level but never at the lower deck.
3 Galleries were always one less than the number of rows of lights, and were never fitted to the lowest row. A 3-decker had two galleries and 2-decked ships had one, but ships with only a single gun-deck never had a gallery.

Occasional exceptions to the above generalisations are known. The *Victory* of 1737 had four rows of lights and three galleries although she was a 3-decker[4].

At first, the galleries were taken round the quarters but the fashion changed quite soon and the galleries were shut off from the quarter galleries and remained so throughout the century. Stern galleries projected beyond the framework of the stern for 3ft or so but the actual width of the galleries was about 7ft. Their inboard side was thus inside the stern's framework and had to be closed off from the cabins by a screen bulkhead set about 4ft in from the frames. With minor variations this arrangement remained in being down to the end of the century, when the outboard parts of the galleries were taken off and the whole area glazed in. As that made a screen bulkhead unnecessary it was abolished. The quarter galleries were always completely closed in except, up to about 1720, where they joined the

280. The *Rettvisan*, a Russian ship of 64 guns captured from the Swedes. The lines were taken off when the ship was at Chatham in 1796. She has many features of the ships designed by Chapman – single level galleries, round-cornered gunports, and a characteristic sharp midship section.

stern galleries. After that date the quarter galleries were shut off by a door from the stern galleries. Quarter galleries were the rule on big ships but small craft had windows on the quarters. The windows had elaborate frames called quarter-badges.

HULL FITTINGS

In this section only those fittings that underwent significant changes, were introduced or were abolished will be discussed, and items not mentioned may be taken to have the same basic form as in the previous century although contemporary models and plans should be consulted about minor changes.

Channels. The seventeenth century practice of setting the fore and main channels on the upper of the pair of wales above the gun-deck and taking the chainplates to the lower member had two serious disadvantages: the channels were liable to damage by waves in storms and the sharp angle at which the chainplates came in to the ship's side reduced their effectiveness. After a few trials, the fore and main channels were moved up to the wales above the middle deck guns on 3-deckers in about 1700 and the chains were fastened to the upper of the pair of wales above the lower gun-deck, ie where the channel had formerly been. The new arrangement led to the disappearance of the spurs that had formerly braced the channels against the ship's side. They were gradually replaced by small brackets, like inverted knees, and had disappeared by 1735. The brackets were abolished a few years later.

On 2-deckers the old arrangement of channels remained in use, the channel being fastened to the wale *below* the upper deck guns. On small vessels with only a single gun-deck the channels were on the wale below the guns. Mizzen channels, on all ships, were a deck higher than the others.

The next change in the position of the channels came in about 1745. Fore and main channels were moved up again, so that they were above the *upper deck* guns, and the mizzen channels were moved up a deck too. The new arrangement was not altogether satisfactory on 3-deckers because the tumblehome of the sides reduced the spread of the shrouds to an undesirable degree. Consequently the channels on 3-deckers, but not on other Rates, were brought back in the late 1750s to their former position and remained there until the 1790s when they were once again raised above the upper deck guns. They stayed in that position until the end of the sailing warship era. During this last phase the mizzen channels were sometimes a deck higher, but sometimes at the same level as the fore and main channels. All channels had their chains taken to a wale a deck lower than the one on which the channel was fastened. It is important to note that, on big ships, channels were never cut by gunports although this was sometimes permitted on small craft.

Accompanying the channels in their migrations were the little 'channels' for the backstays – the backstay stools. These were placed where they would be clear of the blast from the guns. When channels were finally brought up above the guns the stools were abolished and the backstays set up to the channels.

283 **Anchors, cables and associated gear.** As in the previous century anchors were hoisted by a hook and tackle from the cathead. Another tackle at the end of a movable beam, the fish davit, raised the anchor's flukes high enough to allow one of them to be stowed on the fore channel. The fish davit was a strong beam that had two or three sheaves in its outer end from which the tackle fall reeved through a huge block about the size of a deadeye and with a large hook on its lower end.

Anchors had been more or less standardised in shape by 1700: their weight, and therefore their size, was based on the ship's tonnage. Sutherland[8] recommended that the biggest anchor should weigh 1cwt for every 25 tons of the ship's burden for big ships, and 1cwt for every 20 tons for small ones. There was little change in the shapes of either anchor or stock during the century. The most noticeable was the rounding of the ends of the stocks to stop them damaging the copper sheathing.

As for cable sizes, Sutherland states that a 1700-ton ship had a best (ie biggest) cable $22\frac{1}{2}$in in circumference and a ship of 225 tons had one of 12in. Ships of similar tonnage a century later had cables almost the same size (see Chapter 5). The anchor's ring was always wrapped with rope, partly to increase its thickness and thus lessen the strain on the part of the cable bent to the ring, and partly to preserve the cable from chafing on the ring. The 'puddening of the ring', as the wrapping was called, might be a simple one made of one or more layers of old rope, or it might be a 'bosun's special' with the puddening covered with fancy work. The cable was wormed with old rope for a considerable length from the ring and then the worming was wrapped over with rope, the covering being known as keckling. Its job was to save the cable from chafing on the bottom whilst the ship was anchored, or against its side when the anchor was stowed.

Hawseholes. The general rule was to make the diameter of the hawsehole $2\frac{1}{2}$ times the diameter of the biggest cable. The lower edge of the hawsehole was rounded to give the cable a smooth passage.

Copper sheathing. Experimental coppering of ships' bottoms was tried on the frigate *Alarm* in 1761 and on some other small ships. Once the problem of the corrosion of the iron fastenings by electrolytic interaction with the copper had been solved (by substituting copper bolts for all the iron ones below the waterline) copper sheathing became general from 1783 onwards[5].

Stern lanterns. The rather squat lanterns used on 284 English ships at the beginning of the century were replaced about 1715 by a straight-sided pattern that remained standard for the rest of the century. Foreign lanterns were rather more ornate.

Ships' names. Although most European ships had had their names on the stern since at least the seventeenth century, the practice was not adopted on English ships until 1771. The name was to be on the second counter – the one above that through which the rudder passed – and the letters were to be 12in high. The name was to be enclosed in a compartment or 'surround'. A year later it

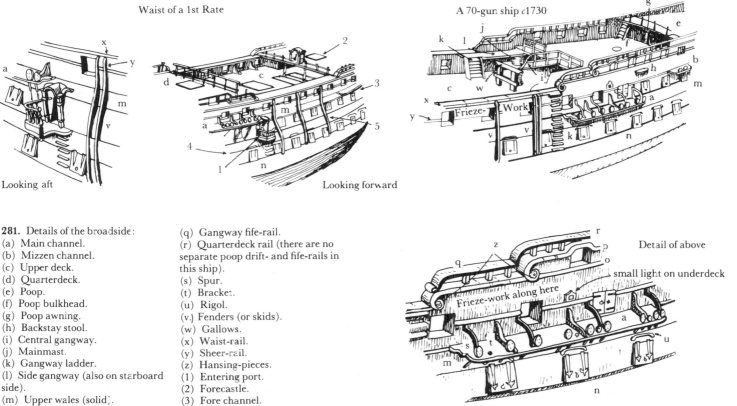

Waist of a 1st Rate

A 70-gun ship *c*1730

Looking aft

Looking forward

Frieze-Work

281. Details of the broadside:
(a) Main channel.
(b) Mizzen channel.
(c) Upper deck.
(d) Quarterdeck.
(e) Poop.
(f) Poop bulkhead.
(g) Poop awning.
(h) Backstay stool.
(i) Central gangway.
(j) Mainmast.
(k) Gangway ladder.
(l) Side gangway (also on starboard side).
(m) Upper wales (solid).
(n) Lower wales (solid)
(o) Gangway drift-rail.
(p) Quarterdeck rail.

(q) Gangway fife-rail.
(r) Quarterdeck rail (there are no separate poop drift- and fife-rails in this ship).
(s) Spur.
(t) Bracket.
(u) Rigol.
(v.) Fenders (or skids).
(w) Gallows.
(x) Waist-rail.
(y) Sheer-rail.
(z) Hansing-pieces.
(1) Entering port.
(2) Forecastle.
(3) Fore channel.
(4) Middle wales (solid).
(5) Fender used as chesstree.

Detail of above

small light on underdeck

Frieze-work along here

282. Details of the stern and quarter gallery:
(a) Taffrail.
(b) & (c). Quarter-figures.
(d) Counter.
(e) Cove.
(f) Lower wales (solid).
(g) Middle wales.
(h) Upper wales.
(i) Lights (2 shown).
(j) Lower finishing.
(k) Upper finishing.
(l) Bearding of rudder.
(m) Stern chase ports.
(n) Position of bust, cypher of arms.
(o) Screen bulkheads.
(p) Quarter galleries.

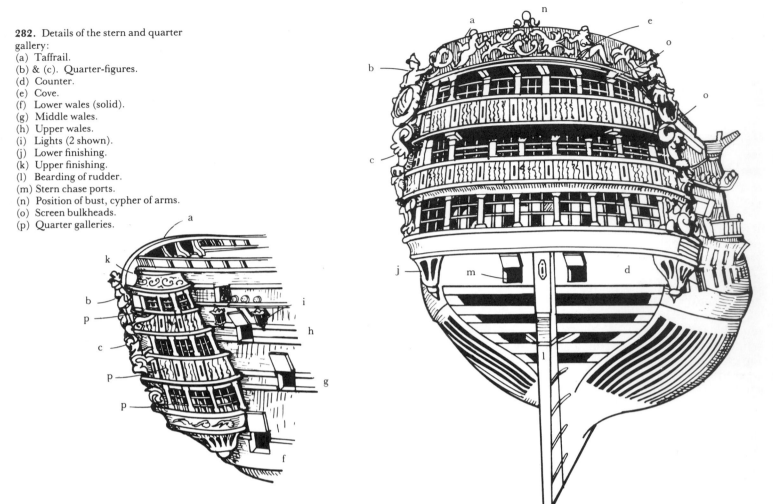

DIMENSIONS OF ANCHORS according to Sutherland's *Ship-building Unveiled* (1717)		
	Size for 1677-ton ship ft in	Size for 364-ton ship ft in
Shank	18 6	12 2
Shank's thickness (max)	11½	7½
Shank's thickness (min)	8 13/20	5½
The square	2 11	1 11
From end of shank to nut	1 11	1 3
Square of nut	2 3/10	1 51/100
Inner diameter of ring	2 1½	1 3
Thickness of ring	4	3
Hole in shank for ring	4 6/10	3 1/10
Length of crown	1 2	8 7/20
Length of arm	7 0	4 0 6/10
Breadth of fluke	2 8	1 9
Length of fluke	3 9	2 5½
Thickness of fluke	2 9/10	1 9/10
Square of arm at fluke	7	4 6/10
Length of bill	10½	6 9/10
Rounding of fluke	1 16/100	76/100
Clutching of arm	3 6	2 4 1/10
Inside meeting	6 6	not given
Outside meeting	6 6	not given
Middle meeting	6 6	not given

Anchors would certainly not be made to such fine dimensions, for the technology of the day was not sufficiently advanced – the nearest ¼in was probably the usual approximation.

was ordered that the letters of the name should be as large as the counter would permit, and there was to be no compartment. This fashion remained in use until about 1815, when it was gradually dropped. Warships never had their names on the bows.

The French and the Baltic nations, together with the Russians, put the ship's name in a compartment but Dutch ships had theirs, at first, just below the Arms on the taffrail though by the 1720s some ships had their names in compartments on the counter.

INBOARD WORKS

Although the basic layout of the decks did not change and few new fittings were added there were, of course, changes in the shapes and decoration of the fittings. These details are not always recorded on plans because many of them were regarded at the time as standard and had no need to be specified on every plan. Curiously enough, 'Navy Board' models often lack details of some fittings because of the practice of leaving the decks unplanked or with only a strip of planking down the middle.

The forecastle. When the Order of 1703 did away with the lavish carving that had characterised seventeenth century ships the timber-heads were given simple and functional shapes, as they were on Continental ships[6].

Catheads. These rose slightly from their inboard to their outer ends and had their arms at about 45° to the centre-line of the ship. As the inboard end, which was called the cat-tail, was set at right angles to the centreline the cathead was curved in two directions. English ships had the cat-tail fastened to the beam just abaft the fore end of the forecastle deck. For most of the century the arm of the cathead was supported by a bracket that was, in effect, an extension of one of the head rails, but towards the end of the century a simple square bracket was used. In the second half of the century a horizontal knee was often fitted between the cathead and the ship's side. The position of the cat-tail on frigates was altered when the round or built-up bow was introduced in the 1760s. The cat-tail was put *under* the deck instead of above it as on ships with the old-fashioned beakhead bulkhead, and the reason for the change was because if the cat-tail was above the deck it interfered with the serving of the bow-chasers.

Companionways. It is rare to find these fitted on models, obviously necessary though they were. Plans show a ladderway between the foremast and the fore end of the forecastle.

Gratings were used extensively for ventilation and to let light into the deck below. On the forecastle there was a grating over the galley stove and another, sometimes, abaft the galley chimney.

Belfries stood at the after end of the forecastle deck. On big ships the belfry was a 'four-poster' but smaller ships made do with an arch. In contrast to the elaborate seventeenth century belfries, those of the eighteenth century were made in a cool, almost severe style. The sizes of ships' bells are rarely met with. One for a 3rd Rate was $18\frac{1}{2}$in in diameter and $15\frac{1}{2}$in high[7].

The galley. With the establishment of the galley on the middle deck of 3-deckers and in the forecastle of smaller ships, the galley chimney made its appearance above the forecastle deck. Its shape varied. Some were sloping-sided (truncated cones), others had a square section and yet others were cylindrical. Some chimneys seem to have had a cowl, presumably one that could be turned away from the wind. By the end of the century the straight, four-sided variety was the normal. Galley chimneys were made of iron after 1748 but before that date either iron or copper might be used. The galley stove was set in brick until about 1752, when iron stoves were brought into use.

Forecastle bulkhead. This is the after bulkhead. At the beginning of the century the bulkhead was sometimes set back under the end of the forecastle deck and could offer

some shelter to men waiting on the deck. On the model of the *Royal William* of 1719 (in the National Maritime Museum) the deck overhangs the bulkhead by the equivalent of about 3ft. Usually, however, the bulkhead was level with the end of the deck. At that time, the bulkhead usually had a door in each half, set almost midway between the bulkhead's centre and the bulwarks. There were no windows in the bulkhead. Although the bulkhead was usually flat, some interesting exceptions are known. A model of a 50-gun ship in the National Maritime Museum has a bay at each end of the bulkhead and three doors between the bays. After about 1740 big ships did not have a complete bulkhead, but only a short one screening off the galley, although on smaller vessels it still went right across the deck.

Capstans. A big ship had two capstans, the fore or jeer capstan that stood about half way between the main hatch and the forecastle, and the main capstan that was under the quarterdeck about midway between the main- and mizzenmasts. Both were drum-headed. According to Sutherland (1717)[8], the jeer capstan had two barrels at the beginning of the eighteenth century but the main capstan only one. William Falconer, on the other hand, whose *Universal Dictionary of the Marine* was first published in 1769[9], says that the main capstan had two barrels but that the jeer capstan had only one. By the end of the century, on big ships, both capstans had two barrels. When the main capstan had only one barrel, this was on the lowest gun-deck, as was the lower barrel of the jeer capstan. The second barrel of either capstan was on the deck above, ie the middle deck of 3-decked ships but the maindeck of 2-deckers and frigates. Consequently the jeer capstan would not be visible on the upper deck of a 3-decker but would be on lesser ships. The main capstan on 2-deckers would be under the quarterdeck. The heel of the spindle of all capstans was stepped on the deck below the barrel.

At the beginning of the century the diameter of the main capstan's barrel was five times the diameter of the biggest cable on the ship. The barrel of a capstan is the solid core to which the riders, called whelps, are fastened. The latter were thick pieces of wood whose

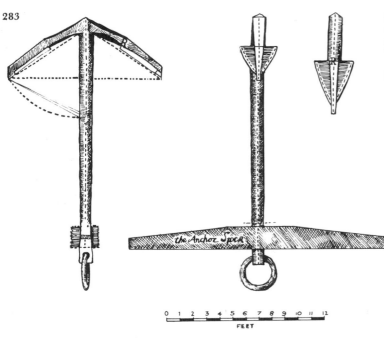

283

0 1 2 3 4 5 6 7 8 9 10 11 12
FEET

283. An anchor for a large 1677-ton warship from Sutherland's *Shipbuilding Unveiled*. Patterns of anchors varied, but the Royal Navy used this 'angle-crown' type until the early nineteenth century when it was replaced by the 'round-crown' type, in which the arms were formed by arcs of a circle.

284. Late seventeenth and early eighteenth century Dutch stern lanterns.

284

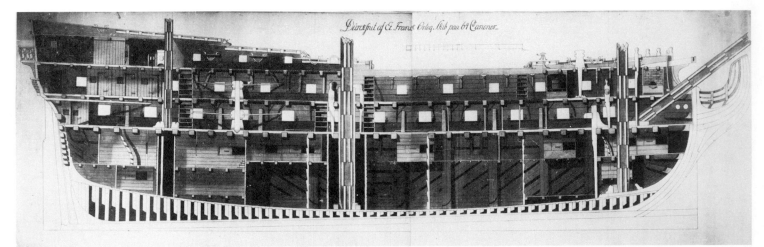

285. An elaborate longitudinal profile of a French 64-gun ship of the mid-eighteenth century from the Danish archives. This pictorial representation of inboard works is almost non-existent in British and French official plans collections. Note the brick hearth under the forecastle.

width at their foot was one-half the diameter of the barrel, and their length was normally a little under 3ft. For the first 2ft of length the whelps sloped inwards $2\frac{2}{3}$in per foot but after that they became wider until they were almost as wide as at the foot. For the rest of their length the whelps sloped backwards $\frac{1}{2}$in in a foot. At their feet, whelps were about as thick as they were wide but tapered towards the top $1\frac{1}{4}$in to the foot. Between each two whelps were chocks. The lower ones were equal in thickness to $\frac{1}{3}$ of the length of the whelps, and were placed high enough to leave space for the pawl to work against the lower part of the whelps. On big ships this space was about 5in. The upper chocks were half as thick as the lower ones and were set 1in above the widest part of the upper end of the whelps. The capstan's head was equal in diameter to the base of the capstan, ie it was twice the diameter of the barrel. The underside of the head was flat but the upper surface was slightly domed and the head's thickness was one-quarter of its diameter. In its edge were 8, 10 or 12 square holes for the capstan bars, the width of each hole being 4/13 the thickness of the capstan's head. The holes tapered inwards $\frac{1}{2}$in per foot of depth. The barrel of single-drum capstans was extended downwards a deck to form the capstan's spindle. This was 19/21 the diameter of the barrel but the lower two-thirds of the spindle were tapered until where they fitted into the lower bearing the diameter of the spindle was only one-half of its upper one.

When jeer capstans had two barrels, as at the beginning of the century, the upper one was like the main capstan's but its diameter was only 6/7 of the main capstan's. The lower barrel had no drumhead for bars but had the same number of whelps as the main capstan. The diameter of the lower barrel was 13/14 of the upper one. By the second half of the century, if not earlier, the lower barrel of the jeer capstan was fitted with a drumhead and at the same time, probably, the second and upper barrel was fitted to the main capstan. As visitors to the *Victory* will have observed, all edges on capstans were bevelled or rounded. On the whelps this reduced the strain on the cable, and elsewhere a blunted edge was less likely to injure a man flung against it in bad weather. In length, capstan bars were about $3\frac{1}{2}$ times the maximum diameter of the capstan head. They were round except where their ends fitted into the drumhead and tapered slightly towards their outer ends. When the bars were placed in their sockets an iron pin, on a chain, was put through holes in the drumhead and the bars' ends. The outer ends of the bars also had holes in them, through which a rope, known as a swifter, was passed and fastened tightly.

Windlass. Only small craft and boats had windlasses. The barrels might be fixed between a pair of stout posts, or between wooden blocks fixed to the inside of the bulwarks. Windlass handspikes resembled capstan bars in shape and were usually $3\frac{1}{2}$ times the diameter of the windlass barrel in length. The bigger boats often had windlasses, fixed amidships, for raising anchors[8].

Bitts. The cable or riding bitts were down on the lower 299 deck. They consisted of a pair of strong uprights (fixed to the bottom timbers of the ship) and a cross-timber, uprights and cross-piece being up to 2ft thick. The cross-piece stood about 4ft above the deck and its end projected 2–3ft beyond the uprights, whose ends stood up nearly 2ft above the cross-piece. On all but the smallest ships there were two pairs of riding bitts, one behind the other and 8–10ft apart.

The jeer bitts and topsail sheet bitts were smaller versions of the riding bitts but lacked the knees that the riding bitts had on their fore sides. Jeer bitts stood just abaft their mast and the topsail sheet bitts just in front of it. The main topsail sheet bitts had their uprights made sufficiently high above the deck to carry a second cross piece at the level of the forecastle deck. Its ends were slightly upcurved and served as support for the spare spars that were stowed between them and the forecastle. The fore-bitts stood on the forecastle deck early in the century but on big ships they were later moved into the forecastle although remaining on the open deck on small ships. By the end of the century, however, the fore-bitts had been brought back into the open.

Pumps. Chain pumps were used on all big English ships 294 but they were less common on Continental vessels. They discharged the water into large wooden cisterns on the 295 lower deck and pipes led the water from the cisterns to the scuppers. Small ships relied on hand pumps.

Gangways and gratings. At the beginning of the century the waist was completely open except for such cover as the spare spars and the boats gave. At each side, from the quarterdeck, a short gangway extended towards the entering place, which was close to the mainmast. By 1714 the gangways finished abreast of the mainmast. During this period another gangway was taken forward from the quarterdeck to the mainmast and finished at the foremost of the main bitts. This gangway was fitted to all ships of over 50 guns. By the 1750s, however, the quarterdeck had grown forward to within a few feet of the mainmast so the gangway virtually disappeared.

286. The construction of a wooden 3-decker, about 1800.

1. Hanging knee (when positioned diagonally – to avoid a gunport, for example – they were known as 'dagger knees')
2. Lodging knee
3. Deck clamp (in French practice this was often more substantial)
4. Waterway timber (in French practice this was usually more substantial and often rebated down on to the beams)
5. Deck beam (formed of two timbers scarphed together)
6. Carlings
7. Ledges
8. Keel
9. Keelson
10. False keel
11. A frame (or 'framed bend', made up to two sets of futtock timbers bolted side by side). The individual parts are as follows: (a) half-floor; (b) floor-timber (the two floor-timbers of a frame, and the space between them and the next pair, are known as 'room-and-space' – a crucial measurement of the lightness or heaviness of construction in any vessel); (c) 1st futtock; (d) 2nd futtock; (e) 3rd futtock; (f) 4th futtock (obscured by the beam knees, but above the 2nd futtock); (g) 5th futtock; (h) Top timbers; (i) Chock (the French used a simple butt-joint without a chock to connect the futtock timbers: this was not as sturdy)
12. Floor riders (there were also riders higher up the full sides known as 'futtock riders' and 'top riders')

(*Drawn by John Roberts*)

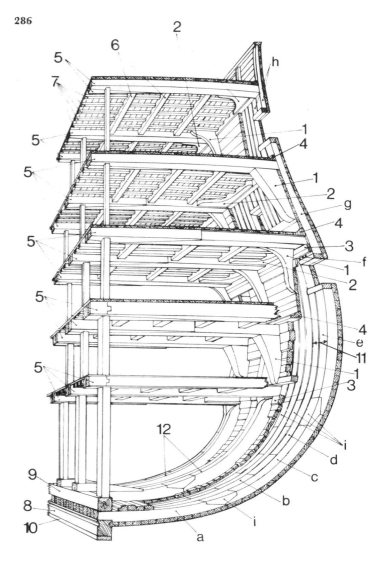

286

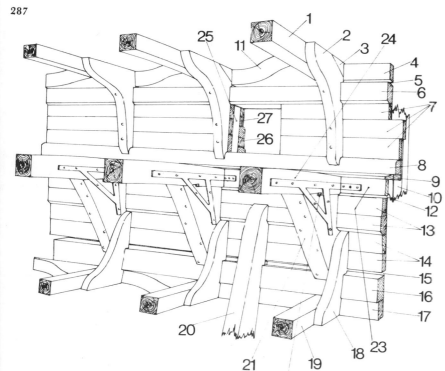

287

287. Interior constructional details
1. Upper deck beam
2. Hanging knee
3. Chock in throat of knee
4. Intercostal packing
5. Air space to ventilate timbers
6. Deck clamp or beam shelf
7. Inner planking
8. Spirketting
9. Waterway
10. Section of frame
11. Lodging knee
12. Ventilation space
13. Deck clamp
14. Ceiling or inner planking
15. Ventilation space
16. Spirketting
17. Intercostal packing
18. Reverse hanging knee or standard
19. Orlop deck beam (note no waterway on this deck)
20. Floor rider
21. Beam chock combined with iron beam knee bracket
22. Iron wedges to take up transverse movement (ie racking stresses)
23. Intercostal packing
24. Gun-deck beams
25. Part of frame exposed at gunport (note that not all small ships had ports on this deck)
26. Main wale
27. Outer planking

1–12 represent standard English practice down to the end of the century; 13 onwards were adopted thereafter, but are comparable with French eighteenth century practice. In both cases the practice reflects the shortages of expensive 'grown' timber for proper knees, a shortage which affected the French Navy much earlier.

(*Drawn by John Roberts, after an original by Keith Hobbs*)

288. English belfries from 1st Rates of about 1720.
289. Dutch belfries.

290. French belfries, from models of:
(a) *Royal Louis*, 1758.
(b) ship-of-the-line, *c*1700.
(c) *'Mars'; c*1805.
(d) *'Hero'*, 1802.
(e) *'Ocean'*.
(f) *'Caledonia', c*1805.
(g) *Protecteur* , 1757.
(Those in inverted commas are attributed but inaccurate names.)

291. English belfries:
(a) *Victory*, 1765.
(b) a 70-gun ship of *c*1740.
(c) a snow of *c*1705.
(d) *Centurion*, 1745.
(e) *Boyne*, 1790.
(c) *'Cleopatra*, 1799'.
(g) a 70-gun ship of *c*1730–5.

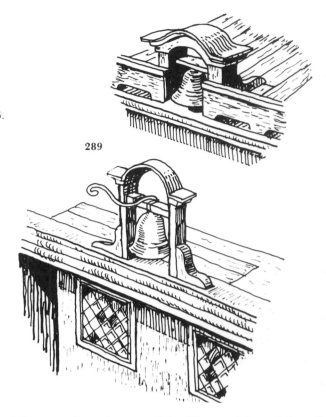

289

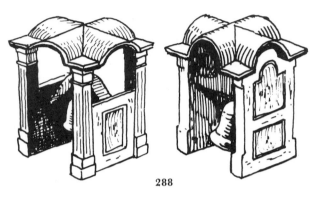

288

The side gangways were first of all extended by temporary structures as far as the forecastle but by 1744 they had become regular fittings on 2-deckers. At first they were narrow but were soon made wider. The gangways were level with the top of the bulwarks in the waist and might be planked over or have a series of gratings. In the 1760s removable beams were laid across the waist, between the gangways, to carry the spars and boats, but by the 1790s the beams had become permanent fittings and the gangways had been widened, so that the scene was set for the complete covering of the waist in the next century.

Besides the gratings already mentioned there were others; over the hatchways, sometimes in the central gangway from the quarterdeck to the mainmast, and in the forecastle deck over the galley stove. Their position is shown on the more detailed Admiralty plans, and on models.

After bulkhead. The position of the bulkhead at first was flush with the fore end of the quarterdeck but after about 1715 the quarterdeck was taken forward so that the bulkhead appeared to have moved aft though in fact it was in its old position. By the end of the century the fore end of the quarterdeck was in front of the mainmast but the bulkhead was approximately abreast the after end of the main channels. The bulkheads were usually flat, but there were sometimes cabins built on them, in front, at each side. There was a door in each half of the bulkhead, the space between being panelled and sometimes, according to models, having windows.

Steering wheel. This made its appearance on English ships some time around 1700. A model in the National Maritime Museum of a ship of *c*1705 has a winch in place of the customary whipstaff. Within a very few years, however, the winch was replaced by the familiar wheel. Until the 1730s the wheel was always abaft the mizzenmast and close to it – rarely more than 6ft on the real ship. The barrel round which the tiller ropes were wound was normally aft of the wheel but two models in the National Maritime Museum have the wheel behind the barrel. After 1745 the wheel was usually in front of the mizzenmast though between that date and 1735 both

positions are found on models. The position of the wheel seems to be governed by the lead of the tiller-ropes. At first they were led somewhat inefficiently allowing the tiller a 4–5° swing, which is about all the whipstaff permitted. In an important paper on early steering wheels J H Harland has shown that until the tiller was fitted with a sweep it was not possible to obtain a wide swing of the tiller by means of a wheel. It has been suggested that it was with the introduction of the sweep that the early steering wheel was moved in front of the mizzenmast[10,11].

The number of models with steering wheels is too few to allow the formulation of a precise rule about which deck the wheel stood on. There seems to have been, as would be expected, some experimenting with different placings. A series of 50-gun ship models, from 1710 to 1750, in the National Maritime Museum have their wheels on the quarterdeck but the 100-gun *Royal William* of 1719 has it under the quarterdeck, as do the 2-deckers from the 1740s onwards. Frigates had their wheel on the quarterdeck.

Binnacles (bittacles). These cabinets that held the compass have a long history (they are recorded from the early fifteenth century) about which we know little. They are rarely shown on models, and descriptions of them by seventeenth and eighteenth century writers have a remarkable similarity of wording – even after making allowance for the probable similarity of the objects being described – that makes one wonder how much is true description and how much is mere copying. The only modern account of the development of the binnacle is to be found in the *'Mariner's Mirror'*, and the following notes are based on it[12].

Contemporary writers agree in describing the binnacle as a 3-compartment cabinet, made of wood, that stood before the helmsman, but as to what went into the binnacle opinions differ. Blanckley, writing in 1750, says that the binnacle held the compass, a candle to illuminate it, and a sand-glass but he omits to tell us which compartments they were in[13]. William Falconer's *Universal Dictionary of the Marine* (1769) states that a binnacle, formerly called a bittacle, had three compart-

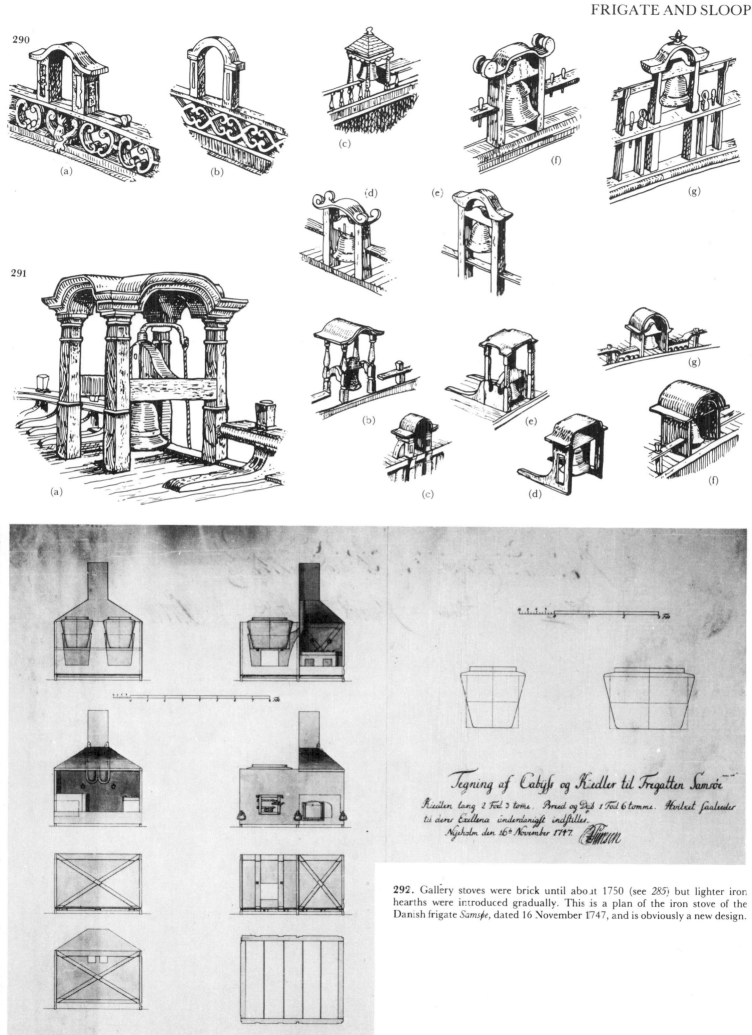

292. Gallery stoves were brick until about 1750 (see *285*) but lighter iron hearths were introduced gradually. This is a plan of the iron stove of the Danish frigate *Samsøe*, dated 16 November 1747, and is obviously a new design.

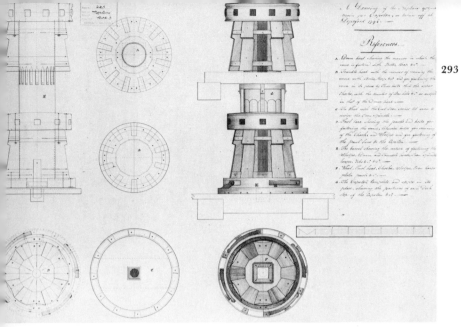

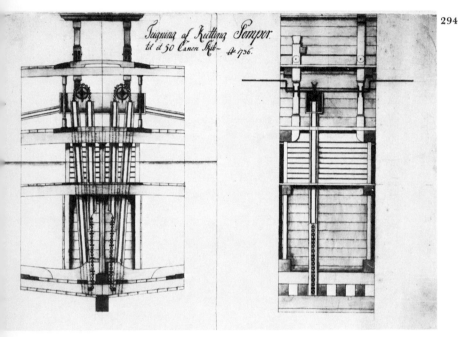

293. A drawing of the main jeer capstan of the *Neptune*, 98 guns, as taken off at Deptford in 1796. Such plans of standard fittings are rare in the Admiralty Collection.

294. A Danish plan of an English-style chain pump for a 50-gun ship, dated 1736. Using such a pump six men could discharge a ton of water per minute and it is a mystery why they were not popular with the French Navy.

295. A Danish plan of a French suction pump. Compared with a chain pump there was one advantage in that a suction pump put the water under some pressure so it could be used for fire-fighting or hosing-down.

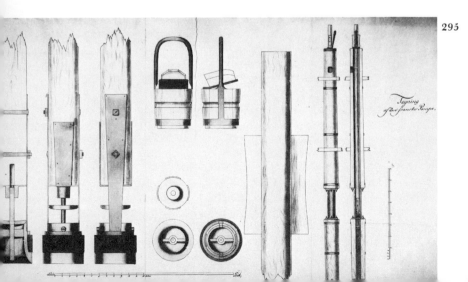

293 ments. The two outer compartments held compasses and the middle one a candle or a lamp which illuminated the compasses through glass partitions. Each compartment had a sliding shutter, apparently a vertically moving one. Binnacles are described in almost the same terms in Steel's *Elements and Practice of Naval Architecture* of 1805 and Burney's revision of Falconer's *Universal Dictionary of the Marine* of 1815.

    The number of binnacles on a ship is uncertain. Seventeenth century writers state that there was only one and so does Blanckley, but Falconer states quite definitely that there were two, one for the helmsman and one for the man watching the steering. Later writers repeat Falconer's statement but none of them tells us where the second binnacle stood. There is some evidence that more than two binnacles were sometimes carried although they were possibly only spares, for in 1779 the Navy Board directed that no more than two were to be allowed to 1st, 2nd and 3rd Rate ships. The available evidence may be summed up as follows:

294 1 In the early part of the century ships had only one binnacle and it stood just before the helmsman.

2 After c1750 there were two but the position of the second is not known.

3 Until 1779 the three biggest rates of ships had more than two binnacles, but their location is not known other than the helmsman's.

Cleats, kevels and pin-rails. Plans rarely show these important fittings because they were standard and every shipwright knew where they ought to be. They are infrequent on models unless the latter are rigged, when it is often difficult to make the fittings' shapes out.

DECORATION

The Admiralty took the first effective step towards limiting the excessive amount of decoration on ships by an Order, in 1700, that the cost of decorating a 1st Rate was not to exceed £500 and, at the other end of the scale, a 6th Rate might only have £25 spent on it. We have to remember, of course, that in the money of those days the sums allowed were substantial. A more drastic Order in 1703 directed 'that the carved works be reduced to only a lion and trail board for the head, with mouldings instead of brackets placed against the timbers; that the stern have only a tafferel [taffrail] and two quarter pieces, and in lieu of brackets between the lights of the stern, galleries and bulkheads, to have mouldings fixed against the timbers; that the joiners' works of the sides of the great cabin, coach, wardroom and round-house of each ship be fixed only with slit deals, without any sort of moulding or cornice, and the painting be only plain colour. . . .'[14]

    The imposition of the Orders brought about a revolution in decoration. The riot of baroque carving and paintwork that had covered the ships was replaced by the neo-Classical style that we call Georgian. As the century

295 progressed there was a tendency for profuseness of carving to creep in again but it was confined to the taffrail and the supporters at the ends of the stern galleries. The decoration of some models from the first quarter of the century reflects the contemporary interest in China. The lion of the figurehead was carved in the Chinese manner and figures of Chinamen were painted on the beakhead bulkhead.

The head. For some 20 years the Admiralty Order restricting figureheads to a lion on all but 1st Rates was adhered to despite its unpopularity. The animal was carved in heraldic style and was given an upright stance so that he could glare over the top of the head knee. After 1727 the Admiralty allowed 2nd Rates to have figures appropriate to their name, and about 30 years later this permission was extended to all but the smallest ships.

As a general rule the 1st Rates, being exempt from the restrictions of the 1703 Order, had elaborate figureheads. These were called 'double heads' because there were figures at the side of the principal one. The latter might be a representation of the person after whom the ship was named, or it might be an allegorical figure.

In the 1770s figureheads were made lighter and simpler and many draughts of figureheads from that period have survived. Later, in face of the growing need for economy, attempts were made to get rid of figureheads altogether and to substitute a scroll for them. The move was so unpopular that figureheads reappeared before long on all but the small ships, which had to make do with the scroll or a 'fiddle-head'.

Figureheads were usually gilded or 'gilt painted' until about the 1760s, when the fashion for painting them in colour, which lasted until the very end of the sailing ship era, came into vogue. The rest of the head – the knee, the cheeks, the head timbers and the rails – was painted in accordance with the Order of 1703, carved work being limited to giving the rails mouldings. The stem knee, like the lowest wales, was painted black, but there was a good deal of variety about the painting of the rest of the head.

The Order of 1703 also deprived the beak-head bulkhead of its carvings, which were replaced by pilasters and arches made of plain mouldings. The compartments so formed were painted with heraldic trophies of arms, floral scrolls and motifs from baroque painting. Examples in colour are to be found in the Science Museum's booklet *Ship Models*[15].

The broadside. According to an Admiralty Order of 1715, ships' sides were to be 'painted of the usual colour yellow, and the ground black, and that both inside and out to be of a plain colour . . . except such parts of the head, stern and galleries as are usually friezed . . .' This is straightforward and the wording 'usual colour yellow' implies a well-established tradition; there is, furthermore, evidence that the order was obeyed. Yet contemporary pictures and models do not accord with the Order, and show the sides 'bright', which means that they have been treated with turpentine or varnish. Some models have their upperworks painted a soft, light blue on which scrollwork and heraldic designs are painted in gilt, and others, although conforming to the Admiralty Order about plain colours, nevertheless have scrollwork etc in gilt along their topsides. This divergence from the official scheme is curious and suggests a certain amount of 'artist's licence' about the decoration of models. After 1740, however, there is no doubt about individual variations in ships' paintwork, for there are references to ships with all-black sides (which would make them look smaller and, so it was hoped, induce the enemy to attack) and to others with the lowest wale and the topside black but the in-between parts red. The history of ship painting for the years 1740–1780 has never been investigated in detail but enough information has come to light to prove that the appearance of a fleet then was far from a uniform one. Official recognition of this fact was given in an Admiralty Order of 1780 that allowed ships to be painted black or yellow, and from then until some years after Trafalgar a fairly wide variety of styles was to be seen[16]. By good fortune a record of the appearance of the British and French ships at the Battle of the Nile in 1798 survives. It was made by Col Fawkes, who was present at the battle[17].

WARSHIP COLOURS – Battle of the Nile 1798

Royal Navy		French Navy	
Alexander Audacious Bellerophon Defence Orion Mutine	Plain yellow sides	Le Guerrier Le Conquerant	Dark yellow sides
		L'Aquilon	Red sides with a black strake between the upper and lower gunports
		Le Franklin	Plain yellow sides
Goliath Leander Majestic Theseus Swiftsure Vanguard	Yellow sides with a black strake between the upper and lower rows of gunports. In addition *Theseus* had her hammock cloths painted yellow, with black 'ports' to make her look like a 3-decker	L'Orient Le Peuple Souverain	Dark yellow sides
		Le Tonnant	Broad light yellow side, with small black strakes on a line with the muzzles of the guns and two between the upper and lower decks
Culloden	Yellow sides with two narrow black strakes between the upper and lower rows of gunports	L'Heureux Le Mercure	Very dark yellow sides
Zealous	Red sides with a small yellow stripe		
		Le Timoleon Le Genereux	Very dark red sides
Minotaur	Red sides with a black strake between the upper and lower rows of gunports	Le Guillaume Tell	Light yellow sides with a black strake between the upper and lower decks
		Frigates	All Yellow

Other examples of ships having been painted in similar styles are known yet models and pictures tell us nothing about them. The implication is clear: in the late eighteenth century, if not earlier, neither Admiralty Order nor 'Navy Board' model, if such exists, can be relied upon as evidence for a ship's actual appearance.

296. A forerunner of the wheel, a steering windlass, from a model of *c*1705.

297. The double steering wheel, winding drum and tiller ropes.

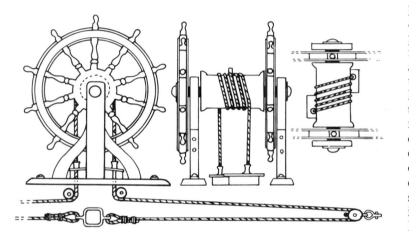

298. The great mechanical invention associated with the wheel was the sweep, shown here with rollers and a tackle to adjust the tension of the tiller ropes.

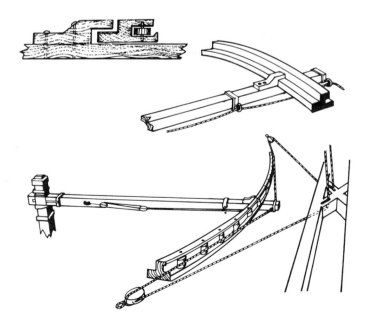

The stern. The changes in the decoration of eighteenth century sterns will be more easily understood from an examination of the examples shown in the accompanying illustrations than from a verbal description. The remarkable thing about the changes in the stern's decoration is the speed with which the 'Georgian' style replaced the Baroque after the restrictive Order of 1703 came into force. Practically the only parts to retain something of the old profusion of carving were the taffrail and its supporters, and only the larger vessels had any extensive carving there. The 5th and 6th Rates had to make do with mouldings and pilaster work, with here and there a little gilding or, more likely, gilt paint. Some contemporary English models have extensively painted sterns (as, for example, the stern of the 60-gun 2-decker *Achilles* of 1757 in the Science Museum, London, which has the flat surfaces painted blue with swags, trophies, drapery motifs and badges in gilt) but the question is whether the ship itself was painted in such an elaborate manner.

There is no doubt, however, that paint was used more widely in the eighteenth century than in any previous age. The raw materials for paints were available in sufficient quantities to allow the preservative properties of paint to be put to good use. Paints were made up on the spot from their component pigments, oil and thinner (turpentine) as they were in fact right down to the beginning of the present century. William Sutherland's *England's Glory: or Ship-building Unveiled* of 1717 lists the materials used in Naval Dockyards: white lead, vermilion, red ochre, spruce (Prussian ochre), English ochre, verdigris (used for greens), calcined smalt (a cobalt compound used in blues) and blue-black. Linseed oil was used as the binder, although instances are known of dishonest contractors using size instead. From other sources we learn that gold leaf was used, though sparingly we may suppose, and red lead, Venetian red and Indian red. The last two would have been used for decoration rather than for mass coverage. A drab paint was made by mixing the leftovers together and was known, appropriately, as 'sad colour'. It was used on the bottoms of boats, in the bilges and on the faces of joints. In the 1780s whitewash began to be used on the interior parts of ships and its application gradually increased until it had to a large extent replaced the traditional red.

Rendering the directions for painting an eighteenth century ship in modern colour terminology presents several difficulties. Not only were the paints lacking in gloss and the shades dull by comparison with modern paints, but the name of an eighteenth century colour, though the same name is in use today, may refer to quite a different hue. For example, the 'yellow' used on eighteenth century topsides was really a yellowish-beige (in present day nomenclature) because it was made with yellow ochre, and as that mineral would certainly not be as pure as the modern material the shade of the paint would be duller than its modern equivalent. The name 'red' did not denote the bright colour used today either, but something not unlike the colour of freshly dried blood. Nor was gilt always what its name suggests. Much of it was the colour produced by brushing varnish or even wood tar over white and was a golden-yellow like the colour seen on old furniture, not at all like the brassy modern 'gold' paint. The differences between eighteenth century and modern paints are important when renovation of an eighteenth century model is to be undertaken. It is not by any means unusual to see a 'restored' model decked out with colours that are much too bright for the period in which the ship was built.

MASTS AND YARDS

The major changes that occurred during the eighteenth century were: the replacement of the seventeenth century spritsail topsail by fore-and-aft headsails and the replacement of the lateen mizzen by a gaff sail; more staysails added until there was one on every principal stay; royals on the fore- and mainmasts of ships-of-the-line, and on the mizzenmasts of the smaller vessels as well; and stunsails on each yard of the fore- and main-masts except the royals. By 1800 the sail plan had reached its maximum development on warships, so that even a comparatively small ship could set 37 sails alto-gether. Development of the fore-and-aft rig did not lag behind, especially along the American seaboard, but the inherent difficulties of enlarging the rig, and its unsuit-ability for the rapid manoeuvring necessary for a war-ship, restricted its application to the smaller support craft[18].

There was little change in the shape of the spars but their proportions in relation to the ship's length and to one another altered, especially in the cases of the upper spars which became longer. Standing and running rigging remained much as it had been in the seventeenth century and its components kept to similar sizes although, as the ships themselves were bigger, there was a diminution in relative size for each rate of ship. None-theless, the rope was thick and the blocks often enor-mous.

As rigging had become more or less standard-ised by 1700 it will not be necessary to go into the same amount of detail as in Chapter 3 and only the significant changes will be discussed at length.

Bowsprit, jibboom and flying jibboom. At the begin-ning of the century the bowsprit rose at an angle of about 36° on the big ships and 33° on small ones. In the 1790s the angle was 36°. Its length as a fraction of the main-mast's length at various dates was: 1711, 2/3 (0.67); 1719, 11/18 (0.61) on 1st and 2nd Rates and 19/32 (0.59) on all others; 1773, 19/32 (0.59); 1794, over 80 guns 7/11 (0.63), 74 guns and under 3/5 (0.6). The maximum diameter was: 1711, 9/10 of the mainmast; 1719, 1 5/9in per yard of length on 1st to 4th Rates, 1 3/7in per yard on 50-gun 4th Rates, 1 1/3in per yard on 5th Rates and 1 2/9in on 6th Rates. The 1773 propor-tion was 1 1/2in per yard of length. In 1794, however, the bowsprits of 64- to 100-gun ships were only 2in less in diameter than the mainmast, whilst on 50-gun ships and under they were the same thickness as the mast. Like masts, bowsprits tapered towards each end. The inter-mediate diameters are given in the table. While the sprit-sail topmast remained in use the outer end of the bow-sprit was cut off perpendicular to the waterline but after-wards, when a cap was fitted to hold the jibboom, the end was cut into a tenon like those on mastheads.

INTERMEDIATE DIAMETERS OF BOWSPRITS
1759 and 1794

Date	Heel	1st quarter	2nd quarter	3rd quarter	Head
1759	3/4	30/31	9/10	3/4	5/6
1794	7/12 athwartships, 2/3 up and down	60/61	11/12	4/5	5/9 (square)

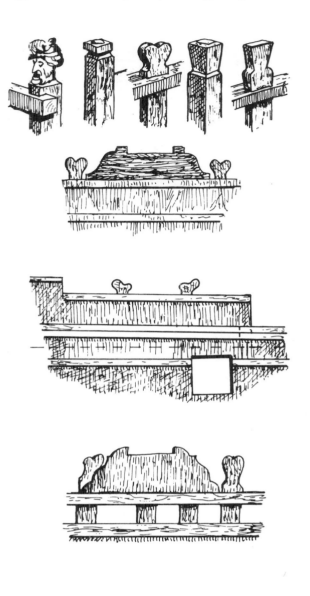

299. English bitts and timber-heads (left to right, from beginning to end of century), fish davit cleats and (bottom) a kevel appearing over a bulwark.

300. Dutch-style timber-heads from a late eighteenth century ship-of-the-line.

301. French-style timber heads, the first and third from the *Soleil Royal* (1690), the second from a ship of 1755 and the last from a training model of about 1800.

302

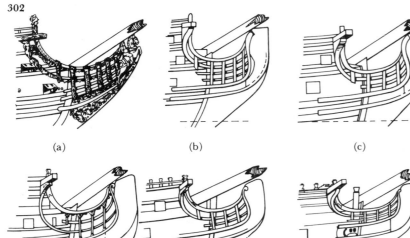

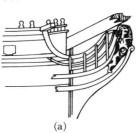
(e)

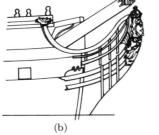
(f)

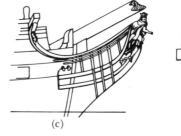
(g)

(h)

302. English heads:
(a) Deane's 1st Rate, *c*1670;
(b) *Ossory*, 90, 1706–11;
(c) *Resolution*, 70, 1708;
(d) *Cumberland*, 80, 1710;
(e) *Ramillies*, 90, 1748;
(f) *Canada*, 74, 1759;
(g) *Albion*, 74, 1778;
(h) *Courageux*, 74, 1796.

303. French heads:
(a) *Berlin*, 64 guns;
(b) *Pompée*, 80 guns, 1793;
(c) *Genoa*, 74 guns, 1815;
(d) frigate *Diane;*
(e) corvette *Vesuve.*

303

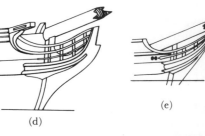

(a)　　　　(b)　　　　(c)　　　　(d)　　　　(e)

305

The date of the introduction of the jibboom (which was known at first as the flying jibboom) is uncertain. It had been authorised in 1705 for small ships and by 1714 had displaced the spritsail topmast on all ships below 60 guns. By 1719 70-gun ships were added to the list but on bigger ships both jibbooms and spritsail topmasts were carried, at any rate officially, until 1745, although, we may suppose, the awkwardness of the combination would have led to the spritsail topmast being taken down and stowed away long before that date. So long as there was a spritsail topmast the jibboom was fastened to the starboard side of the bowsprit, and if there was a spritsail top the jibboom protruded through a hole in it. After the spritsail topmast had been abolished the jibboom was shifted to the top of the bowsprit and secured by a cap. At the inner end of the jibboom was a hole through which a lashing was taken and round the bowsprit, and above the lashing was a sheave for the outhaul. The length of jibbooms gradually increased. In 1719 they were 0.37 of the mainmast's length on big ships and 0.35 on small ones; they were 0.42 of the mainmast in 1773 and 0.455 (big ships) and 0.43 (small ones) in 1794. Unlike bowsprits, jibbooms tapered from the heel to their outer end. The true flying jibboom (in later terminology) only came in at the very end of the century.

TAPER OF JIBBOOMS
1717 and 1794

Date	Heel	1st quarter	2nd quarter	3rd quarter	End
1717	1	30/31	7/8	–	2/3
1794	1	40/41	11/12	5/6	2/3

The maximum diameters of jibbooms were 1/42 of their length in 1719 and 1/41 by 1794.

304. A contemporary model of a 50-gun ship of the 1733 Establishment, with its original rigging. The identity of the ship is uncertain but it is very like the *Gloucester*, built in 1736, that accompanied Anson on his voyage of circumnavigation. The decorative work, and particularly the frieze, is typical of models of this period.

305. The *Boekenroode*, a 58-gun ship built at Amsterdam by the English shipwright Thomas Davis in 1729. The hull combines the flat floor usual in Dutch vessels with the semi-circular shape found on English ships. The figurehead has adopted the upright stance fashionable at the time, and much of the decorative work and general appearance is reminiscent of English ships of the period.

306. In contrast to the decoration of the previous two ships, the Spanish *San Josef* is stark both in colour scheme and because of the absence of carved work. Of 112 guns, the ship was captured by Nelson at St Vincent in 1799, and this draught was taken off the ship at Plymouth in 1799.

306

307

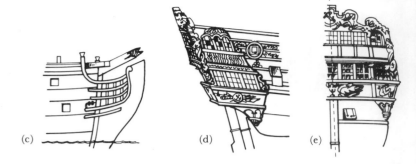

(a) (b) (c) (d) (e)

308

309

308. The stern of a model of an 80-gun ship according to the 1719 Establishment. If this model is compared with that of the *Prince* (**171, 172**) the revolution in decorative style that took place at the end of the seventeenth century can be seen at a glance. The form of stern shown here lasted with only comparatively minor changes for over 100 years.

309. The stern of a model of the 98-gun ship *Boyne* of 1790. Compared with the ship in the previous plate, the stern of the *Boyne* is broader. Note the stern ports hinged on their lower edges, and the huge opening for the rudderhead.

310. The stern of a Russian 66-gun ship of the middle of the eighteenth century. The resemblance of the model to English ships of the same period suggests that is represents the *Lesnoye,* a ship built at St Petersburg (now Leningrad) in 1743 by the English shipwright William Sutherland. The decoration of the upper part of the stern however, is more in the French style than the English. The broadside gunport lids have the Russian double-headed eagle on their inner faces.

311. The stern of the French *L'Aimable* built at Brest in 1725. The highly 'architectural' sterns of French ships persisted down to the 1770s, but were eventually replaced by simpler classical patterns, with a characteristic horseshoe shape enclosing a stern without open galleries.

312. The Danish 70-gun ship *Wenden* built at Nyholm in 1742. Danish ships generally adopted elaborate French-style decoration, but the basic shape of the stern was uniquely Danish.

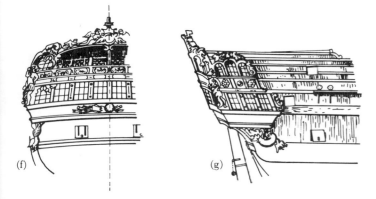

(f)   (g)

307. Dutch heads, quarters and sterns:
(a) a 64-gun ship of 1778;
(b) a ship of 1767;
(c) the *Hercules*, 64, taken in 1797;
(d) and (e) the *Boekenroode*, of 1732 – see also **305**;
(f) and (g) a 64-gun ship of 1749.

Lower masts. The mainmast was placed at about the middle of the lower gun-deck but the positions of the fore- and mizzenmasts were more variable. At the end of the century the position of the foremast had been stabilised at 1/9 of the gun-deck's length from the stem rabbet, the mainmast at 5/9 and the mizzenmast 17/20. Throughout the century both the main- and the mizzen-masts raked aft; the foremast, though sometimes raked, was usually vertical. The amount of rake was not fixed. The extent of it, and sometimes the position of the masts themselves, might be altered in accordance with experience gained from sailing trials. As examples, the *Royal George* of 1723 had the foremast vertical, the mainmast raking aft about 1/25 of its length and the mizzenmast 1/20. Sixty years later the recommended amounts were: foremast, vertical; mainmast, 1in per yard of length (1/36); mizzenmasts, 5/8in per *foot* (1/19). On frigates and sloops, however, the proportions were: foremasts, 1/8in per yard; mainmasts 7/8in per yard; mizzen-masts, 1in per yard.

LENGTH OF MAIN LOWER MAST
(after a 1719 MS)

Ship type	Length
1st and 2nd Rates and 80 – gun 3rd Rates	2.28 × breadth
70 guns	2.32 × breadth
60 guns	2.34 × breadth
50 guns	2.36 × breadth
40 guns	2.38 × breadth
30 guns	2.40 × breadth
20 guns	2.42 × breadth

LENGTHS OF FORE- AND MIZZENMASTS AS FRACTIONS OF MAINMAST'S LENGTH 1711–1794

Date	Foremast	Mizzenmast
1711	7/8–9/10	6/7
1719 and 1773	9/10	11/13
1794	8/9	11/13

Eighteenth century mizzenmasts were stepped in the hold and are therefore longer than many seventeenth century masts that were stepped on the lower deck.

The length of the main lower mast (on which the lengths of the others were based) was calculable in several ways but the commonest was to make it equal to one-half the sum of the gun-deck's length and the extreme breadth. An alternative rule, given in a manuscript of 1719, is shown in the relevant table.

Rope wooldings were put on the masts throughout the century and were augmented by iron hoops. By 1780, and probably for many years earlier, a lower mast for a 74-gun ship had 9 rope bindings and 6 iron hoops, but by the 1790s there was an iron hoop at about every 4ft of a mast's length as well as rope wool-dings. The multiplicity of wooldings and hoops reflected the increasing difficulty of obtaining trees big enough for masts and the consequent necessity of building up a large mast from several pieces.

Trestletrees and crosstrees. William Sutherland's figures (1711) for trestletrees work out at 0.35 of the ship's beam for the main trestletrees, with those of the foremast 7/8 of the main, and the mizzen's 7/16, or as a more general statement the trestletrees were 1.28 times the length of the masthead on fore and main but the

310   311   312

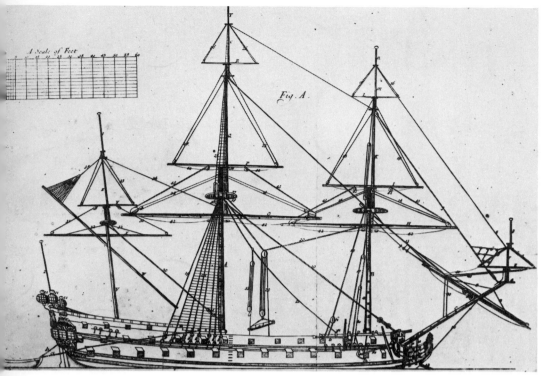

313

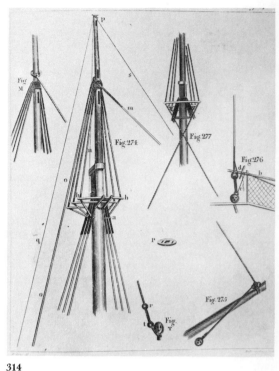

314

MAXIMUM DIAMETERS OF LOWER MASTS 1711–1794				
Date	Ship type	Mainmast (in per yd)	Foremast (in per yd)	Mizzenmast (in per yd)
1711	Large	1	1	2/3
	Small	7/8	7/8	2/3
1773		7/8	7/8	2/3
1794	64–100 guns	1	1	3/5
	32–50 guns	9/10	9/10	2/3
	28 guns and under	7/8	7/8	2/3

313 The spar plan of an English ship of about 1700 from Sutherland's *Shipbuilding Unveiled*.

314. An example of the kind of illustration in contemporary eighteenth and nineteenth century rigging manuals. Many of these have been reprinted recently in facsimile editions.

same length on the mizzenmast. Their depth was very slightly less than 1in for every foot of length and their width 7/8 to 9/10 of the depth. Late eighteenth century trestletrees were equal in length to 1/4 of the topmast, their depth was 1/2 the maximum diameter of the topmast and their width 1/3 of that diameter. Crosstrees had a length that was 6in less than their topmast's length but in depth and thickness they were equal to the trestletrees. Crosstrees and trestletrees had the same shape.

Caps. In shape and proportions caps altered little during the century. The early ones were twice as long as they were deep and their length was 4 times the maximum diameter of the topmast, or half the length of the masthead. Later, ie at the end of the century, the proportions were slightly different, as shown in the table. A typical lower cap had a round hole slightly larger than the diameter f the topmast and lined with leather. A square hole fitted over the masthead. The two holes were separated by 2/5 of the diameter of the round hole. Some ships had a short post between the underside of the cap and the top, in front of the topmast. Its job was to keep the cap level whilst the topmast was being raised or lowered, so that the mast did not jam in its hole.

Topmasts had trestletrees and crosstrees also, but the latter differed in shape from the lower ones. The trestletrees at the beginning of the century were very nearly 1/11 of the topmast's length and were equal to the length of the topmast head; their depth was 1/14 of their

length and the width about 7/8 of the depth. Late-century trestletrees were 7/72 of the topmast length, their depth was 3/32 of their length and their width 1/16. Crosstrees were slightly longer than trestletrees, had the same depth but were very slightly narrower at the beginning of the century. Late-century crosstrees had somewhat different proportions. They were 1/3 longer than the trestletrees, had only 7/8 of the depth but were 1/4 wider. There were three topmast crosstrees, each of which was curved backwards. The middle section was always straight but the outer thirds were set back a little more than 1/3 of the diameter of the topmast.

Topgallant masts sometimes had trestle- and crosstrees for the flagstaff's shrouds. They bore the same proportions to *their* mast as the topmast trees did. The crosstrees differed, however, in that the forward one curved forwards instead of aft as the other one did. Topgallant trestle- and crosstrees had gone out of use by the end of the century.

Tops. Soon after 1700 the round top gradually began to give way to the familiar shape that lasted, with minor changes, until the end of the sailing era. The proportions of the round tops were, according to Sutherland in 1711, equal to a little less than 1/3 of the topmast's length. Many mid-century tops had a length equal to 1/4 of the topmast and a breadth of 1/3 of it. The hole in the top was rectangular and had sides 5/12 of the top's length and width. Tops at the end of the century had lengths and widths of the same proportions as those just given but the central hole had a width 2/5 of the top's breadth and a fore-and-aft length of 13/35 of the breadth. The aft side of the hole was 1/5 of the top's length from its after edge. Tops sometimes had the floor between the crosstrees replaced by a grating.

In action it was customary to fit cloths round the tops to screen the topmen. The cloths were fastened

315. A contemporary engraving of the *Royal George* of 1715.

to stanchions of wood let into the back and sides, but not the front, of the top. The stanchions were sometimes used for mounting swivel-guns, and on small ships those on the after edge of the top might be connected by a rail. Lanterns were sometimes carried in the tops, for night signals. They were fixed to the after side.

Topmasts and topgallant masts. The lengths of these spars, as a fraction of the main lower mast's length, are tabulated, as are the diameters of the caps and the degree of mast taper (the smaller ships had the slimmer masts). Topmast heads were 1/10 of the mast's length in the first part of the century and topgallant masts' were the same. By the end of the century fore and main topmasts' and topgallant masts' heads were 1/9 of the length but on mizzenmasts they were 1/10.

Flagstaffs. The jackstaff on the spritsail topmast and the staffs at the heads of fore-, main- and mizzenmasts were roughly 2/3 the length of the mast below and the ensign staff at the stern was slightly longer than the mizzen topmast. The jackstaff was, in essence, a spritsail topgallant mast and was set up like one of those masts. If the flagpoles on the masts were separate pieces they were set up like topgallant masts, but the flagpole was often a part of the mast that stood up above the shrouds. In this case the 'pole' was between 1/4 and 2/5 of the mast's length. The ensign staff at the beginning of the century was between 7/20 and 2/5 of the mainmast, the main flagstaff was the same, the fore staff about 7/20 and the mizzen staff slightly longer. The jackstaff on the bowsprit was almost 3/20 of the mainmast. The proportions at the end of the century were similar: the length of the ensign staff above the taffrail was 1/3 of the mainmast, the jackstaff 1/6. Their thicknesses were, respectively, 1/72 and 1/48 of the length. The masthead flagstaffs had been replaced by pole mastheads. English flagpoles had circular trucks but those of other navies, at least in the early part of the century, were sometimes of a more ornate shape.

Yards. Only in minor details was there any difference between the shapes of eighteenth and seventeenth century yards. Topsail and topgallant yards had become longer in proportion to the lower yards, and royal yards, unknown since the *Sovereign of the Seas,* reappeared. The major change during the century was the replacement of the lateen mizzen by a gaff sail. The first stage in the changeover was to do away with that part of the lateen sail that stood before the mast. This had happened on the 4th Rate *Tyger* in 1708. A 50-gun ship had a half-mizzen in 1714 and so did the 48-gun *Falkland* in 1721. The substitution of a half-mizzen for the old lateen sail was nonetheless a slow process. By 1747 5th and 6th Rates had half-mizzens and over the next ten years they were supplied to all HM ships of under 80 guns. After 1760 half-mizzens came into use even on 3-deckers although the long yard was retained. In fact, the replacement of the lateen yard by a gaff was not complete until the end of the century although a gaff was fitted to the *Royal Caroline* (a yacht) in 1732 and 6th Rates had them in the 1740s. There was some point in retaining the long mizzenyard, even though only a half-mizzen was set on it, because the yard could be used as a replacement for a

				TAPER OF LOWER MASTS 1711 and 1794				
Date	Heel	1st quarter	2nd quarter	3rd quarter	At hounds	At crosstrees	Head (athwart)	Head (fore & aft)
1711	1	40/41	11/12	–	5/6	2/3	2/3	7/12
1794	1	60/61	14/15	6/7	–	3/4	2/3	–

The mast below the partners tapered similarly to the heel, the diameter of which was 4/5 of the maximum in 1711 and 6/7 later.

316

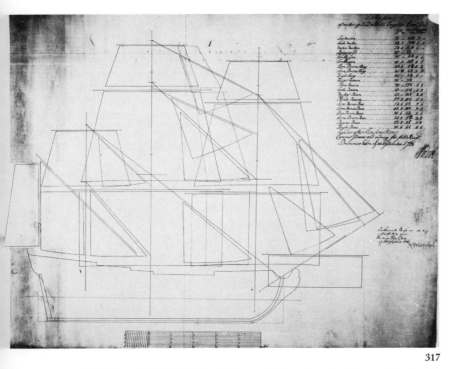

317

316. The official 1745 Establishment rigging plan for 70-gun ships. In the Royal Navy spar dimensions and rigging proportions were all standardised so that rigging plans are rare before the experiments of the early nineteenth century.
317. The Danish Navy, with relatively few ships, designed individual sail plans for most ships and from the middle of the century this was based on calculations of the centres of efforts of the sails. This plan of the sails for the frigate *Stralsund*, dated 30 September 1746 is interesting since it shows fore-and-aft sails, stunsails and a half-mizzen, with the full mizzen in dotted line.
318. Sutherland's plan of the sails and running rigging for a ship of about 1700.

318

PROPORTIONS OF CAPS
– late Eighteenth Century

Cap	Length	Breadth	Depth
Main	(4 × topmast diameter)+3in	(2 × topmast diameter)+2in	4/9 of breadth
Fore	(4 × topmast diameter)+2in	(2 × topmast diameter) +1in	4/9 of breadth
Mizzen	(4 × topmast diameter) +1in	(2 × topmast diameter)	4/9 of breadth

lost spar. At all events, the last British ship to carry a lateen yard is believed to have been Nelson's *Vanguard* at the Battle of the Nile in 1798. A hint of the official reluctance to recognise gaffs is their absence from rigging lists until the last 20 years of the century.

The lengths of yards were based on the length of the mainyard and this might be derived from the length of the mainmast, or more directly from the breadth of the ship or the length of its gun-deck. The diameters of yards at their midpoints were expressed in a variety of ways by contemporary writers but the proportions have been reduced in the table to a fraction of each yard's length, eg 1/51 instead of 7/10in per yd of length.
Mizzen gaff and boom. These spars were not introduced together. Whereas the gaff was in use as early as 1708 on small ships and was gradually brought into use on bigger and bigger vessels, the sail was not extended by a boom except on brigs. Booms did not come into official use until the Admiralty Order of February 1780 directed them to be fitted to frigates, and another Order, issued 3 months later, applied to all other ships.

The lengths of the early gaffs are not known, but since they replaced the upper part of a lateen yard it is reasonable to suppose that the length was the same as that part of the lateen yard, in which case it would be just over 2/5 the length of the mainyard. In 1794 a gaff's length was 0.43 of the mainyard's length; at the same date the maximum thickness of a gaff was 1/56 of its length. Booms were about the same length as the main topsail yard, or 5/7 of the mainyard, and their maximum diameter was 1/56 of their length. Neither gaffs nor booms were uniform in diameter. The thickest part of a gaff was from the jaws to about 4ft aft and from then onwards the gaff tapered: first quarter 40/41, second quarter 11/12, third quarter 4/5 and end 5/9. Booms, like yards, had their thickest part in mid-length and from there tapered: first quarter 40/41, second quarter 11/12, third quarter 5/6, and end 2/3. The main booms of brigs had different proportions. Their length was 0.8 of the mainmast and their maximum diameter 1/51 of their length. This point was 1/3 of the boom's length from its inboard end and the taper towards each end of the boom was: first quarter 40/41, second quarter 11/12, third quarter 5/6, and ends 2/3. Since the boom's length is based on the length of the mainmast it should be noted, in case the actual dimensions for a particular brig are not available, that the length of the mainmast was 1/2 × (gun-deck length + breadth + depth in hold). Cutters, and other vessels that had their lower mast and topmast in one, had a mainmast that was 3/4 × (gun-deck + breadth + depth).

DIAMETERS AT CAPS 1711 AND 1794		
Mast	1711	1794
Spritsail topmast	1/42 of length	
Fore topmast	1/40–1/41 of length	1/36 of length
Main topmast	1/40 of length	1/36 of fore topmast
Mizzen topmast	1/40–1/50 of length	7/10 of main topmast's diameter
Fore topgallant	1/42–1/44 of length	1/36 of length
Main topgallant	1/44–1/38 of length	1/36 of length
Mizzen topgallant	–	1/36 of length

LENGTHS OF TOPMASTS AND TOPGALLANT MASTS as fractions of main lowermast's length 1711–1794			
Mast	1711	1773	1794
Spritsail topmast	8/45	–	–
Fore topmast	24/45	57/100	24/45
Main topmast	3/5	19/31	3/5
Mizzen topmast	2/7	43/100	3/7
Fore topgallant	4/15	29/100	4/15
Main topgallant	3/10	19/61	3/10
Mizzen topgallant	–	11/50	3/14

Stunsail yards and booms. There is still much that is obscure about the development of stunsails in the Royal Navy[19]. In a manuscript dating from about 1719 there are stunsails to the fore- and mainyards and the fore and main topsails. The lower booms were to be 6/13 of the lower yards and the upper ones 5/9 of the topsail yards. The maximum diameter of the booms was to be 5/8in per yard of length. As nothing is said about stunsail yards the sails may have been triangular (see Chapter 3). In another manuscript, of 1759, however, stunsail yards are listed and their diameter is given as 1in for every 5ft of length (1/60) but no length is given. The booms have the same proportions as in 1719. It is curious that notwithstanding stunsails were a regular part of a ship's outfit of sails, their yards and booms do not appear in official rigging lists even as late as 1773, by which time privateers and probably some Navy vessels had added topgallant stunsails to the others. The first reference to dimensions of stunsail yards is to be found in a manuscript of 1785, which states that, in general, stunsail yards were to be 1/3 the length of corresponding square yards and their diameter was to be 5/8in per yard of length. Alternatively, the stunsail yards were to be 4/7 of their boom's length. Main lower booms were 5/9 of the mainyard's length and in thickness 5/16in per yard of their length. There was no fore lower stunsail boom. The topmast stunsail booms were 1/2 the length of the topsail yards and their diameter 1/2in less than that of the lower boom. In 1794 stunsail booms were 1/2 of the yard they went on and stunsail yards were 4/7 of the length of their booms. Both yards and booms were 1in in thickness for every 5ft of length. The mizzenmast never carried stunsails, nor did the royal yards.

The shape of stunsail yards and booms was different from that of the other yards and booms. For one-third of their length from the inboard end the diameter was constant but for the remainder it tapered: first quarter 40/41, second quarter 11/12, third quarter 5/6 and the end 2/3. The early upper stunsail booms were run out through a figure-of-eight iron at the yardarm and the inner end was lashed to the yard. Then a wooden saddle was fitted to the yard to assist the lashing. In the second half of the century the outer iron was replaced by a ring and the lashing by a figure-of-eight iron, the outer ring of which was hinged so that it could be opened to admit the boom's end. The lower booms were hooked into the appropriate channels.

STANDING RIGGING

The basic pattern of rigging having been established in the last century, all that remained to be done was to accommodate new additions to spars and sails within that pattern. Consequently it will be only the new pieces of gear that will be treated as fully as earlier rigging has been, and for the rest, comment will be confined to changes in lead or size.

The bowsprit. The introduction of the bobstay had provided a counter to the upward pull of the newly adopted jib but the bowsprit still lacked adequate lateral support. This was given soon after the eighteenth century opened by the bowsprit shrouds. The date of their introduction is not known, for although they were authorised in 1706 bowsprit shrouds had been an unofficial fitting for some time before that date. The early shrouds had their inner ends hooked to eyebolts on the lower wales and their outer ends set up to the bowsprit with deadeyes and lanyards, at a point just in front of the bobstay's collar. That method remained in use until about 1736, after which the deadeyes were replaced by hearts. The rigging of the bobstay was also altered, the deadeyes being replaced by hearts by 1773. The end of the lanyard had a luff tackle attached to it, the tackle fall being brought in to the forecastle. Big ships were given two bobstays soon after 1700 and before long all but the smallest ships had followed suit. The second bobstay was set up just in front of the first one.

When the jibboom came into use it too was found to need support, yet it was a long time before it was given the equivalent of a bobstay. When the new stay, called a martingale stay, was introduced is not certain but it does not seem to have been before 1790. The stay started from the outer end of the jibboom and passed through a groove in the lower end of a short, stout boom (the martingale) fixed to the lower side of the bowsprit cap and then came in to the head. The stay was set up by a tackle consisting of a double block at the end of the stay and a single block in the head. The tackle-fall was made fast to the single block. At the end of the century there were sometimes two martingale stays, one from the outer end of the jibboom as before, and one

DEGREE OF TAPER OF MASTS 1717 AND 1794							
Date	Mast	1st quarter	2nd quarter	3rd quarter	Hounds	Head	
1717	Spritsail topmast	30/31	11/12	–	2/3	1/2	
	Topmasts and topgallant masts	30/31	7/8	–	2/3	1/2	
1794	Topmasts and topgallant masts	60/61	14/15	6/7	–	9/13 (lower)	
						6/11 (upper)	

319. A contemporary model of the *Ipswich*, a 3rd Rate of 70 guns built in 1730 to the dimensions of the 1719 Establishment. The rigging of the model is largely original.

320. The famous *Victory* as restored to her Trafalgar appearance. Considerable research ensured that as far as possible the ship's hull and rig reflect her 1805 condition.

LENGTH OF MAINYARD 1700–1794

Date	Ship type	Length
c1700		2/3 × extreme breadth
1711		7/8 × mainmast length
c1720		2.25 × extreme breadth
1760–1780	100 guns	0.56 × gun-deck length
	90 guns	0.56 × gun-deck length
	80 guns	0.56 × gun-deck length
	70 guns	0.57 × gun-deck length
	60 guns	0.576 × gun-deck length
	50 guns	0.575 × gun-deck length
	44 guns and smaller	0.56 × gun-deck length
1773		7/13 × mainmast length
1794		8/9 × mainmast length

from about its middle. The stays by this time passed through sheave-holes in the martingale (now called a dolphin-striker) and were made fast one on each side of the bow in the same way as the single stay had been. The dolphin-striker at the end of the century was fixed to the outer face of the bowsprit cap by tight-fitting iron hoops. When the flying jibboom came into use in the 1790s it, too, was given a martingale stay. This went to the outer end of the dolphin-striker and the two jibboom stays' sheaves were slightly inwards from it. Jibboom and flying jibboom were steadied by guys that ran from their outer ends to the spritsail yardarms and thence inboard, where they were set up to ringbolts on the upper edge of the beakhead bulkhead.

The need for a martingale stay is so obvious that it may seem odd that one was so late in appearing. The explanation is that so long as the spritsail remained in use it was impossible to rig a martingale stay because it would foul the spritsail. Only when that sail was abolished did the martingale stay come into use. The spritsail yard was retained, however, as a spreader for the jibboom and flying jibboom guys.

Lower masts. According to William Sutherland, the allowance of main shrouds in 1711 was as shown in the table. Foremasts had one shroud less, mizzenmasts on big ships had 3-4 fewer than the mainmast. The 1794 figures are also tabulated. Shrouds were made of 4-stranded rope. The order of putting them over the masthead was the same as in the previous century.

Topmasts, topgallant masts and flagstaffs. The early ones were set up as in the seventeenth century but by the end of the century some changes had been introduced. Topmasts had breast-backstays set up to the channels with a tackle and shifting backstays that could be moved from one place to another. Topgallant shrouds were set up in a new way. Instead of the usual deadeyes etc the shrouds passed through holes in the ends of the cross-trees, were then taken inwards over the futtock staff and passed down, parallel to the topmast shrouds, to the topmast deadeyes, where they were made fast. Topgallant backstays were set up to the after ends of channels or, in the earlier years, to small brackets called backstay stools. If flagstaffs had shrouds they were made fast, via the topgallant crosstrees, to the head of the topgallant shrouds. The fore topmast stay was set up to a thimble at the jibboom end and belayed round the forestay's collar; the main topmast stay was belayed in the foretop; and the mizzen topmast stay was belayed in the maintop.

RUNNING RIGGING

Like the standing rigging, this changed only to a small extent, and the fully developed pattern is shown in the illustrations. As in the preceding section, only innovations or changes in lead will be commented upon.

Lower yards. Only the small ships still hoisted their yards by the old-fashioned tyes and halliards. The bigger ones had jeers, a pair of them, one on each side of the yard's centre. The jeers might have a pair of double blocks each, a double and a treble block or, on the biggest ships, two treble blocks. The jeer rope might start at the yard, or from the masthead. The falls of the jeers went down to the deck on each side of the mast and were made fast to the bitts on the after side of the mast. On small ships, the jeer's fall had a double block on its lower end and a tackle rove between it and a treble block hooked to a ringbolt in the deck, one on each side of the mast. The tackle fall was secured to the bitts. Tyes, when used, were rigged as already described.

DIAMETERS OF YARDS AT MID-POINTS 1700–1794

Yard	c1700	1711	1760–1780	1794
Spritsail	1/48, 1/54**	1/54	1/50	1/56
Spritsail topsail	1/48, 1/54	1/47	1/59*	1/56*
Fore	1/48, 1/54	1/49, 1/53	1/50	1/51, 1/52
Fore topsail	1/48, 1/54	1/51	1/56	1/56
Fore topgallant	1/48, 1/54	1/51	1/54	1/60
Fore royal	–	–	–	1/56
Main	1/48, 1/54	1/53	1/50	1/51, 1/52
Main topsail	1/48, 1/54	1/51, 1/53	1/56	1/57, 1/63
Main topgallant	1/48, 1/54	1/50	1/54	1/58, 1/59
Main royal	–	–	–	1/56, 1/57
Mizzen	1/76	1/70, 1/74	1/65	1/65
Crossjack	1/76	1/72, 1/77	1/56	1/56
Mizzen topsail	1/48, 1/54	1/49, 1/52	1/59	1/58, 1/59
Mizzen topgallant	–	–	–	1/59

*New spritsail topsail yard set under the jibboom
**When two thicknesses are given the larger fraction is for the yards of big ships

So long as the lower yards had to be lowered to furl sail, the jeers were all that held them aloft, but when this practice fell into disuse in the second half of the century the yards' weight was taken by a sling that suspended them together with the jeers.

The foregoing account refers only to the fore- and mainyards. The crossjack yard, as it did not carry a sail, did not have to be raised or lowered in the ordinary course of sailing and consequently it did not have jeers or tyes and was held aloft by a sling. The lateen yard had a jeer made up of a single or a double block on the yard and a double or treble one from the masthead. The jeer-rope started from the masthead and after reeving through both blocks was made fast to an eyebolt on the starboard mizzen channel.

The old-style parrel with its trucks and sisters disappeared from lower masts once the fore- and main-yards were kept permanently aloft, and was replaced by a truss. The lower blocks of the truss-tackles were hooked into eyebolts in the deck on either side of the mast. The mizzen parrel has already been described (Chapter 3).

Lifts on the fore- and mainyards were rigged as already described. The crossjack lifts, which were fixed (standing lifts), started either from the topsail sheet block or from the yardarm and had their upper ends seized to a ringbolt in the cap.

Braces. Early eighteenth century braces were rigged as they had been in the seventeenth century[20]. By the 1790s, however, some alterations in the braces' leads had been made. The forebrace, after coming back from the pendant block to a single block near the mainstay's collar, went down to a sheave hole in the fore side of the main bitts and was belayed there. The mainbraces started at the quarter-pieces of the stern and, after passing through the pendant blocks from the yardarms, came back to a snatch block near their starting point and were belayed to a strong cleat on the inside of the bulwarks.

The crossjack braces had a different arrangement. The starboard brace started at one of the middle main shrouds *on the port side*, reeved through a pendant block from the starboard yardarm and returned to a single block a little below its starting point, and from there was taken down via a lead block on the middle shroud to the fife-rail. The port brace ran in the opposite direction.

Spritsail yard. The spritsail yard was kept permanently outboard. It was hung from the bowsprit by a sling although a halliard was also rigged to keep the yard up in its place. The braces were rigged much as in the previous century except that they started at the foretop instead of the forestay. The spritsail yard's lifts started at the bowsprit cap, ran through blocks at the yardarms and came back to single blocks at the cap, and from there came in to the forecastle pin-rail. There were also standing lifts.

LENGTHS OF OTHER YARDS AS FRACTIONS OF MAINYARD 1700–1794

Yard	c1700	c1720	1760–1780	1794
Spritsail	0.6	0.5–0.58	As fore topsail yard	As fore topsail yard
Spritsail topsail	0.30	0.30	As fore topgallant yard*	As fore topgallant yard*
Fore	0.85–0.9	0.86–0.88	80–100 guns 0.88, others 0.874	0.876
Fore topsail	0.51–0.54	0.48–0.49	100–80 guns 0.629, 70 guns 0.628, 24 guns 0.635, others 0.625	0.625
Fore topgallant	0.26–0.27	0.24	70 guns 0.44, others 0.43	74 guns and over 0.412, others 0.475
Fore royal	–	–	–	0.313
Main topsail	0.60	0.55	24 guns 0.726, others 0.720	0.71
Main topgallant	0.30	0.27	0.50	74 guns and over 0.48, others 0.43
Main royal	–	–	–	74 guns and over 0.24, others 0.22
Mizzen	0.85	0.85	100–80 guns 0.82, 70 guns 0.847 60–44 guns 0.82, 24 guns 0.84	0.86
Crossjack	0.60	0.56	As fore topsail yard	As fore topsail yard
Mizzen topsail	0.30	0.28–0.30	100–80 guns 0.471, 70 guns 0.482, 24 guns 0.496, others 0.469	0.48
Mizzen topgallant	–	–	–	74 guns and over 0.28, others 0.24

*New spritsail topsail yard set under the jibboom

TAPER OF SQUARE YARDS FROM MIDDLE TO EACH END 1700 AND 1790

Date	Middle	1st quarter	2nd quarter	3rd quarter	Yardarm
c1700	1	20/21	7/8	2/3	2/5
c1790	1	30/31	7/8	7/10	3/7

TAPER OF MIZZENYARD FROM MIDDLE TO EACH END 1700 AND 1790

Date	Arm	Middle	1st quarter	2nd quarter	3rd quarter	End
c1700	Upper	1	14/15	13/15	2/3	1/2
	Lower		20/21	11/12	5/6	3/5
c1790	Upper	1	30/31	7/8	7/10	2/5
	Lower		60/61	11/12	5/6	2/3

Spritsail topsail yard. Only the new spritsail topsail yard, the one below the bowsprit, needs any comment. In contrast to the spritsail yard, the new yard was rigged so that it could be run up and down the jibboom. It had a simple parrel and a simple halliard, the fall of which was made fast to the lower end of the jibboom. The spritsail topsail braces went straight from the yardarms to blocks on the underside of the foretop and from there went to the after end of the forecastle where they were belayed. The lifts went from the yardarms to blocks on the end of the jibboom and back to the rack over the bowsprit and were made fast there.

Fore, main, and mizzen topsail yards. Fore and main topsail halliards on big ships were practically jeers. At the lower end of each tye was a single block. Between that and a single block hooked on to a swivel-bolt on the channel a tackle-fall ran, starting from the bottom of the block on the tye. From the lower block the fall went to a conveniently placed lead block and came inboard. The fore topsail halliards were belayed just abaft the forecastle, the main topsail halliards on the quarterdeck. Mizzen topsail yards on big ships and all three topsail yards on small ones had only a single tye. The lower end of the tye had a tackle like that just described. Its fall was belayed on the starboard side of the poop. All three yards had parrels.

Topsail lifts consisted of a single block on each yardarm and a sister-block fastened to the topmast shrouds near the top. The lift started at the topmast cap, ran through the yardarm block and then through the lower sheave of the sister-block, after which it was taken down and belayed to the deadeyes of the lower shrouds. Fore topsail braces started from the mainstay collar, ran through the usual pendant blocks from the fore topsail yardarms and then passed through lead-blocks on the main stay abreast of the fore hatchway, down to other lead-blocks on the after part of the forecastle and were belayed nearby. The main topsail braces started from the mizzenstay collar, passed through the yard pendant-blocks and came back to lead-blocks on the mizzen masthead below the hounds, from where they went to a sheave-hole in the after mizzen bitts and were belayed there. Mizzen topsail braces were taken to the outer end of the gaff (or the lateen yard) and from there down to the fore side of the taffrail and made fast.

Topgallant yards. All three were hoisted by a single tye that ran through a sheave-hole in the topgallant mast. The falls of the later tackles were belayed to the crosspiece of the bitts abaft the mast. Topgallant yards had parrels that were usually made up of two rows of trucks with ribs, but Falconer states that topgallant yards had only a simple rope without trucks. Probably this was used on small ships.

Braces were rigged in a similar manner to the topsail braces. The fore topgallant braces were taken forwards to lead-blocks at the after end of the foretop and then down to cleats on each side of the belfry. The main topgallant braces were taken down inside the mizzen shrouds and belayed to a cleat on the fourth mizzen shroud. Mizzen topgallant braces were like the corresponding topsail braces. Topgallant lifts were simple – they passed from the yardarm through a thimble in the topgallant shrouds and were belayed in the top below.

Mizzen gaff. The early eighteenth century gaffs were hoisted as shown in the drawings. The halliard started at the jaws of the gaff, ran up to a single block on the after side of the masthead and had a tackle composed of a double (upper) and a single (lower) block on its end. The tackle-fall was belayed to a cleat on the mast. Big ships had a different system. There was a double block at the jaws of the gaff and another one slung from the middle of the after crosstree. The halliard started from the upper block and after reeving through both blocks came down to a lead-block on the deck close to the second mizzen shroud on the starboard side and was made fast to the bulwarks a little further aft. The peak halliards, for holding up the outer end of the gaff, consisted of a block, single or double, at the masthead and a similar one about 2/3 the way out along the gaff. The halliard started at the masthead and was rigged like the throat halliards. Its fall was brought down to the deck on the port side.

To steady the gaff a pair of vangs were fitted to its outer end. Vangs on small ships were rigged like braces: a single block on the ends of each of a pair of pendants and a lead-block on each side of the taffrail. The tackles started at the upper block and were belayed to cleats on the taffrail. On big ships the blocks on the vang pendants were double ones and those at the ends of the taffrail single. The falls started at the lower blocks and were belayed, as before, to cleats. At the extreme end of the gaff there was a single block, fastened to an eye-bolt driven into the gaff axially. This block was for the ensign halliards.

Driver boom. The later form of the rigging of this spar was a parrel, a topping-lift to hold the outer end up, a sheet, and guy pendants to control it laterally. The parrel was a single rope, with trucks, fixed between the ends of the boom's jaws. The topping lift was double, so that the lee lift could be slackened off to prevent it chafing the sail. The lift started at the outer end of the boom and passed through single blocks at the sides of the masthead. A double block was put on their ends and a tackle rigged between it and a single block hooked on to the mizzen channel. The tackle-falls started at the double blocks and were belayed to cleats on each side of the mizzenmast. There was no tackle to hold the inner end of the boom up. The jaws rested on a wooden saddle attached to the after side of the mizzenmast.

The sheet consisted of a double block fastened to the boom at about its mid-length if the boom projected over the taffrail but near the boom's end if it did not, and another double block that was attached either to an eye-

MAIN SHROUDS 1711		
Tonnage	Number	Size (in)
1677	9	$9\frac{3}{4}$
1488	9	9
969	8	$7\frac{1}{2}$
625	7	$6\frac{3}{4}$
364	7	$5\frac{1}{4}$
225	6	4

MAIN SHROUDS 1794			
Number of Guns	Foremast	Mainmast	Mizzenmast
110–74	10 (11in)	10 (11in)	6 (7in)
64	9 ($10\frac{1}{2}$in)	9 ($10\frac{1}{2}$in)	6 ($6\frac{1}{2}$in)
50–36	7 ($8\frac{1}{2}$in)	7 ($8\frac{1}{2}$in)	5 ($5\frac{1}{2}$in)
32–28	7 (8in)	7 (8in)	5 ($5\frac{1}{2}$in)
24	7 ($7\frac{1}{2}$in)	7 ($7\frac{1}{2}$in)	5 (5in)
22–20	6 ($7\frac{1}{2}$in)	6 ($7\frac{1}{2}$in)	4 ($4\frac{1}{2}$in)
18–14	5 (5in)	5 or 6 (7in)	4 ($4\frac{1}{2}$in)

bolt on the deck or to a short, iron thwartships 'horse' just in front of the taffrail. With the first arrangement the tackle-fall was belayed to a cleat near the lower block but when there was a 'traveller' on a 'horse' either the same arrangement was used or, on small ships, the tackle-fall was made fast to the lower block. Booms also had temporary braces, guy pendants, which were a pair of luff-tackles rigged between the boom, from near the sheet block, and a convenient timber-head on each side.

Footropes were regular fittings on all yards, on the jibboom, and on the outboard part of the driver boom. In the later part of the century the inboard ends of the yard footropes were fastened on the opposite side of the yard's centre from their starting point (the yardarm). Footropes hung about 3ft below their yard and were supported by four stirrups on each side. Topsail yards had short footropes called Flemish horses at the yardarms in addition to the ordinary footropes. The jibboom's footropes (known as horses, like all other footropes), ran between the outer end of the jibboom and a point a little inboard from the bowsprit cap. The bowsprit horses were fitted on its upper side and fixed between the forestay collar and either to the fore end of the gangway that led from the forecastle deck to the bowsprit (big ships) or to the beakhead bulkhead on small ships. The driver boom's horses were set up like a yard's footropes and were fixed between the outer end of the boom and the strop of the sheet block.

Blocks and deadeyes. The size of a block was determined by two factors: the minimum size of a sheave that would take the rope and would withstand the crushing strain imposed; and the smallest radius that could be used without overstraining the fibres that made up the rope, for bending a rope too sharply hastens its rate of wear. Of the two factors the first was the most influential because until well into the eighteenth century sheaves were made of native hardwoods – ash and oak – as they had been for centuries, and such sheaves had to be big. The proportions of blocks were thus the outcome of long experience and it had become the practice to express the length of a block as a multiple of the size (circumference) of its rope. The length of a tackle-block, for example, was $2\frac{3}{4}$ times the rope size. The other dimensions are not often recorded. The earliest comprehensive details are found in Sutherland's *Ship-building Unveiled* (1717) from which the examples have been taken.

About the middle of the century new and improved blocks, with iron pins instead of the old-fashioned wooden ones, were introduced by Walter Taylor, a blockmaker, and his son. The new blocks were said to be smaller than the old ones and that HMS *Centurion* (1770) was satisfactorily rigged with blocks only half the size of those normally used. To what extent that claim is justified is not clear. Some reduction in the size of blocks is apparent by the 1770s but not to the extent of 50 per cent.

Deadeyes usually had diameters equal to one-half the diameter of their mast, or alternatively to twice the size of the shroud, at the beginning of the century but the ratio was soon reduced to about $1\frac{1}{2}$ times the shroud's size (there was some variation from one mast to another). Throughout the century deadeyes were bi-convex and circular in outline, but to judge from drawings in contemporary books on rigging the early deadeyes were thicker in proportion to their width than those of, say, the 1790s. Full details of the sizes and kinds of blocks, and deadeyes, will be found in *The Masting and Rigging of English Ships of War 1625–1860*.[18]

ARMAMENT

By the end of the seventeenth century warships' armament had been stabilised to the extent that each complete gun-deck carried guns of only one calibre and successively higher decks carried lighter-shotted guns. A change had come about in nomenclature. The time-honoured names cannon-royal, culverin, falcon and the like were obsolete and guns were classified according to the weight of their shot. Since the proportions of each part of a gun were based on its calibre, and that in turn was dependent on the diameter (and therefore the weight) of the shot, classification by shot weight was convenient, simple and readily understood. For most of the century there were ten standard weights of round shot: 42, 32, 24, 18, 12, 9, 6, 4, 3 and $\frac{1}{2}$lb (this last for swivel guns). In the last quarter of the century carronades were mounted on board and by the 1790s the biggest of them were 68pdrs.

The guns listed in the 1793 table were all carriage guns, but after 1780 ships carried carronades as well as their quota of carriage guns, yet by a curious convention carronades were not reckoned as part of the gun total. The difference between the 'theoretical' and actual gun total sometimes bordered on the ridiculous. The *Victory*, in 1793, had two 32pdr carronades on her quarterdeck, two more on her forecastle and six 18pdrs on her poop, or 110 guns in all. The *Ramillies* (74) had eight 12pdr carronades. But the difference was most marked on frigates and smaller vessels. The *Hyaena*, a nominal 24-gun ship, had ten 12pdr carronades in addition to her 24 carriage guns, and an even more remarkable example is the ex-French frigate *Prevoyante*, which was rated as a 36-gun ship in 1795 but actually carried another 20, uncounted, carronades!

Besides their carriage guns, ships carried a secondary armament of swivels for most of the century until these were rendered obsolete by the carronade. The swivels were muzzle-loaders that were mounted along the rails and sometimes in the tops. They were primarily 'man-killers' but could be used with effect against boats. There were not many swivels on big ships but the smaller ones might have them in considerable numbers. A contemporary model of a 20-gun ship of 1719, in the

DIMENSIONS OF BLOCKS 1717

	Example 1(in)	Example 2(in)	Example 3(in)	Example 4(in)	Example 5(in)
Length	8	8	13	13	12
Breadth	7	6	11	11	9
Width of sheave-hole	$1\frac{1}{4}$	$1\frac{1}{8}$	$1\frac{1}{2}$	$1\frac{1}{2}$	2
Thickness of cheeks	$1\frac{3}{8}$	$1\frac{1}{8}$	$1\frac{3}{4}$	$1\frac{1}{2}$	$1\frac{1}{2}$, 2*
Diameter of sheave	5	5	9	$8\frac{1}{2}$	7
Thickness of sheave	$1\frac{1}{8}$	1	$1\frac{3}{8}$	$1\frac{3}{8}$	$1\frac{7}{8}$
Diameter of pin	1	$\frac{7}{8}$	$1\frac{1}{4}$	$1\frac{3}{8}$	$1\frac{3}{8}$
Total thickness of block	$3\frac{3}{4}$	$3\frac{1}{4}$	5	$4\frac{1}{2}$	$5\frac{1}{2}$

The example marked * has cheeks of different thickness.

National Maritime Museum, has 22 swivel guns mounted along its bulwarks. Swivels were mounted between the jaws of an iron stirrup, the lower part of which might be set into a timberhead or into a special post that was mounted in a step on the deck and bound to the bulwark or rail by an iron strap. The tops of both sorts of mounting posts were iron-bound to prevent them splitting under the gun's recoil. Swivels were sometimes mounted in the tops but the practice was not popular in the Royal Navy because of the risk of setting the sails on fire.

The general shape of carriage guns did not alter but there were changes in detail. The loops for hoisting the gun (the dolphins) disappeared and so did the decoration. A new feature made its appearance: the ring on the upper side of the cascabel, through which the breeching rope was reeved, instead of being lashed to the cascabel as hitherto. The major change was the substitution of cast iron for bronze and brass in gunmaking. The changeover was a gradual one and bronze guns remained in use for many years after bronze-casting had ceased. The huge 42pdr, which was still to be found on a few ships as late as the 1780s, was probably always made of bronze but 32pdrs and under were being made of iron as early as 1743[22]. All cannon, and some of the early carronades, were mounted on wooden truck carriages that at first glance look like those of the seventeenth century but were, in fact, put together in quite a different manner[23]. Instead of the carriage's cheeks standing on a timber bed, they were held together by a thick transom piece at the fore end and another strong piece of timber, laid horizontally, at the rear end. The cheeks were strongly bolted together and rested on a pair of stout axle trees that had a wooden truck at each end. The dimensions of truck carriages are not easy to determine. Information is less plentiful than it is for guns and much of what was published in English in the eighteenth century is unreliable. A few dimensions are known. The length of the carriage was practically 3/5 of the gun's overall length and the height above the deck at the trunnions was 1/3 of the gun-length. The diameter of trucks was, roughly, 1/6 of the gun length (or half the height of the carriage). The trucks were as thick as the cheeks and these and the transom pieces were equal in thickness to the diameter of the shot, at any rate for the bigger guns. At the end of the century the thicknesses were slightly less: a little smaller than the shot diameter down to 9pdrs but slightly more for the smaller guns. Sizes of some late eighteenth century trucks are shown in the table[24].

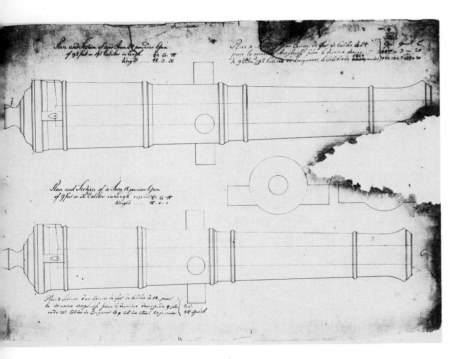

321. Because British naval guns were the province of the Army-controlled Board of Ordnance during the eighteenth century, plans of standard guns are rare in the Admiralty Collection. This is a Danish plan of an English iron 24pdr and 18pdr corresponding to the 1743 Establishment.

DIMENSIONS OF 2- AND 3-SHEAVE BLOCKS 1717

	2-sheave block (in)	3-sheave block (in)
Length	13	13
Breadth	11	11
Width of sheave-holes	$1\frac{1}{2}$	$1\frac{1}{2}$
Intervals (= partitions)	$\frac{7}{8}$	$\frac{7}{8}$
Thickness of cheeks	$1\frac{7}{8}$	2
Diameter of sheaves	$8\frac{1}{2}$	$8\frac{1}{2}$
Thickness of sheaves	$1\frac{3}{8}$	$1\frac{3}{8}$
Diameter of pin	$2\frac{5}{8}$	$1\frac{7}{8}$
Total thickness of block	7	$10\frac{1}{4}$

322. There was a short-lived Establishment of very light guns promulgated in 1753, and this drawing is based on a Danish Navy plan of the 9ft 6in 53¾cwt 32pdr. These guns were not only light but also shorter than previous standard patterns, and were found to be unsatisfactory and were replaced by about 1760.

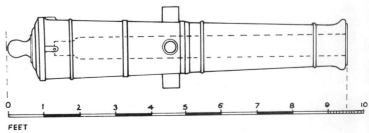

FEET

323. French iron guns established in 1674 and 1689 (see 217) were altered in weight in 1721 and 1733 but not in dimensions. In 1758 the 36pdr was stabilised at 3.20m but it was not until 1766 that a general revision took place in which gun lengths were considerably reduced: 36pdr – 2.88m, 24pdr –2.72m, 18pdr – 2.56m, 12pdr – 2.40m, 8pdr – 2.19m, 6pdr – 1.975m and 4pdr –

1.76m. This was again altered in 1778 to the guns shown here, when short and long versions of the calibres from 12pdr downwards were introduced. The lengths of these guns were: 36pdr – 2.87m, 24pdr – 2.729m, 18pdr – 2.492m, 12pdr – 2.413m and 2.176m, 8pdr – 2.19m and 1.92m, 6pdr – 2.015m and 1.74m and 4pdr – 1.75m and 1.53. (*Drawings by Jean Boudriot*)

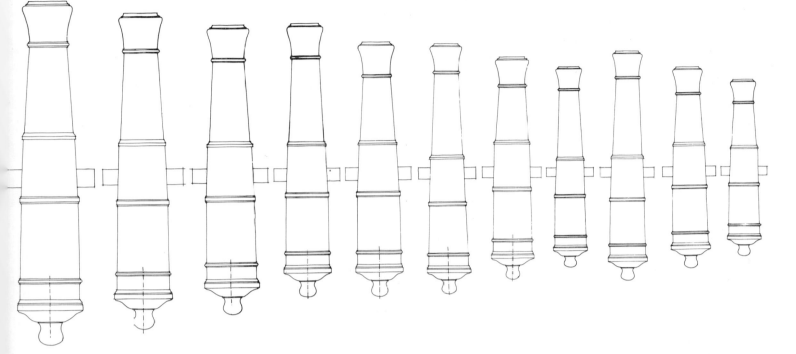

324. In 1786 French gun design was simplified as shown here. The gun lengths were: 36pdr – 2.865m, 24pdr – 2.735m, 18pdr – 2.572m, 12pdr – 2.43m, 8pdr – 2.598m and 2.219m, 6pdr – 2.273m and 2.003m and 4pdr – 1.792m and 1.538m. (*Drawings by Jean Boudriot*)

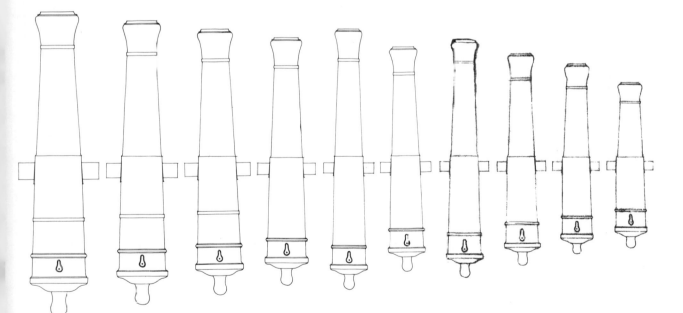

RATIOS OF CONSTITUENT PARTS OF SINGLE BLOCKS 1717

	Example 1	Example 2	Example 3	Example 4	Example 5
Length:breadth	8:7	4:3	13:11	13:11	:3
Length:thickness	15:7	5:2	13:5	20:7	11:5
Breadth of block:diameter of sheave	7:5	6:5	11:9	9:7	9:7
Diameter of sheave:thickness of sheave	31:7	5:1	20:3	25:4	15:4
Width of sheave-hole:thickness of cheeks	10:11	1:1	6:7	1:1	Various
Diameter of pin:thickness of block	1:5	7:40	2:9	3:10	1:4

Sutherland preferred the proportions of example 3

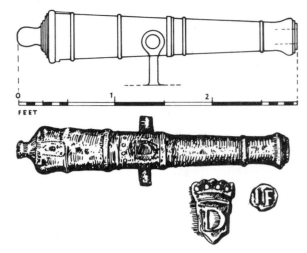

325. Plan and sketch of a British swivel gun recovered from the York River in the USA. Probably cast about 1749.

RATIOS OF CONSTITUENT PARTS OF 2- AND 3-SHEAVE BLOCKS

	2-sheave block	3-sheave block
Length:breadth	13:11	13:11
Length:thickness	12:7	9:7
Breadth of block:diameter of sheave	9:7	9:7
Diameter of sheave:thickness of sheave	25:4	25:4
Width of sheave-hole:thickness of cheeks	4:5	3:4
Width of sheave-hole:thickness of sheave	10:9	10:9
Diameter of pin:thickness of block	4:19	2:13
Thickness of intervals (partitions): thickness of sheave	7:11	7:11

GUN ESTABLISHMENT 1703

	Lower deck	Middle deck	Upper deck	Forecastle	Quarterdeck	Poop
1st Rate (100/90)	**Demi-cannon**	**Culverin**	**Demi-culverin**	**6pdr**	**6pdr**	**6pdr**
Royal Sovereign	28–9ft 9in	28–9ft 6in	28–9ft	2–8ft / 2–9ft 6in	12–8ft	–
Britannia	28–9ft 9in	26–9ft 6in	28–9ft	2–8ft / 2–9ft 6in	12–8ft	2–7ft
Queen	26–9ft 9in	28–9ft 6in	28–9ft	2–8ft / 2–9ft 6in	12–8ft	2–7ft
Royal William	28–9ft 9in	28–9ft 6in	28–9ft	2–8ft / 2–9ft 6in	12–8ft	–
Victory	26–9ft 9in	28–9ft 6in	28–9ft	2–8ft / 2–9ft 6in	12–8ft	2–7ft
London	26–9ft 6in	28–9ft 6in	28–9ft	2–8ft / 2–9ft 6in	12–8ft	2–7ft
St Andrew	26–9ft 6in	28–9ft 6in	28–9ft	2–8ft / 2–9ft 6in	12–8ft	2–7ft
Royal Anne (brass guns)	26–?	28–?	28–?		18–?	
2nd Rates (96-86)	26–9ft 9in	26–9ft 6in	26–9ft	2–7ft 6in / 2–9ft 6in	12–7ft 6in	2–7ft
St Michael (88/80)	26–9ft 6in	26–9ft	26–9ft	–	10–8ft	–
3rd Rates	**24pdr**	**12pdr**	**6pdr**	**6pdr**	**6pdr**	**3pdr**
3-deckers (80/72)	26–9ft 6in	26–9ft	22–9ft	–	6–8ft 6in	–
2-deckers (80/72)	26–9ft 6in	28–9ft	–	4–7ft 6in / 2–9ft 6in	16–9ft	4–5ft 6in
	24pdr		**Demi-culverin**	**6pdr**	**6pdr**	**3pdr**
(70/62)	24–9ft 6in	–	26–4ft	2–7ft 6in / 2–9ft 6in	12–8ft 6in	4–5ft 6in
4th Rates	**Culverin**		**9pdr**	**6pdr**	**6pdr**	
(64/56)	24–9ft 6in	–	26–9ft	2–7ft 6in / 2–9ft 6in	10–8ft 6in	–
	12pdr		**6pdr**	**6pdr**	**6pdr**	
(54/46)	22–9ft	–	22–8ft 6in	2–9ft 6in	8–7ft	–
(50/44)	20–9ft	–	22–8ft	2–8ft 6in	6–7ft	–
5th Rates	**Demi-culverin**		**6pdr**		**6pdr**	
Adventure (42/36)	18–8ft	–	20–7ft 6in	–	4–7ft	–
	Demi-culverin		**6pdr**		**4pdr**	
9 vessels (36/30)	8–8ft	–	22–7ft 6in	–	6–7ft	–
16 vessels (32/38)	4–8ft	–	22–7ft 6in	–	6–7ft	–
4 vessels (28/24)	4–8ft	–	20–7ft 6in	–	4–7ft	–
6th Rates			**6pdr**		**6pdr**	
(24/22)	–	–	20–7ft	–	4–6ft	–

The guns quoted (eg 100/90) are war at home/peace and war abroad complements. Numbers and lengths of guns are given. For *Royal Anne* no lengths are quoted and the disposition of the 6pdrs is vague, but the note mentions that the guns were brass. Some of the 2-decker '80's carried the second battery on the upper deck – they had no middle deck – but the table is simpler in its present form. The 50/44-gun class was small (about 6 vessels) and shortlived: an Admiralty Order of 9 August 1704 uprated them to 54/46-gun ships. Table from *Model Shipwright* No 20, June 1977.

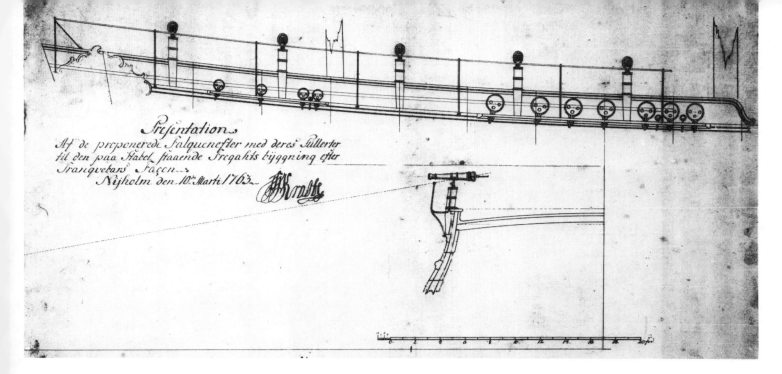

326. A Danish draught showing the mounting of swivel guns along a frigate's quarterdeck bulwarks, and the fitting of the hammock netting cranes. Dated 10 March 1763.

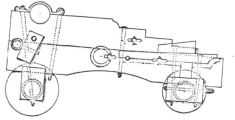
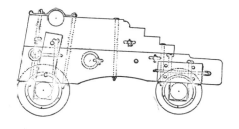

327. A draught contrasting an English 32pdr carriage with a Danish 36pdr carriage, dated 9 June 1766.

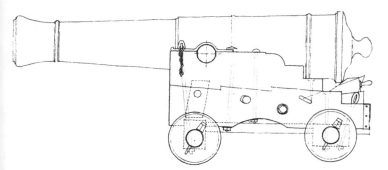
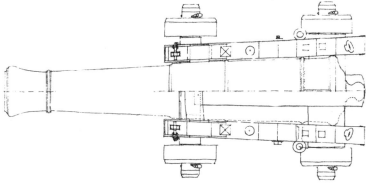

328. A French 36pdr carriage of the type in service between 1763 and 1786. It is 1.72m long. (*Drawing by Jean Boudriot*)

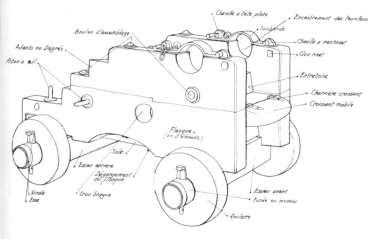
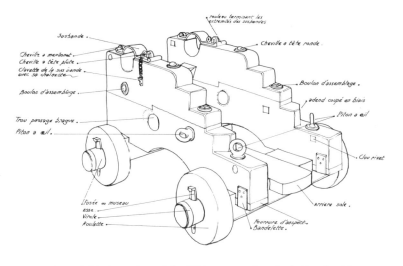

329. A French 36pdr carriage of the 1786 pattern. (*Drawing by Jean Boudriot*).

GUN ESTABLISHMENT 1716

Guns	Lower deck	Middle deck	Upper deck	Quarterdeck	Forecastle
100	**32pdr** 28–10ft/55cwt (or 28–10ft/65cwt 42pdr)	**24pdr** 28–10ft/51cwt	**12pdr** 28–9ft 6in/35cwt	**6pdr** 12–9ft/24cwt	**6pdr** 4–9ft/24cwt
90	**32pdr** 26–9ft 6in/53cwt	**18pdr** 26–9ft 6in/41cwt	**9pdr** 26–9ft 6in/29cwt	**6pdr** 10–9ft/24cwt	**6pdr** 2–9ft/24cwt
80	**32pdr** 26–9ft 6in/53cwt	**12pdr** 26–9ft 6in/34cwt	**6pdr** 24–9ft/24cwt	**6pdr** 4–8ft 6in/22cwt	–
70	**24pdr** 26–9ft 6in/64cwt	–	**12pdr** 26–9ft/32cwt	**6pdr** 14–8ft/20cwt	**6pdr** 2–8ft/20cwt 2–9ft/24cwt
60	**24pdr** 24–9ft 6in/46cwt	–	**9pdr** 26–9ft/29cwt	**6pdr** 8–8ft/20cwt	**6pdr** 2–9ft/24cwt
50	**18pdr** 22–9ft/39cwt	–	**9pdr** 22–8ft 6in/26cwt	**6pdr** 4–8ft/20cwt	**6pdr** 2–9ft/24cwt
40	**12pdr** 20–9ft/31cwt	–	**6pdr** 20–8ft 6in/22cwt	–	–
30	**9pdr** 8–8ft 6in/26cwt	–	**6pdr** 20–8ft/20cwt	**4pdr** 2–7ft/16cwt	–
20	–	–	**6pdr** 20–7ft 6in/18cwt	–	–

Table from *Model Shipwright* No 20, June 1977.

GUN ESTABLISHMENT 1743

Guns	Lowerdeck	Middle deck	Upper deck	Quarterdeck	Forecastle
100	**42pdr** 28–10ft/65cwt	**24pdr** 28–10ft/51cwt	**12pdr** 28–9ft 6in/35cwt	**6pdr** 12–9ft/24cwt	**6pdr** 4–9ft/24cwt
90	**32pdr** 26–9ft 6in/55cwt	**18pdr** 26–9ft 6in/42cwt	**12pdr** 26–9ft/32½cwt	**16pdr** 10–8ft 6in/23cwt	**6pdr** 2–9ft/24cwt
80	**32pdr** 26–9ft 6in/55cwt	**18pdr** 26–9ft/40cwt	**9pdr** 24–8ft 6in/28cwt	**6pdr** 4–8ft/22cwt	–
64	**32pdr** 26–9ft 6in/55cwt	–	**18pdr** 26–9ft/40cwt	**9pdr** 10–8ft/27cwt	**9pdr** 2–9ft/29cwt
58	**24pdr** 24–9ft 6in/49cwt	–	**12pdr** 24–9ft/32½cwt	**6pdr** 8–8ft/22cwt	**6pdr** 2–9ft/24cwt
50	22–9ft/48cwt	–	22–8ft 6in/31½cwt	4–7ft/19cwt	2–8ft/22cwt
44	**18pdr** 20–9ft/40cwt	–	**9pdr** 20–8ft/27cwt	**6pdr** 4–6ft 6in/18cwt	–
24	**9pdr** 2–7ft/24cwt	–	**9pdr** 20–7ft/24cwt	**3pdr** 2–4ft 6in/7cwt	–

Virtually the Establishment proposed in 1733, but that for the '70's and '60's was adopted for '64's and '58's by reducing the number of quarterdeck and forecastle guns (usually thought to be on Anson's initiative). The '24' of 1743 was listed as mounting only the 20 upper deck guns, but many were actually fitted as in the 1733 proposals. Table from *Model Shipwright* No 20, June 1977.

The use of the new carriage spread rapidly from whichever was its country of origin. The French Navy was using it in the late 1750s and a Danish example dated 1771 has been recovered from a wreck. The carriage is 52in long and 29in high. Those are the proportions of an English carriage of the same type.

The gun novelty of the eighteenth century was the carronade, a gun invented by General Melville in 1774 and made by the Carron Iron Company of Falkirk, Scotland. The carronade was originally designed for service with the Army but in 1779 a sea-going version was put into service on frigates and soon afterwards carronades were a regular part of all ships' armaments. The important, and to some extent misleading, influence of the carronade on naval tactics in the wars from 1779 to 1815 is too well known to need re-telling.

The principle of the carronade was a simple one. It had a short barrel and used a comparatively small charge of powder, so that the shot had a lower velocity than one from a normal gun of similar bore. On striking its target a carronade ball caused much more damage that the faster moving cannon shot and produced a shower of splinters that inflicted innumerable casualties among the crew on the crowded decks. The small powder charge used in a carronade – a 68pdr required only $5\frac{1}{2}$lb as against 23lb or more for a cannon – allowed the gun barrels to be made a lot smaller and lighter in weight than ordinary cannon. A 68pdr carronade in 1790 weighed only 35cwt, which was about the same as a 12pdr carriage gun. In length the 68pdr carronades were about the same, 4 to 5ft, as 3 and 4pdr cannon.

The first carronades were mounted on carriages, like cannon, but that method was soon replaced by a novel one. The carronade barrel had a robust, pierced lug cast on its under side at the balance point, and another one, this time threaded and set horizontally, cast on the back end of the gun. The under-barrel lug fitted into a slot in a strong timber bed and was held by a bolt, of iron, that passed transversely through the bed and the lug. At the rear of the gun a levelling screw passed through the rear lug and bore against an iron plate on the bed.

The barrel and its bed were placed on a lower bed that was pivotted at its fore end on a strong iron bolt set into the deck. Down the middle of the lower bed was a slot into which a drop-bolt from the upper bed was set, so that the upper bed could slide on the lower one. The recoil was taken up by a breeching rope. Later, the drop-bolt had its end threaded and an iron plate fitted over it to act as a brake on the recoil. The braking effect was adjusted by a nut on the end of the drop-bolt. For that arrangement to be workable the lower bed had to be raised off the deck, and that was done at first by a transverse timber. That proving inconvenient, it was replaced by a pair of small trucks at the rear end of the bed. Another improvement was to fix the barrel's retaining bolt through a pair of iron pivots bolted to the upper end. The drawings show the arrangements just described.

A weapon of a more specialised sort was the mortar used on bomb-vessels. Only two sizes were in general use, 13in and 10in. Mortars had a fixed elevation of 45° but could be turned on their axis. Good descriptions of how mortars were mounted are to be found in *Model Shipwright*[25].

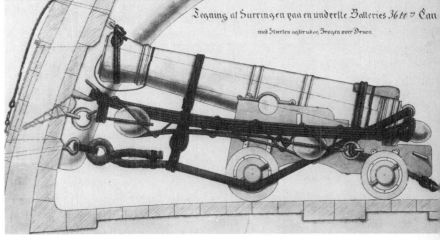

330

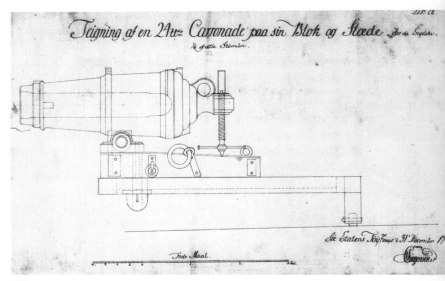

331

330. An illustration from a Danish training manual showing the method of securing a 36pdr at sea.
331. A Danish plan dated 31 December 1795 of the slide for a 24pdr carronade 'in the English manner'. The slide pivoted on a chock under the port (not illustrated) and had lateral 'trucks' (roller) at the inner end to assist in traversing the mounting.
332. A companion plan to 331, of the same date, showing a Danish 36pdr carronade. At first Continental navies did not fully understand the principles of the carronade and the French, for example, used a few howitzer-like *obusiers* instead, but the Baltic navies developed a form of short-barrelled weapon that their inshore flotillas had been using for some time. It was of relatively large calibre, and could be mounted almost like a swivel – in fact it looked like a cross between a howitzer and a swivel and was mainly an anti-personnel weapon. This ancestry can be seen in the shape of this early Danish carronade.

332

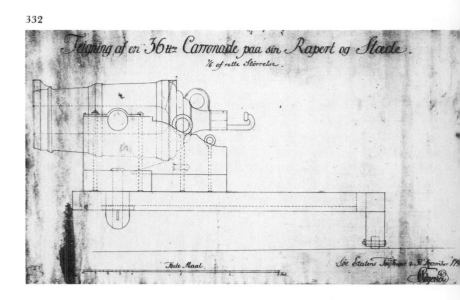

GUNS CARRIED 1761

Guns	Lower deck	Middle deck	Upper deck	Quarterdeck	Forecastle
100	**42pdr** 28–9ft 6in or 10ft/66cwt	**24pdr** 28–9ft 6in/49cwt	**6pdr** 28–9ft/33cwt	**6pdr** 12–8ft/22cwt	**6pdr** 4–9ft/24cwt
90	**32pdr** 28–9ft 6in/55cwt	**18pdr** 30–9ft/40cwt	**12pdr** 30–9ft/33cwt	–	**6pdr** 2–9ft/24cwt
84	28–9ft 6in/55cwt	28–9ft/40cwt	28–9ft/33cwt	–	
80	**32pdr** 26–9ft 6in/55cwt	**18pdr** 26–9ft/40cwt	**9pdr** 24–9ft/29cwt	**6pdr** 4–7ft 6in/20½cwt	–
74	**32pdr** 28–9ft 6in/55cwt	–	**18pdr** 28–9ft/40cwt	**9pdr** 14–7ft 6in/24½cwt	**9pdr** 4–8ft 6in/27½cwt
70 (or 68)	28(26)–9ft 6in/ 55cwt	–	28–9ft/40cwt	12–7ft 6in/24½cwt	2–8ft 6in/27½cwt
66	26–9ft 6in/55cwt	–	26–9ft/40cwt	12–7ft 6in/24½cwt	2–8ft 6in/27½cwt
64	**24pdr** 26–9ft 6in/49cwt	–	**18pdr** 26–9ft/40cwt	**9pdr** 10–7ft 6in/24½cwt	**9pdr** 2–8ft 6in/27½cwt
60	**24pdr** 24–9ft 6in/49cwt	–	**12pdr** 26–9ft/33cwt	**6pdr** 8–7ft 6in/20½cwt	**6pdr** 2–8ft 6in/23cwt
50	22–9ft/48cwt	–	22–8ft 6in/31½cwt	4–7ft/19cwt	2–8ft/22cwt
44	**18pdr** 20–9ft/40cwt 20–9ft/40cwt	–	**9pdr** 20–8ft/26½cwt	**6pdr** 4–6ft 6in/18cwt	–
36 (or 32)	–	–	**12pdr** 26–7ft 6in/28½cwt	**6pdr** 8(4)–6ft/16½cwt	**6pdr** 2–6ft/16cwt
28	–	–	**9pdr** 24–7ft/23½cwt	**3pdr** 4–4ft 6in/7¼cwt	–
24	**9pdr** 2–7ft/23½cwt	–	**9pdr** 20–7ft/23½cwt	**3pdr** 2–4ft 6in/7¼cwt	–
22 (or 20)	–	–	**9pdr** 20–7ft/23½cwt	**3pdr** 2(0)–4ft 6in/7¼cwt	–

This list refers to ships built after about 1750, and earlier ships often continued being gunned on the 1743 model. The '68's and '66's are probably uprated '64's and the '60's reinstated '58's. Table from *Model Shipwright* No 20, June 1977.

333. Early English carronades had a reputation for oversetting in action which is difficult to explain if one assumes that they were mounted on the usual traversing carriage. However, this drawing from a report to the 1796 Committee on carronade mountings shows why. 'A' (far left) shows the original manner of fitting the slide, with four trucks but fixed at the forward corner so that it could not swivel. A limited degree of traverse was obtained by slewing the carronade bed, when it would recoil diagonally across the slide straining the fixing bolts under the port. If these broke, the mounting would be overturned. The other drawings show improvements in the familiar slide including a cut-away rather than a rounded front to obtain more traverse, and two locating bolts ('D'), one for firing and one for securing the gun parallel to the ship's side.

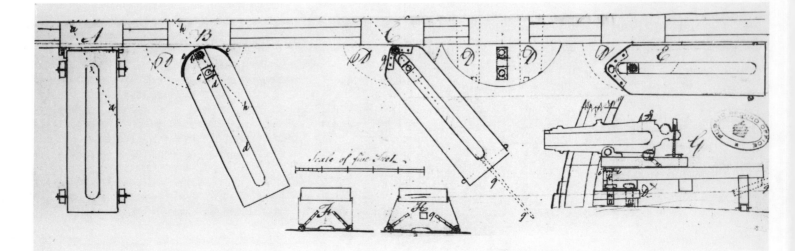

334. A 20-gun ship of the 1719 Establishment – an exceptionally detailed model with its original rigging. Note the numerous swivel guns mounted on the bulwarks, and the 18 sweeps in the lower deck ports. 20-gun ships of later establishments had two gunports a side on the lower deck.

335. Although the English abandoned two-decked 20- and 24-gun ships after 1745, they remained popular with the Dutch. This 24-gun ship of 1767 has a number of oarports and three larger ports on the lower deck. This fashion was known in Holland as 'the English style' and persisted until the 1780s. Note the internal detail, and particularly the Dutch-style capstan. The deep head, brick hearth under the forecastle and cables on the lower deck combine to give the impression that Dutch ship design was rather old-fashioned in the eighteenth century.

336. The last attempts to combine sail, oars and a broadside armament were made by the Swedes and the Russians during the second half of the eighteenth century. Like all other such attempts they were not very successful but produced some interesting warships – particularly those designed by Chapman. This is a model of the *udema Thorberg* which he designed. *Udemas* were 118ft long and 28ft in breadth, with 18 pairs of oars. The main armament of nine 12 pdrs was mounted on traversing carriages on the centreline so as to train on either beam; the bulwarks folded down to allow firing and also acted as outriggers for the oars. *Udemas* also carried pairs of 18pdr bow- and stern-chasers.

334

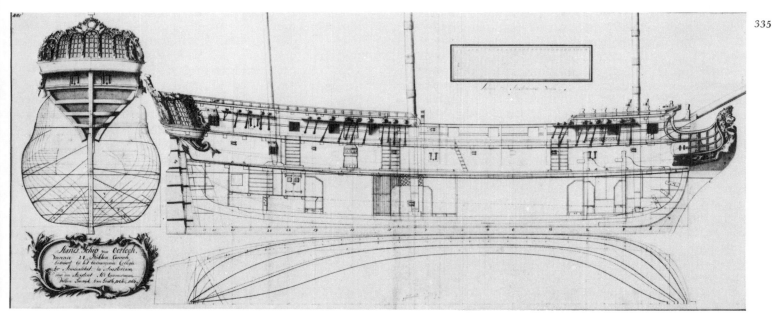

335

336

SUPPORT CRAFT

The doings of the great fleets of 2- and 3-deckers in the long series of wars of the eighteenth century have drawn attention away from the remarkable development of the smaller warships during that period. In the wars of the previous century ships too small to stand in the line-of-battle seem to have played only a comparatively minor part, and consequently we know far less about them than we do about the big ships, so that it comes as a surprise to find the extent to which development of auxiliary craft had taken place by 1700. At what point in the previous century this upsurge began is not yet clear but it is obvious from the early eighteenth century models and plans that have survived that it was under way when the new century opened. Indeed, the eighteenth century might well be called the century of the small ship, for it was in these vessels and not the ships-of-the-line that the most significant advances in naval architecture were made. The development of the various sorts of auxiliary craft has not yet been plotted in detail except in the case of frigates but, as these excellent studies show, the evidence is probably lying in various national archives[3].

20-gun ships. When the eighteenth century began the 'maid of all work' among the smaller warships was the 20-gun ship (and later the 24-gun ship). These were the 6th Rates, 3-masted vessels rigged in the same way as the big ships. The bulk of a 20-gun ship's armament was carried on the upper deck, only a few guns being mounted on the lower deck, but by 1719 all guns had been removed from that deck and the only ports on it were a ballast port amidships on each side. Like most small ships at that time, and for many years after, 6th Rates were often fitted with oarports on the lower deck. Their lids opened sideways, like doors, and they had their hinges on the forward edge. Oarports had, of course, to follow the sheer of the deck, and consequently they sometimes cut across the sheer of the wales towards the after end of the hull. An exceptionally detailed contemporary model of a 20-gun ship of 1719 in the National Maritime Museum has its oarports just above the upper of the pair of wales from amidships forwards, but from a point a little abaft the middle of the gun-deck they cut into the upper wale. If there was only a single wale the oarports were arranged, as far as possible, to avoid cutting it. On the 1719 Establishment the 20-gun ships were to be armed with 6pdrs but from 1743 they carried 9pdrs. Besides their carriage guns the early '20's carried a secondary armament of swivel guns. The model of a ship of 1719 mentioned above had its 22 swivels distributed as follows: waist 12, quarterdeck 6 and forecastle 4.

Swedish oared sailing ships. In the Baltic a remarkable and little-known development of oar-sail hybrids took place in the second half of the century. They were designed for operations in the Gulf of Finland where the sea is too shallow to allow ships of any size to approach the coast but where the rocky and indented shores provide numerous lurking places for small craft. To deal with this problem during their wars with the Russians, the Swedes designed four distinctive types of oared sailing ships. Two of them, the *turuma* and the *hemema*, were virtually oared frigates. A *turuma* was square-rigged but had only courses and topsails. A typical example would be 123ft long and 30ft in beam. The oars, 19 a side, were worked on a narrow outrigger above the lower deck guns. The armament was usually 24 18pdrs and 16 3pdrs. The *hemema* was a similar sort of ship, but bigger, and its guns were carried on the gun-deck, the usual armament being 24 36pdrs and 2 12pdrs. There were 20 oars a side. The third class, the *udema*, was a peculiar design. Its hull was not unlike that of a ship-sloop but the waist's bulwarks were replaced by open rails and the main battery was mounted along the centreline of the deck. The guns were 12pdrs and were mounted on traversing carriages so that they could be trained on either broadside. A typical *udema* was 118ft by 28ft. In addition to 12pdrs on the maindeck, an *udema* carried a pair of 18pdrs forward and two 8pdrs aft. The fourth type of ship was called a *pojama*. The hull resembled that of a large galley but was broader (90ft by 26ft) and carried a ketch rig. There were 16 pairs of oars. For armament a *pojama* had a pair of 24pdrs at each end, on traversing carriages, and a secondary battery of 12 3pdr swivels. Only one recent account of these remarkable craft has been published in English. It is in R C Anderson's *Oared Fighting Ships*[26].

Sloops. The name was given to three kinds of vessel: single-masted sloops, 2-masted sloops (snows and, later, brigs and ketches) and 3-masted ship-sloops. All four kinds were in use in the second half of the century. Single-masted sloops were the oldest sort and had been in use, as yachts, in the previous century. (In this context the term originally referred to the rig.) Not much is known about their role in the Navy in the early part of the eighteenth century but the evidence that has come to light suggests that single-masted sloops were employed to a greater extent than has been supposed hitherto, and that they were remarkably well designed vessels. The *Ferret* (114 tons) of 1711, which was 65ft 7in on the gun-deck, 20ft 10in beam and 9ft deep in hold, had finer lines than was usual at that date and her waterline at the bow had a slight 'hollow', a shape traditionally associated with fast-sailing ships. The *Ferret* was an oar-sail hybrid and had ports for 8 sweeps a side. She had 12 broadside carriage guns and probably 2 more on the forecastle, as well as 10 swivels mounted on stocks fixed to the bulwarks.

Eventually, the term 'sloop' came to represent a type of small unrated warship, and was extended to 2-masted snow or ketch-rigged vessels. The latter is probably the older rig of the two but insufficient is known about the origin of the snow-rig to be dogmatic. The difference between the two rigs is summed up by saying that a snow was a ship without a mizzen-mast and a ketch was a ship without a foremast. A snow's fore- and mainmasts were rigged just as a ship's were, except that the mainmast had a gaff sail. This was set either on a rope 'horse' that was rigged between the after side of the maintop and the deck, or else on an auxiliary mast fixed abaft the mainmast and between the maintop and a wooden step on the deck. The auxiliary mast was known as a snow- or trysail mast. The fore edge of the gaffsail might be laced to the horse or to the trysail mast, or it might be held by wooden hoops. The fore lower corner of the sail, known as the tack, was secured at the foot of the 'horse' or the trysail mast. There was no boom to spread the foot of the sail, the after corner being controlled by a sheet from the taffrail or from an eyebolt in the deck. Some of these sloops had an unbroken sheer from stem to stern, which means that their main deck had a 'fall' or a step at each end to accommodate the forecastle and after cabins, as on, for example, the *Cruizer* of 1732. Other sloops, like the *Hazard,* had a raised forecastle and quarterdeck like 6th Rates[27]. By the 1770s snow-rigged (and ketch-rigged) sloops were being replaced by brigs. The difference between a brig and a snow was that a brig had no main course and her gaffsail was attached to the mainmast instead of to a 'horse' or a trysail mast, and, except perhaps in the earliest brigs, the foot of the gaffsail was extended by a boom. Otherwise the two rigs were the same.

The third kind of 2-masted sloop was the ketch, and in the eighteenth century ketches were square-rigged. The rig was essentially, as already mentioned, that of a ship without a foremast. The early ketches had three sails on the mainmast (course, topsail and topgallant sail) and two on the mizzenmast (lateen mizzen and square topsail). The headsails were a staysail on the mainstay and a jib. The lateen sail was replaced by a gaff mizzen quite early in the century and towards its end a gaffsail had been added to the mainmast as well. If the scarcity of plans and models of ketches is any measure, ketches were not popular as warships except as bomb-vessels.

In common with other warships, sloops grew in size and by the 1750s ship-rigged sloops had appeared. Their sail plan was the same as that of other small warships and does not require comment. Yachts were, on the whole, a sub-division of the class of sloops-of-war and were rigged in the same way. The chief differences were the more elaborate decoration and accommodation on board, because the yachts were frequently used for transporting important people. A good account of English yachts will be found in the National Maritime Museum's booklet *Royal Yachts*[28].

Bomb-vessels. Notwithstanding their unusual armament and function, bomb-vessels have not attracted the interest of students of either naval history or naval architecture until very recently despite the quantity of information available in Britain and abroad. The first modern, English study of bomb-vessels appeared only in 1977, and these notes are based on it[25]. The bomb-vessel was invented to expedite attacks on forts and harbours from the sea. Ordinary gunfire from ships normally struck fortifications at their strongest point – the ramparts – and for the fire to be effective the ships had to be placed within range of the fort's guns. Bomb-vessels carried mortars, which were tremendously powerful guns, with a long range, that fired explosive shells at a high trajectory so that the shells passed over the fort walls and burst inside. Ships moored behind strong harbour walls could be attacked in the same way. Because the mortars were so powerful they had a much greater recoil that ordinary guns and consequently bomb-vessels had to be exceptionally strongly built.

Bomb-vessels were invented by the French in 1683. The idea was quickly copied by the British, who had bomb-vessels by 1687, and by the other maritime States. These early bomb-vessels ranged in size from 60ft long to about 90ft. They were wider for their length than ordinary warships and had, at any rate at first, a shallower draught. Originally English bomb-vessels were usually ketch-rigged (hence the popular name 'bomb-ketch') but ship-rigged examples are known from as early as 1700.

The main armament of bomb-vessels was a pair of big mortars. On English vessels one mortar stood in front of the mainmast and the other between that mast and the mizzenmast; on early French bomb-vessels, however, the mortars were placed side by side before the mainmast. The mortars had a fixed elevation of 45° but their beds, which stood on a strong framework of timber built up from the bottom of the ship, could be rotated. Bomb-vessels also carried ordinary guns. One of the earliest such ships to be added to the Royal Navy (in 1688) was armed with 2 minions, 4 falcons and 2 long bow-chasers. The two mortars were of 12¼in bore. In the eigh-

GUNS CARRIED 1793					
Guns	Lower deck	Middle deck	Upper deck	Quarter-deck	Forecastle
	32pdr	24pdr	18pdr	12pdr	12pdr
112	30	32	32	14	4
100	30	28	30	10	2
100	28	28	28	12	4
	32pdr	24pdr	12pdr	12pdr	12pdr
100	28	28	28	12	4
		18pdr	18pdr		
98	28	30	30	8	2
			12pdr		
98	28	30	30	8	2
2-deckers	32pdr	24pdr	24pdr	12pdr	12pdr
80	28	–	30	14	4
74	28	–	30	14	2
			18pdr		
74	28	–	28	14	4
	24pdr				
64	26	–	24	10	2
			12pdr	6pdr	6pdr
50	22	–	22	4	2
	18pdr				
44	20	–	22	–	–
Single deckers			18pdr	9pdr	12pdr
38	–	–	28	8	2
36	–	–	26	8	2
			12pdr	6pdr	6pdr
36	–	–	26	8	2
			18pdr		
32	–	–	26	4	2
			12pdr		
32	–	–	26	4	2
			9pdr		
28	–	–	24	4	–
24	–	–	22	2	–
20	–	–	20	–	–
			6pdr		
18-gun sloop	–	–	18	–	–
16-gun sloop	–	–	16	–	–
14-gun sloop	–	–	14	–	–
18-gun brig-sloop	–	–	18	–	–

The 42pdr gun had fallen out of use by the 1790s. It was a very heavy piece that needed a big gun-crew, but what led to its abandonment was the realisation that the 32pdr was just as effective, was lighter and was easier to handle.

STANDARD GUN DIMENSIONS 1753 AND 1790

Gun	1753 Brass ft	in	1753 Iron ft	in	1790 Iron ft	in
42pdr	9	6	10	0	9	6
32pdr	9	5	9	6	10	0
24pdr	9	5	9	5	10	0
					9	6
					9	0
18pdr	9	0	9	0	9	6
					9	0
12pdr	9	0	9	0	9	6
					9	0
					8	6
					8	0
9pdr	8	5	8	5	9	6
					9	0
					8	6
					8	0
					7	6
					7	0
6pdr	8	0	7	0	9	0
					8	6
					8	0
					7	6
					7	0
					6	6
					6	0
4pdr	–		6	0	6	0
					5	6
3pdr	6	5	4	6	4	6
½pdr swivel	–		–		3	6

CARRONADE ARMAMENT 1780 AND 1793

Carriage gun total	Carronades Quarterdeck c1780	Quarterdeck 1793	Forecastle c1780	Forecastle 1793
44	8-18pdr	6-18pdr 8-12pdr	2-18pdr	2-18pdr 2-18pdr
38	6-18pdr	4-18pdr	4-18pdr	–
36	4-18pdr	4-18pdr	4-18pdr	–
32	6-18pdr	4-18pdr 6-18pdr 4-18pdr 6-18pdr 4-18pdr	2-18pdr	2-18pdr – 2-18pdr 2-18pdr –
28	6-12pdr	4-18pdr	2-18pdr	2-18pdr

337. A 12-gun 'sloop' of 1720, a 2-masted vessel that would have been rigged as a snow. There are ports on the upper deck for six sweeps a side. Belaying pin rails can be seen opposite the fore and main channels and at the break of the forecastle. The ship's bell stands above the forecastle pin rail. In addition to her maindeck armament the ship has posts for eight swivel guns in the waist. The scroll in place of a figurehead was not unusual in such small ships.

teenth century bomb-vessels might have up to 14 carriage guns as well as swivels but as a rule they were not heavily armed because bomb-vessels were not expected to have to fight warships. The armament was to deal with attacks from small craft and boats.

Frigates. Of all the warships that came to prominence in the eighteenth century the frigate is the one that epitomises, in the popular mind, the exploits of the dashing young naval officer – and rightly so, as any history of the naval operations of the second half of the century makes clear. The new frigates were as effective a development, within the cramping conditions dictated by the need to carry a powerful armament and consequently a large crew, as the clipper ship was a century later. The word 'new' is applied to the eighteenth-century frigate because it was not a descendant of its namesake in the previous century but a separate development. The seventeenth-century frigate, at any rate in its early form, carried a battery on its lower deck, but the new type of frigate had its main armament on the upper (or main-) deck; the lower deck, though it was still called the gun-deck, was devoid of guns and was even, on some ships, set at or below the waterline. In 1941 R C Anderson suggested that the eighteenth century frigate might have been developed from the 24-gun ships that, at the beginning of the century, carried most of their guns on the upper deck, but his hint was not followed up and it was not until 1975 that the origin of the new frigate was satisfactorily worked out by R Gardiner. The notes that follow are taken from his two papers in the *Mariner's Mirror*[3]. The story in brief is that the British frigate derives from a fast-sailing French privateer, the *Tygre*, captured in 1747 and taken into the Royal Navy. The

Tygre carried 26 9pdr cannon on her upper deck but none below it. The lines of the *Tygre* were taken off and used to design two 28-gun ships, the *Unicorn* and the *Lyme*. These were the first true frigates to be built for the Royal Navy. Notwithstanding their French parentage, neither were mere copies of the *Tygre*. Much has been written to the disparagement of British warships without regard to the fact that their builders had to produce ships fitted for the naval tactics employed by the Royal Navy and the conditions under which the ships had to serve, both of which set problems different from those that French builders had to face. So it must be emphasised that the British frigate designs were intelligent adaptations of the French model to the Royal Navy's requirements. As the plans of the *Unicorn* and the *Lyme* show, a good deal of experimenting went into the design of the first members of the class. Even the two ships just mentioned were not identical. In fact, the *Lyme's* design incorporated an important innovation. The bow timbers were taken up to the level of the forecastle deck instead of finishing at the main deck as they did on other ships, thus introducing the round bow to the frigate type. The alteration in the bow's structure conferred two advantages: it provided better protection against end-on fire and it allowed the hawseholes to be brought up to the maindeck, as a result of which the lower deck, where the crew berthed, was a drier and healthier place than it would have been with the cables coming in to it. In the designs of other frigates different midship sections and hull proportions were tried and modified in the light of experience at sea. As to external details, the sterns and quarters of frigates were simpler in construction than those of ships-of-the-line. There was no stern gallery, but instead there was a row

SIZES OF TRUCKS – Late Eighteenth Century		
Gun	Diameter of truck (in)	Thickness of truck (in)
	Fore	Hind	
42pdr	19	16	6.5
32pdr	19	16	6.0
24pdr	18	15	5.5
18pdr	18	14	5.0
12pdr	16	14	4.5
9pdr	16	14	4.0
6pdr	14	12	3.5
3pdr	14	10	3.0

STANDARD CARRONADE DIMENSIONS – Eighteenth Century		
Shot weight	Bore (in)	Length
		ft	in
68pdr	8.05	5	2
	8.05	4	0
42pdr	6.84	4	3½
32pdr	6.35	4	0½
24pdr	5.68	3	7½
18pdr	5.16	3	3
12pdr	4.52	2	2

of windows. These were augmented by what would be called a bay window in a house, placed at each of the after ends of the broadsides.

Frigates were classed by the number of their guns, as other warships were. The first frigates were rated as 24-gun ships but as the usual increase in size took place they were uprated to 28-guns and this class was followed by '32's, '36's and then '38's. The early '24's carried 9pdrs on the maindeck and 4 3pdrs on the quarterdeck. The '32's had 26 12pdrs on the main deck, 4 6pdrs on the quarterdeck and 2 more on the forecastle as chase guns. Besides the carriage guns there would be a variable number of swivel guns. As frigates increased in size so did their guns. The *Endymion* of 1797 had 26 24pdr carriage guns on her maindeck and 2 long 9pdr chase guns on the forecastle. Like all frigates at the end of the century the *Endymion* carried carronades. She had 14 32pdrs on the quarterdeck and 4 more on the forecastle. The extent of the carronade armament in 1780 and 1793 is shown in the table. As will have been apparent from the numbers of guns carried, there had been a great increase in the size of frigates since the launching of the *Lyme* of 581 tons, in 1748. The *Pallas* of 1756 was 718 tons and the *Endymion* of 1797 was 1277 tons. The latter was of the same burthen as the *Prince Royal* of 1612 and far more powerfully armed.

British frigates were not, in point of fact, the first of the type. The French Navy had frigates (in the British meaning of the name) before the Anglo-French War of 1744 opened, and several were captured and taken into the Royal Navy. French frigates were designed for a different purpose, and built in a different way, from the British frigates. The first aspect reflected the different naval tactics of the two Navies. Put in simple terms, the French approach to frigate design was to produce a ship fast enough to overtake possible prey and fast enough to get away again if the opposition proved too strong. To obtain the necessary speed the hulls were given fine lines and comparatively light construction. The British attitude, in contrast, was 'knock 'em down and drag 'em out' and in pursuit of that aim their frigates' hulls were robustly built so that a powerful armament could be carried and the ship fought in almost any sort of weather. Robustness of construction (by British standards) was what French frigates lacked: fast and weatherly though French frigates were, in the right conditions, their lightly built hulls strained and distorted quite soon, to the detriment of their sailing qualities, and because of the light construction French frigates had a lower gun-to-tonnage ratio than British ones. These two factors – light construction and lower fire-power – go some way to explain the higher casualty rate of French ships in fights with British ones. There were other differences between the two countries' frigates besides those just mentioned. The more strongly built British ships could carry a heavier rig and performed better in a seaway and in strong winds. Nevertheless, it is true to say that for the purpose for which they were designed, French frigates were satisfactory ships.

The frigate 'idea' spread rapidly. The Dutch had frigates by 1750 and the Danes by the 1750s, if not earlier. Probably all the major maritime States started to build them at about the same time.

Schooners. Wherever the schooner's prototype may have been evolved, its later development is due to the Americans. The two-mast, fore-and-aft rig was very suitable for voyaging along the east coast of North America where the winds, speaking generally, blow on or off shore. During the eighteenth century two classes of schooner were developed. One was a smallish, fairly full-bodied cargo carrier, but members of the other group had sharper lines and a taller rig than the cargo carriers and were vessels built for fast sailing. They were extensively used in smuggling and privateering, and often downright piracy. A little after the middle of the century the British Admiralty bought some American-built schooners and found them so useful that others, captured during the War of American Independence, were also taken into the Navy. The lines of some of the American schooners were taken off and are now in the National Maritime Museum. No British study of naval schooners has so far appeared but H I Chapelle has a brief study in his *History of American Sailing Ships* and a more up-to-date study has been published in the *American Neptune*[29]. The early schooners had a main topsail and sometimes carried a fore topsail as well. These were square sails. For running before the wind well-manned schooners set square sails to their lower masts. The yards for these were fastened to a rope 'horse' on the fore side of the lower mast, between the trestletrees, and the deck. This arrangement allowed the square sail, or the gaffsail, to be raised or lowered without interference.

The naval schooners were small; some of them were very small. The *Sultana* bought in 1768 was only 50½ft on the deck and 52 tons burthen, and the *Halifax*, bought about the same time, was 58ft long and 83 tons burden. The *Halifax* acquired an unenviable reputation from the part she played in the American War. Another schooner bought in 1768, the *Chaleur*, was twice as big as the *Sultana* at 120 tons. There were no tops on the mastheads of schooners, only trestletrees and crosstrees. The armament of schooners was like that of other small warships: small carriage guns and swivels for the most part, with the addition of carronades in the last 20 years of the century.

Cutters. In English waters the one-masted, gaff-rigged cutter was used for the same sort of work, legal or otherwise, as the schooner was on the other side of the Atlantic, and became popular at much the same time. The early cutters, in naval service, were somewhat bigger than the early schooners but whether this was always so is uncertain. Cutters were clinker-built craft, fairly beamy and having their maximum breadth at about one-third of their length from the stem. They were decked and carried a heavy armament. A contemporary model of a cutter of the late eighteenth century, in the Science Museum, is armed with 10 carronades and 10 swivel guns although she was only 150 tons. Another model, probably of the *Flying Fish* of 1778 (190 tons), has 12 carronades and 12 swivels.

Cutters were very heavily rigged. They had a gaff mainsail, spread at its foot by a long boom, a fore staysail and jib and a square topsail, but other sails could be added according to 'Captain's fancy'. The model of the *Flying Fish*, which was made by a contemporary seaman, Admiral Buckle, has in addition to the basic rig a topgallant sail, stunsails to the topsail and, for running before the wind, a square sail set from a yard at the lower mast's head. Being well-manned, they could get away with it. A peculiarity of rig that distinguished cutters from one-masted sloops was that the former had a bowsprit that could be run in and out quickly. Another difference was that cutters had a straight stem without a head knee or a figurehead.

BOATS

Pictorial and documentary evidence provides a good deal of reliable information about ships' boats although, unfortunately, no boat list corresponding to the various Establishments has come to light. However, two excellent summaries of the available data have been published in a readily accessible form. They are *Boats of Men-of-War* by Commander W E May, available from the National Maritime Museum, and 'Fittings for Wooden Warships. Part two: Boats' by R Gardiner, in *Model Shipwright*[30,31].

So far as may be made out from the rather scanty information on the plans that have survived, there was little change in the shape of boats throughout the century, a degree of stability that is perhaps to be expected since the materials of construction and the uses to which the boats were put remained the same. All boats were open ones and, with the exceptions of yawls and cutters, carvel-built.

A variety of rigs were used. The bigger boats might have two masts but for most boats one sufficed. Gaffsails, spritsails, lugsails and lateen sails were used, sometimes in combination, eg lug- and spritsail (the sort used on a Thames barge, not those set under the bowsprit). According to Sutherland, the proportions of boats' masts at the beginning of the century were: mainmast 3 × breadth of boat; and foremast 2 × breadth. The maximum diameter of the masts was 1/51 of their length, and they would be tapered in the same way as a ship's mast. If the boat was sprit-rigged, the sprit was 1ft longer than the mainmast and its maximum diameter 1/90 of its length. Spar dimensions in the 1770s were:

Sloop-rigged longboats (L = length of mast, B = breadth of the boat). Mast length, $3 \times B$ (to hounds); masthead, $1/6 \times L$; bowsprit, $1/2 \times L$; boom, $7/9 \times L$; gaff $5/12 \times$ boom ($35/108 \times L$). Diameters were: mast, $1/48 \times L$; bowsprit, 3/10in per foot of *total* length; boom, 7/32in per foot length; gaff, 2/5in per foot length.

Two-masted barges, pinnaces and yawls. Fore- and mainmasts, $2.35 \times B$; sprit, $9/8 \times$ mast ($2.77 \times B$). Diameters: mast, $1/48 \times L$; sprit, $1/96 \times L$.

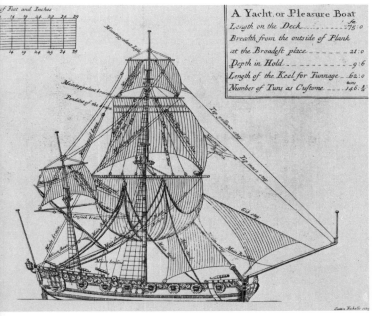

A Yacht or Pleasure Boat
Length on the Deck 75:0
Breadth from the outside of Plank
at the Broadest piece 21:0
Depth in Hold 9:6
Length of the Keel for Tunnage . 62:0
Number of Tuns as Custome 146:4

338. A 12-gun ketch-rigged sloop of 1750. There are the usual sweep ports on the upper deck. In the mid-1750s the ketch rig gave way to brig and ship rigs for sloops.

339. The sail plan of a small ketch (actually a yacht) from William Sutherland's *Shipbuilding Unveiled* of 1711. Bomb ketches were rigged in the same manner, the mortar(s) being placed in the fore half of the ship.

340. A Danish draught of a bomb vessel. The date is uncertain but it is a very early example of the type, and resembles French vessels of the late seventeenth century.

339

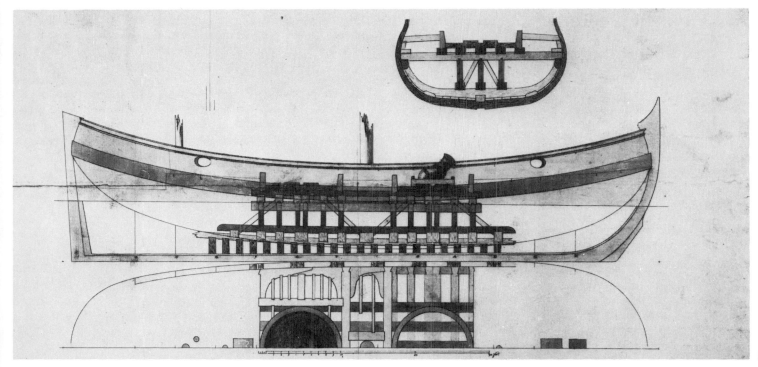

340

Ketch-rigged cutters (lug foresail and sprit mizzen). Foremast, 2.75 × B; mizzen, 1.72 × B; foreyard, 1.375 × B; sprit, 9/8 × mast length; outrigger, 2/3 × mizzen. Diameters: foremast, 1/52 × L; foreyard and mizzenmast, 1/48 × length; sprit, 1/96 × length; outrigger, 5-18in per foot length. The total length of the bowsprit is not given but it seems to have been about the same length as the mast, or a little shorter. About 3/4 of the length was outboard.

The proportions given in the 1794 edition of Steel[32] are:

Sloop-rigged boats. Mast, 2 13/16 × B; bowsprit, 5/9 × mast (1 9/16 × B); boom, 2/3 × mast (1 7/8 × B); gaff, 3/5 × boom (1 1/8 × B).

Lug-rigged longboats. Mainmast, 2 1/2 × B; mainyard, 5/8 × mainmast (1 9/16 × B); foremast, 7/8 × mainmast (2 3/16 × B); foreyard, 5/8 × foremast; bowsprit, 1/2 × mainmast. The diameters of masts and yards were 1/48 of their lengths but bowsprits were thicker, at 5/96 × length.

Lug-rigged launches and cutters. Mainmast 2 3/4 × B; mainyard, 9/17 × mast length; foremast, 8/9 × mainmast; foreyard, 9/17 × mast length; mizzenmast, 5/8 × mainmast; sprit, mizzenmast + 2ft; outrigger, 2/3 × mizzenmast. Diameters of masts and yards were as for sloop-rigged boats but the sprit's diameter was 1/84 × length and the outrigger's 3/84. Lug-rigged boats did not have bowsprits.

Launches and cutters with settee sails (a settee was a quadrilateral sail, like the old lateen with its lower corner cut off). Mainmast, 2 × B; mainyard, 3 1/2 × B; foremast, 17/18 × mainmast (1 8/9 × B); foreyard, 9/10 × mainyard. Diameter of masts: 1/32 × length; of yards: 1/48 × length.

Barges and pinnaces with lateen sails. Masts, 2 × B, plus 8in more; diameter, 5/16in per foot length. (The entry for these boats seem to be incorrect: it has topmasts of 9/8 × mast length and with a diameter of 1/60 × length. As no yards are listed 'topmast' is presumed to be a mistake for (lateen) yard.

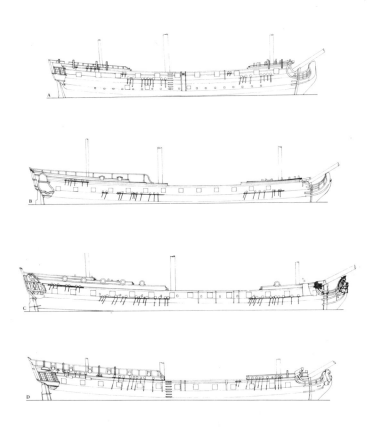

341. Comparative profiles of frigates. The ships are:
(a) *Phoenix*, an English 24-gun ship of the 1741 Establishment. With two gun-ports on the lower deck the ship is a real 2-decker and high out of the water in consequence.
(b) *Renommée*, 30 guns, of 1746, was one of the first French frigates and shows a long and low hull. Although the ship is structurally a 2-decker the lower deck has no guns and was placed at the waterline.
(c) *Ambuscade*, 40 guns, of 1746, was the largest French frigate of the period. She was captured by the English. The design was obviously of great interest since plans of the ship exist in the British, Dutch, Danish and Swedish navy collections. Thus to some extent naval architectural ideas were a common heritage in eighteenth century Europe.
(d) *Lyme*, 28 guns, of 1748, was one of the first English frigates (with her sister *Unicorn*). They were produced because the 24-gun ships like *Phoenix* could neither catch nor defeat the new French frigates.
(*Drawings by John Roberts from originals in the National Maritime Museum*)
342. A contemporary model of the 32-gun frigate *Lowestoffe* of 1761. This was an experimental vessel based on the lines of the Canadian-built French prize *L'Abenakise*.

Sprit-rigged pinnaces, barges and yawls. Main- and foremasts, 2.25 × B; sprits, 9/8 × mast length. Diameters: masts, 1/48 × length; sprit, 1/96 × length.

Information about how boats were painted is scanty. A yacht's boat, in 1705, had the upper parts vermilion but from the thwarts downwards the boat was painted in the drab shade known as 'sad colour'. An Admiral's boat of about the same date was green above the thwarts and had heraldic trophies on the panels and backboards. Below the thwarts 'sad colour' was used. A model of a longboat of 1730 in the National Maritime Museum has its sheerstrake blue with gilt scrollwork but the rest of the hull, except the thwarts, is painted a pale yellowish ochre. The thwarts are red. Another model, of a 4-oared barge c1750, has a dull white underbody, a broad band of dull banana yellow above, then a narrow gilt stripe with a blue strake above that. The inside is red with gilt-edged blue panels; the oars are red.

In 1777 an Order directed that all boats were to be painted below the waterline with white lead and linseed oil, implying that other paints had been in use, but what they were, other than sad colour and the yellow ochre mentioned above, is not known. The next information comes from 1799. A painting of that date shows 11 boats moored in a line. The colours of the outsides, which are all that can been seen, are: no 1 (the biggest) – blue, with a red stripe near the gunwale; no 2 – yellow, with a blue gunwale; nos 3 and 4 – white, with a red gunwale; nos 5, 7 and 9 – yellow, with a red stripe; nos 6 and 11 – all white; nos 8 and 10 – white, with a red stripe. The colours of the boats are not necessarily standard patterns: they are more likely to be 'Admiral's fancy'[33].

342

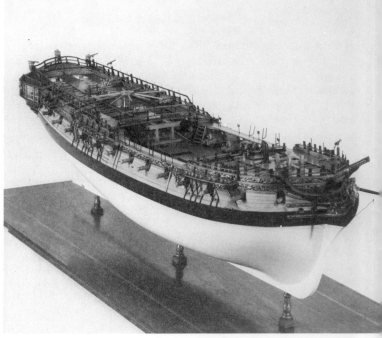

343

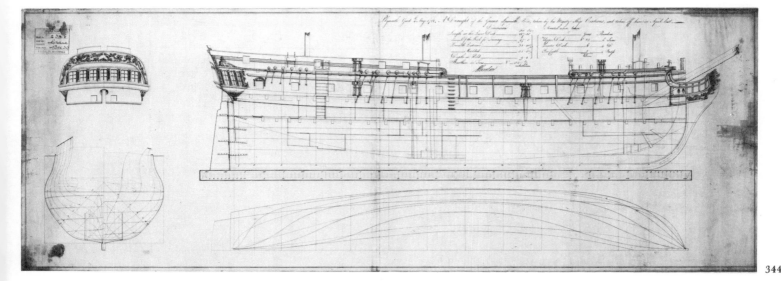

344

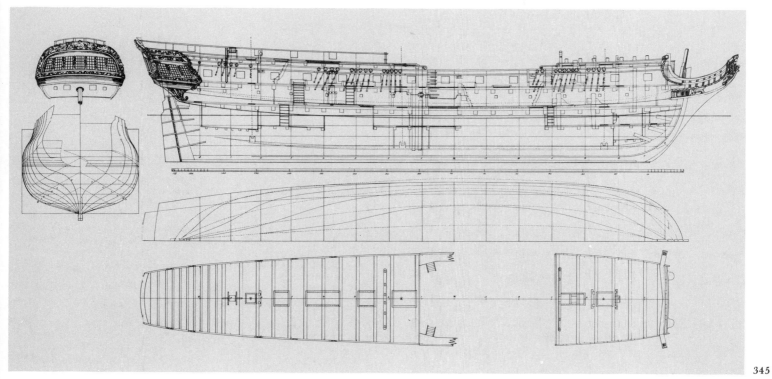

345

343. An *Amazon* class 32-gun frigate of 1793. Armed with 12pdrs, these vessels were developed from the highly successful *Alarm* class of 1757 and were the mainstay of the Royal Navy's frigate force during the American Revolutionary War.

344. The draught of the *Grana*, a Spanish 30-gun frigate captured in 1781. Unlike contemporary English ships the *Grana* has upright stem and sternposts and an almost flat profile. The waist and quarterdeck bulwarks are much higher than those on the Royal Navy's ships.

345. The *Confederacy*, the largest American frigate of the Revolutionary War. She was larger than contemporary English vessels and in many ways a radical design. She was captured in 1783 (as depicted on the jacket of this book) but

having been hastily built of unseasoned wood she was rapidly decommissioned and broken up. (Based on the Admiralty draught, as captured, in the National Maritime Museum.)

346. A plan for a class of Swedish 40-gun frigates designed by Chapman, beginning with the *Bellona* built at Karlskrona in 1782. The sharp section and rounded gunports are Chapman hallmarks, but what made these frigates so different was their main armament of 26 24pdrs. Thus the Swedes were building 24pdr frigates 10 years before the French *Pomone* and over 15 before the USS *Constitution*.

346

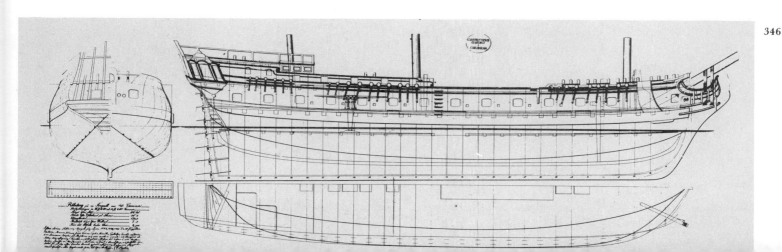

	BOAT ESTABLISHMENTS 1670–1800 – (Read across)						
Date	1ST RATES	2ND RATES	3RD RATES	4TH RATES	5TH RATES	6TH RATES	SLOOPS ETC.
c1670	3 boats (longboat, pinnace, yawl)	3 boats 70-guns and above; 2 boats below 70	2 boats (longboat, pinnace)	2 boats (longboat, pinnace)	2 boats (longboat, pinnace)	4 largest vessels had 2 boats; all 1 only (pinnace)	
1679		*Duchess*, 90-guns, had 32ft longboat, 31ft pinnace, 20ft skiff (yawl)					
1701				3rd boat added – '60's a 6-oared and '50's a 4-oared Deal yawl.			
1702	Additional carvel Deal yawl-type boat (total 4 boats)	Ditto; total, '90's probably 4, '80's probably 3 boats	Ditto; total 3	Total 3 boats	Total 2 boats	Total 1 boat	
After 1710	Tendency for the long boats issued to become shorter, particularly in the smaller ships						
1715						2nd boat added – 27ft pinnace and 17ft Deal yawl	
1719	35ft × 6ft 3in × 2ft 9in pinnace (12 oars); 100-gun ships: 36ft × 10ft 4in × 4ft 1in longboat	90-gun ships: 35ft × 10ft 4in × 4ft 1in longboat; 80-gun ships: 32ft × 9ft 4in × 3ft 11in longboat	31ft × 6ft 2in × 2ft 7½in pinnace (10 oars); 70-gun ships: 31ft × 9ft 4in × 3ft 11in longboat	30ft × 6ft 2in × 2ft 7½in pinnace (10 oars); 60-gun ships: 30ft × 8ft 8in×ft 8in longboat; 50-gun ships: 30ft × 8ft 8in × 3ft 8in longboat	28ft × 5ft 10in × 2ft 6½in pinnace (8 oars); 40- and 30-gun ships: 26ft × 8ft 4in × 3ft 5½in longboat	27ft × 5ft 8in × 2ft 6in pinnace (8 oars)	
17.4.1740	Additional 25ft 6-oared boat, or Deal cutter; total 5 boats	Ditto; total 5 boats	Ditto; also in '70's the 10-oared boat to be lengthened to 32ft *like the larger ships,* and the 8-oared boat to be 28ft; total 4 boats	No change in numbers, but boats of '60's and '50's to be altered like the '70's; total 3 boats			
11.7.1746				Additional 25ft cutter for 1745 Establishment '60's and '50's; total 4 boats	Ditto; for 44-gun ships of 1745 Establishment; total 3 boats	Total 2 boats	
9.4.1755	Additional Deal cutter; total 6 boats	Ditto; total 6 boats	Ditto; total 5 boats				
19.8.1757						All 6th Rates on Channel Service to have a 6-oared boat in lieu of 10-oared boat (pinnace?)	

BOAT ESTABLISHMENTS 1670–1800 – (Read across)						
Date	1ST RATES	2ND RATES	3RD RATES	4TH RATES	5TH RATES	6TH RATES	SLOOPS ETC.
1761					'36's and '32's: 23ft longboat, 30ft pinnace, 24ft yawl; total 3 boats	'28's: 22ft longboat, 28ft pinnace, 23ft yawl; '24's: 21ft longboat, 28ft pinnace, 22ft yawl; total 3 boats	'16's: 19ft longboat, 26ft pinnace; '18's; 18ft longboat, 25ft pinnace; '10's: 16ft longboat, 24ft pinnace
1771			'74's: long-boat, pinnace, barge, yawl and 2 cutters of different lengths; total 6 boats				
1777							'16's of more than 300 tons given an extra 18ft 4-oared cutter
1780			'64's: 30ft launch, 32ft and 28ft pinnaces, two 25ft cutters; total 5 boats		'38's: 26ft launch, 30ft pinnace, two 24ft cutters; total 4 boats		
12.7.1780					'36's: to have two 24ft cutters as '38's have		

7.11.1780 Launches ordered to replace longboats in all vessels being built or repaired

14.6.1781 An additional 4-oared 18ft cutter for all Rates down to and including '20's

| 1781 | Total 7 boats | Total 7 boats | '74's: 31ft launch, 32ft and 28ft pinnaces, two 25ft and one 18ft cutter; '64's: 30ft launch, 32ft and 28ft pinnaces, two 25ft and one 18ft cutter; total 6 boats | '50's: 29ft launch, pinnace (probably 30ft) and two cutters (prob-ably 25ft), 18ft cutter; total 5 boats | '44's: 26ft launch, pinnace (probably 30ft) and two cutters (probably 24ft) and 18ft cutter; '36's and '32's: 23ft or 24ft launch, 30ft pinnace, two 24ft and one 18ft cutter; total 5 boats | '28's: 22ft launch, 28ft pinnace (probably a cutter of about 22ft) and 18ft cutter; '20's: 21ft launch pinnace (probably about 22ft) and 18ft cutter. total 3 or 4 boats | Large sloops: 19ft launch, 26ft pinnace (and probably 18ft cutter); small sloops: 24ft and 16ft cutter (Scout, purchased); (total 3 or 2 boats |

1782–3 Tendency to replace barges and pinnaces with cutters, which were preferred by many sea-officers

1794 A few captains allowed 8-oared cutters in exchange for their pinnaces by special order

From *Model Shipwright* No 19, March 1977, with additions.

347

Stowing the boats is something else about which we lack reliable information. The practice of stowing boats on the spare spars between the forecastle and quarterdeck was probably established by the end of the seventeenth century and it remained in use until beams were laid across the waist, when the boats were stowed on the beams. How this was done is not clear. There are references to stowing boats one inside another, which implies either removable thwarts or some sort of chocks to steady the upper boat. In the last decade of the century davits came into use for hoisting small boats, and it was customary to have a pair of davits on each quarter. It will be more convenient to deal with davits in the next chapter.

347. A model of a naval schooner of about 110 tons. The hull is a contemporary one of the period 1760–80 but the rigging was added in 1902 according to the dimensions in Steel's *Mast-making, Sail-making and Rigging* and is therefore not strictly contemporary in style with the hull.

348. The *Lee,* an American cutter captured on Lake Champlain in 1776 and taken into the Royal Navy, when she carried one 12pdr gun, one 9pdr and four 4pdrs. The *Lee's* rig was probably a gaffsail, one or more staysails and for light winds a squaresail and a square topsail. A reconstruction of the hull and rig is in H. I. Chapelle's *The History of the American Sailing Navy.*

349. A gunboat of 1782. The gun is mounted on a slide-carriage and recoiled along the centreline of the boat. In later versions the carriage could be slid down to the bottom of the boat when the gun was not required for service.

350. A Danish plan of an English fireship of the early eighteenth century (probably a converted merchantman). The door in the quarter is a sally-port from which the crew escaped after setting off the powder train (No 14 on the plan); the downward-hinged ports were blown open by grenades to allow a draught to the fire, and chimneys (No 4) carried the fire to the rigging.

REFERENCES

Abbreviations

MM: The Mariner's Mirror, the Journal of the Society for Nautical Research
MS: Model Shipwright

1 *Le Vaisseau de 74 Canons,* Jean Boudriot, Grenoble: Editions des Quatres Seigneries (1973)
2 *The Ship-Builder's Assistant, William Sutherland (1711)*
3 'The First English Frigates', R Gardiner, *MM* (1975) Vol 61 pp163–172; 'The Frigate Designs of 1755–57', R Gardiner, *MM* (1977) Vol 63 pp51–69
4 *Old Ship Figureheads and Sterns,* L G Carr Laughton, London (1925)
5 'The Introduction of Copper Sheathing into the Royal Navy 1779–1786', R J B Knight, *MM* (1973) Vol 59 pp299–309
6 The Order is quoted in Reference 4, p25, and in *MM* (1913) Vol III p20
7 Quoted by L G Carr Laughton in *MM* (1924) Vol X p173
8 *England's Glory; or Ship-Building Unveiled,* William Sutherland (1717)
9 *An Universal Dictionary of the Marine,* William Falconer (1769 and several reprints)
10 'The Early History of the Steering Wheel', J H Harland, *MM* (1972) Vol 58 pp41–68
11 'The Early Steering Wheel', G F Howard, *MM* (1978) Vol 64 pp188–9
12 'The Binnacle', Commander W E May, *MM* (1954) Vol 40 pp21–32
13 *The Naval Expositor,* T R Blanckley (1750)
14 Admiralty: Navy Board 2507 No 150, quoted in Reference 4, p24
15 *Ship Models: Sailing Ships from AD1700,* B W Bathe, Science Museum, London (1964)
16 Admiralty: Navy Board 2507 No 198, quoted in Reference 4, p266; Navy Board 2508 No 706, quoted in Reference 4, p269
17 'British Ships Painting at Aboukir', L Paul, *MM* (1914) Vol IV pp266–74
18 The dimensions of eighteenth century masts, spars and rigging are set out in *The Masting and Rigging of English Ships of War 1625–1860,* Conway Maritime Press (1979)
19 'The Evolution of Stunsails', D L Dennis, *MM* (1966), Vol 52 pp223–32
20 See *Seventeenth Century Rigging,* R C Anderson, Marshall (1955) and Reference 18
21 'Naval Blockmaking in the 18th and 19th Centuries', G Clark, *MM* (1976) Vol 62 pp137–144
22 'Fitting for Wooden Warships. Part 3: Guns', R Gardiner, *MS* (1977) No 20 pp338–353
23 *Guns at Sea,* P Padfield, London (1973)
24 *British Artillery on Land and Sea 1790–1820,* R Wilkinson-Latham
25 'Bomb Ketches 1670–1700', D Wray, *MS* (1977) No 19 pp242–255
26 *Oared Fighting Ships,* R C Anderson, Marshall (1962)
27 A draught of the *Ferret* is reproduced in H I Chapelle's *The History of American Sailing Ships* (1936) and those of the *Hazard* and the *Cruizer* in his *The History of the American Sailing Navy* (1949)
28 *Royal Yachts,* G B P Naish, National Maritime Museum (1953)
29 'The Schooner Rig', M A Edson, *American Neptune* (1965) Vol XXV pp81–92
30 *Boats of Men-of-War,* Commander W E May, National Maritime Press (1974)
31 'Fittings for Wooden Warships. Part 2: Boats', R Gardiner, *MS* (1977) No 19 pp 235–41
32 *The Elements of Mast-making, Sail-making and Rigging,* D Steel (1794)
33 The details will be found in *MM* (1940) Vol XXVI p305

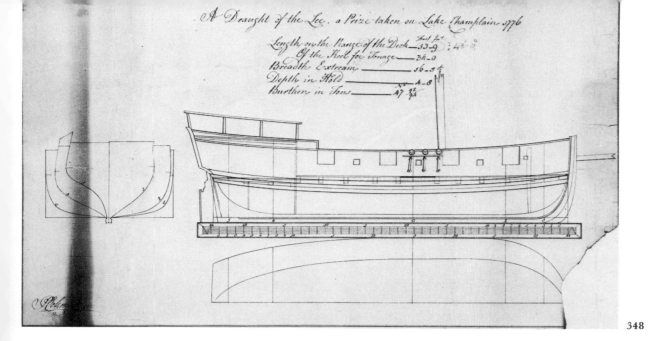

A Draught of the Lee, a Prize taken on Lake Champlain 1776

Length on the Range of the Deck ——— 53–9
Of the Keel for Tonage ——— 34–0
Breadth Extream ——— 16–5¼
Depth in Hold ——— 4–0
Burthen in Tons ——— 47 ²⁴⁄₉₄

348

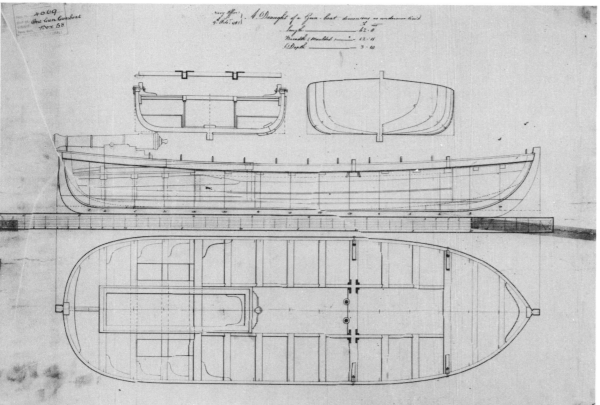

A Draught of a Gun-boat dimensions as underneath

Length ——— 42–0
Breadth (moulded) ——— 12–11
Depth ——— 3–10

349

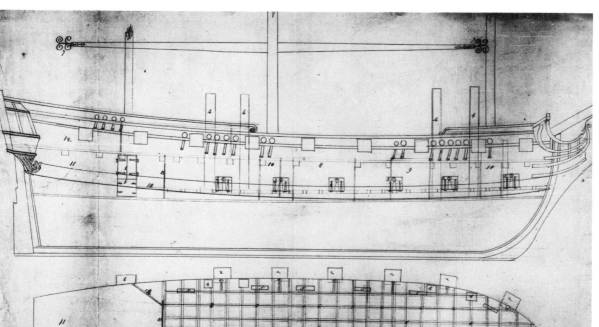

350

351. The *Nelson*, 120 guns, was launched in 1814 and represents the state of the shipbuilding art at the beginning of the century. These beautiful and detailed drawings were made at the time by John Pringle, one of the Woolwich Dockyard draughtsmen. The *Nelson* was 244ft overall, 205ft on the gundeck and 53ft 8in in extreme breadth. In length the ship was very near the limit practicable with the traditional framing but soon after the *Nelson* was completed Sir Robert Seppings introduced his system of diagonal bracing, which allowed longer ships to be built. The *Nelson*'s plan shows the built-up bow that was standard for all ships, but the stern still has the old-fashioned open framework. The top-timbers of the hull have been taken up above the tops of the uppermost gunports to provide strong bulwarks, although the abrupt drops from one level to the next detract from the ship's appearance. Sheer has almost disappeared and the head rails are straighter than they were on the *Victory* in her 1805 form. The waist is still open to the sky but the wide gangways foreshadow its ultimate closing over. A picture of the ship being launched (MacPherson Collection in the National Maritime Museum) shows her with black wales and port lids, and ochre sides.

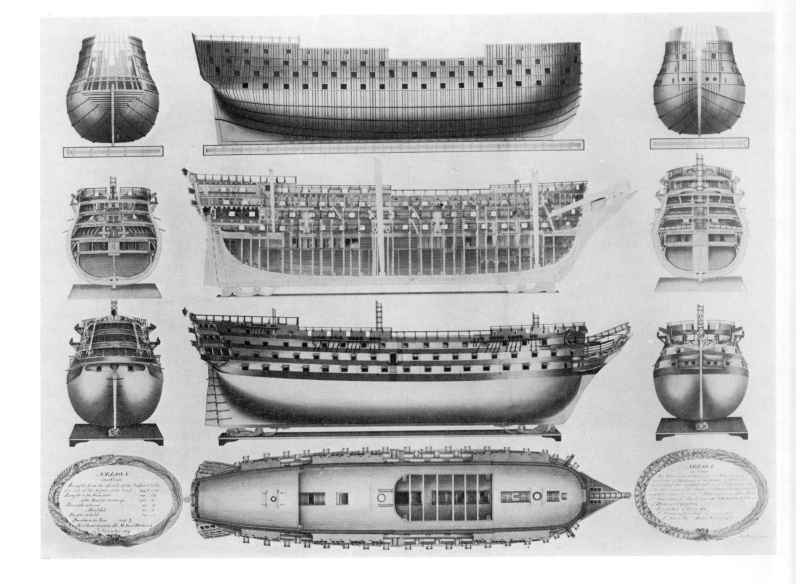

THE LAST
OF THE WOODEN WALLS

In 1815 the long series of wars involving almost every State in Europe, and even the United States, came to an end, and the battle fleets reurned to harbour to be laid up 'In Ordinary', as the phrase was. Only small battle squadrons were maintained, and most of the ships-of-the-line remained laid up for the rest of their days. Indeed, there was only one more major fleet action under sail, namely the destruction of the Turco-Egyptian fleet at Navarino in 1827 by a combined fleet of British, French and Russian ships.

The smaller craft, from frigates downwards, found work to do. In the absence of an opportunity to fight one another the major Navies took up the long-neglected tasks of putting down piracy, policing and surveying the seas, charting little-known coasts and, in the case of the British Navy, suppressing the slave trade from the west and the east coasts of Africa. Much of the work was dangerous as well as difficult, and was carried out in distant and often unhealthy parts of the world. Its successful accomplishment called out the best in men and ships. But for interest and excitement it could not compare with the exploits of daring frigate officers and the battles between great fleets, and in consequence the performance of the nineteenth century sailing warship is little known outside a small circle of naval historians. This is as unfair to the ships and their designers as it is to the crews, for the sailing warship between 1815 and 1860 was as close to perfection as the material and technology of the time permitted. The long wars had weeded out unsuitable types of ship, had shown up weaknesses in design, rig and armament and had forced the development of bigger, more powerfully armed, and better rigged vessels capable of sailing anywhere and withstanding attack from any likely opponent. The eighteenth century had seen a steady growth in the size of every class of warship but by 1800 the biggest of them had reached the limit of size practicable with all-wooden hulls put together in the traditional way, this limit being a gun-deck length of about 200ft, beyond which excessive drooping of the ends was inescapable. The tapering off in length is illustrated by three British 1st Rates: the *Victory* (100 guns) of 1765 had a gun-deck of 186ft; that of the *Queen Charlotte*, also 100 guns and built in 1790, was 190ft; and the *Caledonia* (120 guns), launched in 1808, was 205ft on the gun-deck. The deadlock was broken in 1813 when the Surveyor of the Navy, Sir Robert Seppings, introduced a system of diagonal trussing combined with iron strapping. The new system allowed bigger ships to be built. The *Caledonia* was a 3-decker of 2600 tons but under the new system 84-gun 2-deckers of 2260 tons and 194ft on the gun-deck were built by 1820, and in 1833 92-gun 2-deckers 206ft on the gun-deck were afloat. The 3-decker *Duke of Wellington*, 131 guns, laid down as a sailing ship but given engines before her launch in 1852, had a gun-deck 240ft long and the *Marlborough*, also given engines before she was launched in 1855, was 5ft longer. Ships of such a large size were not unique to the British Navy. The French *Le Valmy* (120 guns), built in 1847, was 210ft on the waterline and displaced 5154 tons whilst the United States had the *Pennsylvania* (120 guns) also 210ft on the gun-deck. None of these huge vessels had their fighting qualities tested in a fleet engagement, and the actions during the Crimean War showed that the shell-firing gun had turned the wooden ship into a death-trap. The end came in 1860 when the steam-driven, armoured iron frigate *Warrior* was launched. Protected by her armour, free to manoeuvre independent of the wind and armed with 26 68pdrs, 10 110pdrs and 4 70pdrs, the *Warrior* could have tackled successfully any squadron of wooden sailing ships afloat at the time[1].

Though the nineteenth century warship was as near to technical perfection as it could be, the ships

352–357. Comparative profiles to the same scale of US warships of the first half of the nineteenth century.
352. *Pennsylvania*, 120 guns, launched in 1837 at Philadelphia Navy Yard. She was not very successful and was destroyed in 1861 during the US Civil War after a very inactive career.
353. *North Carolina*, 74 guns, launched in 1820 at Philadelphia Navy Yard, was a typical US '2-decker' in which the continuous spar-deck provided a *de facto* third deck and many more than the rates 74 guns could be carried. Note the single quarter galleries (the US Navy at this time had no Admirals so required no extra flagship accommodation).
354. *Congress*, 44 guns, launched in 1841 at Portsmouth Navy Yard – the last US frigate designed without engines. The logical development from the *Constitution* type, US big frigates had two complete gundecks and carried at least 50 guns.
355. *Germantown*, 22 guns, launched in 1846 at Philadelphia Navy Yard. A large '1st Class' ship sloop which another navy would have rated a corvette.
356. *Dale*, 16 guns, launched in 1839 at Philadelphia Navy Yard. A smaller ship sloop, rated '3rd Class'.
357. *Porpoise*, 12 guns, launched in 1821 at Portsmouth Navy Yard. A topsail schooner, designed for anti-piracy duties in the West Indies.

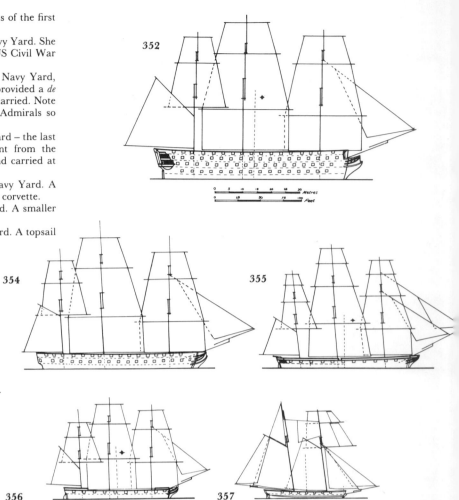

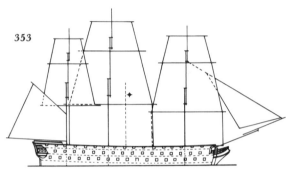

were by no means always things of beauty. In the opinion of many people, then and now, their appearance compared unfavourably with that of eighteenth century ships. The reasons for this opinion are, probably, the flat profile (sheer had almost disappeared), the plain stern galleries and the short, high beak with a bust instead of a figurehead. The biggest ships often had an ungainly appearance, the beakheads and stern galleries looking as though they had been clapped on as an afterthought. Frigates and small craft were more attractive in appearance and compare well with the later clipper ships. Neither in rig nor in armament (except for the number of guns on the biggest ships) were there any striking differences between eighteenth and nineteenth century ships although in both spheres small but important changes took place. In the middle of the century a new feature appeared when many of the bigger ships were fitted with engines: the funnel. The early funnels were telescopic and when they were lowered the ship looked like a sail-only vessel.

The lack of interest in nineteenth century warships is not due to a shortage of information, for there is probably more readily accessible and detailed information about them than about any other period of the same length in the history of the sailing warship. The most able naval architects of the era wrote about the design and rig of ships, and for the general public as well as their technical colleagues the Admiralty produced comprehensive reports on the ships' performance[2] – and from about 1845 there are photographs of the ships themselves. All these sources, together with the collections of plans in the Admiralty archives, provide a wealth of information that has scarcely been touched.

THE HULL

Until the 1830s the underbody of the hull retained the shape developed during the previous century but above the waterline extensive changes were made. The first was the building-up of the bows of 2- and 3-deckers to the level of the forecastle deck. Until 1802 the fore end of the forecastle of these ships ended in the old-fashioned flat beakhead bulkhead, which was lightly built and offered no protection from raking fire. The flat bulkhead was originally devised to allow the chase guns to fire forwards, but by the middle of the eighteenth century, at the very latest, there were no gunports in the bulkhead. The retention of the comparatively flimsy bulkhead, in view of its successful incorporation into frigate hulls in the middle of the eighteenth century, is difficult to understand, but the fact remains that the first British ship-of-the-line to have her bow timbers taken up to the forecastle deck's level was the *Blenheim* (74 guns) in 1802. Nine years later the round bow, as it was called, was ordered for all ships. Besides giving better protection, the round bow enabled more guns to be fired forwards and allowed the head to be made lighter and placed higher, changes that led to a drier ship and increased safety for men working in the head.

The bows having been strengthened, attention was turned to the stern. For more than two centuries the upper part of the stern had been little more than a mass of windows that could not offer protection from even the smallest gun-shot. To that disadvantage was added the lack of fire astern. Captains sometimes attempted to remedy the defect by having guns taken into the stern and fired through the window openings but this, of course, was only a temporary expedient. The problem of how to provide protection and stern-fire was first solved in 1821 by Sir Robert Seppings when he introduced what was called the circular stern, which was constructed by taking the hull timbers between the quarters and the sternpost up to the level of the poop deck. Gunports were made in the new stern just as they were in the broadside and the whole structure was strongly timbered. Galleries were built on to the outside of the stern's framework, access to them being through doors that could also be used as gunports. For all its advantages, the circular stern was an unsightly affair with its galleries sometimes resembling the windows of a lighthouse, and it was so disliked that a modified version was introduced within a few years. This was elliptical in plan and besides allowing as many guns to fire astern as the circular one did, it had the aesthetic advantage of permitting the construction of stern and quarter galleries that resembled the traditional ones. It is curious that so advantageous an improvement was so long in coming. Conservatism, and even blockheadedness, have been given as reasons, but we ought not to underrate the intelligence of the Admiralty or the shipwrights without good evidence. It is likely that the difficulty of working out, on paper, the shapes of the stern timbers was a major factor. As the drawing from a contemporary work by one of the chief naval architects of the day, Augustin Creuze, shows, drawing the parts of a 'round' stern was a complex business, and until draughtsmanship had developed sufficiently to reproduce the curves on a plan, and until shipwrights were able to work from such a plan, the construction of a 'round' stern may have been thought impracticable except by 'hit-or-miss' methods. Furthermore, the construction itself was complicated and difficult.

Changes in the broadside's appearance accompanied the alterations to bow and stern: the sheer of the rails was reduced until the profile of the hull seemed to be almost a straight line; the sheer of the decks, too, was reduced almost to vanishing point. The change in the profile of the hull was brought about, for the most part, by building up the bulwarks. The first step was to build up the forecastle, quarterdeck and poop bulwarks to a little above the tops of the gunports. As the waist already had solid bulwarks the innovation provided a protective belt from one end of the ship to the other. The height of the bulwarks was gradually increased until, on big ships, they were 6ft or more. The ends of the bulwarks were taken down vertically to the next level and made an ugly 'step' in the ship's profile, a fashion that lasted until about 1850, when the abrupt break from poop to quarterdeck was replaced by a curve.

Two other changes affected the broadside's appearance: the age-old concave curve of the topsides was straightened out and the amount of tumblehome reduced until the latest ships were practically wallsided; and between 1800 and 1820 the wales disappeared from view as a result of their edges being tapered off to fair in with the planking.

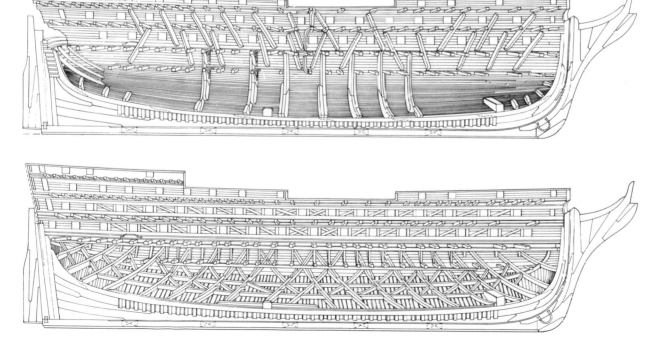

358. Two sectional drawings showing the traditional method of framing (top) and the system of diagonal framing introduced by Sir Robert Seppings. His system undoubtedly produced stronger ships but led to complaints about the excessive amount of timber needed, and later variants employed iron braces and trusses which were stronger and lighter.

359

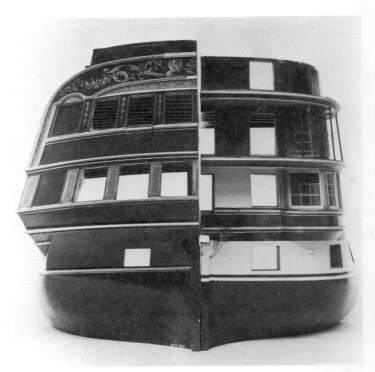

360

359. *Unicorn* also has the round stern and, in fact, all of Sepping's most important structural innovations can be seen in the ship.
360. A comparative model of the vulnerable traditional galleries and the more robust circular stern.

The change in the shape of the underbody of the hulls, at any rate those of the biggest classes of ships, was slower in coming and was brought about, to a considerable degree, by a prolonged controversy over the alleged inferiority of the Royal Navy's ships to those of the United States. The background to the dispute was the successful development in the USA, in the eighteenth century, of a class of fast-sailing ships that had a 'V' or 'peg-top' shaped midship section and fine lines. Although the 'V'-section was certainly not unique to American ships it was developed most intensively in the United States and the reputation for speed of ships based on it, such as the famous Baltimore clippers, attracted a good deal of attention from the general public in Britain, although the fact that the Americans did not themselves use the 'V'-section hull for their big warships was overlooked. A secondary factor was the effects of Seppings' structural improvements, which made British warships stronger and more robust but tended to make them slow.

The adoption of the 'V'-section in designing ships for the Royal Navy was enthusiastically advocated by Captain William Symonds (he was later knighted), who succeeded Seppings as Surveyor of the Navy in 1832. Symonds had several ships built to his plans between 1832 and 1848. All had steeply rising floors and had their maximum beam at about the load line. As the underbody of Symonds' ships was finer than that of the older style craft the requisite buoyancy was obtained by making the hull wider in proportion to its length. A ratio of 1:3.25 was not unusual, compared with 1:4 on other vessels. 'Symondite ships' (as they were known) were able to carry a lot of sail and were fast, but they were found to roll more quickly than other ships, behaviour that adversely affected gunnery. Some of them, moreover, were given to excessive and even dangerous heeling in strong winds. On the whole, Symonds' designs did not come up to expectations as far as big ships were concerned although the smaller craft were often satisfactory.

366

In his later designs Symonds reduced the steepness of the floors but the tendency to excessive rolling and pitching remained. In consequence the 'V' midship section fell into disfavour and in the 1840s it was superseded by one in which the floors rose steeply at first and then curved outwards and upwards to give a full bilge, a design that remained in use until the sailing warship era came to an end. The 'new' design was, in fact, a partial reversion to an older form, for Augustin Creuze wrote in 1851 that the recently built British ships, and also some of the most modern French warships, approximated in hull form to that recommended by the eighteenth century Swedish naval architect Frederick af Chapman[2].

The need for bigger ships, and the increasing difficulty of obtaining large timber, especially curved timbers and knees, led to changes in the way the hulls were put together[3]. Seppings' diagonal trussing has already been mentioned. It was accompanied by iron strapping set diagonally across the frames and by improved methods of joining the sections of each frame. A variety of iron knees or brackets came into use and to give greater longitudinal strength the upper frames were bolted together laterally.

FITTINGS

The trend of the times was towards a 'smoother' hull, from which some of the traditional protuberances were removed. As already mentioned, the edges of the wales had been faired off, and as there were no longer any projecting edges to catch the boats as they were hoisted in, there was no use for the riders on the ships' sides and they were abolished. The entry ports, one on each side, remained, though in a less ornate form than in the previous centuries, and because the amount of tumblehome had been reduced the canopy over the port was made smaller. The steps up the side remained as before. In their final form entry ports were merely enlarged gunports.

Fore and main channels were still fixed, as in the eighteenth century, just above the top of the gunports on the uppermost gun-deck, and the mizzen channels were a deck higher.

The most important alteration to the external fittings was to the rudder, if that vital piece of gear may be called a fitting. On the old-established rudder the axis of rotation lay forward of the rudder's edge so that a sizable opening had to be made for it in the counter, and although this opening was covered over with a canvas or leather rudder coat it was difficult to keep the water out. On small ships the rudder hole could be a source of danger in severe weather. The solution to the difficulty was provided, according to the scanty evidence, by Gabriel Snodgrass, the Surveyor to the East India Company, who in 1779 constructed a rudder that had its upper part cranked forward so that the axis of rotation of the rudder-head passed through the centres of the gudgeons and pintles. The neck of the rudder could then be made circular and be passed up through a circular hole in the counter, in which the rudder's neck would be a close fit. Although it was claimed to have been in use for many years in the East India Company ships, the round-headed rudder was not in use in the Royal Navy when the nineteenth century opened, notwithstanding that the United States Navy had used it since 1794[4]. In fact, the precise date of its introduction into the British Navy has yet to be determined. The *Victory*, as restored to her 1805 form, has the old-fashioned rudder; E W Cooke's etching of the stern of the *Asia,* built in 1821, shows the old style, and in view of Cooke's accuracy in nautical detail it may be taken that, at least in big ships, the round-headed rudder had not come into use by that date. It was fitted to the *Albion*, built in 1842, and so it must have first appeared in the twenty or so years between the *Asia* and this ship.

Another development was the general adoption of davits for hoisting the smaller boats. Davits came into use first in the 1790s and were in common use within ten years or so. The early ones were removable, and because they were so simple and effective they remained in use for a long time. It was not until nearly the end of the era that the familiar inverted-'J' davits, made of iron, replaced them, although iron davits were tried as early as the 1820s. Davits were also fitted over the stern on single-decked ships by the early 1800s and were later on added to 2- and even 3-deckers, if pictures may be relied upon. Like the quarter davits, those over the stern were at first straight and resembled catheads set up on the ends of the bulwarks. Curved wooden ones gradually came into use and, finally, iron ones. No dimensions of davits have been found but they must obviously have been long enough to allow the boats to clear the ship's side.

At the other end of the ship the head underwent changes. The building up of the bow to forecastle deck level and the raising of the head allowed the hawse-holes to be set on the middle deck on 3-deckers and on the upper deck of 2-decked ships. The catheads retained their former shape but because the head had been raised it was no longer possible to bring one of the head rails round to support the cathead, which was thus given a simple bracket.

Anchors retained the traditional shape that had proved its value over many decades. Alternative shapes were, in any case, hardly practicable as long as the anchorsmith had only primitive water-driven hammers to forge his bundles of wrought iron rods. After about 1825, however, a new pattern of anchor, with arms that were an arc of a circle, came into use and this soon became the standard shape. Iron stocks had been fitted to small anchors as early as the 1780s and their use was extended in the 1800s but they never replaced the old-

361–363. The timbering of the square (361), round (362) and elliptical (363) sterns. These drawings reveal the difficulty in constructing a circular stern, and indicate that the introduction of the elliptical stern was much more likely a result of its simpler framing than a conservative desire for a more elegant shape.

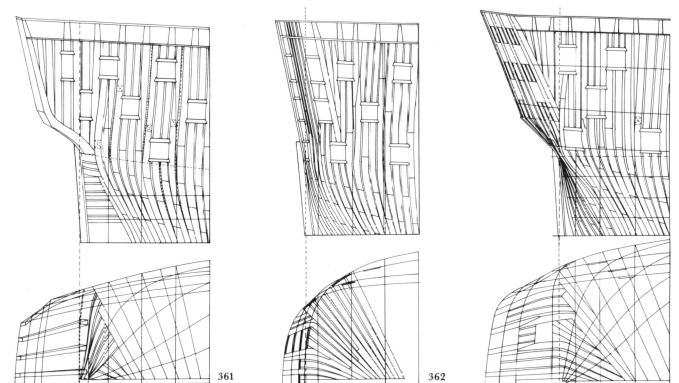

361   362   363

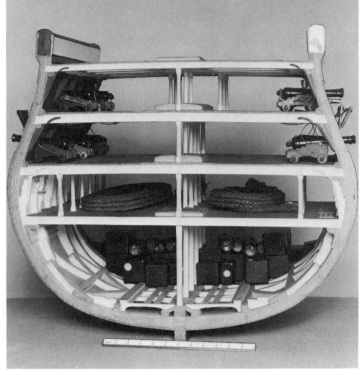

364

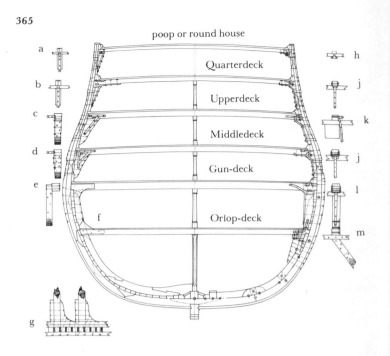

fashioned wooden stock on the biggest anchors. All but the smallest ships had three sorts of anchor: bower (usually 4), stream (1) and kedge (1). The small craft had 2 or 3 bowers.

ANCHOR SIZES *c*1840				
	Best Bower			
	Shank		Arms	
Ship	ft	in	ft	in
100–120 guns	17	0	5	7
80–92 guns	16	6	5	5
72 guns	15	4	5	1½
Frigates				
50 guns	15	2	5	0
40 guns	13	10	4	7½
38 guns	13	0	4	4
Razee	12	8	4	3
Corvettes	11	7½	3	10½
Sloops				
16 guns	10	10	3	7½
8 guns	9	2	3	0

From *Naval Architecture*, John Fincham.

Hemp cables remained in use to the end but chain cables, which had been introduced at the beginning of the century were gradually supplanting them. The cables were still brought in by capstan and, as before, a messenger was necessary with all but the small cables. Chain cables, too, were brought in with a messenger.

There are two points to be noted about gunport lids. After 1809 British ships had their lower-deck port lids fitted with glass 'bull's-eyes', which were called illuminators. They were not needed on middle decks because some of the ports had half-lids hinged vertically or horizontally. These are rarely shown on models but may have been more common than is generally realised. A careful drawing of the Danish 46-gun frigate *Freya* (launched in 1819) by the marine artist

C W Eckersberg shows the ship with all her ports closed by horizontally hinged half-lids that fit round the protruding barrels of the guns.

The principal alteration to the decks of the ships was the closing in of the waist. At the beginning of the century there were side gangways in the waist and these were gradually widened until, by 1813, the gangways took up about one-third of the width of the waist. During the next few years they spread further across and by 1820 what was left of the open waist was almost covered by the boats stowed on the beams. The final step was taken in 1832 when the waist on the big ships was completely covered, so that forecastle and quarterdeck were part of a continuous deck, and in some cases protected by a continuous solid bulwark. No guns were mounted there, although guns had been mounted on the gangways of the large frigates built in 1813. The experiment was not a success and was not repeated. French ships, on the other hand, mounted guns over the waist so that, with the forecastle and quarterdeck guns at the same level, the ships were *de facto* 4-deckers though rated as 3-deckers, as *Le Jemmappes* (106 guns), launched in 1840, and *Le Valmy* (120), launched in 1847, were rated. The latter, incidentally, was the last 3-decker sailing warship to be built for the French Navy.

There were, of course, changes in the style of the various fittings – rails, companionways, capstans and so on – but in a book of this nature it is impossible to go into all the details. As an example of the small changes from one class of ship to another the length of capstan bars will suffice. On the biggest ships they were 14ft long, and diminished by 6in on each successively lower class of ship.

DECORATION

By comparison with ships of the previous century, those of the 1800s were decidedly plain. The need for economy dictated the limitation of ornamentation during the Napoleonic Wars and the succeeding years, and the shift in public taste from the exuberant baroque and roccoco styles to the cooler Regency fashion supported the change. The bow was the first to be affected, for the introduction of the round bow was accompanied by a

364. A model of the midship section of the *Rodney*, 92 guns, launched in 1833, demonstrating the Seppings structural improvements including the prominent diagonal bracing. With these improvements a 2-decker like *Rodney* was 25ft longer and could carry the same number of guns as a 3-decker 2nd Rate of 30 years earlier.

365. A midship section of a 3-decker showing the methods of fastening utilised about 1800 (on the left half of the drawing) and Seppings' improvements.

Key. (a) plate bolt, (b) iron knee under beam, (c) plate knee, (d) Roberts' plate knee, (e) timber hanging knee, (f) timber standard knee, (g) plan view of knees, (h) 'T' plate knee, (j) forked knee, (k) 'side cast' (lodging) knee, (l) Seppings' forked knee and chock, (m) side plate (knee). Seppings' diagonal stiffening is well known, but he also introduced coaked frames (note the absence of chocks in his method), which allowed shorter timber to be used, and employed more ironwork to reduce the requirement for compass timber for knees, which was associated with his system of fastening the beams to the frames with more substantial deck clamps and waterways. This was a more sophisticated version of a system in use by European navies for half a century, and most of Seppings' innovations were prefigured in some way by earlier experiments. Hohlenberg's stern on the Danish *Christian VII*, for example, was regarded as the inspiration for his round stern, but Seppings' work went much further than all previous attempts, was much more practicable, and was universally accepted as a radical improvement, so he fully deserves the credit for the innovations associated with his name.

366

366. A model of the midship section of the *Vanguard*, a 2-decker designed by Sir William Symonds and launched in 1835. The model shows the V-shaped underbody favoured by Symonds. It made his ships faster sailers than those built in the older style but they were less stable gun platforms and were prone to pitch and roll more. In this model the diagonal wooden struts seen on the *Rodney* model have been replaced by iron straps and the spaces between the longitudinal timbers fitted over the floor timbers have been filled with closely packed pieces of thick plank. The waist bulwarks are hollow, the space being filled with rolled-up hammocks when preparing for a fight. Although only an 80-gun 2-decker the *Vanguard*'s measurements were slightly bigger than those of Nelson's *Victory*, and she mounted a single-calibre armament, namely: lower deck, thirty large 32pdrs; maindeck, twenty-eight medium 32pdrs and six 40cwt 32pdrs on the quarterdeck and another six on the forecastle.

raising of the head and a general lightening of its construction. The net effect of the change in position and shape of the head was to make the head rails less curved, so that by 1840 they were nearly straight. The flatness of the head was accentuated by boarding in the space between a rail that ran from the back of the figurehead to a point at the level of the forecastle and the main rail of the head.

Figureheads were drastically simplified after 1796 and only the very biggest ships were given anything more elaborate than a bust. Other 1st Rates could have a bust with supporting figures or a suitable emblematic device in place of a bust. The *Victory's* figurehead of the Royal Arms with supporters is well known. The smaller ships were supposed to make do with only a scroll or a 'fiddle-head' ornament. The new regulation was so unpopular that its rigour was relaxed to allow the first four Rates to have three-quarter length figures, but lesser ships were still expected to have a scroll head. However, even this was altered to allow all but the smallest craft to sport an emblematic figure within the limits laid down. After about 1828 a few of the biggest ships were given full length figures, but busts and half-figures became the general rule and they were usually intended as a portrait of the person after whom the ship was named. Figureheads were painted in naturalistic colours, and splendid examples are to be seen in the Neptune Hall of the National Maritime Museum. The economy drive affected the stern and quarter galleries as well as figureheads. Carved figures vanished and were replaced by painted designs on pilaster-work.

The broadside depended on paint for decoration. The experiments in styles of paintwork that had appeared in the 1790s gave way to the 'Nelson fashion' in which the hull was painted in alternating bands of black and yellowish ochre that followed the lines of the decks instead of the sheer of the hull. The ochre bands were set at the level of the gunports but these had their lids black on the outside and ochre inside, so that when the lids were shut the hull presented a checker appearance, with lines of black squares set in an ochre band between black bands. The first version of the post-Trafalgar 'Nelson fashion' had the yellowish ochre bands slightly wider

than the gunports, so that the black lids of the ports were separated from the black bands above and below. A variant that had a narrow white band above and below the port lids and marking off the yellow from the black bands is recorded from 1813 but it is not known how common the fashion was. At all events, a few years later the yellow bands were replaced by white ones, the port lids being black outside and white on the other side. The next step was to shift down the lower edge of the black bands so that they faired with the top edges of the ports, a style which remained in use until the end of the sailing warship's days and survived on merchant sailing ships until the twentieth century. In the last version of the Navy's black-and-white style the colour bands were taken right to the fore edge of the stem so that, seen from a short distance, the bows sometimes seemed to have an odd twist.

For inboard decoration the traditional red colour had been giving way to whitewash below decks since the 1780s. Above decks the red had been superseded by a yellowish ochre about 1800 and that, in turn, was replaced by a soft green shade. Finally, about 1830, the bulwarks inboard were painted white. How cabins were decorated remains to be discovered – those on the restored *Victory* are not typical because, as a flagship, her main cabins would have had a more elaborate style of decoration and probably a better finish than was usual on ships of lower rank.

367

MASTS AND YARDS

By 1800 rigging had reached the limit of its development in all but minor features. Only fore and main trysails, skysails and an extension to the gaff mizzen were added during the last 50 years of the sailing warship. A few sails went out of use although they remained 'on strength' for many years longer. The minor changes were numerous and although each one was small, in total they added substantially to the efficiency of the rigging. A simple example is the substitution of iron hoops for the traditional rope wooldings on the lower masts, a change that came opportunely since the supply of the huge American trees that had been used for masts for over 200 years was failing, and indeed, had been discontinued completely during the Wars of American Independence and of 1812-15. It was one of Sir Robert Seppings' claims to fame that when he was Surveyor of the Navy he had devised a built-up mast that could be made from smaller timber and was stronger than any other in use at the time. Another change was the shortening of the bowsprit (thereby making that important spar relatively stronger), a change that could be made because ships by the early 1800s had both a jibboom and a flying jibboom. At about the same time the dolphin-striker, which up to then had been fixed to the bowsprit cap, was given jaws like a gaff and fastened directly to the bowsprit. Besides making it easier to shift the dolphin-striker, it is likely that the change, because it gave the dolphin-striker a little play, lessened the risk of the martingale stay being carried away. The time-honoured spritsail yard was retained but it was fixed permanently to the bowsprit and served as a spreader for the jibboom's and the flying jibboom's shrouds. The spritsail itself was not officially abolished in the Royal Navy until 1830 although for some years before that the yard had been replaced by a pair of spreaders that resembled gaffs. The spritsail topsail disappeared from sight in the early years of the century although the yard may have been carried as a spare spar. How either sail could have been set when there were martingales set up is not clear[5].

367. A model of the *Albion*, a 90-gun 2-decker designed by Sir William Symonds and launched in 1842. Her dimensions were: gun-deck 204ft, breadth 60ft and draught 18ft 8in; burthen was 3111 tons. On the lower deck the *Albion* had twenty-eight 32pdrs and on the maindeck were twenty-six 32pdr guns and six 8in shell guns. The quarterdeck carried sixteen 32pdrs and two 8in guns and the forecastle had eight 32pdrs. The model exhibits the principal features of an early Victorian battleship: the built-up bow, the covered-in waist and the strong bulwarks fore and aft. Although the stern has some resemblance to an eighteenth century stern it is in fact the 'elliptical stern' introduced in 1827, a design that gave better protection to the after end of the ship and allowed more guns to be directed astern. The quarter galleries are built outside the framework of the stern and inside them the timbering of the hull is carried round the stern. Note also the round-headed rudder.

368. The sheer and profile draught of the *Brilliant*, a 20-gun ship of 1846, an example of the last phase of the sailing warship. Sheer has almost vanished, the head rails are nearly straight and there are high bulwarks from one end of the ship to the other. The cranked rudder stock shows that the round-headed rudder had come into use. On the quarters are curved iron davits.

369. The deck of the *Brilliant*. The waist is almost completely covered, giving the ship a superficial appearance of a 2-decker. The circular tracks around the bow and stern chase guns allow the guns to be trained in any direction. The guns' carriages have a pair of transversely mounted trucks under each end that run on the iron tracks laid in the deck, the carriage being held at its point of rotation by a pivot. This can be moved from one end of the carriage to the other so that the gun can be swung from either end. Note the 'round crown' anchors.

370. The deck plan for the *Banterer* class (22 guns) ordered in 1805 show the penultimate step in the covering over of the waist. The gangways are now integrated into the forecastle and quarterdeck planking, and the transverse beams are fixed.

371. However, the *Neptune* (120 guns) of 1833 has virtually no waist at all. The midships beams are as much a part of the hull structure as those under the forecastle and quarterdeck but further apart since they support no guns. There are still openings in the planking (under the boats) to allow light and air into the 'upper deck' below.

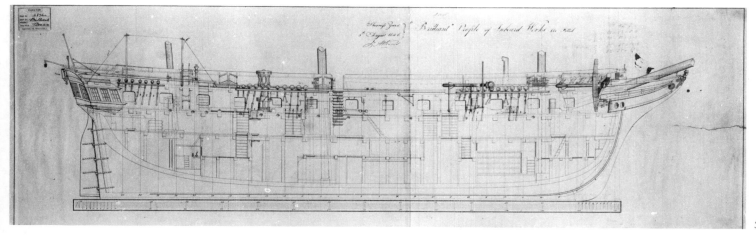

368

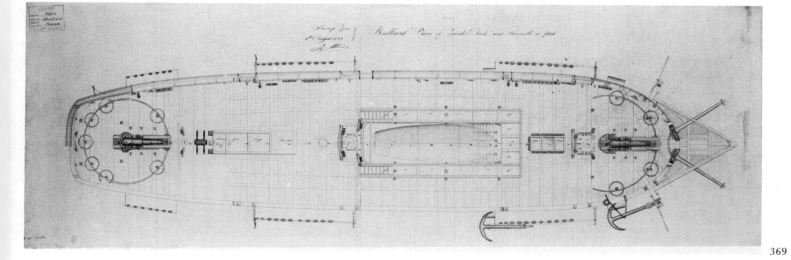

369

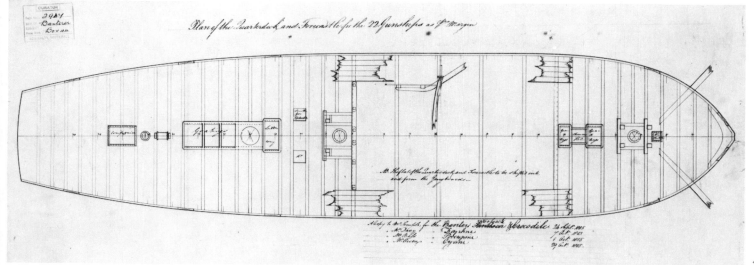

370

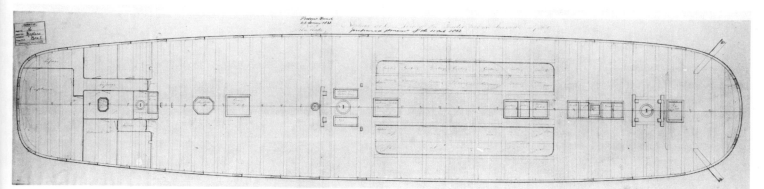

371

Aloft, three valuable innovations appeared. The lower yards were held up permanently by chain slings, the jeers being unreeved after the yards had been hoisted. At much the same time iron jackstays were fitted to the yards and the sails fastened to them instead of being lashed to the yard as they had been for centuries. The third innovation was to bring the topmast futtock shrouds down to an iron necklace round the mast below the top, instead of to the lower shrouds. By this simple arrangement a good deal of strain was taken off the lower shrouds, and off the tops, which were relieved of the racking strains set up as the lower shrouds slackened and tightened with the ship's rolling[6].

The introduction of trysails has been mentioned. These were gaff sails, like the gaff mizzen, and were set from a trysail mast fixed between the top and the deck, as a snow's trysail mast was fixed. The main trysail came into use about 1815, replacing the old mizzen staysail, and soon afterwards a fore trysail was added in place of the main staysail. These sails did not have booms. A few changes were made to the stunsails but their basic rigging was not affected.

One long overdue reform took place between the late 1820s and 1838 – a reduction in the bewildering medley of different sizes of spars for ships of even the same class. Few masts or yards could be interchanged between ships, so that the Dockyards had to carry stocks of spars far in excess of what would have been required under a rational system. The difficulties caused by the multitude of mast sizes had been recognised for a long time but little progress towards simplification took place before the end of the Napoleonic Wars. Even as late as 1829 and after some reforms had been made, different sizes of masts were still being fitted to ships of practically the same size, as these examples from John Fincham's *Treatise on the Masting of Ships* demonstrate: two ships, each 50ft in breadth, had main lower masts of 97 and 99½ft whereas two other ships, each 50½ft in breadth, required masts of 98 and 100ft. The list could be

372

extended to many times that number. Since the sizes of the other masts, and the yards, were based on the size of the main lower mast, there was a similar profusion of lengths among those spars. The explanation is that the length of the main lower mast was calculated either from the gun-deck length (later, the length of the load waterline) or the extreme breadth, so that a slight and inconsequential difference in those dimensions on two ships resulted in two different sizes of mast and therefore of all the other spars. Fincham's attempt to codify mast sizes had only a limited success and it was not until 1838 that Sir William Symonds was able to set up a *Classification of Masts and Spars* that standardised the Navy's rigging.

Partly because of the search for better systems of masting and partly because of the nineteenth century urge to disseminate useful knowledge, there is plenty of information about rigging. Besides Fincham's book, and the others mentioned in the bibliography, there is a remarkable report, published in 1847, that was written by three of the most eminent naval architects of the time after they had spent two years studying the construction and rigging of the whole Navy[7]. Both the report and Fincham's *Treatise on the Masting of Ships* are crammed with data[9].

Lower masts and bowsprit. In the 1820s and 1830s a good deal of thought was given to finding the best position for a ship's masts. The problem was more difficult to solve because scarcely two ships of a Rate were identical, and what suited one ship was not necessarily satisfactory on another. It is for this reason that Fincham, in his book on masting ships, gives a range of positions designed to suit the differing requirements of members of a class. From a modelmaker's point of view, however, this is irrelevant since mast positions are usually marked on the original plan.

There were two ways of calculating the length of the main lower mast, from which the lengths of the other masts were derived. One was to add the straight-line distance between the stem rabbet and that on the

sternpost, at the level of the waterline, to the extreme breadth of the ship. Half the sum was the length of the mast for a full-bodied ship. For fine-lined ships 17/40 was the preferred proportion. The other basis was the extreme breadth, which was the dimension that Fincham used. His figures are the fullest and most systematic up to his day, and we have included a selection in this book (see separate table). Instead of merely giving the total length of a mast, Fincham also worked out the lengths of the masts from their heels to the waterline – this last series is useful when one is reconstructing the profile of a ship.

All masts had some rake. The foremast usually leaned forwards about 3in in 12ft of length, the mainmast aft about 6in in 12ft and the mizzenmast aft about 10in in 12ft. Small ships and schooners had more rake. On brigs the foremast usually raked forwards about 3in in 12ft but the mainmast leaned aft 10in in the same length. Schooners had much more rake but there seems to be no general rule governing it, although both masts leaned aft.

The diameter of the mast at the partners was between 1/36 and 1/41 of its total length, the masts of the smaller ships being the thinner ones. The Establishment of 1807 laid down a proportion of 1/38 for a 100ft mast, 1/40 for an 80-footer but 1/40-1/41 for masts shorter than 70ft. In the 1830s a 120ft mast had a diameter of 1/36 of its length and a 73ft mast one of 1/38. These proportions remained in use but it is sometimes found that masts of slightly different lengths had the same diameter, a piece of standardisation that made the exchange of masts easier because the partners did not need altering. Slight changes were also made in the degree of taper (see tables).

Trysail masts rarely appear in rigging lists but a mizzen trysail mast should have been between 1/3 and 1/2 the diameter of the mizzenmast and without taper. The heel was secured either to a cleat or to a step on the deck and the head through a cap on the mizzenmast head, or else the trysail mast was suspended from an iron fid that rested on the trestletrees. Main and fore trysail masts were presumably fitted in the same way and had similar proportions.

Bowsprits resembled lower masts. Two factors come into account: the total length of the spar and its outboard length, the latter being much more variable than the former. To complicate matters further, the bowsprit's length might be based on the total length either of the foremast or of the lower mainmast, perhaps on their hounded length or even, as in the Symonds Establishment, on the length of the mast above the partners. Both Edye's and Fincham's proportions are given in the accompanying tables.

372. *Impregnable*, one of the last 3-decker 2nd Rates launched in 1810, photographed as a training ship (with reduced rig) about 1880. Note the 'modernised' bow and stern and the austere black and white colour scheme of the last period of the sailing navy.
373. An official draught of the Royal Navy's classification of masts and yards, 1836.
374. A Danish Navy draught of the maintop and topmast top of a French ship-of-the-line of about 1830.
375. Fittings of the yards, gaff, boom, bowsprit and crosstrees of the ship in 374.

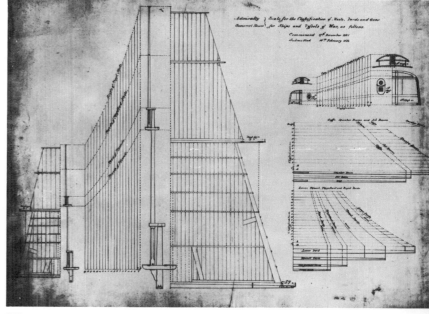

373

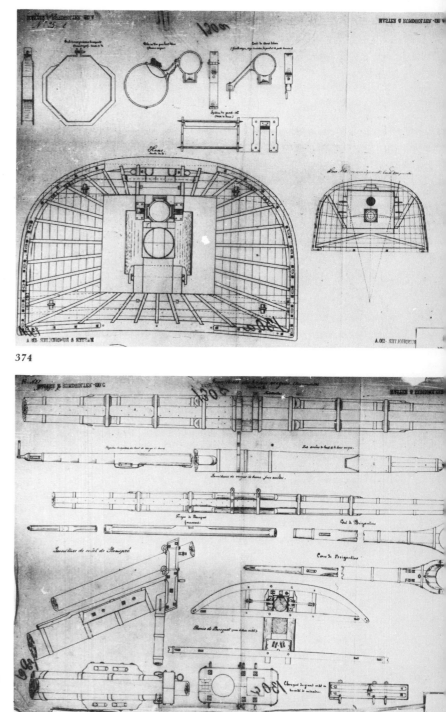

374

375

PROPORTIONATE DIMENSIONS OF MASTS AND SPARS (after Fincham)

Length as a proportion of:	Corvette (i)	(ii)	Frigate (i)	(ii)	(iii)	(iv)	2-decker (i)	(ii)	3-decker (i)	(ii)
Lengths of lower masts										
Hounded length of main lower mast — Ship's breadth	1.99	2.02	1.94	2.05	1.94	1.93	1.93	1.97	1.992	1.94
Main masthead — Hounded length of lower mast	0.1933	0.1933	0.1933	0.1933	0.1933	0.1933	0.1933	0.1933	0.1933	0.1933
Hounded length of fore lower mast — Hounded length of mainmast	0.91	0.903	0.91	0.91	0.917	0.92	0.91	0.91	0.93	0.89
Fore masthead — Hounded length of lower mast	0.1933	0.1933	0.1933	0.1933	0.1933	0.1933	0.1933	0.1933	0.1933	0.1933
Hounded length of mizzen lower mast — Hounded length of mainmast	0.85	0.863	0.773	0.754	0.73	0.737	0.7	0.7	0.69	0.71
Mizzen masthead — Hounded length of lower mast	0.161	0.156	0.156	0.156	0.156	0.156	0.156	0.156	0.156	0.156
Proportionate lengths of masts from waterline to heel										
Foremast — Total length	0.206	0.22	0.25	0.24	0.23	0.24	0.24	0.29	0.31	0.31
Mainmast — Total length	0.28	0.3	0.3	0.25	0.3	0.31	0.31	0.33	0.34	0.339
Mizzenmast — Total length	0.26	0.266	0.06	0.055	0.005	0.0	0.09 Above wl	0.09 Above wl	0.09 Above wl	0.09 Above wl
Proportionate lengths of bowsprits										
Total length of bowsprit — Hounded length of foremast	0.643	0.65	0.8	0.81	0.77	0.758	0.75	0.75	0.75	0.75
Inboard part of bowsprit as fraction of ship's length — Hounded length of foremast	0.5	0.4	0.46	0.54	0.39	0.37	0.5	0.5	0.42	0.43
Steeve (rise) in 12ft — Hounded length of foremast	64	50	63	54	60	60	72	72	72	75
Proportions of topmasts 1829										
Hounded length of main topmast — Ship's breadth	1.26	1.27	1.15	1.29	1.16	1.11	1.18	1.55	1.21	1.16
Main topmast head — Hounded length of topmast	0.154	0.154	0.156	0.156	0.156	0.156	0.156	0.156	0.156	0.156
Hounded length of fore topmast — Hounded length of main topmast	0.87	0.895	0.91	0.893	0.9	0.9	0.88	0.9	0.911	0.89
Fore topmast head — Hounded length of fore topmast	0.154	0.154	0.156	0.156	0.156	0.156	0.156	0.156	0.156	0.156
Hounded length of mizzen topmast — Hounded length of main topmast	0.702	0.725	0.77	0.737	0.755	0.72	0.736	0.71	0.67	0.71
Mizzen topmast head — Hounded length of mizzen topmast	0.154	0.154	0.156	0.156	0.156	0.156	0.156	0.156	0.156	0.156
Topmasts as proportions of lower masts										
Main topmast — Main lower mast	0.596	0.592	0.6	0.617	—	—	0.587	0.566	0.591	0.58
Fore topmast — Main lower mast	0.541	0.518	0.52	0.552	—	—	0.507	0.5	0.535	0.515
Fore topmast — Fore lower mast	0.6	0.574	0.571	0.6	—	—	0.563	0.56	0.577	0.58
Mizzen topmast — Main lower mast	0.386	0.375	0.483	0.466	—	—	0.43	0.41	0.421	0.41
Mizzen topmast — Mizzen lower mast	0.466	0.455	0.581	0.586	—	—	0.643	0.6	0.643	0.59
Lengths of topgallant masts										
Hounded length of main topgallant mast — Ship's breadth	0.7	0.683	0.61	0.657	0.6	0.57	0.61	0.6	0.61	0.6
Main topgallant pole — Hounded length	0.75	0.72	0.75	0.735	0.75	0.8	0.75	0.75	0.75	0.75
Hounded length of fore topgallant mast — Hounded length of main topgallant mast	0.9	0.93	0.9	0.92	0.9	0.9	0.85	0.882	0.91	0.89
Fore topgallant pole — Hounded length	0.75	0.72	0.75	0.735	0.75	0.8	0.75	0.75	0.75	0.75
Hounded length of mizzen topgallant mast — Hounded length of main topgallant mast	0.7	0.648	0.75	0.75	0.75	0.74	0.72	0.7	0.67	0.66
Mizzen topgallant pole — Hounded length	0.7	0.72	0.75	0.735	0.75	0.8	0.75	0.75	0.75	0.75

PROPORTIONATE DIMENSIONS OF MASTS AND SPARS (after Fincham)

Length as a proportion of:	Corvette (1)	(ii)	Frigate (i)	(ii)	(iii)	(iv)	2-decker (i)	(ii)	3-decker (i)	(ii)
Proportions of lower yards										
Mainyard — Ship's length on wl	0.54	0.541	0.553	0.59	0.54	0.53	0.54	0.53	0.53	0.53
Foreyard — Mainyard	0.9	0.88	0.873	0.87	0.876	0.872	0.872	0.86	0.86	0.86
Crossjack yard — Mainyard	0.784	0.708	0.74	0.719	0.726	0.72	0.721	0.72	0.72	0.71
Proportionate lengths of topsail and topgallant yards										
Main topsail yard — Mainyard	0.708-0.784		0.726-0.74				0.72		0.71-0.72	
Fore topsail yard — Main topsail yard	0.9		0.87-0.946				0.87		0.86	
Mizzen topsail yard — Main topsail yard	0.65-0.744		0.66-0.77				0.65-0.66		0.66	
Main topgallant yard — Main topsail yard	0.65-0.7		0.6-0.63				0.62-0.65		0.65-0.66	
Fore topgallant yard — Main topgallant yard	0.9		0.86-0.88				0.84-0.87		0.87-0.89	
Mizzen topgallant yard — Main topgallant yard	0.67-0.69		0.658-0.76				0.69-0.73		0.67-0.69	
Proportionate lengths of royal yards										
Royal yards — Respective topgallant yards	0.7		0.7				0.7		0.7	
Lengths of gaffs and booms										
Driver boom (mizzen boom) — Gun-deck length	0.37-0.4		0.348-0.41				0.362-0.37		0.36	
Gaff — Boom's length	0.754-0.774		0.724-0.759				0.75		0.75	

The bowsprit's maximum diameter, where it was fixed between the knightheads, was usually, on the biggest ships (ie those above 74 guns), the same as the mainmast's, and sometimes an inch wider, but on ships below 74 guns the general practice was to make the diameter 1½-2in less than that of the mainmast. Like masts, bowsprits tapered from their widest part to both head and heel. The heel of the bowsprit was cut to a tenon. This fitted into a mortice in a thick bed of timber, set at right angles to the axis of the bowsprit, that stood on the middle deck in 3-deckers but on the lower deck in smaller ships. At the outer end of the bowsprit was a cap similar to that at the lower mastheads but set at an angle to the bowsprit so that the cap was vertical when the bowsprit was in place. There were different ways of calculating the size of the bowsprit cap. In the early 1800s the cap's length was 5 times the diameter of the jibboom, the breadth twice the diameter of the jibboom plus half the diameter of the jackstaff, and the depth was 4/9 of the cap's breadth. Towards the middle of the century the general rule was: length, 5 × jibboom diameter; breadth, 2 × jibboom diameter; and depth, jibboom diameter less 1in. Bowsprits were hooped and woolded like lower masts.

Trestletrees, crosstrees, tops and caps. As the shapes of these are given in the previous chapter, it is only necessary to have the dimensions. These are summarised in the table, although it should be noted that Fincham has an alternative way of calculating the dimensions of trestletrees and crosstrees, namely that trestletrees are 13/14 of the fore-and-aft length of the top (and, conversely, the length of the top is 14/13 times the length of trestletrees), their depth is 1/8 of their length and in width they are 1/12. Crosstrees are 15/16 of the top's width, they are as wide as the trestletrees, but their depth is only 2/3 of their width. In the centre part of the crosstrees a piece of wood is left standing up to hold the top in place.

The trestletrees were supported by the usual bibs (brackets), the length of which was 5/6 of that of the hounds and the fore-and-aft width 2/5. Tops retained the 'D'-shape that they had in the eighteenth century and their rims slightly overhung the trestletrees and crosstrees. Some representative dimensions of tops and their supporters are given in the relevant table.

Topmasts and topgallant masts. Nineteenth century masts differed little in shape from those of the 1790s, but Rees[8] and Fincham quote some interesting dimensions, which are summarised in the tables[9]. The latter also include proportions which show the relationship between a topmast's total length and the lower mast's length, information which has been arrived at by combining the data from both sources. The topmast proportions for the Symonds Establishment have not been worked out as the mast sizes were standardised.

Topgallant masts were smaller versions of top-masts but differed in that they terminated in a pole, ie they were of round instead of square section. The pole might only be long enough for a flag-pole or it might be, in effect, a royal mast. Fidded royal masts do not seem to have been in use in the Royal Navy although they were to be found on merchant ships towards the middle of the century.

The dimensions of topgallant masts (as fractions of the main topmast) at the beginning of the nineteenth century were: fore topgallant 0.44, main topgallant 0.5, and mizzen topgallant 0.37. A simpler rule was that the topgallants were half as long as their topmasts. The lengths do not include the pole head, which was 2/5 of the foregoing lengths for a short pole and 2/3 for a long one that acted as a royal mast. Brigs had slightly different proportions. Expressed as fractions of the topmast, these were: 0.7 × foretopmast for the fore topgallant mast and 0.66 × main topmast for the main topgallant mast (18-gun brigs); and 0.66 × fore topmast and 0.63 × main topmast respectively (10-gun vessels). The taper of topgallant masts was the same as that of

PROPORTIONS OF TRESTLETREES, CROSSTREES AND CAPS – Nineteenth Century

	Source	Length	Depth	Width
Trestletrees	Rees	0.25 of topmast	0.5 × diameter of lower mast	0.33 × diameter of lower mast
	Fincham	0.23 of topmast	0.5 × diameter of lower mast	0.33 × diameter of lower mast
Crosstrees	Rees	0.33 of topmast, less 6in	2/9 × diameter of lower mast	0.33 × diameter of lower mast
	Fincham	fore: 0.33 of topmast, less 3in; after: 0.33 of topmast, less 15in	2/9 × diameter of lower mast	0.33 × diameter of lower mast
Caps (1800-1830) (Main)	Rees and Fincham	4 × diameter of topmast, plus 3in	0.25 × length	0.5 × length
(Fore)		4 × diameter of topmast, plus 2in	0.25 × length	0.5 × length
(Mizzen)		4 × diameter of topmast, plus 1in	0.25 × length	0.5 × length
	Symonds Establishment	4 × diameter of topmast	10/11 × diameter of topmast	0.5 × length

The Symonds proportions for trestletrees and crosstrees are the same as those of Rees and Fincham.

376. A 32pdr on a pivoting slide carriage of about 1830. (Compare with 370).
377. A 32pdr carronade from the last days of the sailing warship. The lower bed is privoted on a bracket fixed to the top of the waterway. There are no trucks, the lower bed resting on chocks, but the rear chocks have axles for a pair of transverse trucks. The gun has a loop for a breeching rope, fixed to the gun close to the socket for the elevating screw. The plan is dated 21 July 1859.

378. A large sharp-lined Dutch frigate of 46 guns, designed in 1803. Note the retention of lower deck oar-ports even at this late date.

376

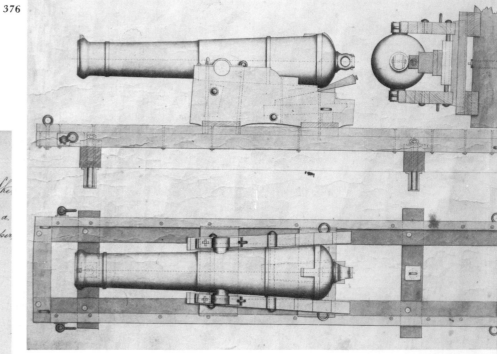

377

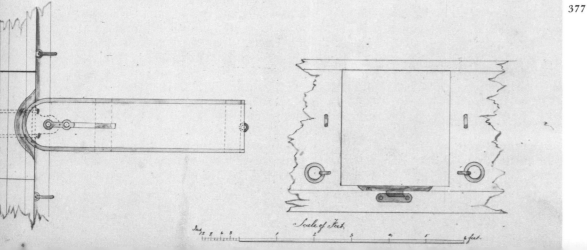

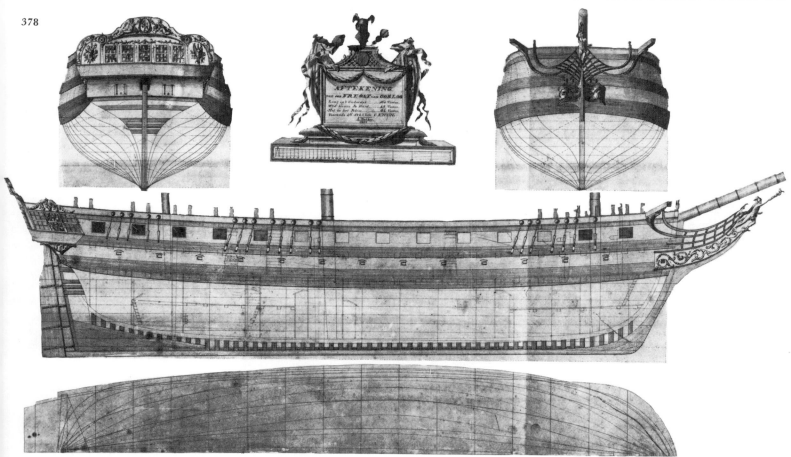

topmasts up to the rigging stop (a shoulder that took the place of the hounds), and from the stop the mast tapered to 5/9 of the topgallant mast's maximum diameter.

On the Symonds Establishment the lengths of topgallant masts ranged from 0.7 times the topmast on the biggest ships to 0.8 on the smallest. This length included the pole, which was 0.4 of the total length.

Jibbooms and flying jibbooms. The Fincham proportions for a jibboom, as a fraction of the bowsprit's length, are 0.78-0.797 for corvettes, 0.71-0.733 for frigates, 0.7-0.74 for 2-deckers and 0.7-0.75 for 3-deckers. The measurements given in Edye's *Naval Calculations* have been converted to fractions for the purposes of the tables in this book[10].

Flying jibbooms are not often listed among spar dimensions. Fincham states that their lengths relative to the jibboom were 1.2-1.22 for corvettes, 1.02-1.2 for frigates, 1.13-1.37 for 2-deckers and 1.12 for 3-deckers. In 1848 the 50-gun frigate *Phaeton*, a ship similar

to the *Vernon*, had a flying jibboom that was 1.07 times the jibboom. The spars tapered both ways from their point of maximum diameter, which, of course, would be just inboard from the cap on the end of the jibboom, and Symonds Establishment versions projected beyond the jibboom end to a length equivalent to 2/5 of the jibboom's total length. Flying jibbooms tapered in the same proportions as jibbooms except that their outer ends were 2/3 of the maximum diameter and their inner ends 3/4. The heels of the early flying jibbooms were probably lashed down but after they became established it was usual to step the heel on the jibboom's cap.

Yards, gaffs and booms. The shape of yards had been standardised by 1800 and the only change in outward appearance was the fitting of an iron jackstay on the upper surface, to which sails were bent. Jackstays were introduced in 1811, and in the same year chain slings, to hold the lower yards permanently aloft, were adopted.

REPRESENTATIVE DIMENSIONS OF TOPS AND SUPPORTERS – Nineteenth Century

Source	Topmast Length ft	Topmast Length in	Top Length ft	Top Length in	Breadth ft	Breadth in	Trestletrees Length ft	Trestletrees Length in	Depth in	Width in	Crosstrees Length (fore) ft	Crosstrees Length (fore) in	Length (after) ft	Length (after) in	Depth in	Width in
Fincham	73	0	–		–		16	$11\frac{1}{4}$	19	$12\frac{5}{8}$	22	$9\frac{3}{4}$	23	$9\frac{3}{4}$	$8\frac{3}{8}$	$12\frac{5}{8}$
	65	0	–		–		15	1	$16\frac{7}{8}$	$11\frac{1}{4}$	20	$0\frac{1}{2}$	21	$0\frac{1}{2}$	$7\frac{1}{2}$	$11\frac{1}{4}$
	60	0	–		–		13	11	$15\frac{3}{8}$	$10\frac{3}{8}$	18	9	19	9	$6\frac{7}{8}$	$10\frac{3}{8}$
	55	0	–		–		12	9	$14\frac{1}{4}$	$9\frac{1}{2}$	17	$2\frac{1}{2}$	18	$2\frac{1}{2}$	$6\frac{3}{8}$	$9\frac{1}{2}$
	52	0	–		–		12	$1\frac{1}{2}$	$13\frac{3}{4}$	$9\frac{1}{8}$	16	3	17	3	$6\frac{1}{8}$	$9\frac{1}{8}$
Symonds	73	6	15	10	26	6	–		21	14	–		–		$9\frac{1}{2}$	14
Establishment	65	6	14	2	23	6	–		$18\frac{3}{4}$	$12\frac{1}{2}$	–		–		$8\frac{1}{4}$	$12\frac{1}{2}$
	59	6	12	11	21	6	–		$17\frac{1}{4}$	$11\frac{1}{4}$	–		–		$7\frac{3}{4}$	$11\frac{1}{2}$
	55	0	11	10	19	9	–		$15\frac{1}{4}$	$10\frac{1}{4}$	–		–		$6\frac{3}{4}$	$10\frac{1}{4}$

The proportions of the square hole in the top were: length, 0.6 of the fore-and-aft length of the top; width, 0.36 of the top's width.

SIZES OF TOPMASTS (after Rees)

| Topmast | 74-gun ship | | 40-gun ship | |
	As fraction of mainmast	As fraction of own mast	As fraction of mainmast	As fraction of own mast
Fore	0.522	0.596	0.527	0.591
Main	0.596	0.596	0.591	0.591
Mizzen	0.44	0.516	0.45	0.545

PROPORTIONATE DIAMETERS OF TOPMASTS
(ratio of greatest diameter to length)

Ship	Fore	Main	Mizzen
74-gun ship	1:35	1:39.5	1:40
40-gun frigate	1:35.5	1:40	1:42.5

PROPORTIONATE DIAMETERS OF TOPMASTS
– typical examples (after Fincham)

Topmast	Diameter in	Length ft	Ratio
Fore and main	24	80	1:40
	22	73	1:40
	18	60	1:40
	15	50	1:40
	12	38	1:38
	10	31	1:37
	8½	26	1:37
Mizzen	15	54	1:43
	14	50	1:43
	11	39	1:42.5
	9	30	1:40
	8½	28	1:42

DIMENSIONS OF JIBBOOMS
– early Nineteenth Century

Size as a fraction of:

Ship	Bowsprit	Foremast	Mainmast
74-gun ship	0.744	0.5	0.45
40-gun frigate	0.7	0.47	0.42

TAPER IN SPARS – Nineteenth Century

Date	1st quarter	2nd quarter	3rd quarter	Ends
Jibbooms				
Before 1820	40/41	11/12	5/6	2/3 outer, 5/9 inner
Symonds Establishment	60/61	13/14	5/6	2/5 outer
Yards				
Early 1800s	30/31	7/8	7/10	3/7
Early 1830s	40/41	9/10	3/4	1/2
Gaffs				
Early 1800s	40/41	11/12	4/5	5/9
Booms				
Early 1800s	40/41	11/12	5/6	2/3

Jibbooms tapered from a point 1/3 of the length from the inner end to the outer end (and sometimes to the inner end); yards tapered from the centre to the ends; gaffs tapered from the splice of the jaws to the end; and booms tapered in each direction from a point 1/3 the distance from the outer end.

Although yards did not change in appearance they were increasingly made from several pieces of timber as the supply of huge trees formerly used began to slow down. Even topsail yards were sometimes built up. The information in the previous chapter will serve for nineteenth century yards if the appropriate alterations are made to their proportions. All that is necessary here is to give those proportions at the significant dates.

The lengths of all yards derived, directly or indirectly, from the length of the main lower mast. In the early part of the nineteenth century the lengths were as follows: mainyard, 8/9 of the mainmast; foreyard, 7/8 of the mainyard or 7/9 of the mainmast; lateen mizzen-yard (obsolete), 6/7 of the mainyard or 16/21 of the mainmast; and crossjack yard, 5/9 of the mainmast. The yards' diameters at the slings were 1/48 of the yard's length for the fore- and mainyard and the same diameter as the fore topsail yard for the crossjack yard. Pre-1820 proportions for topsail and topgallant yards were as follows: main topsail yard, 5/7 of mainyard or 40/63 of the main lower mast; fore topsail yard, 7/8 of main topsail yard or 5/9 of the mainmast; and mizzen topsail yard, 2/3 of the main topsail yard. Topgallant yards on 74-gun ships and upwards were 2/3 of the respective topsail yards but on ships below 74 guns they were 3/5, whilst royal yards were half the length of the topsail yards. The diameters at the slings were: topsail yards, 5/8in per yard of length; topgallant yards, 3/5in per yard; and royal yards, 5/16in per yard. Other details are given in the tables. The diameters of the yards at the slings was 1/56 on the big ships and 1/58 of the yard's length on the small ones. The taper was in the same proportions as for the lower yards. Spritsail and spritsail topsail were the same size as the fore topsail and fore topgallant yards.

Although they are not listed in official rigging inventories, skysail yards, usually thought of as specialities of the clipper ships, were in use early in the nineteenth century. The British 20-gun ship *Bacchante* carried skysails in 1808 and, moreover, she had a 'lateen' sail set above her main skysail[11]. Presumably this was the sort of triangular sail later known as a raffee. US warships had skysails by about the same time, if not earlier – the frigate *President* had skysail yards on all three masts at the time of the 1812-15 War[12].

Nineteenth century sources have surprisingly little to say about stunsail yards and booms. Rees' *Naval Architecture* merely repeats Steel's tables, and Fincham gives only the length of the main stunsail boom – 0.6 of the mainyard – although he states that the diameter of stunsail yardarms was 3/7-1/2 of the maximum diameter of the stunsail yard. Fortunately the Symonds Establishment gives full dimensions, and from these it may be calculated what proportions the yards and booms bear to the length of the mainmast above the partners.

Gaffs and booms differed in shape in that gaffs tapered from the jaws outwards but booms tapered towards each end from the point of maximum diameter (see previous chapter). The length of the driver boom in about 1800 was 30/41 of the mainyard, and the gaff was 11/20 of the length of the boom. Later booms and gaffs were long spars. A contemporary model of an 84-gun ship of about 1820 in the Science Museum, London, has a boom that is about 0.3 of the ship's waterline length and a gaff that is about 0.2. These figures approach those given by Fincham. Trysail gaffs on mainmasts were 1/3 the length of the mizzen gaff, and fore trysail gaffs were 1/2. There were no booms to the trysails.

RIGGING

The only new standing rigging to be introduced during the last 60 years of the sailing warship was that for the flying jibboom and the chain slings for the lower yards. Minor changes were no doubt made to all parts of the rigging but they have not found their way into our authorities' books, except for the change in the setting up of the topmast shrouds. A general comment that applies equally to running rigging is that because of improvements in the manufacture of rope, and probably in the quality of the raw material, nineteenth century rope was stronger, size for size, than before and consequently, although ships were bigger than they had ever been, the size of their ropework differed little from what it was in the 1790s.

Lower masts and bowsprit. Up to the 1820s, and perhaps later, the number of shrouds for each class of ship was the same as it had been in the late eighteenth century, but under the Symonds Establishment there was actselly a slight reduction in the number. The widths of fore and main deadeyes ranged from 0.43 of the mainmast's diameter on big ships to 0.48 on small ones. Mizzen deadeyes' widths were 0.46 of the mizzenmast's diameter (big ships), 0.42 (frigates) and 0.39 (corvettes). Deadeyes were somewhat flatter in cross-section than those of the previous century but were still bi-convex in the early nineteenth century. After the establishment of the block-making machines, (see below), the shape was standardised as only slightly bi-convex, but with well-rounded edges.

A few experiments were made with wire rope but it was not taken up by the the Royal Navy. This was not due solely to the difficulties of handling wire rope but, no doubt to a great part, to the problems of obtaining replacements overseas.

There were no changes to the bowsprit's rigging, but the jibboom was rigged as it was at the end of the eighteenth century and the flying jibboom was set up in a similar manner.

Topmasts and topgallant masts. Until about 1811 the topmast futtock shrouds were set up to the lower shrouds in the traditional way, but after that date the practice of securing them to a chain necklace round the lower mast came into general use. The necklace was set round the mast at the level of the futtock staff. No new running rigging appeared. When extra sails such as fore and main trysails were added their rigging was similar to that of sails already in use.

Blocks and deadeyes. Improvements in block-making in the second half of the eighteenth century had brought about some reduction in size, easier running and some degree of standardisation, but blocks (and deadeyes) were still made largely by hand. Mechanisation and standardisation came in 1805 when Marc Brunel set up his revolutionary block-making machinery in Portsmouth Dockyard. In a very short time the machine-made article established its superiority over the old-style block: not only did the machines produce blocks at a much greater rate, but the sizes and quality were uniform and the machines could be quickly adjusted to make blocks of any desired size. Furthermore, the new blocks had improved metal bushes and pins and consequently lasted longer. Brunel's machinery is still in existence at Portsmouth[13].

The standard dimensions of nineteenth century single blocks, which were based, of course, on the size of the rope to be led through them, were:
Thickness of sheave: 1.1 x diameter of rope
Diameter of sheave: 5 x thickness
Depth of groove in sheave: 1/3 thickness of sheave
Width of sheavehole in block: sheave's thickness+1/16in
Length of block: 8 x width of sheavehole
Breadth of block: 6 x width of sheave (6.6 x diameter of rope)
Thickness of block: 4 x width of sheavehole.
If the block was flat sided instead of bi-convex, the thickness was only 3 x width of sheavehole.

The sizes of sheaves and sheaveholes for multi-sheave blocks, and the length and width of these blocks, have the same relation to the rope's size as in single blocks, but the thickness is governed by the number of sheaves and the partitions between them, each partition being, in thickness, 5/6 of that of the sheave.

A table given by Fincham supplies the required information to enable the actual sizes of blocks to be worked out, but it should be noted that Fincham makes his sheaves 1 1/8 times the rope's diameter.

Like blocks, deadeyes were produced to standardised sizes by the Brunel machinery. Their widths are commonly to be found in rigging lists but for some reason the thickness of deadeyes is not given. Judging from models, however, the thickness of a deadeye was about twice the diameter of its shroud.

SAILS

With the introduction of the flying jib the spritsail and spritsail topsail disappeared. The flying jib was rigged in the same manner as the jib. Fore and main trysails took the places of main and mizzen staysails and were rigged as the mizzen gaffsail except that they lacked a boom to their lower edges. Otherwise the sail's gear was the same as at the end of the eighteenth century.

ARMAMENT

Until the very end of their days sailing warships carried the same sort of smooth-bore guns that had been in use in Henry VIII's time. Solid iron round shot were still the principal missiles but by the 1850s explosive spherical shells had come into use. Although guns and carriages were much the same as those of the eighteenth century, changes did, of course, take place. As with rigging, progress towards standardisation was slow, and as late as 1820 ten calibres of cannon and 29 gun lengths were officially in use with the Royal Navy, together with seven calibres of carronade and two of mortar, although to what extent such an assortment of sizes was in actual use is another question[14,15].

Shorter barrels did not mean lighter guns. On the contrary, nineteenth century guns were often heavier than the older ones of the same calibre because improvements in powder quality made it necessary to strengthen them. After 1820, shell-firing guns gradually came into use. They were 8in bore and were nominally rated at 68pdrs although an 8in shell did not weigh as much as that.

Notwithstanding the multiplicity of calibres and lengths, steps had been taken towards a standardised armament before the century opened although many years passed before that aim was fully realised. Up to about 1811, 3-deckers, for example, had 32pdrs on the lower deck (a few still had the old 42pdrs), 24pdrs on the middle deck, and 18pdrs on the upper deck, whilst on the forecastle and quarterdeck were 12pdrs and 32pdr carronades. 68pdr carronades were sometimes carried, as the *Victory* did at Trafalgar. Even in 1815 the new 3-decker *Nelson* was to have had 32 32pdrs on the lower deck, 34 24pdrs on the middle deck, and 34 18pdrs on the upper deck, with 6 12pdrs and 10 32pdr carronades on the quarterdeck and forecastle and 6 18pdr carronades

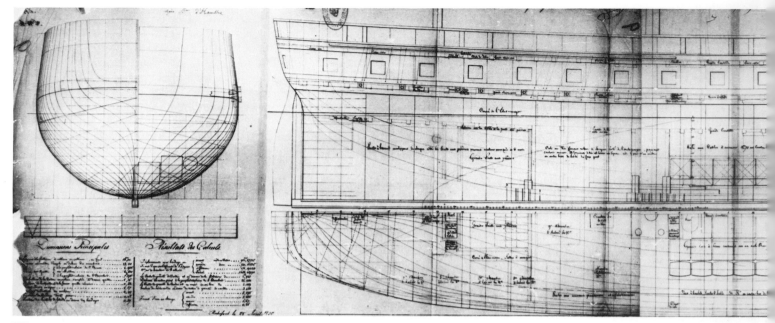

379

379. The design draught fot a French frigate of 46 guns dated 25 April 1830. With little sheer, no stern galleries and a built-up bow the ships of this generation lost much of the grace of their predecessors – which may partly account for the lack of interest in the last half-century of sailing warships.

380. The British 50-gun frigate *Vindictive*. Launched as a 74-gun ship in 1813, she was cut down to a frigate in 1832, when she was given an elliptical stern.

380

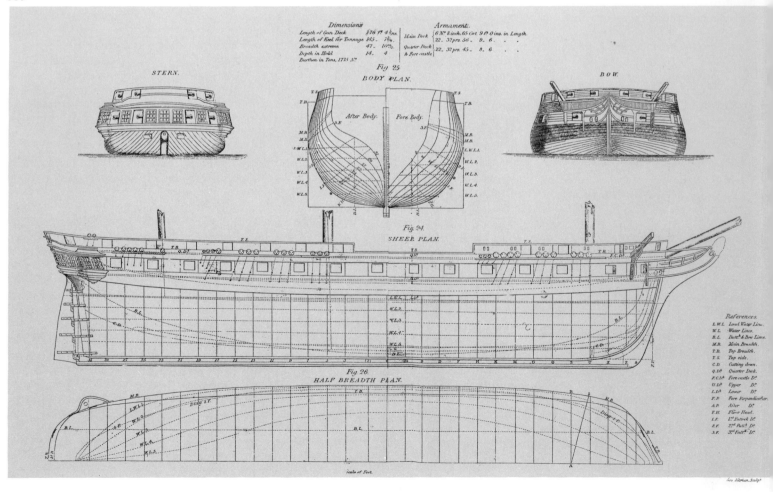

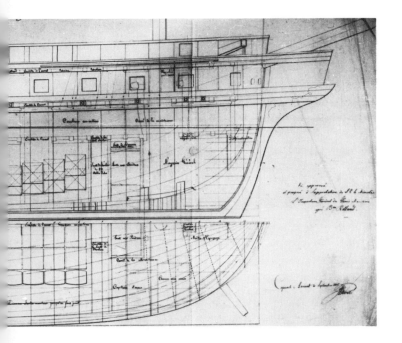

Like guns, truck carriages changed only slightly. The explanation is that the truck carriage, for all its cumbrousness, was well fitted for its purpose and for the conditions likely to be met with in service. The carriage was easy to make and repair, and the raw materials were available almost everywhere. The superior strength of iron carriages was recognised but the difficulty of repairing them away from a dockyard told against their general use. Of the changes that took place between 1800 and 1860 the most obvious was the replacement of the rear pair of trucks by wooden slide blocks. The friction between the blocks and the deck slowed down the gun's recoil and took some of the strain off the breeching rope. What happened to the deck planking is another matter, and so is what the gun crews had to say about the extra effort needed to run the guns out.

The carronade remained a feature of ships' armament right to the end, but it is surprising to find, as late as 1840, ships still being armed very largely with carronades even though the American War had shown the necessity of having an adequate battery of long range guns. The multiplicity of calibres and gun lengths was as typical of carronades as it was of cannon: in 1820 there were seven calibres and nine barrel lengths in service.

The shape of carronades changed little, the principal modification being the screw elevator fitted to the cascabel. A foresight was also added and was cast with the barrel. Some carronades were mounted on truck carriages but most were on non-recoil beds fixed on a pivot close to the bulwarks. One variety of bed had small trucks at its rear end, set with their axles parallel with the gun's axis, so that the gun could be traversed more easily than by levering with crowbars. Swivel guns fell out of use early in the century, being replaced by small carronades.

At the beginning of the nineteenth century there were a number of experiments with very short barrelled cannon – sometimes referred to as 'gunnades' – mid-way in length between carronades and long guns. These are best known because of the lightweight 24pdrs which were fitted in lieu of 18pdrs on a few British 38-gun frigates during the War of 1812. However, they were not designed in response to the challenge of the US 24pdr frigates as is often thought, but were already in existence at that time. Indeed, the oldest type, Gover's Patent, had been in widespread use with the East India Company since the end of the eighteenth century and had been

on the poop. As a result of the experience of the American War of 1812-1815, however, enthusiasm for the carronade waned, and before the *Nelson* was commissioned her poop carronades were scrapped and she was given 24pdr guns on the upper deck instead of the original 18pdrs. Large frigates were armed with 24pdr guns and 32pdr carronades; smaller frigates, such as the *Amethyst* of 1811, had 26 18pdr cannon on the gun-deck and 12 32pdr carronades on the quarterdeck, as well as 2 9pdr cannon and 4 32pdr carronades on the forecastle. After 1820 there was a gradual reduction in the number of calibres until by 1840 only six were in use and many ships had all their guns of the same bore though not the same length.

Except for the shortening of the barrel there was little change in the shape of the guns until the end of the 1840s. Nevertheless, as in previous centuries, there were small differences that mark out a gun of one decade from one of another. A new feature of nineteenth century guns was a sight. Fixed foresights on ship guns were undesirable because of the risk of their catching on the top edge of a gunport. The new sights were not an integral part of the gun but were detachable fittings that were taken off when the gun was not in use.

TAPER IN MASTS – Nineteenth Century					
Date	Heel	1st quarter	2nd quarter	3rd quarter	Head
Masts					
Before 1820	6/7	60/61	15/16	7/8	Lower: fore-and-aft 3/4, thwartships 7/8; upper: 5/8
Symonds Establishment	5/6	60/61	20/21	8/9	Lower: 4/5; upper: 2/5
Bowsprits					
Before 1820	2/3	60/61	11/12	4/5	5/9 (cap)
1820s	5/6	60/61	14/15	5/6	2/3 (cap)
Symonds Establishment	5/6	40/41	10/11	7/9	5/9 (cap)
Topmasts					
Before 1820	6/7	60/61	14/15	6/7	3/4 at hounds, 5/8 at cap
After 1830	–	60/61	20/21	8/9	4/5 at hounds, 9/12 at cap

Masts and topmasts tapered from the partners to both head and heel; bowsprits tapered from the bed (3/10 the length from the heel) to both cap and heel.

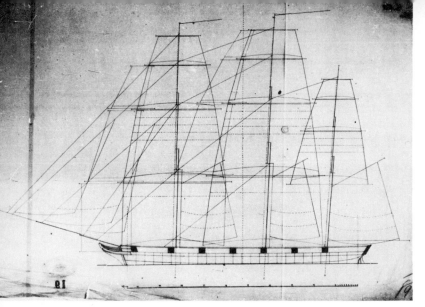

381

381. An example of the lofty rig applied to small craft in the nineteenth century – a Danish sail plan for a 12-gun ship sloop.

382. The profile draught of the *Columbine* brig built in 1834 to the design of Sir William Symonds. The *Columbine* is an example of the extreme 'peg-top' section used in Symonds' early designs. To compensate for the fineness of the underbody the *Columbine* was made broader than full-bodied ships of the same length. Her gun-deck:breadth ratio was just over 3:1 compared with proportions of up to 3.6:1 for earlier brigs. Although they were fast sailers ships of this form were unsatisfactory gun platforms because of their tendency to excessive pitching and rolling.

383. The 12-gun brig *Daring* built to the design of William White in 1844. The *Daring* was one of the Experimental Squadron of seven ships, built to different designs, that were subjected to extensive sailing trials in 1844–5. The *Daring* was one of the fastest and had excellent all-round qualities. Although she was very similar in size to the *Columbine* the *Daring's* hull was fuller, though with a good deal of deadrise, and there was less rake at bow and stern.

under discussion by the Admiralty since 1797. The first short 24pdrs were ordered to be tested in a 36-gun frigate in June 1800, and in December 1806 several of the smaller '74's were given a homogeneous armament of 'long' 24s, Gover's Patent 24s (6ft 6in long and weighing 39cwt) and 24pdr carronades.

However, the War of 1812 certainly spurred developments of two further 24pdr types, General Blomefield's 7ft 6in 40cwt gun and Congreve's 7ft 6in gun of 40½cwt. A parallel trial was organised in 1813 between two sister '38's, the *Cydnus* carrying Blomefield's guns and the *Eurotas* with Congreve's. The latter were considered superior and 300 were ordered. In the following decade a short 32pdr was also introduced, thus allowing ships-of-the-line to carry a homogeneous armament based on the 32pdr calibre, but this was a short-lived development since guns rapidly became larger and were fitted to fire explosive shells.

The mortars on bomb-vessels were of two sizes only, 10in and 13in. Their lengths were 4ft 8in and 5ft 3in respectively.

MORTARS: dimensions of beds				
	10in		13in	
	ft	in	ft	in
Length	7	0	7	10
Breadth	3	11	4	6
Depth	2	5	2	11

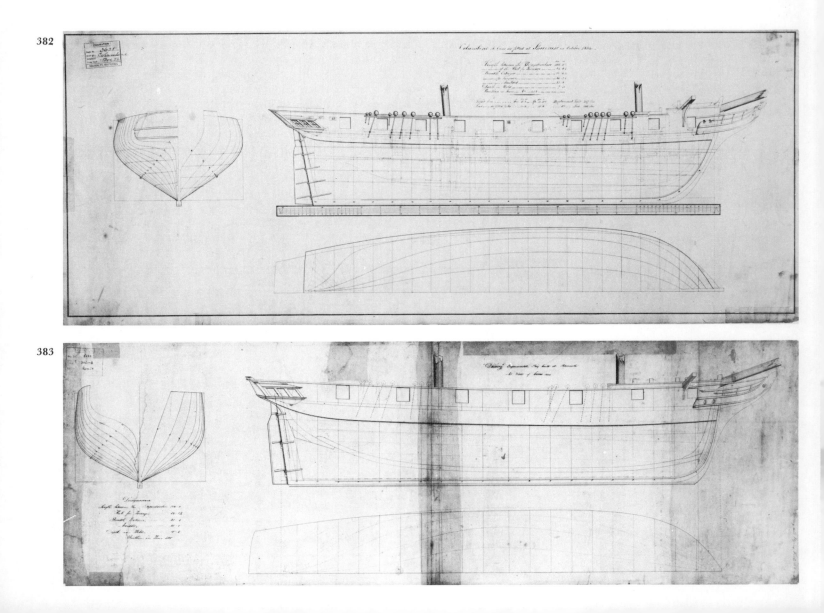

382

383

DIMENSIONS OF SPARS (after Edye)

Spar	Length as a fraction of:	120 guns	80 guns	74 guns	50-gun razee	52 guns	46 guns	40 guns	26-gun razee	18-gun corvette	18-gun brig	10-gun brig
Bowsprit	Foremast	0.68		0.66				0.66			0.73	0.77
	Mainmast	0.623		0.61				0.62			0.63	0.66
Jibboom	Foremast	0.48	0.46	0.49	0.49	0.53	0.48		0.48	0.51	0.45	0.57
	Mainmast	0.44	0.42	0.5	0.5	0.48	0.44		0.42	0.46	0.42	0.5
	Bowsprit	0.7	0.714	0.73	0.73	0.76	0.73		0.72	0.74	0.67	0.75
Foreyard	Mainmast	0.76	0.75	0.77	0.78	0.85	0.8		0.8	0.78	0.8	0.88
Mainyard	Mainmast	0.87	0.86	0.9	0.89	0.98	0.9		0.9	0.89	0.81	0.9
Crossjack yard	Mainmast	0.61	0.62	0.65	0.65	0.71	0.66		0.66	0.66		
Fore topsail yard	Mainyard	0.62	0.63	0.64	0.64	0.62	0.65		0.65	0.65	0.77	0.81
Fore topgallant yard	Mainyard	0.41	0.38	0.42	0.48	0.41	0.41		0.4	0.4	0.5	0.53
Main topsail yard	Mainyard	0.71	0.73	0.73	0.73	0.71	0.72		0.73	0.74	0.77	0.77
Main topgallant yard	Mainyard	0.47	0.45	0.47	0.47	0.47	0.46		0.46	0.45	0.5	0.4
Mizzen topsail yard	Mainyard	0.47	0.46	0.47	0.47	0.47	0.5		0.49	0.49		
Mizzen topgallant yard	Mainyard	0.35	0.33	0.33	0.33	0.32	0.37		0.38	0.34		

ARMAMENT 1800–1839

Calibre/ weight of shot	Length ft	in	Calibre/ weight of shot	Length ft	in	Calibre/ weight of shot	Length ft	in
1800			*1820 continued*			*1820 continued*		
32pdr	10	9	18pdr	9	0	$\frac{1}{2}$pdr swivel	3	0
24pdr	10	0	18pdr	8	0			
18pdr	10	0	18pdr	6	0	*1839*		
12pdr	9	3	18pdr carronade	3	3	68pdr (nominal 8in)	10	10
9pdr	8	3	18pdr carronade	2	4	68pdr (nominal 8in) carronade	5	4
6pdr	7	8	12pdr	9	0	8in	9	0
4pdr	5	9	12pdr	8	6	8in	8	10
			12pdr	7	6	8in	8	0
1820			12pdr carronade	2	2	8in	7	0
68pdr carronade	5	2	9pdr	9	0	32pdr	9	6
68pdr carronade	4	0	9pdr	8	6	32pdr	9	0
42pdr carronade	4	4	9pdr	8	0	32pdr	8	6
32pdr	9	6	9pdr	7	6	32pdr	8	0
32pdr	8	6	9pdr	7	0	32pdr	7	6
32pdr carronade	4	0	6pdr	8	6	32pdr	6	6
24pdr	9	6	6pdr	8	0	32pdr	6	0
24pdr	9	0	6pdr	7	6	32pdr	5	4
24pdr	8	0	6pdr	7	0	32pdr carronade	4	0
24pdr	7	6	6pdr	6	6	24pdr carronade	3	9
24pdr	7	0	6pdr	6	0	18pdr	6	0
24pdr	6	6	6pdr carronade	2	8	18pdr	5	6
24pdr	6	0	4pdr	6	0	18pdr carronade	3	4
24pdr carronade	3	8	4pdr	5	6	12pdr carronade	2	8
24pdr carronade	3	0	3pdr	4	6	6pdr	6	0

GUN CARRIAGES AND SLIDES c1800

Gun	Gun carriage Length ft	in	Overall length of axle ft	in	Height to underside of gun ft	in	Carronade slide Height ft	in	Thickness ft	in	Thickness of chock ft	in	Breadth ft	in	Length ft	in	Diameter of bolt ft	in
68pdr							1	$9\frac{3}{4}$	0	$7\frac{3}{4}$	0	5	2	$6\frac{1}{2}$	8	0	0	2
42pdr							1	$9\frac{1}{2}$	0	7	0	$5\frac{1}{2}$	2	$2\frac{1}{2}$	6	$10\frac{1}{2}$	0	$2\frac{3}{4}$
32pdr	6	3	4	9	2	9	1	7	0	6	0	3	2	0	6	6	0	2
24pdr	5	10	4	7	2	8	1	6	0	$5\frac{3}{4}$	0	$3\frac{1}{4}$	1	9	6	4	0	1
18pdr	5	$8\frac{1}{2}$	4	4	2	$4\frac{1}{2}$	1	7	0	5	0	4	1	8	5	4	0	1
12pdr	5	3	3	10	1	10	1	4	0	5	0	4	1	8	5	7	0	1
9pdr	4	10	3	$6\frac{1}{2}$	1	$10\frac{1}{2}$												
6pdr	4	5	3	$3\frac{1}{2}$	1	10												
4pdr	3	6	3	0	1	9												

SUPPORT CRAFT

At the end of the eighteenth century the frigate had reached a stage of development from which it might have seemed that any further growth in size, though to be expected, would not take place soon nor to any great degree. Developments in the United States upset those expectations. In the late 1790s the US Navy built several frigates that were, by contemporary standards, almost line-of-battle ships. The three biggest, *Constitution*, *President*, and *United States*, measured 173ft on the gun-deck, 44ft in breadth and were of 14ft depth in hold, corresponding to a burthen of just over 1500 tons. Nominally rated as 44-gun frigates, they carried 30 24pdr 'long' guns and 20-22 carronades (42-pdrs). Because of its preoccupation with the French and allied naval forces the British Admiralty were slow to react to the potential menace of these huge frigates and it was not until a war with the United States appeared on the horizon that active steps were taken to provide a counter to them, and to the slightly smaller but very powerful companion classes that the US Navy had built. War broke out before the Admiralty's designs had been put into practice. The American frigates scored several successes over smaller and less powerful British ships and, naturally, the most was made of them in the resulting publicity and propaganda. The British Admiralty's first counter-move was to convert three 74-gun ships into 2-decked frigates by cutting away the quarterdeck and forecastle but retaining the guns on the upper deck. The armament was 28 carriage guns and 28 carronades (42pdrs) as well as two 'long' 12pdr chase guns. Then, in 1813, two 2-decked frigates were launched. The design of the *Leander* and the *Newcastle*, of 1572 tons, pre-dated the outbreak of war but are usually regarded as 'answers' to the *Constitution* and her sisters. Each was armed with 30 'long' 24pdrs on the maindeck and 26 carronades (42pdrs) together with two (later 4) 'long' 24pdrs on the upper or spar deck. These 2-decked frigates were not a success and no more were built after the Peace of 1815. Instead, the 'classical' frigate was developed into a 50-gun ship. These 'heavy frigates', as they were called, were the battlecruisers of their day. One of the last of them, the *Constance*, built in 1846, was 180ft on the gun-deck (only 6ft less than the *Victory's* gun-deck) and her breadth was actually 15in more than that ship's. The two ships were almost the same in tonnage: the *Constance* measured 2132, the *Victory* 2162. The *Constance's* armament was 10 8in shell guns, 22 32pdrs and 18 small 32pdrs. 'Heavy frigates' were sometimes made from cut-down '74's after 1815 but they were all single-decked. The 50-gun frigate *Vindictive* is an example. She was launched in 1813 as a 74-gun ship with a gun-deck of 176ft, a beam of almost 48ft and a depth in hold of 21ft. In 1832 she was cut down a deck and converted into a frigate of 1775 tons burthen. The *Vindictive's* armament was six 8in guns 9ft long, 22 32pdrs 9½ft long and 22 32pdrs 8½ft long. 'Heavy frigates' were not, of course, the only members of the class to be built. There were 26-, 36-, 38-, 42- and 46-gun ships. The frigate class was the focus of much of the experimentation in design during the 1830s and 1840s and careful comparisons were made of the performance of the different hull forms. As with the clipper ships, however, perfection was attained almost at the moment that the type became obsolete.

384

| | | | | BRIGS OF THE EXPERIMENTAL SQUADRON | |
Ship	Date	Length (ft)	Breadth (ft)	Depth (ft)	Tonnage	Designer
Mutine	1844	112	32	13½	428	Fincham
Flying Fish	1844	103	32⅓	14⅓	445	Symonds
Espiegle	1844	104⅓	31	13	443	Read, Chatfield & Creuze
Pantaloon	1831	92	29⅓	12½	323	Symonds
Daring	1844	104	31⅓	15	426	White
Osprey	1844	101½	32	13¾	425	Blake
Cruizer	1818	100	31	12	384	After a design by Rule

385

Below the frigate class were sloops and corvettes, brigs and brigantines, and schooners and cutters. Sloops and corvettes were ship-rigged vessels but differed in build – a sloop had a raised quarterdeck and forecastle but corvettes were flush-decked. Both classes mounted 14-18 guns. Brigs were classed with sloops and, like those ships, were armed with 14-18 guns. Brigs were the subject of a good deal of research into hull design and in the 1840s an experimental squadron of seven of them, each built to a different design, was put through an extensive series of trials (see table). The trials showed that none of the designs had an overall superiority in sailing properties. The Symonds ships did best in smooth water but in a head sea the *Daring* was the most weatherly. This ship was also the best in strong breezes. With a beam wind the three fastest brigs were the *Daring*, *Espiegle* and *Flying Fish* but before the wind the oldest vessel, the *Cruizer* outsailed the others.

The rig of nineteenth century brigs differed slightly from that of the previous century. The mainmast had a square mainsail (which the earlier brigs lacked) as well as a gaffsail. It was possible to set a square mainsail because the mainyard was kept permanently aloft – this allowed the gaff to run on the mainmast and the gaffsail to be hooped to the mast instead of to a horse or a trysail mast as it was on snows.

The search for the best proportions for brigs' masts and spars attracted as much attention as that for their best hull form. John Fincham devoted a whole section of his book *On the Masting of Ships* to brigs.

A brig had the distinction of being the only sailing warship built of iron for the Royal Navy. The ship was the *Recruit*, built in 1846. She was 114½ft on the gun-deck, 30½ft in beam and 12½ft in draught. The *Recruit* was a victim of the prevailing prejudice against iron for building warships and her qualities were never tested.

Brigantines were a class of vessel that enjoyed a brief spell of popularity in the 1830s and 1840s. They were small ships, and some were used off the west coast of Africa in suppressing the slave trade. The *Bonetta*, of 319 tons, was the pattern for the group: she was 90ft 7in long, 29ft 3in in beam and 14ft 6in deep. The armament was one large and two small 32pdrs.

Schooners were more popular than brigantines. They were used mostly in American waters and many British examples were, in fact, captured American vessels although schooners were built in Britain for the Navy and were used down to the end of the sailing warship era. British schooners were usually small ships. The *Express*, 92 tons and built in 1815, is such an

384. A model of the 16-gun brig *Fantome*, launched in 1839. Carrying four 32-dr guns and twelve 32pdr carronades, she was one of a class of 14 brigs designed by Sir William Symonds. All had steeply rising floors and the fine lines that characterised his designs. The hull of the model is a contemporary one but the rigging was added in 1902 and is to the dimensions established for the class by Symonds in 1836.

385. A model of a naval schooner of about 1850: a small vessel, only 74ft on the deck and 47½ft keel. The breadth was 18ft 7in and the depth in hold about 8ft 9in. The schooner was thus much the same size as the cutter represented in 396. Although there are 18 ports it is unlikely that so small a ship would carry 18 guns unless they were very light. The hull has virtually no sheer, the head knee is set high up and the head rails are nearly straight. The round head of the rudder is clearly seen as are the simple hand pumps beside the mainmast.

NUMBERS AND LENGTHS OF BOATS 1842–1844

Class of ship	Barge	Launch	Pinnace	Yawl or cutter	Jolly-boat	Gig	Dinghy
3-deckers	1 × 32ft	1 × 38ft or 40ft	1 × 30ft or 32ft	2 × 25ft or 26ft	1 × 20ft	1 × 28ft	–
2-deckers	1 × 32ft	1 × 38ft or 40ft	1 × 30ft or 32ft	2 × 25ft or 26ft	1 × 20ft	1 × 28ft	–
Razees and frigates over 1400 tons	1 × 32ft	1 × 38ft or 36ft	1 × 30ft or 32ft	2 × 25ft or 26ft	1 × 20ft or 18ft	1 × 28ft or 24ft	–
Frigates under 1400 tons	1 × 32ft	1 × 34ft	1 × 30ft or 28ft	2 × 25ft or 26ft	1 × 18ft or 16ft	1 × 28ft or 24ft	–
26-gun frigates of 913 tons	–	–	1 × 30ft or 28ft	2 × 23ft	1 × 16ft	1 × 22ft	1 × 14ft
Frigate-built sloops of 600 tons	–	–	1 × 30ft or 28ft	1 × 25ft or 23ft	1 × 16ft	1 × 24ft or 22ft	–
Sloops under 600 tons	–	–	1 × 30ft or 28ft	1 × 25ft or 23ft	1 × 16ft	1 × 24ft or 22ft	–
18-gun corvettes & brigs	–	–	1 × 28ft or 26ft	1 × 23ft	1 × 16ft or 14ft	1 × 22ft	–
Small brigs	–	–	–	1 × 26ft or 25ft	1 × 16ft or 14ft	1 × 22ft	–

example. She was 64½ft on the deck, 18ft extreme beam and 8ft deep in hold. The minor role of schooners in the Royal Navy is reflected in the paucity of information about their rigging in contemporary British sources. Only Fincham gives much detail and he divides his schooners into two groups: common schooners, which are presumably merchant vessels, and Bermuda schooners, which were the fast-sailing sort used in American waters. Bermuda schooners were fine-lined and heavily-sparred vessels used in a variety of unsavoury trades. Their history has been set out in H I Chapelle's definitive book *The Baltimore Clipper*[16][17].

One of the most remarkable underwater discoveries is the recent find of a pair of British naval schooners on the bottom of Lake Ontario, in 300ft of water. Their state of preservation is extraordinary: even the boats' oars are still lashed in place. The schooners had been captured by the Americans and were in their service when they sank during a storm in 1813[18].

The cutter had the same role in British waters that the schooner had on the other side of the Atlantic. The original cutter was a one-masted, gaff-rigged vessel with a clinker-built hull, but during the nineteenth century changes were made to both hull and rig. The

386

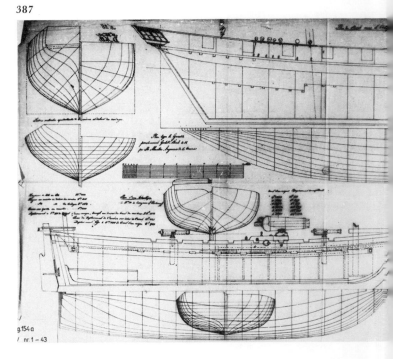

387

386. A model of a naval cutter of about 1830. The dimensions of the hull, which is a contemporary one, correspond to a length over the deck of 70ft, a keel of 60ft 10in, a breadth of 20ft and a depth in hold of about 8ft, which in turn correspond to 130 tons. The rigging, however, was added in 1902 and is based on the proportions in force at the time the vessel was built. By 1830 cutters were carvel-built and had less rake to stem- and sternpost than they did in the late eighteenth century. The square topsail formerly carried had been replaced by a gaff topsail but the square foresail, which was set 'flying', was still used when running before the wind. When the sail was not required its yard was stowed upright in front of the mast.

hulls were sometimes a hybrid construction, with clinker planking up to the wales and carvel above them. The rig was enormous for the size of the hull, for in addition to the basic canvas of gaffsail, foresail and flying jib a cutter might carry a squaresail on her lower mast, a topsail and a topgallant sail as well as stunsails, and a ringtail on her gaffsail. Later cutters had hulls that were entirely carvel-planked and the rig was increased to two and sometimes three masts. There was even a class of cutter brigs, about which, however, little is known[19]. In fact, the name 'cutter' lost its original meaning and acquired the sense of a fine-lined and speedy vessel. According to Fincham, cutters were masted in the same proportions as schooners.

BOATS

Being unspectacular objects, boats attracted no more attention from artists in the nineteenth century than they had done in the previous one, notwithstanding the many heroic 'cutting-out' attacks made with boats during the long wars. The only publications dealing with men-of-war boats are the monograph by Commander W E May already mentioned[20] and a short but informative article by Robert Gardiner in *Model Shipwright*[21].

The early nineteenth century boats differed little in shape from their predecessors, for they had to perform the same sort of duties and were propelled by oar or sail. Changes did, of course, take place. When the freeboard was increased by adding an extra strake, called a wash-strake, the thwarts remained at the old level so that, to keep the oars at their original angle, square openings were cut in the wash-strakes. In 1826 a new way of placing the oars was introduced. This was the now familiar metal crutch which allowed the oars to trail alongside the boat when they were not in use. The crutches proved so convenient that they were soon adopted for all boats with single-manned oars. Boats were made with finer lines and only the launch retained the old-fashioned bluff bow. Standardisation was as slow in coming to boats as it was to rigging: fifty-seven sizes of boat were in use in 1817, and a few years after this date dinghies were added to the Boat Establishment. By the 1840s the number of sizes had, however, been reduced to 20.

Most boats were carvel-built, clinker-building being confined to the smaller craft. In 1820, however, an attempt was made to combine both methods. Some quarter-boats were constructed with carvel bottoms and clinker topsides. The new boats were found to be stronger and easier to repair than wholly clinker-built boats, although they were heavier. Paradoxically, the outcome of the experiment was to increase the popularity of the wholly carvel built boat, and the hybrids were not taken up.

The painting of boats is rarely mentioned, although in the early years of the century it seems likely that 'Captain's fancy' was still commonly to be seen. Two examples from the 1840s are probably typical of that period: the boats of the *Queen* (a 3-decker) were black outside and white, with buff thwarts, inside; the *Constance*, a frigate, had boats that were black outside and greenish-grey inside. The sizes of boats' masts are rarely mentioned but Fincham has given some useful data about the thicknesses of masts and spars. Taking the maximum diameter of a boat's mast as 1, the proportionate thicknesses are: masts 0.66, at the head or the stop, 0.4 at the end of the pole head, 0.55 at the heel; bowsprits: at outer end 0.75; outrigger (old outligger) or boomkin, 0.75 at outer end; booms: 0.8 inner end, 0.75 outer end; gaffs: 0.55 outer end; yards: 0.6 at arms or end; sliders or gunters: 0.5 at end, the lower third of the gunter to be parallel sided; sprits: 0.7 upper end, 0.9 lower end, the greatest diameter of sprits to be 1/3 of the length from the lower end.

At the beginning of the century launches were armed with carronades: the launches of 100-, 80-, and 76-gun ships had 24pdr carronades and those of ships below 50 guns carried 12pdrs. The carronades were mounted on slides that originally ran the whole length of the boat but, the arrangement proving inconvenient, the slides were shortened so that they reached only to the third or fourth thwart, and were hinged at about 1/3 of their length from their fore end, so that the gun could be run back to the bottom of the boat. Apparently only launches had carronades at the beginning of the century, smaller boats relying on swivels as before. Under an Order of 1823, however, the launches of ships-of-the-line were to carry an 18pdr carronade, on a slide, at each end and the launches of frigates and all barges and pinnaces were to be armed with a single 12pdr apiece. The Order was modified in 1828 so that the launches of frigates had two 12pdr carronades, whilst all smaller boats were to carry Congreve's rocket launchers. The 1839 Establishment is shown in the table.

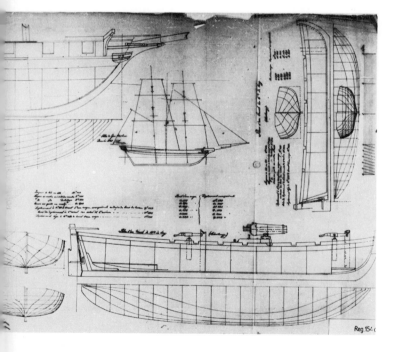

387. An interesting composite draught of about 1840 showing three French ships' boats, but armed with swivels and a carronade. The brig is the *Volage*, launched at Toulon in 1825.

GUN ESTABLISHMENT FOR SHIPS' BOATS 1839

| Class of ship | Brass Guns | | | Carronades For launches | | | Other boats | | |
	No	Length ft in	Calibre	No	Length ft in	Calibre	No	Length ft in	Calibre
120–70 guns	1	6 0	6pdr	2	3 4	18pdr	2	2 8	12pdr
50–36 guns	1	6 0	6pdr	2	2 8	12pdr	2	2 8	12pdr
26–3 guns	–	– –	–	1	2 8	12pdr	–	– –	–

REFERENCES

Abbreviations
IJNA: International Journal of Nautical Archaeology
MM: The Mariner's Mirror, the Journal of the Society for Nautical Research
MS: Model Shipwright

1 *Sailing Ships of War 1800–1860,* A H Moore, London (1926) has an excellent general account of the ships of the first half of the century
2 *An Introductory Outline of the Practice of Shipbuilding* (1821) and *A History of Naval Architecture,* J Fincham, and *Treatise on Naval Architecture,* A F B Creuze (1851), reprinted from the seventh edition of *Encyclopaedia Britannica,* are outstanding examples
3 *The Timber Problem of the Royal Navy 1652–1862,* R G Albion, Society for Nautical Research, London (no 5 in the *Maritime Miscellany* series)
4 See R C Anderson, *MM* (1944) Vol 30 p112; L G Carr Laughton, *MM* (1944) Vol 30 p167; and M V Brewington, *MM* (1945) Vol 31 p46
5 'The *Victory's* Spritsail Topsail Yard and Dolphin Stiker', J H Harland, *MM* (1977) Vol 63 p8; and 'The *Victory's* Dolphin Striker', W P Dunphy, *MM* (1978) Vol 64 p44
6 *The Young Sea-Officer's Sheet Anchor,* Darcy Lever (1827 and later editions)
7 *Reports on Naval Construction 1842–4,* Read, Chatfield and Creuze (1847)
8 *Naval Architecture 1819–20,* Abraham Rees, a reprint by David & Charles from Rees' *Cyclopaedia: or a Universal Dictionary of the Arts, Sciences and Literature*
9 *On the Masting of Ships and Mast-making,* J Fincham (1829)
10 Quoted from the article 'Naval Architecture' in the *Encyclopaedia Metropolitana* (1834)

11 *The Naval History of Great Britain,* William James (1837 edition) Vol 5 p51
12 See *The History of the American Sailing Navy,* H I Chapelle (1944) p267
13 'Naval Blockmaking in the 18th and 19th Centuries', G Clark, *MM* (1976) Vol 62 pp137–144
14 *British Artillery on Land and Sea 1790–1820,* R Wilkinson-Latham (1973)
15 'Naval Gunnery Tables of 1813 and 1832' N A M Rodger, *MM* (1975) Vol 61 pp408–11
16 *The Baltimore Clipper,* H I Chapelle, Massachusetts Marine Research Society (1930)
17 *Fast Sailing Ships,* D R MacGregor (1973)
18 *IJNA* (1976) Vol 5 pp266–8, with a photograph
19 'More Cutter Briggs', J Lyman, *MM* (1972) Vol 58 p102; gives references to earlier articles
20 *Boats of Men-of-War,* Commander W E May, National Maritime Museum (1974)
21 'Fittings for Wooden Warships. Part 2: Boats', R Gardiner, *MS* (1977) No 19 pp235–41

388. Sail, unassisted by steam, survived in the Royal Navy long after 1860 but not for regular warships. However, even after warships abandoned auxiliary sail power altogether, seamanship training under sail remained highly valued and special training brigs were built and kept in commission until the early years of this century. HMS *Sealark* shown here under full sail was built in 1843 and sold in 1898.

GENERAL BIBLIOGRAPHY

Abell, Sir Westcott: *The Shipwright's Trade* (Cambridge University Press, 1948). A superficial survey of the development of shipbuilding in Britain.

Albion, Robert: *Forests and Seapower*. A remarkable account of the difficulties of getting enough ship-timber. The sections on the supply of masts are specially valuable.

American Neptune. A journal founded in 1941 specifically for American nautical history.

Anderson, R & R C: *The Sailing Ship: 6000 years of history* (Harrap, London, 1926). A general if somewhat outdated introduction to the development of the European sailing ship.

Anderson, R C: *The Rigging of Ships in the days of the Spritsail Topmast*. Published in the USA by the Massachusetts Marine Research Society, 1927. The English data is available in the same author's *Seventeenth Century Rigging* published by Percival Marshall.

Anderson, R C: *Oared Fighting Ships* (Percival Marshall 1962). A survey of the development of galleys from the earliest times to the oar-and-sail hybrids of the sixteenth to the eighteenth centuries.

Bass, G (Editor): *A History of Sea-faring from Underwater Archaeology* (Thames and Hudson, London, 1972). Informative accounts, well illustrated and with background history, of the recovery of the remains of ships of all ages.

Bathe, B W: *Seven Centuries of Seafaring* (Barrie & Jenkins, London, 1972). A general account, with many illustrations of all kinds of ships.

Bathe, B W, de Cervin, R, Taillemite E and others: *The Great Age of Sail* (Edita Lausanne, 1967). Full of interesting illustrations, mostly of Continental ships. Some of the texts, however, do not match the standard of the illustrations.

Boudriot, Jean: *Le Vaisseau de 74 Canons* (Obtainable from Meridian Books, Greenwich). A superbly illustrated work in four volumes, covering every conceivable aspect of the construction, armament and rigging of a French 74-gun ship.

Boudriot, Jean: *L'Artillerie de Mer de la Marine Francaise, 1674–1860* (Triton, 1968, vols. 84, 85, 86). Of the same high standard as the previous work by Boudriot, this series of articles deals with guns, carriages, fittings, installation, ammunition and their use of board ship.

Bugler, A: *HMS* Victory: *Building, Restoration and Repair* (HM Stationery Office, 1967). An authoritative account of the ship in her present Trafalgar guise.

Chapelle, H I: *A History of the American Sailing Navy* (Bonanza Books, 1947). A well-illustrated account, by a famous naval architect and historian, of the ships of the United States Navy and their colonial forebears. The author's earlier book *A History of American Sailing Ships* (Putnam, 1936) also has chapters on the sailing warship from the early 1600s to the middle of the nineteenth century, as does the later *Search for Speed under Sail* (Norton, 1967).

Cipolla, C M: *Guns and Sails in the Early Phases of European Expansion* (Collins, 1965). A general account of the part played by the gun-carrying ship but having little about construction or rig.

Cowes, G Laird: *Sailing Ships: their history and development* (HM Stationery Office, 1932). The former Catalogue to the collection of sailing ship models in the Science Museum, London. Part 1 describes the sailing ship's development and Part 2 describes the exhibits as they were at that date. A valuable account of how the sailing ship, and particularly the warship, developed. Out of print.

Corbett, Sir Julian: *The Successors of Drake*. Originally published in 1900 and reprinted about 1972 by Burt Franklin, New York. The concluding chapter has an excellent account of the improvements made to English warships during Queen Elizabeth I's reign, though some parts are now out of date.

Creuze, Augustin F B: A Treatise on Naval Architecture. A reprint (1851) of Creuze's article on shipbuilding in the 7th Edition of *Encyclopaedia Britannica*. His treatise gives an account of the development of shipbuilding in England, and of the various methods of ship design and construction. Useful tables of dimensions, and plans.

Deane, Sir Anthony: *A Doctrine of Naval Architecture* (1670). A manuscript book written at the request of Samuel Pepys, in which Deane, one of the foremost English shipwrights of his day, explains how the lines of a ship were drawn out. There are plans of ships of several rates, together with their rigging sizes. The manuscript is in the Pepysian Library, Magdalene College, Cambridge; Conway Maritime plan to publish the complete work in 1980.

Falconer, William: *A Universal Dictionary of the Marine* (1769 and editions down to 1815). A valuable source of information although the information is not always up to date, even in the first edition, and later ones often repeat the earlier ones without amendment. A *pot-pourri* of the various editions was produced in the 1930s by C S Gill under the title *The Old Wooden Walls*.

Fincham, John: *An introductory Outline of the Practice of Shipbuilding*. First published in 1821, this authoritative book by one of the chief naval architects of the period ran to several editions.

Fincham, John: *On Masting of Ships and Mast-making* (1829). An exhaustive treatise on the subject. Many tables of spar dimensions for every sort of warship and some merchantmen.

Fragments of Ancient English Shipwrightry. Pepysian Library. Magdalene College, Cambridge. A collection of coloured draughts of ships, scale drawings and plans, together with an extensive collection of working notes on many aspects of shipbuilding, traditionally believed to have belonged to Matthew Baker, a principal shipwright of the later sixteenth century, who died in 1613. The date of the plans is uncertain: they have been assigned as early as 1585 and as late as the early 1600s.

Laughton, L G Carr: *Old Ship Figureheads and Sterns* (Halton & Truscott Smith, 1927). The pioneer work on ship decoration from the earliest times to 1860. Published in a limited edition and now difficult to find.

Lees, J *The Masting and Rigging of English Ships of War 1625—1860* (Conway Maritime Press, Greenwich, 1979) A comprehensive and authoritative survey of the subject by a Senior Conservation Officer at the National Maritime Museum.

Lengths of Masts and Yards of the Navy in Anno 1600; Lengths and sizes of Rigging for the Navy, 1611. Two contemporary manuscripts in the Pepysian Library, Magdalene College, Cambridge.

Lever, Darcy: *The Young Sea Officer's Sheet Anchor* (1827?) A rigging manual for young officers. Many editions.

Longridge, C N: *The Anatomy of Nelson's Ships* (Percival Marshall, 1955) Despite the title the book is concerned only with making a model of the *Victory* in her restored 1805 state.

MacGregor, D R: *Fast Sailing Ships* (Nautical Publishing Co, 1973). An interesting account of the search for speed under sail.

Mariner's Mirror, the journal of the Society for Nautical Research, London. The journal was first published in 1911. The sixty-four volumes contain authoritative articles on every aspect of nautical history and ship development.

Moore, Sir Alan: *Rig in Northern Europe.* Originally published in the *Mariner's Mirror* Vol 42 (1956). An offprint is obtainable from the Society for Nautical Research c/o the National Maritime Museum, Greenwich.

Moore, Sir Alan. *Sailing Ships of War 1800–1860* (Halton & Truscott Smith, London 1926). A selection of prints from the magnificent MacPherson Collection at the National Maritime Museum, Greenwich. The introductory essay is an excellent but all too brief account of the ships of the last half-century of the sailing warship. Issued in a limited edition and now rare.

Nance, R M: *The Ship of the Renaissance.* Originally published in Vol 41 of the Mariner's Mirror (1955). An offprint is obtainable from the Society for Nautical Research, c/o the National Maritime Museum, Greenwich.

Naval Architecture from the *Encyclopaedia Metropolitana* (1834). A popular account of the subject but has some useful data and plans, such as the elliptical stern of the *Hamadryad* frigate.

Navy Records Society publications: *The Spanish War, 1585—7,* published 1898; *The Defeat of the Spanish Armada* Vol 2, published 1894. Both contain useful information about the size, rigging and armament of Elizabethan warships. *The Life and Works of Sir Henry Mainwaring* Vol 2. Published 1921. Contains *The Seaman's Dictionary,* the standard source for early seventeenth ship construction and rigging. Contains much information applicable to the last quarter of the sixteenth century.

Oppenheim, M: *A History of the Administration of the Royal Navy 1509–1660.* Although published as long ago as 1896 this book is still an unsurpassed source of information, and of references to original documents.

Padfield, P: *Guns at Sea* (Evelyn, London, 1973). A great deal of interesting material but chiefly about the way guns were used at sea.

Pope, Dudley: *The Gun* (Weidenfield, 1965). A copiously illustrated account of the development of the gun. Mostly about land artillery but having many illustrations of early guns.

Rees, Abraham: *Naval Architecture, 1819–20.* A reprint by David and Charles from the *Cyclopaedia; or A Universal Dictionary of Arts, Sciences and Literature.* Based on Steel and other writers of the last quarter of the eighteenth century but not brought up to date and consequently unreliable for naval architecture and rigging *c*1820.

Robertson, F L: *The Evolution of Naval Armament* (Constable, 1921). A general account of the subject, but now surpassed by more detailed books on the subject.

Robinson, M S: *Van de Velde Drawings in the National Maritime Museum* (Cambridge University Press, 1958). Many pictures of English and Continental warships of the middle of the seventeenth century.

Salisbury, W: *A Treatise on Shipbuilding written about 1620–25.* Describes the parts of a ship's hull, gives their proportions and explains how to draw a plan of the hull. Published together with a contemporary *Treatise on Rigging,* edited by R C Anderson, by the Society for Nautical Research.

Sandahl, B: *Middle English Sea Terms.* (University of Uppsala, Sweden). Vol 1 (published 1951) deals with the hull, Vol 2 (1958) with the masts, spars and sails. Quotes the occurrence of 450 items between 1290 and 1550 and discussed their meaning. Throws light on the dates when innovations were introduced. A third volume, on rigging, is in preparation.

Steel, D: *The Elements of Mast Making, Sail Making and Rigging* (1794 and 1806). The standard source for late eighteenth century rigging. Packed with information and copiously illustrated. An edited conflation of the two editions was produced by C S Gill and published under the same title in 1932 and has recently been republished by E Sweetman, New York.

Steel, D: *The Elements and Practice of Naval Architecture.* Originally published in 1805 and reprinted in facsimile by Sim Comfort Associates, London (1977). The principal source of information about late eighteeneth century naval architecture.

Sutherland, W: *The Shipbuilder's Assistant* (1711 and many later editions). Has details of lengths and sizes of rigging and ships' fittings. The later editions often contain out of date information, some of it as old as the 1650s!

Sutherland, W: *England's Glory; or Shipbuilding Unveiled* (1717). Deals comprehensively with designing, building and fitting out ships.

Wilkinson Latham, R: *British Artillery on Land and Sea 1790–1820.* Within the dates set a good though short account of the guns and their ammunition. Many useful references.

Mortier en Bedding Proviel te Sien,